THE HUMANIST CHRISTOLOGY OF PAUL

JESUS OF NAZARETH YESTERDAY AND TODAY

THE HUMANIST CHRISTOLOGY OF PAUL

JUAN LUIS SEGUNDO

*Edited and Translated from the Spanish
by John Drury*

ORBIS BOOKS
Maryknoll, New York

SHEED AND WARD
London, England

Originally published as Part 2 of *Historia y actualidad: Sinópticos y Pablo,* which is Volume II/1 of the series of works entitled *El hombre de hoy ante Jesús de Nazaret,* copyright © 1982 by Ediciones Cristiandad, S. L., Huesca, 30-32, Madrid, Spain

English translation copyright © 1986 by Orbis Books, Maryknoll, NY 10545
Published in the United States of America by Orbis Books, Maryknoll, NY 10545
Published in Great Britain by Sheed and Ward, Ltd., 2 Creechurch Lane, London

Manufactured in the United States of America

English manuscript editor: William H. Schlau

Indexes compiled by James Sullivan

Library of Congress Cataloging in Publication Data

Segundo, Juan Luis.
   The humanist christology of Paul.

   (Jesus of Nazareth, yesterday and today; v. 3)
   Translation of: Historia y actualidad—Sinópticos
y Pablo
   Bibliography: p.
   Includes index.
   1. Jesus Christ—History of doctrines—Early church,
ca. 30–600. 2. Bible. N.T. Romans—Criticism,
interpretation, etc. I. Segundo, Juan Luis. Historia
y actualidad—Sinópticos y Pablo. English. II. Title.
III. Series: Segundo, Juan Luis. El hombre de hoy ante
Jesús de Nazaret. English; v. 3.
BT198.S393   1986   232   86–8480
ISBN 0–88344–221–3 (v. 3: pbk.)

SHEED AND WARD / ISBN 07220-4270

Somewhere in this world there exists a group, a community of persons, with whom I discussed the themes of these volumes one night a week for almost twenty years. We, the members of that group, became more than friends. We became brothers and sisters. By now it is almost impossible for me to say which thoughts are my own and which I owe to others in the group.

Participating in that group were people who became Christians only in adulthood, who were not yet Christians when we were talking about the topics that fill these volumes. But all of us were equally captivated by Jesus of Nazareth, and the quest for him made us even more brotherly and sisterly.

Some members of that community are now far removed in space, though not in affection. Others became part of that reflection and affection at a later date. To all of them I dedicate these volumes, not as a personal gift from me but as a duty honored: a work returned to those who brought it to life.

JUAN LUIS SEGUNDO

Contents

Translator's Note

In Volume III all biblical citations in English are translations of the author's own Spanish text unless otherwise noted specifically. Other basic English translations of the Bible have been consulted, but the deciding factor in doubtful cases was the underlying Greek text of the New Testament. The reasons for this approach should become clear in reading the author's text and notes. Here at the start readers may wish to consult section (4) of the author's Introduction (pp. 1–11) as well as notes 23 and 25.

INTRODUCTION

The Transition to 'Christology' in Paul

After one has spent a great deal of time exploring the most reliable historical data about Jesus in the Synoptic gospels, one does not find it easy to plunge into the 'christological' world of Paul: i.e., into the interpretation of Jesus that Paul offers even before the final redaction of the Synoptic gospels. Paul's world is a strange one, and it doesn't help any to realize that our switchover is anachronistic, at least at first glance. From the documents at our disposal we know that Paul's *interpretation* came first, before the *recollection* put down in the gospels. When we step into the christological world of Paul—into Romans, for example—we seem to be separated from the Synoptics by a century of reflection; but in reality we are ten or fifteen years before their final redaction.

The reality here is more complicated, however. It is true that behind the Letter to the Romans, for example, there was a long process of creative thinking by Paul, a man of undoubted genius. But it is equally true that behind the final redaction of the Synoptic gospels there was a long process of fixing the memory of the community. That process was not devoid of interpretive creation, even though its origins bring us back closer to events surrounding Jesus himself. So rather than facing an anachronism, we are confronted with a question. Paul undoubtedly was familiar with the *data* transmitted by the Synoptics before he began his own interpretive work. Why, then, do we find that the Synoptic data are almost completely absent from Paul's finished effort?

Less than thirty years after the events narrated in the Synoptics—which deal with the life, proclamation, death, and resurrection of Jesus—Paul goes into a lengthy and profound exposition of what Jesus signifies. But he apparently retains only two specific events: Jesus' death and resurrection. Paul does not cite his words[1] or recall his teachings. Gone are the key terms employed by Jesus to designate himself, his mission, and the immediate objects of that mission: the Son of man, the kingdom of God, the poor, etc.

Here readers may rightly point out certain things that balance the picture. We must not confuse or equate Paul with only one of his ecclesial functions: his letter-writing. In his own mission, moreover, Paul was probably accompanied

1

by two of the Synoptic evangelists: Mark and Luke.[2] And in all the churches to which he wrote letters, Paul undoubtedly presupposes the existence of an ongoing catechesis based specifically on the gospels (at least those of the two evangelists just mentioned).[3]

Even granting all that, we cannot readily see how those communities could move from an understanding of "the elementary teaching about Christ" (Heb 6:1) to Paul's abstract categories. Without clarifying explanations or bridges, Paul uses those abstract categories to deal with Jesus explicitly, apparently attributing no importance whatsoever to the events and teachings that the Synoptics took so much trouble to record and explain.

To be sure, Paul himself writes: "If we did know Christ according to the flesh, we no longer know him that way" (2 Cor 5:16). But quite aside from the fact that we are not sure what he is talking about, Paul does not offer us any data on this other kind of knowledge "according to the Spirit," or the ways in which it is created and verified. That would certainly have shed some light on how we are to interpret Paul; and such light seems all the more necessary today, given the time that has elapsed between Paul and us. Using theology, we can throw up bridges *much too easily* between the Jesus of the Synoptic gospels and (e.g.) the 'new Adam' of Paul's Letter to the Romans: i.e., the one who confers decisive justice on those who believe in him, who declares the Law abolished.

That is not the only problem. Jesus himself spoke about imitating the heavenly Father, who "makes his sun rise on the evil and on the good, and sends rain on the just and on the unjust" (Mt 5:45; RSV), and who "is kind to the ungrateful and the selfish" (Lk 6:35; RSV). Paul, on the other hand, writes about pagans in a very different tone. Since they did not deign to maintain true knowledge of God, he calmly notes, God "handed them over to . . . the cravings of their hearts . . . passions that bring dishonor . . . a reprobate mind" (Rom 1:24.26.28).

After what we have seen in Volume II, we are not going to succumb to the silly extreme of calling Paul 'the inventor of Christianity'. But the fact remains that his data cannot simply be *added* to that of the Synoptics.[4] We sense that we are dealing with a profound difference in literary genre, something that goes far beyond the difference between narrative and letter-writing. Let me explore this whole issue a bit more since it may help me to frame my own, necessarily limited, effort to interpret Paul and, through him, Jesus.

(1). Certain letters are generally regarded as belonging to the authentic *Pauline corpus*. There is little doubt, in other words, that they are Paul's thinking dictated to someone or even written down by him in some instances. These letters are divided into three periods.

The *first* period, situated around the year 50, takes in the two letters to the Thessalonians. The *second* and central period, dating from approximately the year 57, takes in the letters to the Corinthians (1 and 2 Corinthians), the Galatians, and the Romans. The *third* period, situated during Paul's captivity in Rome (the years 61–63), takes in the letters to the Colossians and Philemon.

On a secondary level of certainty[5] with regard to date or the direct authorship of Paul, we have the letters to the Philippians and the Ephesians and the so-called Pastoral Letters (to Timothy and Titus). Thus the Letter to the Philippians, which is commonly attributed to Paul, alludes to Paul's present captivity. If he is in Ephesus, then we are talking about the central period that includes the letters to the Romans, Corinthians, and Galatians. But if Paul is in Rome, that would make Philippians contemporary with the letters of the third period noted above. There is debate about Paul's direct authorship of the Letter to the Ephesians, which does seem to date from his Roman captivity. Perhaps he used a secretary or disciple; perhaps some disciple of his presented himself under Paul's name. The Pastoral Letters would belong to a later period (65–67), which included a second Roman captivity, if they are to be regarded as Paul's. There is no unanimity on this matter.[6]

So we have three definite periods of known apostolic activity, separated by two gaps of five to seven silent years insofar as we are concerned.

(2). We may now ask if those three periods reveal 'stages' in Paul's creation of a christology. Despite the inherent limitations of the data available to us, it seems that the obvious answer is 'yes'. And since I am going to limit my focus to the central period in the following chapters, let me briefly touch upon the three periods and what we can glean from the data despite the limitations.

The limitations themselves are part and parcel of the epistolary genre. Paul's letters originate in particular problems facing the communities known to him. Those problems are often occasional ones, and usually practical in the broad sense of the term. There is one exception to this general rule, but even it is only partially an exception as we shall see in this volume. From the standpoint of general teaching or doctrine, then, Paul's letters lack balance. They are heavily geared toward partial emphases and urgencies of the moment. Sometimes this partiality is made expressly clear, sometimes our perception of it depends on our ability to reconstruct the context and its corresponding problems.

Nevertheless it is plain that Paul always finds an opportunity to express thoughts, however fragmentary, about the significance of Jesus' life, death, and resurrection. This may be due to the fact that the community was only recently founded, or that Paul's stay there was brief, or that new, complicated, and even hazardous circumstances surrounded the insertion of Jesus' message into contexts outside Palestine. And no matter how fragmentary our data are, particularly for the first period, we have enough to justify talk about *a process of christological creation*.

The two letters to the Christians of Thessalonica, our scanty material from the first period, probably represent the first Christian documents to come down to us.[7] To be sure, nothing in them heralds the great christological syntheses of the later periods. If it were not an anachronism, we could say that Paul is still dependent on the Synoptics—if not on the gospels as finally redacted, then on the material that they record and that was probably written down to some extent from a very early date.

Although they do not offer direct citations of Jesus' teaching, the two letters to the Thessalonians are the only Pauline letters in which we seem to hear direct echoes of that teaching. In them we find the term, 'the kingdom of God' (2 Thes 1:5; see also 1 Thes 2:15). They hint at the similarity between the persecutions being suffered by Christians and those suffered by the prophets (1 Thes 2:15). The coming of the Lord is like that of a thief in the night (1 Thes 5:2.4). Christians are not to repay evil with evil (1 Thes 5:15). And a divine justice will convert present suffering into joy, and vice versa (2 Thes 1:6-7).[8]

These echoes, however, should not lead us to imagine that the first period of Pauline christology was lacking in originality, that no creative transposition was required at the very least. Of necessity the first Christian document is already applying to pagans a message that Jesus himself obviously addressed to a Jewish audience. Most of those who made up the Christian community of Thessalonica, thanks to Paul's work of evangelization, came from paganism. If we did not have clear proof of this from the letters themselves, we would still have the explicit testimony of Luke (Acts 17:14). Today we are much too inclined to view the shift from Jew to pagan—by way of 'the human being'—as easy and natural. We think it is simply a matter of stripping away the limits from something that was restricted at that time in order to move out into the universal where we now find ourselves, and where we naïvely imagine we can read and interpret the message of Jesus without further ado.

There is another fact about Paul that is initially a source of many difficulties, even though it may later prove to be very enriching. Paul is a *Pharisee* who has converted to something that as yet has no name (and that will later be called Christianity), and who must talk about that something to pagans of Greek culture. Today the media of social communication are more or less universal. They have made us insensitive to the cultural barriers existing in Antiquity—at least those of us living in urban civilization. It is very difficult for us to have an adequate idea of the chasm that separated Jewish culture from Greek culture at the time Paul took his decisive step.

What about Jesus could interest pagans of Greek culture unless they were first put through the whole process of the Jewish religious tradition? Practically nothing said by Jesus has to do with them, certainly not in general. Some sort of transposition had to be invented, and it had to be a faithful transposition.

From where we stand, with only the two letters to the Christians of Thessalonica[9] and Luke's allusions in Acts, it would not be wise to devise elaborate hypotheses about the preaching that might have served as the founding basis for the Christian community of Thessalonica. It does seem certain, however, that Paul must have placed very heavy emphasis on the imminence of eschatological judgment, i.e., on the proximate return of the risen Jesus to save his own from the coming wrath of God's judgment (see 1 Thes 1:10; 2:16-19; 3:13; 4:6.13-18; 5:1-2.8-9.23; 2 Thes 1:5.6-10; 2:1-2).[10] We find, particularly in the second letter, a 'small eschatological discourse' (2 Thes 2:3-12) that seems to echo data reported as prophecies of Jesus by the Synoptics.

This would be closer to John the Baptist than Jesus (see Volume II, Chapter

X), if it were not for a note of joy we detect in the two letters. As I pointed out in the previous volume, that note of joy is characteristic of Jesus and hard to reconcile with the idea of the 'coming wrath' and the 'axe laid to the root of the tree'.

The note of joy has shifted direction, however. In Jesus' preaching it is closely bound up with the approaching happiness of his friends: the poor and sinners, who constitute one and the same group. In the two letters to the Thessalonians, and we may assume in many other new Christian communities, we get a different picture: what for other people is the day of wrath is, *for the disciples of Jesus*, the day of salvation and rehabilitation (1 Thes 1:9–10; 2:16.19; 4:14; 5:4.9.16–18; 2 Thes 1:5–12; 2:13–14).[11]

On this matter it might well be interesting to compare the Paul of these two letters to the Thessalonians and of Luke, but I cannot delay any longer on this first period of Pauline christology. It has nothing to do with the scantiness of the material, but rather with my main purpose here. I brought up the first period solely to stress the surprise that awaits us when we approach his major letters of the second period and their treatment of the same theme. It is some seven years later, and we are now in the central period of the formation of Paul's christology. If we can appreciate the difference in this second stage of Paul's christology, we should be able to better delineate the specific object and method of our own quest here.

In this second period we encounter the most extensive letters of Paul that we possess.[12] To be sure, occasional problems do appear in them (especially in 2 Cor), having no specific connection with christology: concrete moral questions, order in their assemblies, etc. But some of the problems which the communities have posed directly or indirectly to Paul, and to which Paul devotes whole chapters, are specifically points that were left murky in his preaching on the significance of Jesus.

We find a clearcut example of this in Galatians: i.e., the alleged obligatoriness of circumcision for new Christians. That ultimately leads to the crucial christological question: What exactly is the difference, and hence the novelty, of Christ vis-à-vis the Old Testament revelation?[13] Another example is the problem of Jesus' resurrection and its relationship with the eschatological resurrection of (all) the dead, which is taken up at the end of 1 Corinthians. At the start of the very same letter we find another crucial issue: How are people to evaluate the insertion into the Christian faith of religious ideologies (as I define the latter term) stemming from paganism or the basic tendencies of the human being?

In this central period we also come across a letter that in some respects resembles a little treatise: the Letter to the Romans. It is the only letter expressly stating that it was written by Paul to a community he did not yet know personally, because he had neither founded it nor visited it. In principle, that should allow him to present 'his gospel' in a way that is freer of occasional problems. We should not, however, underestimate Paul's possible knowledge of the Roman community and its problems. Traces of such knowledge are evident in the letter itself, which is far from pursuing one and the same line of argument from beginning to end.

The Christian community of Rome was undoubtedly made up of both converted Jews and converted pagans. In all likelihood Paul's protestations of personal unfamiliarity with the community were largely a rhetorical device to win their good will. He was trying to suggest his own impartiality toward the conflicts that may have already existed in the community, or that may have arisen in connection with his projected visit to it.

Moreover, Paul was not a theoretical thinker. More than anything else, then, the comings and goings of his argumentation in Romans are the watermarks of a dialogue that he has already had to carry on with similar audiences in similar contexts of his whole apostolic praxis. So while the Letter to the Romans is less 'circumstantial' in concrete details and problems, it is not so in spelling out the milestone that Paul has reached in his christological thinking: i.e., the possibility of employing *one single* (hence *new*) idiom to speak to Jews and pagans (i.e., humanity as a whole) about the significance of the Christ, Jesus of Nazareth.

Before I come back to Romans, let me briefly say something about Paul's christological thinking in the third period, which takes in the letters that Paul wrote about seven years later, from his first imprisonment in Rome.

On the one hand those letters are brief. Even leaving aside the Pastoral Letters, we can say that they are made up mostly of exhortations. While they may allude to specific practical problems, they do not expatiate on any specific problematic as did his letters of the second period. On the other hand these letters do possess great christological importance. Besides invoking Jesus Christ, they present highly structured, brief compositions about Jesus of Nazareth: who he is, what he means and, in particular, what his relationship is to God and God's universal plan.[14]

These compositions are highly poetic in form and endowed with a distinctive rhythm that sets them apart from Paul's ordinary prose even at its most exalted. So we do not know for sure to what extent they derive from him or are citations of hymns already existing in Christian communities. They are christological documents of primary importance in any case, since they predate the redaction of the Synoptic gospels. I do not intend to treat them in detail here. I mention them simply as part of my effort to survey the christological case of Paul's third period.

In general, we detect a shift of accent between Paul's second and third periods. It is somewhat comparable to the shift between Jesus' prepaschal preaching and the postpaschal preaching of his disciples, or between the Synoptic gospels and John's gospel. Remember that Jesus announced *the kingdom*, focusing attention on the fulfillment of a divine plan for the world. After Pentecost, however, his disciples preached *Jesus*, focusing on who and what he is: Messiah, Son of God, Word of God, God (without the definite article: *theòs*, not *ho theòs*).

In a less clear and conclusive way we can detect a parallel shift of emphasis between Paul's second (and first) period and his third period. In the second or central period, and even though he uses different terms,[15] you could say that Paul was trying to define the kingdom of God, or at least God's plan for the world and humanity. In the third period his attention shifts to identifying the nature and attributes of the one who brings it: Jesus, the Christ (the Messiah of Israel). It is true that the hymns mentioned above, which are the chief christological element of the third period whether or not they come from Paul, do refer to both things. They never set aside the divine plan within which Jesus and his relationship with God are to be understood. But their literary form is unmistakable, and it has no parallel in Paul's major letters.[16] They are clearly hymns, or whatever you may choose to call them, *about* Jesus as being somehow identified with the Divinity.

In contrast, I think we can say something different about the major letters of Paul's central period. They do talk about Jesus, and sometimes even about one or another of his attributes: 'son of God', 'son of David', 'son of woman, born under the law'. But they always do so within a context structured around a broader question of a different order: i.e., What exactly is the transformation that the human being is to expect from Christ? The difference may seem subtle, but it is unmistakable nevertheless.

(3). Let us now go back to the central period and Paul's Letter to the Romans.

We must *make a choice*, you see. Dozens of volumes would not suffice to explore one by one the different christological efforts contained in the New Testament.[17] When I referred to my effort in Volume II as an *anti-christology*, I had in mind specifically the impossibility of elaborating one meaningful tract out of data deriving from differing creative efforts to understand Jesus and talk about him in different cultural contexts. To try to elaborate such a tract would be to lose the very thing that is most worthwhile for us: i.e., discovering what mental mechanisms, what human keys, and what literary genres were employed in this creative work of interpretation—work that is not already finished once and for all, or without us.

Among the many such efforts available to us, I have chosen that of Paul. And since his first and third periods do not offer us enough elements to be sure of the process followed—aside from those mentioned above—I think we must cut into that process and slice out a section of it. I have chosen to take my slice from the central period, and to focus specifically on *the first eight chapters of the Letter to the Romans*. This choice necessitates several brief considerations.

The letters of Paul's central period certainly do not directly contradict the perspectives of the first period (1 and 2 Thessalonians). We find reliable testimony to that fact in 1 Corinthians, where Paul reaffirms his hope of being *alive* here on earth to witness the *parousia*, the second coming of Jesus (1 Cor 15:52). That comes down to reaffirming the near end of history, as some Thessalonian Christians had done in an earlier period. They went on to conclude, quite logically, that there was no longer any point or value in working.

Paul's response to them at that point in time was relatively superficial. He pointed out that the end was not *that* close, that the main signs forecasted in Jesus' eschatological discourse[18] had not yet surfaced. In his central period Paul offers a more profound response. When we examined the Synoptic gospels (Volume II, Chapter X), we saw that eschatology increasingly made room for history. This was not so much because Christians sensed the delay of the end and used history to fill the interim, but because they discovered something more basic and essential. They came to see that the kingdom proclaimed by Jesus had its roots and causality in this world. We find much the same sort of shift when we move from Paul's earlier letters to the Thessalonians to those of his central period (Romans, 1 and 2 Corinthians, Galatians).

In their own way, you see, the letters of the central period are a new kind of eschatological discourse and even 'apocalypse', substantially similar to the last book of the New Testament though no one would suspect that on the basis of surface appearances. In the Apocalypse (or Book of Revelation) 'the adversary' is personified in multiple and diverse images of animals and other things. In the letters of Paul's central period, 'the adversary' is depicted in a more or less complicated struggle where different entities play their own specific and personalized role. In our modern vernacular languages, those entities are common nouns. Indeed we could almost attribute to the Paul of that period the present-day German usage of capitalizing all nouns. Paul addresses questions to the character, Death. He asks a personal question—Who?—and answers with nouns such as Grace, Tribulation, Sword. He attributes ambiguous intentions to Law, human actions or reactions to Sin, and ineffectual orders to our Inner Humanity. He gives active, universal dimensions to the experiences undergone by individual persons such as Adam, Abraham, and Christ. In this conflict there are incidents, skirmishes, ambushes, strategic retreats, counterattacks, Pyrrhic victories, and even decisive victories that, surprisingly, give rise to new battles.

Thus the (causal) *complexity* of this *final* struggle ends up almost completely substituting the complicated interplay of those grand and cunning characters for the earlier expectation of an immediate end effected by God. Here again, as we shall see, the historical instruments that give concrete shape and finish to their specific roles end up clarifying and explaining the 'final' value of history, its mechanisms, and its appointed periods.

(4). Finally, the characteristics pointed out above have prompted me to adopt a specific method in my analysis. It will be spelled out more clearly in the following chapters, of course, but I would like to say something about its whys and wherefores right now.

In the Synoptics we encountered material that was recorded fragmentarily, rearranged in different ways, and focused around different objectives; here we encounter a line of thought that moves in accordance with its own creative rhythm. Dealing with the Synoptics, we moved in concentric circles in our effort to unify the material and thus give it complete historical sense; here fidelity to the thinking of Paul requires that we follow his own process of argumentation. Since that process is more fully developed and universal in Romans, we will follow its thread in that letter, bringing in passages from Galatians and Corinthians when it seems appropriate or necessary.

For the reasons noted in section (3), we will focus only on the first eight chapters of Romans. The problematic dealt with in those chapters is more universal and theoretical than the issues tackled in the remaining chapters of the letter (e.g., Jewish opposition to Christianity, moral exhortations, and questions of church order). Moreover, insofar as they embody the most complete and complex synthesis offered by Paul about the significance of Jesus Christ for the human being, they have had a profound and fruitful impact on Christian thinkers of all ages. We live in a culture where any ideological dispute, however superficial it may be, must take account of the fact that in past centuries people opted, polemically and explicitly, for one or another possible interpretation of those eight chapters in Romans. Such well-known authors as Max Weber and Erich Fromm have stressed the importance of those choices for areas of life that might seem far removed indeed from theology: e.g., economic systems.

Nevertheless I will claim a certain freedom in my effort to follow the living, developing thought of Paul and interpret it. My exegesis will divide up according to the major units of meaning in his discourse.[19] Those units will often, but not always, coincide with the chapters into which his letter was artificially divided at a later point in time. Within the major units I will look for smaller units of meaning as well, though I will never get down to a verse-by-verse exegesis of Paul's text.[20]

That still leaves us with a much more important problem to be considered. In dealing with the Synoptic gospels, I was trying to unite the fragments of the Synoptic mosaic into a coherent whole. The very fact or effort of ordering suggested the use of a certain *key* and verified it, so to speak. Here the unity is given by Paul himself, so I must start by getting in tune with *his* key. That does not mean we are to maintain a wholly passive attitude towards the text, but it does mean that Paul tells us much more about the key he is using.

It is certainly not the political key that helped us with the Synoptic gospels, nor could it be. The term 'kingdom' has disappeared, and so has the central position of 'the poor'. The term 'sinners' no longer serves as an ideological label for a specific social group; that is why the unexpectedly positive or favorable sense of the term in Jesus' message disappears in Paul's letter. That does not reflect unfavorably on our use of the political key to interpret the Synoptics, nor does it mean that Paul invented a Christianity cut to his own measure. But it does indicate that he used a different key, a different set of mental and literary instruments, to ponder the very same message and communicate it to a different audience.

What is this new key? It is clear enough, I think, if we take a close look at Paul's personification of the conflicting forces, which is a 'theatrical' device in the good sense of the word. In the context of those forces Paul makes clear the unique place of Jesus, the Christ, and his importance for the human being.

What does Paul personify? He personifies *the forces that intervene signifi-cantly in every human life*, the forces that any human being will detect when it looks into the depths of its own existence, regardless of outer circumstances or religious background. Such terms as sin, grace, justification, law, inner human being, etc., compel us to assay an *anthropological* or existential key in Paul. And if a specific conception of the human being merits the name of humanism, then readers will see the justification for entitling this volume: "The Humanist Christology of Paul."

My actual implementation of this interpretive key will help to clarify it and give it more content. In our use of language today, you see, terms like 'anthropological' and 'existential' are often used in contrast to the 'historical' or 'political' (the latter being a substantial part of the historical). But we will see that in Paul the existential and the anthropological open out into historical causality and politics[21] by virtue of their own inner dynamics and fidelity to the Jesus of the gospels.

This brings me to another important observation about the setup of the chapters in this volume. In choosing to study Paul's christology of a certain period, from among the many ones to be found in the New Testament, I do not mean to imply that it represents the best of the lot or the one that is preferable for us. From the very start of Volume II, I have been insisting that it is not a matter of formulating one christology out of all the available material on Jesus. What *is* a matter of life and death for our human (and Christian) existence today is our ability to create christologies that are valid for our own context and, at the same time, faithful to Jesus of Nazareth, the historical Jesus.

Here I am presenting Paul as an example of *christological creation*. Chapters I–IV are divided into two basic sections. The first section of each chapter attempts to understand Paul and his work of christological creation. The second section, equally important, attempts to spell out what Paul did to arrive at those conclusions on the basis of the initial data about the historical Jesus that we examined in Volume II. Thus section I of the chapters will tell us what Paul believed, and section II will tell us how he came to that belief. Realizing that Paul worked at a high level of creativity, one would suspect that the second section of those chapters will require much more effort from us. That particu-lar sort of analysis, by the way, is almost completely absent from our usual christologies, even those that rely heavily on Paul.

My procedure will change somewhat once we get to Chapter V, because we will then be considering Pauline interpretations based on the paschal realities of Jesus (see note 114 and section II of Chapter V).

That brings me to my final methodological observation of importance. Readers approaching Paul through modern-language translations of his letters tend to be unaware of the traps laid for them by the version they are using. To settle for one example, consider the most controversial term in those chapters of Romans: the noun traditionally translated as 'justification', and the verb traditionally translated as 'to justify'. Both words refer to what God effects with those who believe in Jesus. Inadvertent readers will tend to equate 'justification' with 'salvation'. Since the reference is to God's judgment, they assume that the 'just' will likewise be 'saved'. Although this assimilation of justification and salvation is currently disputed (without foundation, in my opinion), there still remains the far more important question: In the life of the human being, what does it mean to be *justified* by God?

Ingenuous readers will tend to assume that God 'justifies' someone because God recognizes that the person in question *is* just. But that does not solve the problem because Paul reiterates that we all are sinners. Does God first *make* a human being just and then *declare* him or her to be so? Exegetes inform us that the Greek verb in question (*dikaioō*) never means 'to make just'. We should translate it as 'to *declare* just'. And in this context it certainly is applied to one who *is not* just. Certain statements of Paul, then, are terribly ambiguous: e.g., "God justifies the impious person" (Rom 4:5). We automatically tend to think that God will do this *after* making the person just. Now it is certainly possible that Paul is coining his own new terminology here, and the matter deserves study. But otherwise the phrase most likely means that God, moved to compassion by the sacrifice, merits, and justice of Christ, declares just someone who continues to be impious.[22] To retain the note of strangeness that the reader of the original Greek text must have felt, wouldn't it be better to translate the verse: "God *declares just* the impious . . ." (Rom 4:4)?

Our translations generally seek to facilitate the reading of the text in modern terms. They tend to avoid 'literary' (rather than literal) versions that today would be inexplicable, incomprehensible or, even worse, systematically misunderstood. Thus such terms as 'flesh' and 'fleshy', which are central to Paul's thought, are disguised in our modern translations because they now have connotations of sensuality and lust. In Paul, however, they refer to something like human 'nature' or our creaturely 'condition'. When we translate such terms with different words in different contexts, we bypass one of the most interesting processes in Paul's thinking: the gradual shift or variation in the meaning of a given term.

To help readers, then, I have chosen to begin each chapter with my own translation of the Pauline text under consideration. It is translated as 'literally' as possible,[23] so that they may get a fairly accurate idea of the *difficulties* and *riches* in the text itself. Thus I leave 'flesh' where Paul wrote it, and I consistently translate the verb *dikaioō* as 'declare just'.

With these methodological observations,[24] which readers could probably dispense with if they so chose, we begin our study of Paul's christology and our effort to pick apart its creative mechanisms.

CHAPTER I

Sin, Enslaver of Paganism

Romans 1:16–32

(16) I am not ashamed of the gospel. For it is the saving power of God for everyone who believes, for the Jew first and (also) for the Greek. (17) Because in it the justice *that proceeds* from God is being revealed from faith to faith, as it is written: "The one who is just by faith will live."

(18) For the wrath of God is being revealed from heaven against every *type of* impiety and injustice of human beings who are holding truth shackled in injustice. (19) For what is knowable of God is manifest in their midst, because God has made it manifest to them. (20) The fact is that since the creation of the world invisible (____p1.) of his are seen intellectually by means of (his) works, both his eternal power and divinity, so that they have no excuse, (21) because even though they have known God, they did not glorify him as God or give him thanks, but have become entangled in their own reasonings and their uncomprehending hearts have been darkened.

(22) Claiming to be wise, they have shown themselves to be fools, (23) and exchanged the glory of the incorruptible God for the likeness of the image of (the) corruptible human being, birds, quadrupeds, and reptiles. (24) For this, God handed them over to the cravings of their hearts, *delivered over* to the impurity of dishonoring their bodies among themselves.

(25) They actually exchanged the truth of God for the lie, and adored and worshipped the creature instead of the Creator, who is blessed forever, amen. (26) For this, God handed them over to passions that bring dishonor: for, on the one hand, their females have exchanged natural relations for anti-natural ones (27) and, on the other hand, the males, having abandoned natural relations with the female, have burned with cravings for one another, males with males committing the unseemly and receiving in their own selves the due *negative* consequence of their aberration.

13

(28) And since they did not deign to recognize God, God handed them over to a reprobate mind, to do the unsuitable, (29) replete with every injustice, wickedness, outrage, full of envy, murder, quarreling, deceit, malice, gossipers, (30) slanderers, haters of God, insolent, haughty, boastful, inventive in wickedness, disobedient to their parents, (31) senseless, disloyal, unloving, pitiless. (32) They know the just *decree* of God, that those who practice such things are deserving of death; but not only do they do them, they also approve those who do them.

After greeting those to whom his letter is addressed, Paul lays down a principle of salvation in a single phrase. Though it is not completely clear without subsequent elaborations, it is clear enough that it is based on faith. It is also clear that Paul expects his readers to withhold their judgment and restrain their curiosity about this principle, since he does not proceed to explain it. Instead he takes up the whole problem of humanity from further back: i.e., from its basic religious division into pagans and Jews.

I

In talking about a principle of *salvation* (1:16), Paul invites us to examine the context of his remark. Its usage here differs from the use of the term in the Synoptic gospels. In Paul it does not point to an event that is merely final or outside history. Instead the term raises the grammatically obvious question: *salvation from what?* In Romans 1 the answer is: from the world enslaved to Sin that is found among 'the Greeks'. In Paul's terminology 'the Greeks' means the world of pagans or Gentiles.

We cannot deny that Paul's description of that sinful world shocks us. Unless we are historians, we cannot say for sure what level of corruption might have been reached by pagans in the Rome of Paul's day. Even more important, however, is the fact that Paul is not talking about extreme cases of moral degradation. We must realize that he is talking about the behavior of the average human being, the average *pagan,* if you will.

Now it is true that Paul, after his first two chapters, draws a more general conclusion. He tells us: "We have already made the accusation that *we all,* Jews and Greeks, are under Sin" (3:9).[25] But despite this general accusation, and his assertion that the Jews "do the same things" (2:1), we cannot avoid the suspicion that Paul is painting the sins of pagan idolatry in excessively dark colors. Even if we grant his general accusation that all human beings are under Sin, isn't it likely that certain pagan extremes—e.g., the widespread homosexuality described in verses 26 and 27—were not to be found among the children of Israel?

That pushes us back to a logically prior question. Since Paul was trying to show that *all human beings* are under the bondage of Sin, why did he bother to write *two* distinct chapters or sections? Our present chapter divisions are artificial, of course, but they do fit in with an obvious transition in Paul's development of his theme. Why didn't he offer one general, unified description of the enslavement experienced by both groups?

It is easy enough to offer a provisional, and valid, response to that question. It was not just a matter of speaking to each group in its own language when he wrote to them. There was something else. While Sin is essentially the same for both, the *mechanisms* it uses to enslave the human being will differ greatly, depending on whether human beings do or do not possess or recognize a *law* outside themselves that tells them what is licit and what is sinful. Paul makes a distinction between those who 'hear' a law coming to them from outside, and those who have it 'written in their hearts', in their 'conscience', in their 'inner thoughts' (2:13.15).

That brings us back to our original question: Doesn't Paul exaggerate the general conduct of pagans in this first chapter? If we are to answer the question, we must keep in mind two important elements that are imbedded in the structure of the chapter but not obvious at first glance.

Let me explain *the first* with an example. Any outsider who has travelled to one of the 'developed' countries, or spent some time there without running into any particular conflict, can testify that most of the people they met there were fine, sensible, generous, and open-hearted. But if it comes down to judging the global politics of that country vis-à-vis poor and 'underdeveloped' countries, that same visitor might well feel obliged to use much the same terms as Paul: "replete with every injustice, wickedness, outrage . . . insolent, haughty, boastful . . . senseless, disloyal, unloving, pitiless." And the contradiction is all the more obvious to the extent that political policy is arrived at by democratic means.

Why is it that the visitor must use such terms in the latter case, when he or she would not use them to describe the concrete persons they came to know in the developed country? Between one plane and the other, you see, we are forced to recognize the existence of a *mechanism* that is more or less unconscious and inevitable; and it is a mechanism of Sin, for sure. On one plane it leaves individuals alone at some level of relative goodness; but it steps in to blacken the picture when those same individuals become an active part of the other plane, as they cannot help but do.

Politics is obviously not the only area where these two different planes are apparent, where some sort of unbalancing mechanism has room to operate. Paul himself is proof of that fact. If we knew nothing more about him than the fact that he had extraordinary success in converting pagans to Christianity, we could still assume that he must have had good, cordial relations with those people. Paul did not win friends and influence people by lambasting everyone around him, although the first chapter of Romans seems to be written in that vein. His other letters to Christian converts from paganism express sentiments of mutual affection and esteem, and we have testimony about Paul and his relationships in the Acts of the Apostles as well.

So the first point we must keep in mind is that Paul is not offering a sociological description in Romans 1. He is trying to point up a *mechanism,* specifically, a mechanism of deceit and alienation, which explains why its victims are people whom we might well classify as well intentioned if we knew them personally.

On the personal level Paul recognizes the virtues of many pagans, even in Romans (see 2:10.14–16.26).[26] But between that level and the *culture* of the pagan world there has intervened a mechanism against which the good will of the individual can do little or nothing. In varying degrees all the people immersed in that culture succumb wittingly or unwittingly to the mechanism. It is impossible to live in and *by* that culture, says Paul, without approving to some extent what that culture sets up as normal, even though one may not accept it as an individual and may even condemn it in secret.

Using today's terms, we could say that one level is the level of spontaneous intention and the other is the level of concrete performance. Between them comes *Sin,* which for Paul is always a *mechanism,* not an isolated, conscious violation of the law. Sin sets in motion a process that deforms the human being, so that the result is something inhuman.

The second important structural element in Romans 1 has to do with the adjective I just used: 'inhuman' (or 'infrahuman', if you prefer).

I raised the question whether Paul might not have painted too lurid a picture of pagan moral conduct. But if we look more closely at what Paul attributes to them, we are surprised to find something very different. What exactly is the *injustice* Paul has in mind when he writes *"replete* with every *injustice"* (1:29)?

Somewhat to our surprise, we notice that his list does not contain the main headings we would almost automatically include on the basis of the Old Testament decalog. Paul makes no mention of false testimony, stealing, murder, or adultery, for example.[27] He does deal with the concrete realm of sexuality, but note the absence of sins that we would consider more blatant and unjust: fornication and adultery. Instead Paul deals at length with homosexuality.

Now it is true that terms such as 'natural' and 'anti-natural' have certain resonances in our society that we may have introjected. We may well feel that the practice of homosexuality is much more serious than adultery is. That is not a 'moral' judgment, however; it is an evaluation of comparative repugnance. In any Christian morality, moreover, everything acquires meaning insofar as real, effective love enters the picture. Thus a Christian morality is logically compelled to attribute much greater gravity to adultery, and even to fornication, than to homosexuality.

From the same standpoint it is pertinent to note the literary fact that Paul, in talking about this sort of sexual relationship, uses the category, natural/anti-natural (1:26–27)[28] rather than some other category directly involving the contrast, moral/immoral. He does not stress the offense against God or a human being, but rather the mutual 'dishonoring' of their bodies (1:24). They strip the *human* body of the honor due to it as a means of relating to others. In short, Paul stresses the dehumanization of the body.

We find much the same thing if we look at the list offered by Paul. The attitudes described there could hardly be considered *serious sins* in most instances: e.g., "full of envy . . . malice, gossipers . . . insolent . . . senseless, disloyal . . . pitiless" (1:29–31). If we again attempt a strictly *moral* evaluation, we would have to say that pagan human beings have dishonored their interpersonal relations, that they have *dehumanized* them.

If we equate 'animal' and 'subhuman' for our purposes here, we can say that the generalized pagan conduct described by Paul is not so much humanly immoral conduct as a reversion to the bestial conduct of the jungle, to a subhuman level. Except that in this case it involves interpersonal relations and employs human powers and instruments.[29]

Keeping these two elements in mind, let us move on to the central question: What *mechanism* produces this picture of dehumanization as the end result, a result which Paul describes as enslavement to Sin? How does Sin manage to take control of human conduct and degrade it?

From our written text the answer seems clear enough. Paul repeats the same explicative structure three times, as readers can see by noting his triple use of the verb 'hand over' (1:24.26.28). We find the same three elements in exactly the same order: (1) the human being deviates from acknowledging God; (2) God hands the human being over to the deviation of its desires and passions; (3) this results in dehumanized conduct in one's relations with other human beings.

Here is the first element in Paul's terms: "Even though they have known God,[30] they did not glorify him as God or give him thanks, but have become entangled in their own reasonings and their uncomprehending hearts have been darkened. Claiming to be wise, they have shown themselves to be fools, and exchanged the glory of the incorruptible God for the likeness of the image of (the) corruptible human being, birds, quadrupeds, and reptiles" (1:21–23). "They actually exchanged the truth of God for the lie, and adored and worshipped the creature instead of the Creator, who is blessed forever, amen" (1:25). "They did not deign to recognize God" (1:28).

The second element, causally linked to the first, finds its central affirmation in the key word, 'hand over': "*For this,* God *handed them over* to the cravings of their hearts . . ." (1:24). "*For this,* God *handed them over* to passions that bring dishonor . . ." (1:26). "And *since they did not deign* to recognize God, God *handed them over* to reprobate a mind" (1:28).[31]

The third element is Paul's description of the interpersonal conduct between human beings once the 'handing over' has taken place.

What is the logical process linking the three elements? What is the mechanism—religious or anthropological—that produces such results?

My readers might feel that this question is superfluous once we have ascertained the phases of a fairly clear process: disavowal of God in favor of idolatry, divine punishment leaving the human being abandoned to itself,[32] and, finally, the aberrant and dehumanized conduct of the human being in its interpersonal relations. I don't think there is any doubt that this is the first reading one can and should take of the chapter.

My question is designed to suggest both the possibility and advisability of a second reading or interpretation, which would not be surprising where Paul is concerned. He himself tells us that he often began his explanations with 'infantile' expressions and reasons. Depending on their own capacities, his readers or listeners could comprehend things on a more superficial level or move on to a deeper level of understanding (see 6:19; 1 Cor 3:1–2; 2 Cor 11:16–21; etc.). Paul, in any case, takes pains to provide the elements needed for a more profound and mature reading by those capable of it (see 1 Cor 2:6).

That might be the case with us today. The three-phase scheme described above might well seem infantile to us, picturing a God who *punishes* humanity's bad relationship with God (idolatry) by abandoning human beings and letting them dehumanize their interpersonal relations, as if God were tired of keeping the leash on them. The fact that such a scheme might *seem* infantile *to us* is not enough to go on, however. By itself our way of thinking cannot serve as the criterion of what Paul meant to say in his day and in terms of his categories.[33] But it is an inducement to be a bit suspicious, to see if Paul himself offers us indications that he has a deeper line of thought that goes beyond the superficial scheme: idolatry/punishment/dehumanization.

In fact, we do have such indications. The main ones show up in later chapters of Romans and culminate in the latter half of Roman 7. I think they will convince my readers that a more realistic reading of Romans 1 is in order. But since I cannot reverse the order of the chapters, I will refer here to the indications present in Romans 1 and, on that basis, formulate my hypothesis of an alternative reading.

First of all, if we look closely we will see that it is not correct to say that the enslavement of pagan human beings to Sin begins with idolatry,[34] that the initial triggering of Sin's dominion lies in the refusal to worship the true God and the turn to idols or false gods. If that were correct, then *impiety* (the generic sin against God, which would include accusations of idolatry, sacrilege, etc.) would not cede first place to *injustice* (the generic sin against all that is due to any human being), as in fact it does in Paul's text.

There are two parts to the verse in which Paul sums up pagan enslavement to Sin[35]: "The wrath of God is being revealed from heaven against every type of *impiety* and *injustice* of human beings who are holding truth fettered in *injustice*" (1:18). In the first part Paul cites two possible types of sins that can be committed and undoubtedly are: sins vis-à-vis God (*impiety*) and sins vis-à-vis human beings (*injustice*). In the second part, however, Paul drops any mention of impiety. Injustice alone is left as the mechanism of enslavement to Sin.[36] And so we get the curious opposition that becomes central in Romans 1: *truth/injustice.* Not truth/lie (as in 1:25), nor even justice/injustice, the two obvious oppositions between good and evil. Even if we had nothing more to go on than this summary formula—"holding truth shackled in injustice" (1:18)— we could cautiously advance certain observations as being of some importance.

It is *injustice,* and injustice alone, that subjects the human being to Sin. Injustice, not impiety (or the lie), is the enslaving power, the main actor, the protagonist. This is confirmed by the transition from 'impiety' to 'holding truth shackled'. Impiety is a category of sinning; the shackling of truth alludes to a mechanism on the level of consciousness or conscience. It refers to a (ridiculous) effort at self-deception by the human being. That is how the main actor operates. This does not mean that the effort is not culpable or sinful. But the point is that the real culpability does not lie in the visible result but rather in the very effort of the human being to disguise and excuse that result.

Not surprisingly, this sort of sinner bears little resemblance to a rebellious Lucifer. Paul's description is more ironic than indignant: "*they . . . have become entangled* in their own [obviously self-justifying] reasonings and *their uncomprehending hearts have been darkened*. Claiming to be wise, they have shown themselves to be *fools*" (1:21–22). Already at this stage we have the *sub*human quality that characterizes the result.

Thus, exchanging "the truth of God for the lie" of idols shows up less as a serious sin than as a stupid effort at self-deception on the part of the human being.[37] Incredibly enough, however, this effort is successful. We must not forget that behind it lies the power of the protagonist: injustice.

We find a second and complementary indication for an alternative reading if we ask ourselves: What is the point and purpose of the human being's ridiculous effort at self-deception vis-à-vis God? Paul certainly does regard the effort as ridiculous, because what can be known about God is manifestly clear since the creation (see 1:19–20).[38] Why, then, this gratuitous effort to become entangled in one's own reasoning, with the result that the heart—the seat of judgment in biblical language—is darkened, and the human being foolishly worships images "of the corruptible human being, birds, quadrupeds, and reptiles" (1:23)?

The only sensible conclusion is that the desire for idolatry is not the mainspring of this attitude or behavior. The self-deception that draws the human being from worship of the *super*human to worship of the unworthy *infra*human is a *means* for something else: i.e., injustice. That is what the desires of the human heart are really aiming at. In the idolatry depicted by Paul the real intention of human beings is to justify, on the basis of the divine, the dehumanized relations they want to have with other human beings.

Closely related is a third indication of a crucial nature. It has to do with the sequence in which the factors operate. Paul tells us what is present from the very beginning, though held in check: i.e., the desires and passions of the human being, who is inclined toward the infrahuman.

Paul attests to this pre-existing element when he tells us three times that God 'hands over' the human being to itself or to something inside it.[39] As he sees it, this human tendency to fall back into the infrahuman is restrained by recognition of an Absolute, who reminds the human being of its ought-to-be: God. The human being needs only a minimum of sincere thinking to have a clear knowledge of God as its suprahuman ideal.

There is no doubt that people have tried to see some sort of 'natural theology' in this passage: i.e., a spontaneous, correct philosophy of the divine, based on the fact of creation, as opposed to the theology 'revealed' in the Bible. But there is every grammatical indication that creation is only the temporal starting point for the 'works of God'. Unlike John, in his treatment of God Paul never seems to adopt the *essentialist* viewpoint of Greek culture. It is hard to interpret the 'works of God' in Paul as something opposed to the typically historical vision of Hebrew and biblical thought. Rather, the phrase refers to the way divine providence operates in actual events so that a norm governing human action is made transparent. At two points in Romans (2:14–15; 7:16–22), Paul stresses the basic harmony between this ought-to-be and the inner self of the human being (as opposed to its desires or passions).[40]

A fourth and final indication of a possible alternative reading comes to us from Paul's list of the 'unjust' attitudes of the pagan world that has fallen into idolatry. According to those exegetes who seem to have the best reasons on their side, all those attitudes or traits apply to human interrelations except for one, the only one that relates to God: "haters of God" (1:30).[41] This goes deeper than mere idolatry. Active hatred of a clear and complete conception of the divine must be rooted in something even more basic: i.e., the fact that the true God disturbs the human being in its effort to carry out its unjust desires. Here we have one more reason for thinking that idolatry is not the source but rather a means, an essential component in the process of self-deception whereby the human being attempts to reassure itself as it goes about its dehumanizing activity.

Why does the human being shackle the truth? Because truth interferes with what the human being wants to do. Twisting its reasoning and darkening its heart, the human being seeks and manages to fabricate an Absolute after its own desires. It is not that God takes the initiative in *punishing* and hands the human being over to its own cravings. The cravings are unleased because the human being has cunningly contrived to rid itself of the one and only thing that could hold them at bay: i.e., the norm it recognized as absolute.

In the first, infantile reading, Paul seems to have God saying something like this: "So you don't want to recognize me and render me proper worship, eh? Well, then, I am going to let you be delivered over to your craven heart, your base passions, and your defective mind" (see 1:20–24.26.28). The anthropomorphism is not the problem here, because it is present in either reading. The disturbing thing is the reaction attributed to Yahweh, or, God. The God 'full of grace and truth'—or the God of 'mercy and fidelity', to use the old Hebrew terms—reacts with a mixture of punishment and base vengeance.

I say 'punishment' and 'vengeance' because they are different from a mere *result*. The difference lies in the fact that in them we cannot see any intrinsic, causal relationship between one thing and the other. When the chain of causality is not broken, when the good or bad result dovetails with the causes at work, no one attributes the outcome to punishment or vengeance by another person (not even a supernatural person). We don't talk about such punishment when a person eats too much and then gets indigestion; but we may do so when a miser comes down with a toothache.

Picking up the aforementioned indications, I think we can and should replace the first, infantile scheme of interpretation with a different one. Instead of the scheme, idolatry/punishment/dehumanization, we will use another one in subsequent chapters: i.e., desire or craving for injustice/self-justifying and self-deceiving reasonings/creation of an infrahuman idol[42] that justifies injustice and, finally, the fall into infrahuman mutual relations. There would be no enslavement, you see, if the human being were master of its actions, no matter how bad those actions might be. But by stopping their ears to the truth that disturbs them, human beings become enslaved beings, beings driven by an alien power. Their works serve the purposes of another; and that other is *Sin,* which is the negation of God's project.

II

Now the question is: What relationship is there between this sort of evaluative definition of paganism, certainly a negative one, and the historical message of Jesus of Nazareth?

At first glance the answer would seem to be clearcut and final: none. It is not just that Paul nowhere cites Jesus in this chapter dealing with paganism as a whole. The more important fact is that it would be impossible for him to do so. It is no accident that in Jesus' message we do not find any judgment of the overall relationship between pagans and God (or the kingdom of God). By deliberate choice his message always refers explicitly to the God of Israel, the plans of that God for Israel, and Israel's situation before God. Nothing permits us, by way of mere *addition,* to move from Jesus' specific listeners to human beings in general.

It has become classic to talk about the so-called *universalism* of Jesus. But as we saw in Volume II, the most one can say is that such universalism was *virtual.* One would have to creatively deduce what Jesus *would have said* if he were in Paul's situation: i.e., confronting a humanity stripped of its classical divisions, which is how Paul wants the Christian community of human beings in Rome to be.

Let's spell out the question, then: What data in the historical preaching of Jesus might be significant and relevant here, suggesting how the God of Jesus would regard the general situation of pagans?[43]

One such datum is 'the kingdom of Satan' that is opposed to the coming kingdom of God. We tend to view the diabolic as a source of temptations to our freedom. But as we noted in Volume II, Jesus sees Satan as a 'force' or 'strong one' who keeps the human being enslaved in an infrahuman situation. This may range from privation of the physical functions of relationship to the psychic impossibility of establishing the most basic social ties. It is interesting to note that the Synoptic account in which this is brought out most clearly has to do with the 'dispossession' of a pagan specifically. It may only be a coincidence, but even in that case Paul may have noticed it and used it for his purposes. The Synoptic account clearly suggests that the contest between the two strong ones—one an enslaver, the other a liberator—is not restricted to Israel.

The Satan of the Synoptic account is not associated with any voluntary breaking of the law, but rather with some sort of possession or enslavement. Similarly, Paul's Sin, the anthropological personification of Satan, does not signify a person's free choice of some concrete evil; it signifies a power that takes possession of the human being and enslaves it.[44]

Viewed from that standpoint, Paul's message is clearly in continuity with that of Jesus. The shift from 'Satan' to 'Sin' is very easy to make; it is little more than a first attempt at demythologization. And it is also justified by the change of cultural context.

But we are still far from grasping the creative coefficient entailed in that shift. To begin with, there is a shift in emphasis. *Sin* is no longer held responsible for the physical evils that are attributed to the power of Satan in the Synoptic gospels. At first glance this may seem to be a secondary matter, but it has important consequences.

When Jesus chose disciples, he did so to send them out to preach the good news; and he gave them the *consequent* power to expel demons and cure illnesses. Those expulsions and cures, you see, were the signs that God was once again present in Israel's history and that God's kingdom was close at hand or already inaugurated. It is worth noting, therefore, that this anti-satanic function *in the physical realm* disappears in the Pauline churches. On the other hand, the charism of *prophecy* takes on major importance (1 Cor 14:24–25). Exercise of that charism becomes the sign that "God is truly among" the faithful. Why? Because another basic human need (besides physical integrity), which cannot be met under the enslavement to Satan-Sin, is thus satisfied completely. The human being "will be called to account and judged by all; *the secrets of its heart will be laid bare*" (1 Cor 14:24–25).[45]

From the very first chapter of Romans we notice that knowledge (judgment) of Sin and its mechanisms is equated with discovery of the truth about the 'heart' and 'mind' of the human being.

That brings us to the second datum permitting Paul's transposition. If my analysis of the Synoptics in Volume II was correct, if the political key did succeed in unlocking the more or less occult meaning of much of Jesus' preaching, then his message was far from being ingenuous. In parables and direct debates with his adversaries, Jesus located the *root* sin elsewhere than in the superficial sin that could be attributed to the poor. He located it in the ideological use of God and God's Law to oppress people. To put it another way: hardness of heart[46] paralyzes the truth so that it does not come to the aid of suffering people who need it. Indeed we could say that the accusation of sin levelled by Jesus at his opponents is that they "are holding the truth (about God) shackled in injustice."

What must Paul do to transpose this basic proclamation of Jesus to pagans—or better, to a humanity composed of both Jews and pagans? *Two* things, obviously.

First, he must exchange the political key, valid for Israelite society, for an anthropological key. That is what he does, moving from the accusation of oppression to the more general accusation of social relations devoid of truth and humanity. To grasp and verify this change of key, readers can compare the list of epithets that Jesus hurls at the Pharisees in Matthew's gospel (Mt 23:1–32), or that might be culled from his polemical parables, with the list of epithets that Paul applies to pagans in general.

Second, and this step might look easy for an expert in Scripture such as Paul, he must move from the ideological use of God by means of a mistaken interpretation of God's Law to (pagan) idolatry. I use the general term, 'Scripture', because the historical Jesus does not seem to have shown any interest in the problem of formal idolatry. That would fully accord with his intention to address his message to "the lost sheep of the house of Israel."[47] And despite the abundant biblical material on idolatry, Paul's thinking, particularly in Romans 1, is far from being a mere repetition of traditional judgments of the subject. That fact is noteworthy. Paul's analysis of idolatry cannot readily be culled from Scripture because his analysis somehow 'equates' the idolatry existing both *outside* and *within* the religion of Yahweh.

We can distinguish two major periods in the biblical treatment of idolatry. The first period, which extends up to the Exile, tends to deal with the topic from the standpoint of *monolatry.* The second period, from the Exile on, deals with it from the standpoint of *monotheism.* In both periods the Bible detects very human (non-religious) motives in the mechanism that leads to idolatry, but the motives differ in the two periods.

In the first major period of implicit polytheism, the danger facing Yahwism is human greed. People are inclined to break the covenant with Yahweh, as one might betray a friend or spouse, if some other deity promises to provide them with what they are seeking in even greater measure: "I will go after my lovers, who give me my bread and my water, my wool and my flax, my oil and my drinks" (Hos 2:5).[48] It is not theological orthodoxy that is at stake in choosing one or another deity, but such things as fecundity, fertility, and victory in war.[49]

A new literature on idolatry surfaces when the crisis of the Exile forces the prophets to explicitate a profounder view of Yahweh as the sole creator of the universe who transcends all earthly and heavenly powers (see the view of Deutero-Isaiah in Is 40:1–18f.). Jealousy, the hallmark of the implicit polytheism opposing Yahwist monolatry in the earlier period, is no longer the dominant trait of Yahweh as depicted in the Bible. Irony characterizes Yahweh's view of the deliberate efforts of human beings to forge an image in their own perishable likeness and then worship it (see Is 40:19–20; 41:6–7; 44:9–20). But this satiric presentation of the material *origin* of idolatry tells us nothing about the human mechanism that leads to it. Indeed, the more inexplicable idolatry seems, the better the satire works.

We are forced to conclude, then, that Paul's thinking on idolatry in the first chapter of Romans does not coincide exactly with any of the biblical treatments of the theme, even though there might be some traces of similarity, more apparent than real, with the second chapter.[50]

The fact is that the first chapter of Romans is intimately connected with the second chapter and 'magnetized' by it, so to speak, even though this may not be readily obvious. Paul wants to show us that *all humanity* is 'under Sin' (Rom 3:10). He is not trying to classify sins by groups. He is trying to show that the *same* slavery and the *same* inhuman mechanisms are at work in 'sins' that seem very different in terms of their objects. In the very first chapter, then, Paul must logically provide an analysis of idolatry that will serve as the basis for his later accusation that the Jews "do *the same things*" (Rom 2:1).

Viewed in these terms, Paul's logical process is much closer to the approach of Jesus of Nazareth and his critique of religious *ideology*, of the way human beings use their relationship with the divine.

Paul seeks and finds a common substrate for two very dissimilar situations: pagan polytheism on the one hand, Jewish monotheism on the other. Both do 'the same things'. Such an approach means that Paul has already chosen to shift his emphasis away from the plane where the two situations confront each other as *opposites*: i.e., the plane of orthodoxy. Thus Paul makes a creative leap with respect to Scripture, pointing out that pagans, in a conscious way, are basically just as orthodox as Jews in their knowledge of divine reality (see Rom 1:19-21.25.28) and their moral obligations (see Rom 2:14-15). It is precisely in the *transition from that orthodoxy to praxis* that *both* go astray, becoming enslaved to the same *Sin* even though they commit different sins.

In trying to establish the basic orthodoxy to be found in paganism, Paul faces a new and difficult problem.[51] In the message of Jesus he can find only a proof against the contrary view (see Volume I, Chapter II, section III). Jesus teaches that the crucial factor for an *authentic* relationship with God is a heart sensitive to the signs of the time and what is best for the human being.[52] And to underline the potential danger of using religion to harden one's heart, Jesus cites two examples of better sensitivity than that of Israel in his own day. One has to do with pagan people, the Ninivites; the other has to do with a pagan individual, the queen of the South.

This confirms the hypothesis that injustice takes precedence over idolatry, needless to say. But in the general context of paganism Paul must obviously offer some explanation for one cultural fact of great importance: i.e., the difference between adoration of Yahweh in a formally orthodox way, however corrupt it may have become, and adoration of pagan idols. To do this, Paul must show:

(a). That the religious deviations of paganism are *secondary* by comparison with the *primary* datum—a basic religious unanimity that is correct.
(b). That humanity, not God, was responsible for the concrete evils represented by idolatry.
(c). That Sin gained control, not over the knowledge that is the *basis* of

religion, but rather over the *use* made of religion. To use my terminology, Sin gained control over religious *ideology*, not over *faith*.

In the *use* of religion and attitudes associated with it there are mechanisms that are intimately linked to Sin. This point was made repeatedly by Jesus in his parables and his polemics with the Pharisees. It was made again by Paul in this same general period of his life with respect to two different Christian communities: the Galatian community of largely Jewish origin and the Corinthian community of largely pagan origin.[53] This means that even the message of Jesus and his warnings were not enough to immunize people's use of religion against the anthropological mechanisms of sin, even in the earliest Christian communities.

The difference in context between Galatians and Corinthians may well be the reason why the close parallelism of Paul's argument in both cases has not been given enough attention. He uses the same vocabulary in both cases, and he starts from the same basic point: the proclamation of Jesus conveyed by Paul and accepted in faith is accompanied by the presence of the Spirit of God (see Gal 3:1–2; 1 Cor 2:1–5; etc.).

Starting out from there, however, things have taken a wrong turn in both communities; and this is no accident in Paul's view. There must be an anthropological root to the problem, a radical human mechanism leading people into an inferior situation, a situation that is more facile, 'human', and 'natural' (see 1 Cor 3:3; 2:14; Gal 4:29). What attracts our attention, however, is the fact that this situation is also, perhaps even 'more', *religious*. There is a strange mechanism at work, one which we might erroneously judge to be absent from our secularized world. It is what Paul has in mind when he addresses himself to those Galatians who "want to be subject to the Law" (Gal 4:21) when that is unnecessary. In the case of the Galatians, the mechanism leads to the useless multiplication of 'observances'. In the case of the Corinthians it leads to the useless pursuit of religious 'efficacy', "boasting of human beings" (1 Cor 3:21), and human practices. The Corinthian discussions that Paul calls 'infantile' (1 Cor 3:1) deal precisely with the different degrees of religious efficacy associated with the preaching of different apostles and the Baptism received from them (see 1 Cor 1:11f.).[54]

There must be some anthropological mechanism to account for the tendency of human beings to place themselves 'under' the religious sphere.[55] Paul uses various terms to designate this tendency, one of the vaguer ones being 'human' as opposed to 'grace'. For example, Paul tells the Galatians who want to submit anew to religious law that those who would be justified by the Law "are severed from Christ . . . fallen away from *grace*" (Gal 5:4; RSV).

These 'designations' take a back seat when Paul gets down to more accurate and authentic definitions. Two new characters appear that are crucial in the human struggle: the *Flesh* and the *Spirit*. We have already noted that the correct basis and starting point of religious faith, both in 1 Corinthians and Galatians, is the operative presence of the Spirit. Now we learn that the misguided religious behavior of the two communities, their mistaken use of religion, is labelled with the same epithet by Paul. It is 'of the flesh' or 'fleshly' (1 Cor 3:1-4; Gal 3:3).

The meaning of the two terms, Flesh and Spirit, in the Bible is no secret to any exegete, and their meaning remains the same for Paul and John. To biblical authors, particularly from the Exile on, 'flesh' means the human being or any living creature left to its own capacities, to its created substratum as such. 'Spirit' means the power of God, either operating alone or (more frequently) giving the creature both the basic preconditions for existence and survival as well as the loftiest and most characteristic embodiments of human qualities. When exegetes want to translate 'flesh' into modern vernacular terms, they use different circumlocutions to convey the root biblical meaning of the term.[56]

Unfortunately many exegetes go no further than that, even though it is only a start in trying to grasp Paul's meaning when he uses the term. Remember that Paul is trying to explain what mechanisms are responsible for the fact that an originally authentic religious faith tends to degenerate in all humanity, and due to something he calls *the Flesh*, into a religion 'under Sin'. The work of the Flesh described in Romans 1 is akin to that of the Flesh described in 1 Corinthians, whereas the work of the Flesh described in Romans 2 is akin to that of the Flesh described in Galatians.

Now in the Old Testament 'flesh' was a factor of sin only when it led people to place their confidence in human, created, political, and historical means *instead of* Yahweh (see Is 31:1-3). When the creature ('flesh') recognized its creaturely character and its radical indigence, sensing the profound terror and total adoration it should show toward the transcendent, the term 'flesh' tended to have a positive meaning. As a synonym for the creaturely condition, therefore, the term 'flesh' could have either a negative or positive meaning. It was negative when it turned into an element of *secularization,* positive when it became an element of *religiosity.*

When we look at the term in the letters to the Galatians and Corinthians, however, we are surprised to find that it seems to refer to an excess of religiosity. We are forced to conclude that the human being's deep awareness of its creaturely condition leads it to place religion above itself, to use the religious realm as an intermediary between the intangible transcendent on the one hand and the insecurity of its condition as a creature on the other. The creature tries to lay hold of the transcendent and use it for human purposes. For Paul, then, the term 'Flesh' means just the opposite of a tendency towards secularization.

It was Jesus' criticism of the religion of the Pharisees that enabled Paul, an ex-Pharisee, to effect this revolution in the terminology of the Old Testament. Flesh now signifies that the creature is afraid to confront God with criteria (ontological and epistemological premises) deriving from the human being. Thus it is opposed to an authentically religious faith, seeking to use the religious realm ideologically and placing that realm under the enslavement (and the mechanisms) of Sin.

It is of the utmost importance that we discover what this mechanism concretely comprises for human existence. Otherwise its anthropological anti-dote, *Faith,* as used in Paul's text, will come across to us as a merely magical element with supernatural efficacy and without any connection to a transformation of the whole human being.

Let us not rush ahead too fast, however. Another anthropological character must now appear to incarnate and clarify the mechanism that places religion in the service of Sin.

CHAPTER II

Sin, Enslaver of Judaism

Romans 2:1-28

(1) For *all* that you have no excuse, human being, whoever you may be, you who judge *others,* for in judging the other *person* you condemn yourself because you pass judgment *in spite of* doing the very same things *the other* does. (2) And we know that God's judgment, in accordance with the truth, is levelled against those who do such things. (3) You, human being, who pass judgment on those who do such things and do the same yourself, do you think you will escape God's judgment? (4) Or do you think little of the wealth of his kindness, patience, and forbearance, not *choosing* to recognize that his kindness *seeks* to lead you to conversion? (5) Because of the hardness and impenitence of (your) heart, you are storing up wrath for yourself on the day of wrath and the manifestation of the just judgment of God, (6) who will give to each *human being* according to its works. (7) To those who seek glory, honor, and incorruption, (God will give) eternal life. (8) But for those who (are) egotists, indocile to the truth but docile to injustice, (there will be) wrath and indignation. (9) For every human person who works evil, the Jew first and also the Greek, (there will be) tribulation and anguish; (10) glory, honor, and peace, on the other hand, for everyone who works good, for the Jew first and also for the Greek. (11) Because there is no partiality on God's part.

(12) Those who have sinned without law will perish without law, and those who have sinned in *the system of* the law will be judged by *the criterion of* the law. (13) For it is not those who hear the law who (are) just before God, but *only* those who practice it will be declared just. (14) For when *some* Gentiles, without having law, naturally do *what is commanded by* the law, they are law for themselves *even* without having law. (15) They prove thereby that they have the work of the law written in their hearts, witness being provided by their own conscience and their inner thoughts, which will accuse and even defend them (16) on the day when

28

God will judge the secrets of human beings through Christ Jesus, as per my good news.

(17) But if you call yourself Jew, and rely on the law, and glory in God, (18) and know his will, and discern *the essential*—having been instructed by the law, (19) and claim to be guide for the blind, light for those who dwell in darkness, (20) *moral* educator of the foolish, teacher of uninformed beginners, because in the law you have the very pattern of knowledge and truth— (21) well, teaching others, you do not teach yourself; preaching one should not steal, you steal; (22) saying one should not commit adultery, you commit adultery; *claiming* to abhor idols, you commit sacrilege. (23) Glorying in the law, you dishonor God by transgressing the law; (24) and so, on account of you, God's name is blasphemed among the Gentiles, as it is written.

(25) Circumcision is certainly useful if you fulfill the law; but if you are a violator of the law, your circumcision becomes uncircumcision. (26) Now if uncircumcision keeps the just precepts of the law, will not that uncircumcision be reckoned as circumcision? (27) Physical uncircumcision that fulfills the law will judge you who, possessing the letter *of the law* and circumcision, (are a) transgressor of the law. (28) Because being a Jew is not in the outer, nor is circumcision the outer in the flesh; being a Jew (is) in the inner, and circumcision of the heart (is) in the spirit, not in the letter, and its praise (comes) not from human beings but from God.

Chapter 2 of Romans deals mainly with the universality of Sin within the Jewish people. At first glance it seems much easier to understand—perhaps too easy.

I

In this chapter it seems that Paul is saying that those who have the Law—i.e., the Jewish religion based on biblical revelation—do "the very same things" (2:1) the pagans do. Indeed they add a new sin insofar as they pass judgment on those things from a vaunted religious superiority (see 2:1–5.17–24).

Is that the case and, if so, why? To answer those questions, we must begin by considering two preliminary matters. The first has to do with the actual boundaries of the 'chapter' in which Paul alludes to Judaism and its enslavement to Sin. The second is what Paul means by the three examples of sins that are committed in the Jewish world even though they are judged as sins: stealing, adultery, and sacrilege.

Insofar as the first matter is concerned, we know that the division of Paul's letters into chapters is a later and largely arbitrary device. It normally signals a more or less noticeable change of subject in the author's train of thought. As such, the division into chapters is a practical and useful tool for reading and interpreting Paul. By the same token, however, someone dividing a written piece into chapters cannot help but try to make divisions of relatively equal length. It would hardly be suitable to designate three lines as a chapter simply because they contain a theme different from the ones treated in the preceding and following lines.

We have already noted that Paul's purpose in the early chapters of this letter and any corresponding material is to prove that both pagans and Jews are 'under Sin' (3:9). So we are naturally led to seek a sort of diptych, a picture with two panels. One panel would contain a description and proof of the sinfulness of pagans; and we found it in Romans 1, where Paul specifically dwells on the accusation of idolatry throughout that chapter. The other panel would contain Paul's treatment of 'the Jew' as a religious category characterized by possession of the revealed Law; and we expect to find it in Romans 2.

Right away certain questions crop up. To begin with, the appellation 'Jew' appears for the first time in 2:17. Up to that point Romans 2 contains the general term 'human being' (2:1.3.9). So it is at least possible to say that Paul continues to talk about pagans up to 2:12 at least, then discusses the judgment that God will pass on both pagans and Jews (2:12–16), and only then begins to address himself to Judaism (see ICC 2:138).

There is one item that might seem to lend support to such an hypothesis, though in fact it works against it as we shall see later. It is the repetition, in very similar terms, of the key phrase used to describe the Sin of paganism: i.e., holding truth shackled in injustice. Describing human beings whom he does not specify exactly, Paul says that they are "indocile to the truth, but docile to injustice" (2:8).

It is more likely, however, that whoever divided Paul's letter into its present chapters was correct in identifying the human being who judges others (2:1) as the "you call yourself Jew" of 2:17. So the second panel of the diptych would begin with 2:1. Indeed judging others is the central feature noted by Paul throughout Chapter 2, and certainly the most serious factor in the enslavement of the Jewish world to Sin.

What causes the ambiguity here is the fact that Paul makes the *transition* from the first to the second panel of his picture by interjecting the assertion that *all* human beings are subject to the same critierion of judgment, without alluding as yet to Judaism specifically (see 2:11). Thus the sinfulness that dominates paganism is not avoided by people who merely condemn it while doing "the same things" themselves. Paul goes on to speak of God's judgment based on a just and universal criterion; it will certainly take such differences as inner law or revealed law into account, but it will not permit any of those differences to function as a *privilege* (see 2:12–16). This is an at least implicit allusion to Judaism, and Paul then proceeds to mention the Jew explicitly.

There is another question about the termination of the chapter, and we shall see that it is an important one. The fact is that Romans 3 continues the panel devoted to Judaism right up to verse 20. There is no break in continuity between 2:28 and 3:1. Moreover, the first part of Romans 3 (verses 1 to 20) permits Paul to arrive at the conclusion he wants to draw, providing him with the most relevant materials. Only there do we see clearly that in his second panel Paul pretty much repeats the same structure he used for his first panel. *Only there,* for example, does Paul provide his catalogue of Jewish behavior that corresponds to his catalogue of pagan conduct in the first chapter.

Now our second question, which would become rather minor if Romans 3:1–20 were incorporated into Romans 2, is this: If the Jew does "the very same things" (2:1), why does Paul charge the Jew with three specific sins, none of which he attributed to pagans in Romans 1? And this is quite aside from the fact that it is hard to see how those three sins—stealing, adultery, and sacrilege (2:21–22)—could have been typical in the Jewish world, even in the diaspora.

To begin with, the inhuman 'falsification' of interpersonal and intergroup relations that Paul attributes to pagans contrasts sharply with the three offenses attributed to the Jews, even if the latter are cited only by way of example. Looking at the matter from a sociological standpoint, we must admit that Paul does not depict Jewish society as profoundly corrupt and inhuman, even though he specifies three sins. We might almost say that he depicts Jewish society as a pretty normal one. So there must be some key that will lead us to another level, one where Paul can detect a grave situation akin to that which is so obvious in his description of the pagan world. And remember this: Paul must prove, not that the Jews commit sins, but that they are *slaves* to Sin.

More than one hypothesis presents itself here, so let me consider them briefly. A first hypothesis would suggest that Paul offers these specific examples of sins because they are expressly prohibited in the Law, the Mosaic decalog. For his examples Paul chooses a direct violation of the first commandment, a direct violation of the seventh commandment, and a direct violation of the eighth commandment, as those commandments are presented in Exodus 20:3.14–15. In the case of pagans, Paul describes the *overall* disorder of their conduct because he must point up its gravity without being able to appeal to an explicit law, which they do not possess. In the case of Jews, on the other hand, one might assume Paul need only point out how they are clearly and directly violating the commandments of their own law, letter and all. And here again one transgression noted by Paul has to do with *impiety,* two have to do with *injustice.* Although these transgressions might seem minor compared to those that characterize pagan life, they would suffice to support Paul's basic argument that "all have sinned and lack the glory of God" (3:23).

But do they suffice to support Paul's other conclusion, which goes much deeper: "We have already made the accusation that we all, Jews and Greeks, are *under Sin*" (3:9)? It is difficult to see how the three sins of the Jews could be anything but explicit and conscious. Hence it is difficult to discern the 'enslavement to Sin' that is so closely bound up with holding truth 'shackled' in Paul's line of argument. Indeed so true is this of Paul's argument that in the end we find that not even Christians are free not to sin; at best they have been freed from the necessity of being slaves to Sin.[57]

There are two additional reasons for rejecting this first hypothesis. One is the fact that in this same chapter Paul makes another accusation against the Jews: because of their conduct, "God's name is blasphemed among the Gentiles"

(2:24). It is hard to see how such sins as stealing, adultery, and sacrilege could lead people to despise or hate the God of Israel unless they were a universal and distinctive constant among the Jews, and unless the Gentiles could boast of better conduct, which is even more unlikely.

The second reason for rejecting this hypothesis is that there is no historical proof for such conduct among the Jews, contrary to the case of the pagans as depicted in Romans 1. Some exegetes interpret the word 'sacrilege' here in the strict sense of sacking the temples of idols. They do not seem to realize how historically unlikely it is that around the middle of the first century Jews, either in Palestine or in the diaspora, were in a position to loot pagan temples frequently. In short, exegesis cannot offer any historical evidence of facts that Paul might have assumed to be widely known (at least among the Romans), culturally significant, and influential.

A second hypothesis about these three sins as examples interprets them in a figurative sense. That would obviously be easy in the case of *adultery*, a word whose metaphorical use for 'idolatry' is amply attested in the Bible. Indeed this usage is even more noteworthy in the New Testament because at that point in time it no longer had to do with any *real* or pervasive idolatry among the Israelites, as it did in the time of Hosea, for example. When Matthew's gospel has Jesus using the expression, 'wicked and *adulterous* generation' (Mt 12:39; see also Mt 16:4 and Mk 8:38), Jesus is not accusing his listeners of any *formal* idolatry; he is accusing them of disfiguring the face of the true God by their thoughts and actions. And that conduct is perfectly compatible with the strictest Yahwist orthodoxy.[58]

The sin of *stealing* could be interpreted in a similar way, though such an interpretation would be far less likely. Jesus accused the Pharisees—or more probably the scribes, whose official function was to interpret the Law—of taking advantage of piety and religion to gain control over the goods of the weak and the needy (Mk 12:40). According to Matthew, he also made the more general accusation that they were using religion as a means of oppressing the multitude of the poor (Mt 23:4). Those accusations, however, are too closely bound up with the socioreligious structure of Palestine to be readily applied to the Jews of Rome.

A metaphorical interpretation of the third sin, *sacrilege*, would be even more difficult to find, unless one interpreted it in the strict sense of robbing temples and assumed that here it meant that the Jews of the diaspora were charging exorbitant prices in selling animals and other products for cultic use in pagan temples.[59]

That brings us to a third hypothesis. The unknown nature of the three sins mentioned by Paul is solved, or loses its importance, when we perceive their proper place in the overall scheme of Romans 2, which reiterates the scheme of Romans 1 in broad outlines.

That brings us to the second phase of our exegesis of this chapter. If we take Chapter 2 as a whole and add to it the first part of Chapter 3, we arrive at the general conclusion that embodies Paul's intention in his diptych of Sin among both pagans and Jews: "We have already made the accusation that we all, Jews and Greeks, are under Sin" (3:9).[60] All, in other words, are enslaved to that anthropological character named Sin, which is not to be confused with any specific sin, however serious the latter may be.

Now in the first part of Romans 2, Paul reminds Jews that they cannot appeal to any privilege because they do "the very same things" (2:1) that other human beings do. And because "there is no partiality on God's part" (2:11), Jews must consider themselves subject to the same negative judgment passed on all those who, by their deeds, are "indocile to the *truth* but docile to *injustice*" (2:8). My readers will recall that 'holding *truth* shackled in *injustice*' (1:18) was practically Paul's shorthand definition of the pagan enslavement to Sin.[61]

Starting from this base, we will find in the material of Romans 2 and 3:1–20 elements that closely parallel those of Romans 1. One difference must be duly noted, of course, with respect to the religion of the Jews and their specific enslavement to Sin: i.e., their possession of the Law as both a norm and a positive divine revelation.

It is true that Romans 2 is not so obviously structured in three parallel parts, as is Romans 1; but if we look closely, we find that the elements are there.

If we assume that in this chapter, too, injustice is distorting truth, we must ask ourselves what sort of injustice Paul has in mind. Once again we find that this injustice is not composed of sins consciously accepted as such, no matter how serious they may be.[62] It is characterized by a dehumanization of human relationships.

This is made clear right at the very start. Paul presents the Jew as someone who 'judges' others, who clearly *despises* other human beings. This is not regarded as a *sin* by the Jew, whose scorn goes hand in hand with the realization that the Jews have been favored by God with a revealed norm. Paul makes this clear in refuting any such pretensions (see 2:11 and, in more general terms, 2:6–11).

We begin to see that the Jews, on the basis of something proper and exclusive to them, have ended up with some of the characteristics that Paul attributed to pagans. We can and should assume that they are "slanderers . . . insolent, haughty, boastful . . . unloving, pitiless" (1:30), because all that is to be included under the heading of 'judging'. The proof, adduced by Paul, is the fact that "*on account of you*, God's name is blasphemed among the Gentiles" (2:24). This general accusation can have only one cause: namely, the hatred provoked by Jewish 'religious' conduct towards other human beings.

If there were any remaining doubts about this, it is spelled out clearly with biblical testimony in the part of the second diptych that matches the description of pagan dehumanized and 'unjust' conduct in the first chapter. The only thing is that we must go beyond the limits of Romans 2 to find it, as I have already mentioned. In Romans 3:9-19 we find a list of behavioral practices that are more dehumanized than formally sinful, and that Paul finds not only in observable reality but also in a series of biblical passages.

The list is preceded by Paul's general conclusion: "We have already made the accusation that we all, Jews and Greeks, are under Sin" (3:9). As if this accusation were not adequately grounded in observable reality, Paul adds a series of biblical passages: "as it is written" (3:10). It is clear why Paul has recourse to this biblical listing to document the basis for his accusation, rather than to mere sociological observation. He wants to rule out any claim by Judaism that it is in a more favorable position vis-à-vis divine judgment. The Bible is no argument for the pagans; there one must adduce facts. But it is an argument when it comes to the Jews. And so Paul's list ends with these significant words: "But we know that whatever the Law says, it says it *speaking to those who are in the system of the Law,* in order that every mouth be stopped . . . " (3:19). Here the first mention of 'the Law' is synonymous with Scripture or divine revelation as a whole, and the phrase in italics obviously refers to the divine norm dictated to Israel specifically. Thus Israel itself, which has turned the Law into a privilege, must recognize its enslavement to Sin (see 3:19).

It is instructive and highly interesting to see the parallel between this biblical listing and Paul's list of pagan forms of conduct. "There is no one who is just, no one who has sense," parallels "replete with every injustice . . . senseless" (3:10-11 and 1:29.31). "No one who seeks God" parallels "haters of God" (3:11 and 1:30). "All have gone astray, all together have become useless" parallels "to do the unsuitable" (3:12 and 1:28). "There is no one who does good, not even one" parallels "replete with every . . . wickedness" (3:12 and 1:29). "An open grave is their throat, with their tongues they are in the habit of deceiving, snake poison is under their lips" parallels "full of . . . deceit, malice, gossipers" (3:13 and 1:29). "Their mouth is full of curses and bitterness" parallels "slanderers . . . insolent, haughty, boastful" and "full of envy" (3:14 and 1:30.29). "Their feet are swift to shed blood" parallels "full of . . . murder, quarreling" (3:15 and 1:29). "Destruction and misery pile up along their ways and they have not known the way of peace" parallels "replete with every . . . wickedness, outrage . . . inventive in wickedness . . . pitiless" (3:16-17 and 1:29-31).

Looking closely, we can see that the parallelism is surprising[63] and can hardly be accidental. Selected from among many other possible biblical accusations, these must be equivalent to "the *very same* things" that are both the initial trigger and the ultimate result of the mechanism of enslavement. And again we should note that these "very same things" are not conscious serious sins but major factors in the dehumanization of mutual relationships between human persons. Left to themselves, human beings tend toward this *sub*human state.

For a true enslavement to Sin, however, there must be something more than a list of deeds. As we have already seen, it is essential that the human being imprison or shackle *the truth that links it to God,* i.e., to an ideal of humanity. This was the second element at work in the process Paul observed among the pagans. It must show up again in the case of the Jews to trigger the desires or cravings in question.

But it is obvious that the relationship of the Jews to God is *different* from that of pagans. (Paul will discuss whether or not it is a radical difference.) The Jews have been the object of a gift from God, who has given them a *Law*. And here the word has the twofold sense meant in Scripture and in Paul. It is a revelation, and it is a normative revelation.

These two senses are clearly brought out by Paul in Romans 2 and the first part of Romans 3. "God's oracles were entrusted to their faithfulness" (3:2). Those oracles embody the ought-to-be that dovetails with God's will and that should orientate the human being in its actions. Thus Paul tells the Jew: "You call yourself Jew . . . and know his will, and discern the essential—having been instructed by the Law" (2:17-18). Here we have the one and only difference between the pagan's knowledge of God (1:19.21) and that of the Jew. But this difference is "a great deal" (3:2). In itself or in terms of God's universal plan, it represents a big 'advantage' and has much 'usefulness' (3:1). God will certainly take this 'usefulness' into account when passing judgment on those to whom it was given as a norm (2:12).

Logically enough, if the Law was given, it was given in the first place to be *fulfilled*—even if God did have later plans for it, as we shall see (3:4.20; 5:20; Gal 3:19.22). Acting in compliance with it would have meant the avoidance of the 'unjust' patterns of conduct listed by Paul. At the very least it would have provided *"knowledge of Sin"* (3:20).[64]

Now Sin enslaves by *shackling* that revealed and normative truth. To do that, it must darken the heart of the Jews and cause them to become entangled in their own reasonings.[65] How is this accomplished precisely under the prompting of dehumanizing cravings or desires?

Here is what Paul says in this first stage of his analysis of the Law. Sin accomplishes this by turning Jewish attention from the *fulfillment* of the Law to the *privilege* they enjoy by virtue of having the Law. This means that the Law ceases to provide the disturbing knowledge of Sin and at the same time enables the Jews to justify their dehumanized relationships with people of other religions and non-Jews in general.

At this point, in any case, Paul stresses that the important thing was to fulfill the Law (2:13.25).[66] How does the human being manage to delude itself about the Law, driven by its cravings for injustice? By taking the Law as a possession, one which serves as the basis for a disdainful attitude and relationship— ideological oppression—vis-à-vis those who do not possess the Law. This point surfaces right from the start. Paul clearly points to this dehumanizing distortion with a key word: "you who *judge* others" (2:1). The heart and its knowledge of God is darkened thereby. It is *used* to dominate others, or to compensate for oppressing others on a different level. And the means is disdain. One regards others as "blind . . . in darkness . . . foolish . . . uninformed beginners" (2:19-20).

Now it is important to realize that this God, who is thus misused by the unjust cravings of the heart, ends up being 'blasphemed'. And with good reason. Because no matter how much literal orthodoxy may be involved, this God is in fact an *idol:* a deity whose judgments are based on the outer trappings of the human being—its nation or race—rather than on its heart (2:27–28); a deity who grants odious privileges and advantages (2:11), thereby causing pagans to hate the image of that deity as they see it reflected in the conduct of such believers (2:24).

Here, then, is the great paradox. The Jews, making use of God's own normative revelation, commit the very same sin of idolatry that pagans do, and for the very same reasons: i.e., to set free their cravings and dehumanize their relationships with other human beings. Deceiving themselves, they end up entangled in their own self-deception and enslaved to the power that wields that self-deception against God: i.e., Sin.

II

Now let us once again consider Paul's creative effort in connection with the message of Jesus as presented in the gospels.

With Romans 2 we enter the second panel of Paul's diptych depicting the enslavement of all humanity to Sin. Here it is Judaism's turn to be analyzed by Paul. Yet we find a curious situation.

In Romans 1, remember, Paul faced a difficult situation and had to be very creative because a 'Christian' judgment of paganism could find only rudimentary and implicit data in the message of Jesus. Dealing with Judaism in Romans 2, we assume that Paul's discussion of the mechanisms of Sin there could benefit from the rich, profound, and explicit treatment of the same theme in the gospels. Instead we find that Paul's treatment seems to be relatively poor and inferior by comparison with what Jesus had to say in the Synoptic gospels. Moreover, Paul's statement that the Jews "do the same things," that they steal, commit adultery and sacrilege, seems to be sheer invention on his part, and hardly very creative by comparison with Jesus' profound and radical analysis of Israel's real sins.

I think two things must be kept in mind here, which might help to offset that initial impression. First of all, Paul is addressing people of Jewish origin living in Rome; he cannot merely parrot Jesus' judgment on the sinfulness of Jews living in Israel. It is not just that their sin may be different. Even if Jesus' criticism of his Israelite contemporaries were valid for them too, the main problem is that Paul's *audience* is a different one.

Paul is not trying to address two different groups in turn, first pagan converts to Christianity and then Jewish converts to Christianity, using different arguments to persuade each group of its sinfulness. His letter is addressed to a community made up of both groups, and both must grasp one and the same argument that Paul uses to place them both on an equal footing vis-à-vis God's radical and universal judgment.

Unlike Jesus, Paul does not argue from *within* the context of Jewish revelation. Instead he points his guns much more directly at the *function* performed by religious Jews in the world. Jesus proves that they 'blaspheme'. Paul proves something else that can be verified by pagans, since it affects them: namely, that the Jews *cause* God's name *to be blasphemed* by the Gentiles (2:24).

If we grasp this limitation imposed on Paul by his overall audience, we will better appreciate why he is forced to be more original vis-à-vis Jesus' message in the Synoptics. And we will also better appreciate the creativity he needed to overcome the second factor that imposed limitations on him. The fact is that the Jewish people of the diaspora, in sociological terms at least, occupied a morally higher place in the general pagan milieu. It is precisely because of this moral superiority, or the assumption of it, that Paul feels compelled to discover in their works "the very same things" that God will impute to the pagans. In short, Paul must prove that the supposed morality which the Law gives to the Jewish people, and which they follow more or less, leads other people to 'blaspheme' the God of Israel.

The two factors described above rule out any literal transcription of the gospel message and its political key. On the surface they would also seem to bar Paul from concluding that Sin holds all of humanity enslaved. If we keep that in mind, Romans 2 will not seem to be as impoverished as it might seem at first glance.

As a matter of fact, we are forced to recognize that the whole chapter is suffused with a line of thought that is clearly evangelical in origin. I am referring to the polemical assertion that connects the end of the parable of the murderous husbandmen with the parables of the talents and the sower: "That is why I tell you that the kingdom of God will be taken away from you and given to *a people who will produce its fruits*" (Mt 21:43; 13:11–12; 25:29 and par.).[67] And the fact that this failure to produce fruit is the result of bad faith, of people's self-serving deformation of the truth ("indocile to the *truth* but docile to *injustice*"—Rom 2:8) is made clear in the same Synoptic passages which record the polemic (see Mt 21:38; 13:13–15; 25:24–27 and par.).

If we follow this line, we will see that Paul's argument in Romans 2 makes sense. As yet we do not get the full sense because Paul must go much deeper in his analysis.

Paul's argument goes something like this. Israel's function is to serve as the universal witness to Yahweh's divinity. It assumes that its own special characteristic is knowing the divine will and hence being able to distinguish good from evil.

But what is the actual situation? Only if the will of God is rightly interpreted and fully carried out, says Paul, can this witness serve to attract the whole world to Yahweh. It will achieve its purpose only if a group of human beings, a people, act as Yahweh would act on earth. If it is carried out only partially rather than *totally*, which is the normal case, the result is a hateful and counterproductive *religious* division that estranges the world from Yahweh.

Here two things must be noted. *First*, we do not yet know, nor does Paul explain in this chapter, *why* the Jews do not fulfill the Law completely as Deuteronomy assumes they would. Nor does 'their' Sin lie in that fact. If the

Jews, like the pagans, are 'under Sin', the reason is something that has to do with religion, truth, and justice.

In that sense it is possible that we exaggerate the importance of the three 'sins' or violations of the Law mentioned by Paul as examples. They may not even have been sociologically characteristic. Perhaps Paul chose them at random from the prescriptions of the Law to demonstrate that the Jewish people, for all their declarations of principle, always end up violating their Law. Perhaps we might even reverse Paul's statement of the issue and put it this way: "If you commit adultery, you still continue to maintain that one should not commit it."

Second, it is also worth noting that Romans 2, for the most part, does not focus on the inner attitude of the Jew towards self or the Jewish community; instead it focuses on the Jew's attitude towards the pagan, an attitude based on the possession of the Law even though the latter is only partially obeyed.

Pursuing the gospel line, we find in such an attitude all the traits of a *privilege* that has become disengaged from its accompanying *responsibility*, from its functionality vis-à-vis the outside world: "you who judge others" (2:1); "do you think you will escape God's judgment?" (2:3); "egotists, indocile to the truth but docile to injustice" (2:8); "those who hear the Law" (2:13); "you call yourself Jew, and rely on the Law, and glory in God" (2:17); "and claim to be guide for the blind, light for those who dwell in darkness, moral educator of the foolish, teacher of uninformed beginners" (2:19-20); "glorying in the Law" (2:23).[68]

Remember that Paul's explicit intention in these first two chapters is to prove that the two religious groups of humanity "do the very same things." We can then say that his statement about the pagans in Romans 1 applies even more to the Jews: "For what is knowable of God is manifest in their midst, because God has made it manifest to them" (1:19). But even though this supplementary knowledge of the divine has always been formally "re-cognized" (1:28) in Israel, the same mechanisms noted by Paul among the pagans are operative among the Jews. As the pagans "hold truth shackled in injustice," so the Jews are "indocile to the truth but docile to injustice" (2:8). We could say that "the cravings[69] of their hearts" (1:24) and "a reprobate mind" (1:28) turn that divine revelation into an instrument of injustice and egotism, thus making the name of Yahweh hateful.

We note two significant differences, however, when we compare Paul's argument in the second chapter with his argument in the first chapter.

First, the deviant conduct of the Jews remains on the religious plane. Remember the exact nature of Paul's accusation. He does not simply say that the Jews commit theft, adultery, and sacrilege. He says that the Jews pass judgment on other people from the standpoint of their religion *as if* they did not do the same things. The emphasis does not shift from the religious realm to the realm of human interpersonal relations, as it did when Paul was talking about the pagans in Romans 1. Many of the adjectives and characteristics applied to pagans certainly could be attributed to the Jews as well; but even then they would lose the general, secular tone they had in the first chapter and refer to attitudes directly bound up with the Jews' conception and practice of religion.

Second, in the case of the Jews there is no validity to the hypothesis that would suggest we take literally the explanation of dehumanized attitudes offered in Romans 1. Remember how that explanation went. The process of deviation (in mythical terms) supposedly involves *three* stages: natural revelation of God, theoretical and practical disregard of that revelation, and divine punishment opening the doors of the human heart to its inhuman tendencies.

In the case of the Jews we do not find the intermediate stage that would explain divine punishment: i.e., a transition from the evil of idolatry to the evil of injustice. This should help us to see that Paul did not intend his readers to take literally the explanation he offered in the first chapter. In the case of the Jews, Yahweh could not punish ignorance or disregard of revelation. Yahweh's revelation was always formally acknowledged, especially in eras devoid of syncretism and idolatry such as the era of Jesus and the era of Paul. Nevertheless 'the cravings of the heart', 'passions that bring dishonor', and a 'reprobate mind' did not cease thereby to be at work in the Jewish world. They were the *cause*, not the *effect*, of Jewish perversion of God's revelation.

Even in the first chapter, then, we are not dealing with a divine decision to punish a deliberate, conscious, sinful act against God on the religious level by denaturalizing interhuman relations. Romans 2 seems to suggest that God never managed to get the full, authentic sense of divine revelation recognized by Israel. At least there is no mention of a period when that was the case. We are faced, then, with a thorough critique or criticism of 'the religious' as such.

We can begin to understand the mechanism involved if we look at Paul's criticism directed against another community. It is not exactly his criticism of the Galatians for 'going back' to a religious element that no longer makes any sense. Rather, it is his criticism of the Corinthians for their almost instinctive tendency to turn elements that should serve faith and revelation into 'religious means'.

It is here that a new anthropological character surfaces, one that I alluded to at the end of the previous chapter and that will prove to be crucial in Paul's christology: i.e., the Law.

Every 'religion' is a system of beliefs or practices, of revelation and moral norms. That is precisely what Paul is referring to in Romans 2, under the name of Law. It is here he begins his discussion with this complex character.

As we have already had occasion to see in abstract terms, and as Paul's comments to the Galatians and Corinthians bring out more clearly, a divine *revelation* to human beings can take place only through human means, through the one kind of language that a human being understands. The beings who express it, the words and formulas they use, and the gestures they make, are all human. And human, too, are the means they use to transmit that revelation to future generations: creedal formulas, religious authorities, moral norms, rites, and sacraments.

Unfortunately, human beings do not readily take to the deeper process of molding their existential values in accordance with God's revelation. They tend to short-circuit the process.[70] Clinging to the values they already hold or serve, they try to bolster them with the allegedly *sacred* (*value-free*) *efficacy* of the human elements that necessarily accompany any and every revelation from God.

The specific danger of this system of efficacy is brought out by the gospel message. People cannot rest content with merely using supposedly effective (magical) means to carry out their intentions. Insofar as *religious* means are considered sacred and placed above the human being, they are *absolutized*. The 'heart', the center of practical judgment, hardens and closes itself to the values that challenge us *from the locale of (secular) history*, however much it may acknowledge those values in theory. The field of human activity is necessarily defined by an economy of energy, and so the use of those absolutized means displaces every other sort of interest; and this is done in God's name. The result is 'judging' and 'glorying'.

This critical-minded conception of the Law is profoundly faithful to the historically verifiable message of Jesus, and it forms the meaningful core of Romans 2.

The Jewish religion has proved to be sterile in carrying out the universal function that God bequeathed to it. And the cause lies in the whole religious system that has been built up under the name of *the Law*. It is not a chance occurrence, nor is it due to any particular weirdness in the Jewish people. It is due to an underlying tendency in the human being as such. The roots of 'egotism' and 'injustice' tend to darken human judgment about 'the truth'. Confronted with a revelation designed to fulfill human beings, the latter lay hold of religion rather than faith as their tool.[71]

And they do it in a way that is just as odious as other acts of egotism or injustice: e.g., stealing, adultery, or plundering the temples of other people.

The point is clear, and Paul states it explicitly in Romans 2. God will judge human beings, not in terms of their religion (2:1), but in terms of what they 'seek' (2:7). As the gospel message tells us, God will judge them in terms of their inner reality (2:25–28), in terms of the intentions that come from their heart and are not later belied by their 'works' (2:6).

Only when we view the Law from this standpoint of the inner human being (2:28) can we appreciate the fact that the Law *in principle* can represent *faith:* i.e., the adherence of the human being to the values that God proposes in God's revelation. This holds as true for pagans as it does for Jews (2:12–16).[72] Further on we shall consider the concrete history of the Law.

Romans 2, then, establishes the complete *universality* of God's judgment. From the standpoint of human enslavement under Sin, it neither sees nor makes a distinction between pagans and Jews. Before the judgment of God there now stands only *the Human Being* (2:1–3.7–11).

Anticipating a bit on the basis of our analysis so far, we can say that Paul has at least paved the way for further study of the concrete course taken in history by these two anthropological characters, *Faith* and *Law*. In Abraham and Jesus we shall see God's revelation comprehended and assimilated without distortions as a source of values structuring a human life and its activity; we shall see *Faith*. And we shall also see the religious realm in all its ambiguity, simultaneously a formulation of God's will and a religious instrument used by human beings to avoid seeing the truth: i.e., *the Law*.

CHAPTER III

Between Law and Faith

Romans 3:1–31

(1) What is the Jew's advantage, then? Or what is the usefulness of circumcision? (2) A great deal, from every point of view. First of all, God's oracles were entrusted to their faithfulness. (3) So if some of them were unfaithful, does their unfaithfulness render ineffective the faithfulness of God? (4) Never! God must be true, though every human being be false, as it is written: "That you may be declared just in your words and win out, on being judged."

(5) But if our injustice sets the justice of God in relief, what *are we to say* then? (That) God is unjust when he inflicts his wrath on us?—I am speaking in human terms— (6) Never! Because, otherwise, how is God to judge the world? (7) But if the truthfulness of God *is made manifest* even more to his glory by my lie, why am I still judged as a sinner? (8) Might it not then be the case, as some people slanderously allege that we say: "Let us do evil that good may come (of it)"? The condemnation of such people is just.

(9) What then? Do we *Jews* have a head start? Not entirely. Because we have already made the accusation that we all, Jews and Greeks, are under sin, (10) as it is written: "There is no one (who is) just, (11) no one (who has) sense, no one who seeks God. (12) All have gone astray, (all) together have become useless, there is no one who does good, not even one. (13) An open grave is their throat, with their tongues they are in the habit of deceiving, snake poison (is) under their lips. (14) Their mouth is full of curses and bitterness. (15) Their feet (are) swift to shed blood, (16) destruction and misery *pile up* along their ways, (17) and they have not known the way of peace, (18) there is no fear of God before their eyes."

(19) But we know that whatever the law says, (it says it) speaking to those who are in *the system of* the law, in order that every mouth be stopped and the whole world present itself guilty before God. (20) Because no flesh, through the works of the law, will be declared just

42

before him. Since with the law *comes* knowledge of sin.

(21) But now, independently of the law, the justice of God has been manifested, in accordance with the testimony of the law and the prophets, (22) that is, the justice of God through faith in Jesus Christ for all who believe. There is no distinction, you see. (23) Because all have sinned and lack the glory of God, (24) being declared just by the gift of his grace through the redemption *accomplished* by Christ Jesus (25) whom God destined to be, in his own blood, expiation through faith, so as to prove the justice of God in overlooking earlier sins (26) during the patience of God: *i.e.,* to prove his justice at the right moment, so that he might be just and declare just one who believes in Jesus.

(27) Where, then, the glorying? It has been ruled out. By what law? By the law of works? No, but by the law of faith. (28) We maintain, you see, that the human being is declared just by faith independently of the works of the law. (29) Is God (God) only of the Jews, and not of the Gentiles as well? Of course of the Gentiles as well! (30) So if God is one (and only), (it is God) who will declare just circumcision in accordance with faith, and uncircumcision by means of faith. (31) Do we then invalidate the law with faith? Never! Rather, we make it stand.

Here Paul comes to a thorny question: Why did God entrust the Law to Israel? In other words, what is the place of the Jewish Law in God's plan for humanity?

"What is the Jew's advantage, then? . . . *A great deal, from every point of view*"(3:1–2). "What then? Do we Jews have a head start? *Not entirely*" (3:9). Paul's way of thinking, all his creativity and earnest desire to get to the bottom of things no matter what the cost, is embodied in the flagrant contradiction between his 'yes' answer in verse 2 and his 'no' answer in verse 9 of the very same chapter.

As if that were not enough, we find a similar contradiction in the last ten verses of the chapter. "But now, *independently of the Law,* the justice of God has been manifested . . . through faith in Jesus Christ . . ." (3:21–22). "*Do we then invalidate the Law* with faith? Never! Rather, *we make it stand*" (3:31).

These two contradictions, one at the start of the chapter and the other at its end, indicate that Paul is somewhat uncomfortable with the question at hand, one which will recur time and again.

This is the apparent theme of Romans 3, which justifies it as a distinct chapter. My earlier remarks might seem to suggest the contrary. Remember that the first half of the chapter continues Paul's treatment of Jewish enslavement to Sin (3:1–20), whereas the second half introduces the character that God sets up as a counterweight to *both* Jewish and pagan enslavement to Sin: namely, *Faith*. The subsequent chapters of Romans will show how Faith permits God to declare just those who found themselves enslaved. Nevertheless, throughout Romans 3 Paul confronts the problem of the Law and its function.[73] In the first half of the chapter he challenges the Jewish pretension that the Law constitutes a privilege and an advantage for them. In the second half of the chapter he denies that God's declaration of justice can in any way depend on the fulfillment of the Law.

Discussion of the Law, then, provides the apparent unity of the chapter.[74] Appearances may be deceiving, of course, but that does not excuse us from taking a careful look at the inner logic of the chapter and its two sections.

I

Obviously, the *first part* of Romans 3 has already been the object of our analysis. As I pointed out, it continues and concludes the second diptych in Paul's treatment of human enslavement to Sin. Why bother to pursue the matter further in this chapter? Because Paul, in expounding his thought, broaches new themes that are worth noting and that will recur again and again.

One of those themes is the role of the Law given to the Jewish people in God's universal plan for humanity. It is closely associated with another major theme that surfaced in Chapter 2 and that can be summed up in Paul's own question: "How is God to judge the world?" (3:6)

One significant indication of the unity of these two themes is the fact that Paul's first obvious contradiction has to do with this divine judgment, and the Law is involved. First Paul tells us that God is going to use the criterion of the Law to judge those under it (2:12); then later he tells us that God will use the same criterion of judgment for all, and that this criterion will be independent of the Law (3:30).

But let's not go too fast here. Let's take our time and see what we find. Perhaps the theme of divine judgment will enable us to salvage data from Romans 2 that we bypassed in our analysis of the core of that chapter.

The first datum is that God's judgment shows no partiality, gives no advantages to anyone (2:11). To ground this assertion, Paul says that in judgment God "will give to each human being *according to its works*" (2:6).

It should be noted that this is not merely a biblical citation (Ps 62:12). It is a constant preoccupation of Paul: see 6:19-23; 8:12-13; 13:8-10; 1 Cor 6:9-11. And the proof is the fact that Paul is not satisified with a mere biblical quote. He proceeds to elaborate his own thinking right away: "To those who seek glory, honor, and incorruption, God will give eternal life. But for those who are egotists, indocile to the truth but docile to injustice, there will be wrath and indignation. For *every human being who works evil*, the Jew first and also the Greek, there will be tribulation and anguish; glory, honor, and peace, on the other hand, for *everyone who works good*, for the Jew first and also for the Greek" (2:7-10).

It is precisely after this explanation, which makes *working* good or evil the criterion of universal judgment, that Paul states that God shows no partiality (2:11). Then Paul goes on to say that God will take the Law into account in passing judgment, not to upset his impartiality but to confirm it in the face of dissimilar situations. Since some have been granted greater discernment for working good (2:18), it is only logical and fair that greater good should be demanded of them.[75]

Paul's preoccupation to point up the absolute universality and impartiality of God's judgment, based on one and the same criterion *for all* (working good), must be kept in mind as we try to interpret the second half of Romans 3, where Paul seems to make faith in Jesus Christ the criterion governing the very same divine judgment.

This preoccupation leads to another consideration about the Law, one that is important for Paul and for us. In order to prove the even-handedness of his judgment of all humanity, God had to leave the Law susceptible *to the same mechanism of self-deception* that subjected the pagan's 'natural' knowledge of God to Sin. So after stating that God entrusted God's revelation to the Jews, he goes on to say: "God must be true, though every human being be false, as it is written, *'That you may be declared just* in your words and win out, on being judged' " (3:4).

Thus "our" injustice—that of the Jews, who possess the Law—"sets the justice of God in relief" (3:5). Because the most important thing of all is fairness, one and the same divine attitude towards all human beings. To the Galatians Paul writes: "If in fact we had been given a Law *capable of giving life*, then *justice would really come from the Law*" (Gal 3:21). In that case God's judgment would favor some over others. "But, in fact, Scripture *has locked all under Sin*" (Gal 3:22).[76] This is almost an exact parallel to what Paul says in Romans 3. God gave a specific Law to a specific people. If God's judgment is to be even-handed, then it must be clear that this Law does not change the Jewish people's situation vis-à-vis the criterion of divine judgment: i.e., working good. So Paul goes on to say: "We have already made the accusation that *we all*, Jews and Greeks, *are under Sin*" (3:9). Then he proves his assertion with the list of sins drawn from the very Law that makes Jews to be Jews in religious terms.

A second datum is implicit in what we have just seen, laying the groundwork for the real meaning of the latter half of Romans 3. Paul will spell it out later in insistent terms, but we can read it here between the lines.[77]

Up to 3:20, Paul has been presenting a diptych of humanity's enslavement to Sin in terms of its two religious components: the Greeks (pagans) and the Jews. I have already noted that it would be wrong-headed to ask why he did that instead of presenting one single picture of humanity, since "there is no distinction . . . all have sinned and lack the glory of God" (3:22–23). But why is that a wrong-headed approach for us to take? Because even though Paul suggests that the two situations are the same (both parties "do the very same things"), and even though the same basic mechanism is operative (both hold "truth shackled in injustice"), we still cannot figure out why God would entrust the Law to a specific people—particularly when we realize that Paul is hinting that *it was not God's intention* that the Law be carried out as an effective norm (see 2:5; 5:20; Gal 3:19)![78]

There is only one logical solution to the puzzle, you see. We must convert

Paul's diptych, which comes across as a static presentation of two simultaneous pictures, into a *dynamic process* involving two stages. The representatives of the two stages are both present in Paul's time, to be sure, but the process itself awaits a third and definitive stage. And the third stage is what Paul focuses on in the latter half of Romans 3.

The figures who represent the start of each stage in God's plan for humanity are Adam, Moses, and Jesus (see 5:14).[79]

In the first stage (Adam to Moses), Paul sees an advantage that will be regained only in the third stage: i.e., universality. Though enslaved to Sin (the negative aspect), all human beings are clearly confronted with the same criterion: working good or working evil. No one can claim to possess divine privileges. If people do make such a claim, they cannot help but know that they are indulging in self-deception—at least at the start. Thus no one can succumb to hardness of heart simply and solely on the basis of an inner voice by which God tries to keep the human heart open and sensitive.[80]

In the second stage (Moses to Jesus) there appears the Law, promulgated by a 'mediator' (Gal 3:10-20): Moses. Now remember that in these early chapters of the Letter to the Romans Paul's main aim is to convince the Jews that they, too, are under bondage to Sin. For this reason Paul concentrates on discrediting the Law as a possible way of escaping the common lot of humanity and the criterion by which all will be judged. By his own admission, then, Paul puts less emphasis on the positive side of this second stage, a stage that seems doomed to failure from the very start.

But there are important indications of the positive purpose of the second stage. To begin with, by attacking Judaism's distortion of the Law and its purpose, Paul indirectly hints at the positive purpose God had in mind for it. God let God's voice be heard *from outside* the human being, through a 'mediator', so as to raise the level of humanity's moral *discernment* (see 2:18). The outside word clarifies the inner voice and elevates moral concern by refining and explicitating it. At least that is what God intended by entrusting divine oracles to people and expecting fidelity from them (see 3:2).[81]

The most important indication that this is a unique and universal process lies in the fact that God's intention *will not fail*: "So if some of them were unfaithful, does their unfaithfulness render ineffective the faithfulness of God? Never!" (3:3-4). Thus when pagans convert to the faith, they do not assume the dead letter of the second stage (see 2:27) but its life-giving sap. They are not branches of the olive shoot that have been broken off, but *wild* shoots *grafted* on to the trunk (see 11:16-18).

For all its positive aspects, however, the second stage could only be a stage, because it introduces a negative element into the universal picture: i.e., its particularity. And a sacral particularity of that sort is always provisional and dangerous. That is why its fulfillment (not of its letter) will also be its termination.

The final stage must combine the positive elements of the first two stages: the universality of the first stage with the moral level of the second stage. And it must do away with the unsuitable aspects of the first two stages: the moral confusion of those depending solely on subjective conscience and the moral conceitedness of those who regard their objective, sacred particularity as a privilege vis-à-vis God. So this dialectical process will culminate in the third stage, the Christian one. Paul begins to discuss it in the latter half of Romans 3 when he writes: "But now . . ." (3:21). Let us look at this 'now'.

The *second half* of Romans 3 deals with what has been called 'Paul's system' by some exegetes. I shall show later why I do not agree with that expression, but it does reflect the surprise we feel upon reading the letter. For we suddenly find ourselves before a strange, new way of picturing how God saves the human being enslaved to Sin, a conception we do not find in the rest of the New Testament. God still passes judgment on human beings enslaved to Sin, yet somehow manages to declare them just.

Our surprise is all the greater because Paul's conception here is novel, not only compared with the rest of the New Testament writers but also with his own presentation in Romans 2, where he tells us that the sole basis of God's judgment is whether human beings have worked good or evil. Here in Romans 3 we are suddenly confronted with a new criterion: *Faith*. All human beings are and remain sinners, but God declares just those who believe in Jesus.[82]

Paul states this principle repeatedly in the last ten verses of Romans 3, and it is worth noting that he does so in *abstract* terms. Concrete examples will come in the following chapters. Herein lies the importance of Romans 4, for example, where he discusses the Faith that justifies Abraham.

Some readers might ask: Why do we need examples at all when the principle itself is so clear? Let me answer that question honestly right here. We need examples for two reasons: (1) In laying down his principle here, Paul does not seem to be consistent with what he wrote earlier (Chapter 2) and what he will write later; (2) his later examples show us that the principle, seemingly so clear in the abstract, is actually more complicated when applied to concrete cases.

Having said that, let me get back to the last ten verses of Romans 2 and analyze them as if they were all we had. I will introduce supplementary data only insofar as the basic terms of his principle are ambiguous and force us to look for clarification.

Let us begin with one restatement of his principle that is more important, I think, because it embodies a serious personal commitment embraced by Paul: "*We maintain* . . . that the human being is declared just by Faith independently of the works of the Law" (3:28).

(1). Here we are told about the judgment that God passes on the *human being* as such, on humanity rather than on the Jew or the pagan. We are in the third stage, where odious particularities disappear and all humanity is treated in the same way. And if anyone has doubts about that fact, Paul does away with them right away. He rejects particularity and makes it crystal-clear that God will use the same criterion, Faith, to judge all human beings: "Is God (God) only of the Jews, and not of the Gentiles as well? Of course of the Gentiles as well! So if God is one (and only), (it is God) who will declare just circumcision in accordance with *faith*, and uncircumcision by means of *faith*" (3:29-30).

Notice that up to this point the principle applies to humanity *only insofar as faith has arrived* (see Gal 3:25), only to the *now* of which he is speaking in Romans (3:21). Without further data on the time of "the patience of God" or the time of the Law, we must for the moment restrict the principle to the third stage that begins with Jesus Christ. From that point on, at least, all humanity will once again be judged equally on the basis of faith.

(2). Remember what I have already said about the Greek verb translated as 'declare just'. It is a judicial term, referring to the court judgment that declares a defendant innocent or guilty. Obviously it does not *make* a defendant innocent or guilty, it simply declares that person innocent or guilty. Paul certainly could be using the term in a new way, but we have no *a priori* reason to assume that he is. Up to this point, at least, we cannot justify such an assumption on the apparent contradiction between a declaration of innocence based on faith and his earlier statement that God's judgment is based on working good or evil.

What should be kept clear in our minds right now is that the *judicial* context of the Greek verb connotes the divine judgment that is passed on all human beings to decide their ultimate fate.[83]

This is the way, says Paul, that God judges all humanity by the same standard (see 3:29-30). By being *declared just* in this judgment, human beings obtain *redemption* (3:24) and expiation for all "earlier sins" (3:25). They are then at peace with God (5:1) and saved (5:9), because those who are in Christ Jesus will not be condemned (8:1).

All these interpretive precautions, which might seem curious or exaggerated, are necessary because of the final part of Paul's assertion. He tells us that the reason behind our being declared just is "Faith, independently of the works of the Law" (3:28).[84]

Let us begin, then, with *Faith*. Perhaps the best thing for us to do right now would be to suspend judgment, since this is the first time we meet the term aside from an equally mysterious reference to it near the start of Paul's letter (1:17). In any case it is clear that the term 'faith', unlike the stricter term 'justify' or 'declare just', opens out in all directions, even as it does in our vernacular languages today. It can connote trust in a person, hope in some future, certitude about the affirmation of certain truths, and so forth. We might as well assume at the start that Paul's use entails all these connotations, and that only the context will set us on the right track.

Faced with this first appearance of the term, the only thing we can safely assume is that by 'faith' Paul means something opposed to 'works of the Law' insofar as God's judgment is concerned. Trite as this observation may seem, it can help us because Paul has already referred more than once to such 'works'.

Before we delve into that contrast, however, we must note something else about Paul's use of the word 'faith' in this chapter. It may shed light on the term or, alas, it may only confuse matters more. In 3:28, which embodies a very personal stand on Paul's part as far as I can see, he talks simply about 'faith' as something independent of the works of the Law. But the first time Paul sets forth his principle in this chapter (3:22), he talks more specifically about "faith *in* Jesus Christ." This faith is held by "all who believe," a clear reference to the Christian community, to those who "are in Christ Jesus" (8:1), as Paul will put it later. The point is all the more important insofar as Paul, after particularizing his universal principle in Romans 3, goes on to say that it is through this "expiation through faith" (3:25) that God is able to "declare just one who believes in Jesus" (3:26).

At this point in our study, then, we can only note the *two extremes* of faith and its meaning: the vaguest and the strictest.

In Romans 4, Paul tells us that Abraham was declared just because he believed *in* God (4:3.17). Here is faith in the vaguest sense. Abraham was declared just, and he obviously could not have had faith 'in Jesus'. We find the other extreme, faith in the strictest sense, when Paul writes further on of "*the word* of faith that we proclaim" (10:8). He tells us: "If you confess with your mouth *that* Jesus is Lord and believe in your heart *that* God resurrected him from among the dead, you will be saved" (10:9).[85] Clearly we are dealing with the same general theme, but here the word 'faith' is used in its narrowest or strictest sense and has almost dogmatic content. Note the use of 'that'. Exegetes agree that its basic content, embodied in the formula 'Jesus is Lord', was one of the earliest and most widely preferred *faith-formulas* in the Church. It marked the Christian as such, and martyrs used it to signify their perseverance in the faith unto death (Bultmann: 81,125,312).

We cannot easily tell in each individual case whether Paul is using 'faith' in a very strict or very loose sense, but we do well to keep in mind the two poles of meaning within which the word operates.

Even more helpful to us in pinpointing the meaning of 'faith' would be the thing that Paul sets up in opposition to it. Once again, however, Paul's usage is imprecise. In the ten verses we are examining here, Paul contrasts 'faith' with three terms: 'works of the Law' (3:28), 'works' (3:27), and 'Law' (3:21).[86]

Are the three terms referring to the same reality? It can hardly be doubted since the ten verses in question reiterate the same basic principle in different ways. Then which term is the best for following Paul's line of thought? One could say that there is no need to choose between them, that it would be better to keep all three in mind as we wait for further explanations and applications from Paul. Several observations might help us a bit here, in any case.

First, in his most solemn formulation of the basic principle (3:28), Paul uses the fuller and more explicit terminology: 'works of the Law'. Barring evidence to the contrary, then, it is quite likely that we should assume both 'works' and 'Law' as going together whenever we find Paul discussing the same theme and using one of the terms by itself.

Second, let us consider the seeming contradiction between the principle set down here by Paul and his discussion of God's universal judgment in Romans 2. In Romans 2, the criterion was 'working' good; in Romans 3, the criterion shifts from 'works' to faith. Notice that the use of the verb in Romans 2 reduces a series of 'works' to a process in the singular: 'working good' (2:10). In Romans 3, by contrast, we have the *plural* of the noun, 'works'; and it is further specified by the term 'Law', which prescribes or forbids many works. This may be a big help to us in trying to resolve the apparent contradiction, especially since we can refer here to 1 Corinthians for a similar use of words. Paul is talking about 'the day' of divine judgment, and he writes: "*The work* of each one will be made manifest . . . and *the quality* of each one's *work* will be tested by fire . . ." (1 Cor 3:13). Here we have Paul's thinking about divine judgment once again, and he is referring to Christians (see 1 Cor 3:11). Once again he seems to be referring to the work of a person as a process, and he uses the noun 'work' in the singular. We would do well to keep this in mind as we explore the further elaboration of Paul's thought in Romans.

Third, I want to say something about the capitalization of 'Law' in this chapter, both in the term by itself and in the expression 'works of the Law'. Remember that I did use capitalization systematically for Romans 2 and the first half of Romans 3, with one exception.[87] My purpose was to point up what Judaism had turned into an instrument of Sin: i.e., *the Law,* the normative divine revelation summed up in the decalog of Moses and presented more amply throughout the Old Testament. Now when Paul uses the expression, 'works of the Law', is he really referring to the same divine Law or Revelation contained in the Bible? The question is important and deserves a careful answer.

At first glance we might be inclined to answer: no. Paul has already laid down the principle that all human beings are enslaved to Sin, so we would expect his new principle to apply with equal relevance to pagans and Jews. But it turns out that the new principle does not seem to greatly affect the situation of pagans. If we are dealing with *the Law,* then the substitution of faith for 'works of the Law' would have to do with the mainspring of Sin operative exclusively in Judaism. The Jews are the ones who 'glory' in possessing the Law (3:27). And if my remarks above are correct, they are also the ones more closely associated with the plural 'works', since one would need some exterior law, such as that of Moses, to keep tabs on both sinful acts and good works (see 5:13).

Despite the seeming merit in these arguments for a 'no' answer to our question, I think that 'the Law' to which Paul is referring here is indeed the Law of Moses and should be capitalized. My reason is very simple. The same thing is required of both pagans and Jews: i.e., faith.[88] Only faith, in a way we have yet to spell out, is capable of leading the human being, enslaved to Sin, to a declaration of justice and hence reconciliation with God. If Paul contrasts faith with something, that something refers solely to Judaism to the extent that only Judaism had a different way of viewing God's judgment. Only in Judaism could sin be reckoned on the basis of works performed according to the Law or in violation of it (see 5:13).

Thus the positive side of the principle (the declaration of justice, thanks to faith) applies to both Jews and Greeks; but the negative side of the principle (elimination of the works of the Law as the criterion of judgment) applies only to those who can appeal to the Law of Moses as their distinctive criterion. If Paul were addressing himself solely to converted pagans here, he could have said simply that one is declared just *through faith*. In fact, that is precisely what he does say in Romans 3:30.

Now even if our statements are exegetically sound so far, we cannot help but raise one final question with regard to the principle just set forth. Faith, as something opposed to 'the works of the Law', clearly has a direct connection with the *mechanism* that subjects the Jews to the bondage of Sin. But the pagans, too, have their own *mechanisms* for falling into the same bondage, thanks to the 'cravings of their hearts'. In the case of both parties, the mechanisms lead to enslavement by way of self-deception and the shackling of truth. So the question is this: Isn't *the faith* mentioned by Paul opposed, in principle, to the 'entangled reasonings' of the pagans just as it is opposed to the 'works of the Law' of the Jews? Paul does not deal explicitly with that question in the verses under examination here. But it may have been on his mind as he elaborated his thinking, and its unconscious influence may show up in what he writes further on: in Romans 7, for example. So far I have simply broken ground in our effort to understand Paul's basic principle and avoid simplistic rehashes of it.

II

So far we have seen that in the first two chapters of Romans Paul managed to find in the historical message of Jesus the capital idea that *Sin* exercises its enslaving power over all. An element of lying, inherent in *the Flesh*, takes control of all religious revelation, systematizes it, and puts it in the service of human interests. It is not just that religious revelation is turned into an ideology. As a 'sacred' ideology, it perverts human judgment to the point where human beings unwittingly and naturally use religion to justify their unjust relationships with other human beings.

Paul uses the case of the Jews as his example. Among the various religious elements that have been placed in the service of Sin, Paul selects one and uses it for his demonstration: i.e., *the Law*.

From that point on, it is more difficult for Paul to pursue the continuation of his *anthropological* argument in the gospels—or, to be more exact, in the fragments of the gospels that were available to him at the time. In a real sense Paul must now risk pursuing the logic of the premises he has already laid down.

The first conclusion that seems to follow from those premises is this: if God's plan was to remedy the situation of pagans through a supplement of knowledge (i.e., a revelation to the Jewish people), through the Law,[89] then God failed miserably in that effort. The fact is that both Jews and pagans 'do the very same things' and 'hold truth shackled in injustice'.

Hence it is obvious to Paul that this was not God's plan, or at least God's *whole* plan. The seeming mistake has to be part of a much bigger and more complicated plan. To discover this plan, Paul must once again depart from the letter of the gospel message, where only Jesus' ambivalent thinking about the Law can be found. Indeed he must also depart from the more literal sense of Old-Testament Scripture because it focuses on the theme of the chosen people soon after discussing the creation of the rest of the world's peoples.

Paul's intended re-reading, which is designed to embrace all humanity in God's plan, must necessarily go back to a stage preceding Sinai, the place where the people of Israel were 'religiously' constituted through the promulgation of the Law of Moses. For the former Pharisee Paul, moreover, circumcision and Law go together. The former is the sign of one's total acceptance of the latter (see Gal 5:3). Because the priestly source retrojects the circumcision back to the patriarchal period and even a period in the life of Abraham (see Gn 17:1f.), for his argument Paul can use only the first seventeen chapters of Genesis: i.e., from the creation of the world and humanity to the circumcision of Abraham.

I am getting a bit ahead of myself, however. The point here is that Paul's creative interpretation demands a re-reading of God's plan, which he will eventually rediscover in Jesus of Nazareth and thus be able to verify as a complete process.

To get back to Romans 3, it is obvious that in it Paul is compelled to adopt an hypothesis in support of his argument that God's plan was always broader than any mere victory of the Law. And with all the precautions involved, his hypothesis is nevertheless scandalous. It is the idea that *it suited God* that the Law should fail to make the human being just.

If Paul had used a political key, such an assertion might seem obvious enough because it would very much dovetail with the fate of Jesus himself. All great politicians are such because they fight the great vices of society. If Israel's religious law had succeeded in building a solid and just society, little or no interest would have been evoked by the human being named Jesus. The fascinating thing about him was his fight against those who were using the Law to justify a great injustice. That is what Paul writes to the Galatians, even though he does not express himself in the political key: "If in fact we had been given a Law capable of giving life, then justice would really come from the Law. But, in fact, Scripture has locked all under Sin *in order that* the promise might be granted to believers through faith in Jesus Christ" (Gal 3:21–22).

However cynical, the basic idea is obvious enough in a political key. But in an anthropological key—or a religious-anthropological key, if you wish—the same idea is hard to express, harsh, and even scandalous. It is not very easy to say that both sinning (the breaking of the Law) and even Sin (the enslavement of human beings through their bad faith) *are suitable to God*. It is even harder to say that God actually operated in accordance with this suitability.

But the fact is that the Law, automatically understood by the human being in a 'religious' sense, is a wrong road, a dead end; and only when human beings realize that can they set out to look for the true import of the Law, which is something very different. Such is Paul's argument.

As I mentioned in the previous chapter, this argument is spelled out clearly in the Letter to the Galatians. Before being circumcised, Abraham received God's basic and gratuitous *Promise* of being an unlimited, universal blessing for humanity. Four hundred years later, by biblical reckoning, the Law came along with Moses. How did human beings receive it? With their almost natural tendency not to put too much credence in vague promises whose fulfillment they cannot keep close track of. So their conception of the Law was that of a contract: if you do this, you will gain the blessing.

Paul uses a legal comparison. The Promise was like a *testament*: i.e., the anticipated certainty of a gift. The Law was mistakenly pictured as a *codicil* added to that testament much later, a codicil which stipulated the *conditions* that the presumed heir had to fulfill in order to get the gift promised in the testament. Thus while it might have seemed to be a testament (a promise and free gift or grace), it was actually a *contract*. At least that is how the teachers of Israel interpreted the Law, says Paul.

How, then, will it be possible for God to carry out God's pristine, universal plan? That is possible only insofar as the contract *cannot possibly be carried out*. That is why Paul so frequently uses one argument that makes sense only if the Law is regarded as a contract: i.e., that even *a single infraction* is enough to make sure that nothing can be expected from the Law.

In his Letter to the Galatians Paul ridicules the assumption that God first made an unconditional promise and then, alarmed by the imprudence of such generosity four hundred years later, conditioned the gift with moral clauses based on the Law. But then how do we explain the fact that people succumbed to such ridiculousness?

Here again Paul's answer is the same: it is the natural, spontaneous tendency of human beings to believe only in that which they can control and calculate. That is why they cast their net of calculation over that which is most powerful of all: the religious realm. Once a Law came into existence, sin was calculable (see 5:13) and so was justice.

That is precisely what God has to demolish; and God cannot do it 'from above', through another 'revelation', because the latter would fall prey to the same distorting mechanisms. Humanity must pursue the trajectory of its mistake to the end and finally see that it is a mistake.

Paul's argument in Galatians is capsulized more vaguely in Romans 3 when he writes: "No Flesh, through the works of the Law, will be declared just before him" (3:20). The phrase, 'through the works of the Law' obviously alludes to the conception of the Law as a contract whose clauses are mandatory and must be carried out completely if the goal mentioned in the contract (being 'declared just') is to be achieved. By using *Flesh* instead of *human being*, Paul is also alluding to the inherent tendency of the creature to use the religious realm for its purposes, to desperately assure itself of divine benefits that are certain and calculable.

In Galatians Paul writes that these benefits are to be expected as a gift. He makes the same point in Romans 3 when he says that the justice of God, sought in the Law conceived as a contract, "now, *independently of the Law* . . . has been manifested . . . (all human beings) being declared just *by the gift of his Grace"* (3:21-24). Paul also alludes here to the fact that this is not a surprise but the fulfillment of a Promise, as he does in Galatians. Note his phrase, "in accordance with the testimony of the Law and the Prophets" (3:21), which is a shorthand term for Scripture in general. In the next chapter of Romans Paul will examine in greater detail that testimony as it relates to the promise made to Abraham.

The certain failure of the Flesh in trying to make the law operate as a contract is thus confirmed in two ways. First, the gift is actually given 'independently of the Law'. Second, efforts to achieve justice by means of the Law are doomed to failure, when judged by God's own revelation. This is made clear when Paul presents a long list of sins of which *all* are guilty, as was true of the pagans, but which in this case is further sanctioned by God's own judgment since the list comes from Sacred Scripture itself (3:10-18).

At this point we can sidestep the false conclusion, described as such by Paul himself, that we should collaborate with God's plan by committing sins of our own; or that we cannot be held responsible for them because God wants us to be sinners. But that still leaves us with another question. Is the *sole* function of the Law to show itself as a wrong road, so that we may then take the right road?

To this question Paul repeatedly answers 'no'. The Law should, and undoubtedly did, represent a step forward. I would say that Paul sees such progress in every area but one. The Law could not affect the fact that we all are under Sin.

Now at first glance Paul would seem to be a bit atavistic in trying to find some other purpose in the Law besides the one of confronting human beings with their own impotence, with their silly efforts to negotiate a declaration of justice with God as if it were their acquired right. As the difficulties of the passage make clear, it is not easy for Paul to attribute to the Law some value *that could not be denaturalized* by the Flesh and turned into a privilege or a negotiable commodity. That would seem to be the fate of any revelation that falls subject to creaturely mechanisms; and when we read Paul, we often cannot help but suspect that there is a radical pessimism in his thought.[90]

So we are at a crucial point. What *positive* function could the Law have vis-à-vis the gratuitousness of a gift? How could it have any such function without *conditioning* the gift and hence stripping it of its nature as a gift?

The Letter to the Galatians may help us here once again. In it Paul describes the Law metaphorically as our *paidagōgos* ('pedagogue': the slave who went with a boy from home to school and back again; hence, 'tutor') until Christ came (Gal 3:24). With the arrival of *Faith*, the new and decisive character that steps on stage here in Romans 3, "we are no longer under the pedagogue" (Gal 3:25).

What, then, is our present situation vis-à-vis this 'pedagogue' or 'tutor'? We can assume that the tutor has not disappeared just because we are no longer *under* it. Instead, as Paul makes clear, we must find another function for the tutor, one that is new for us but actually the *original function* of the tutor. And as the metaphor itself suggests, especially in the context of the Greco-Roman world of Paul's day, that function is for the tutor to be *under us*.[91] The Law is under the human being, not the human being under the Law. Is there any reader who does not hear an echo of the gospel message here?

1 Corinthians provides a nice complement to Galatians here. It teaches us to convert a moral but infantile question into a mature, adult one. Instead of asking what is 'lawful', we should ask what is 'suitable' (see 1 Cor 6:12; 10:23). Why? Because we are no longer *under the pedagogue*, under the Law, so "everything is lawful."[92]

When they come of age, a change takes place in those who were 'owner of everything' (Gal 4:1) by testament, by virtue of the Promise. They now effectively take possession of their inheritance: the whole universe (see, for example, 1 Cor 10:26). As owners, it would not be logical for them to ask their tutor—who was always in their service, though once capable of giving them orders—what is lawful for them to do in their own house. What help might the tutor still have to offer? The tutor can still give them guidance on the question of the 'suitability' of various means for achieving the goals they seek.

That does not mean that the teachings of the tutor have lost any of their guidance-value. They may still remain *true* (see 3:2; 7:12.14.16) as an indispensable stage on the journey towards truth; but they represent an 'infantile' stage when the pupil has reached the point of maturity.

To use Paul's terminology, we could say that the tutor's truth is one we learn with the Flesh. As we have already seen, for Paul 'fleshly' and 'infantile' are synonymous (see 1 Cor 3:1) because fear is still the mechanism operative in comprehending that sort of 'truth'. Those who worry about what is 'lawful' are afraid of doing something that will bring punishment, not about doing something that will undermine their plans and goals. Or else they are seeking to merit some reward for their conduct.

The maturity of which the Letter to the Galatians speaks so clearly is not a trial or a feat of magic. It comes at the proper time with Christ, to be sure, but it is a result of the *Spirit*. Contrary to the Flesh, the Spirit liberates human beings from fear and gives them the sense of being sons and daughters (Gal 4:4–7). They can now venture into the realm of what is 'suitable'. Leaving aside thoughts of rewards, punishments, and contracts, they can implement an historical praxis based upon loving service to others.

To get back to Romans 3, we find the same argument expressed in such succinct terms that it might well give rise to the worst possible sort of misunderstanding. Paul clearly says that the Law in itself represents a truth, even though it may be systematically distorted by the Flesh and even though it does not position the Jew any better than the pagans insofar as Sin is concerned. That is evident in his statement that *"God's oracles* were entrusted to their faithfulness" (3:2). Since God remains ever faithful, those oracles will never be taken back no matter how unfaithful the Jews might be. But the fact remains that they gave those oracles a bad reception, turning what was Promise and Grace into a contract involving merits, rewards, and punishments. In short, they operated at the 'infantile' and 'fleshly' stage.

The new stage inaugurated by Jesus Christ is mentioned only briefly at this point. Paul will deal with it in greater detail in later chapters.

We saw that in Galatians the new and decisive stage marked the passage of the child and heir to adulthood and full possession of its inheritance. In Galatians this new anthropological *status* is given a name, one which introduces another decisive character in the life of the human being with all its tensions and compromises. It is the stage of *Faith*: "Now that faith has come, we are no longer under the pedagogue" (Gal 3:25; see also 3:26).

The same term, Faith, is used to describe the same stage in Romans: "But *now*, independently of the Law [i.e., we are no longer under the pedagogue], the justice of God has been manifested . . . that is, the justice of God through *faith* in Jesus Christ" (3:21-22). A little further on Paul writes: "Where, then, the glorying? It has been ruled out. By what law? By the Law of works? No, but by *the law of faith. We maintain*, you see, *that the human being is declared just by faith* independently of the works of the Law" (3:27-28).

In that compact synthesis there lies a danger that is greatly reduced in the explanations of Galatians and Corinthians, which are so close to the gospel message. The danger is that readers might interpret *Faith* in a magical, mythical, and indeed infantile sense, just as *the Law* was so interpreted. They might see Faith as an act required by God so that God might gift us with something, precious to be sure, but nevertheless external to us and given as a gift only when we make that act.

If we get the point of Galatians, we will see the matter more clearly. God does not want to give us a declaration of justice that would place us somewhere we have no right to be. The gift that God gives human beings in Jesus Christ is the possibility of a coherent maturity, of complete fulfillment as human beings; and this presupposes replacing the mechanisms of the Flesh with those of the Spirit.

It is not without reason that Romans 8 will reiterate almost word for word the crucial passage in Galatians as to what the Spirit effects deep down in us through Faith: "The fact is that all who are led by the Spirit of God are children of God. For you have not received a spirit of slavery in order to fall back into *fear*. You have received a spirit of adoption as a child, by which we cry: 'Abba! Papa!' The Spirit itself joins to assure our spirit that we are children of God, and if children, heirs as well . . ." (8:14-17). So there is no question of associating us with some unmerited justice, thanks to the merits of Jesus Christ. Faith is something very different. In Faith, the Spirit for the first time lays down the initial foundation for a completely new existence, one opposed to the mechanisms of the Flesh. Only this new life is capable of the creative boldness proper to children of God, of achieving something new in the history of the universe, which is the Creator's heritage.

Finally, readers might ask why this new anthropological character is given the name 'Faith', a term that does not seem at first glance to be related to the vocabulary of the gospel message. We find in Paul three implicit and interrelated answers to that question.

In one sense, *Faith* is the *yes* of the human being to God's pure revelation, God's revelation devoid of the 'religious' use that the Flesh tries to make of it in order to win advantages, privileges, glory, and security. If the term in that sense seems absent from the Synoptic gospels, the reason is that Jesus attacks 'hypocrisy' without ever giving a specific name to the opposed attitude.

In a second sense, *Faith* is not an act but rather one's adherence to the person and message of Jesus. As the parables and debates in the Synoptic gospels make clear repeatedly, by this adherence we accept our status as children of the Father and heirs of the world created by him.

In a third sense, *Faith* is the attitude that enables us to overcome the fear of the Flesh. The latter prompts us to try to negotiate a declaration of justice with God, to read the clauses of the Law as if it were a contract and interpret them with as much neutrality as possible. Jesus made it clear that we must first get over that radical fear if we want to understand what God is trying to say to us. Still knowing that we are sinners, we must then plunge into the problems of a truly mature and adult life, into the task of creating a love that is truly inventive and effective in history.

These three senses make up the spectrum of meaning applicable to the term 'Faith' in Paul. We might well find it surprising, then, that we do not find the same term with the same senses in the Synoptic gospels. But do we find the same thing expressed in other terms or images?

Consider the opposite of Faith in the Pauline passage we have already examined: i.e., the works of the Law. Now recall how Jesus reacted to the interpretation of the Law made by the scribes and Pharisees, as we saw in Volume II. Both in the debates recorded by Mark and in the fourth group of parables, Jesus launched an *attack* on their interpretation; and his attack was crucial and *central* to his message. In his attack we find things very close to what Paul has to say about the works of the Law.

First, Jesus attacks a certain type of attention directed first and foremost to the Law and its letter. He says that this 'hardens the heart' and makes human beings insensitive, enabling them to mistakenly justify their lack of love and respect for their fellow human beings.

Second, in his polemics Jesus suggests that there is only one correct way to interpret the Law in line with its Spirit. Forgetting about its works, people should read and interpret the Law in terms of the dire needs of human beings. And the only way to recognize those needs is to rely on the impact of the signs that history shows us and then judge for ourselves 'what is right' to do for those in need.

Third, the conclusion we reach from Jesus' view is that human beings must have the audacity to place another criterion ahead of the letter of God's word and stake their whole life on it. And that criterion is the dictates of their own heart. If the true and correct hermeneutics of the Law demands this risk, then only those who take that risk can understand the true import of the Law and derive profit from it.

Now the fact is that *Jesus does not give a name* to this crucial, decisive attitude. But if we try to picture to ourselves the human being who acts thus before God, then it seems to me that we cannot help but regard that person as a *human being of Faith* in Paul's threefold sense.

Of course we must be careful. We must not push Paul's statements in Romans 3 too far, trying to make him say something that he does not say. But I think we have every right to say the following, to offer it as a reasonable and logical hypothesis. Paul's declaration of justice based on Faith might seem to have no parallel in the Synoptics. But when we comprehend it fully, in depth, and in an anthropological key, it turns out to be the very attitude, the crucial and decisive attitude, that the historical Jesus taught his disciples.

CHAPTER IV

Abraham, First Synthesis of the Christian

Romans 4:1-25

(1) Then what shall we say happened in the case of Abraham, our ancestor according to the flesh? (2) Because if Abraham was declared just by works, he has ground for glorying. But *it is* not *so* before God. (3) After all, what does the Scripture say? "And Abraham had faith in God, and it was credited to him as justice." (4) Now to one who works, the wage is not counted as a gift but as something due. (5) But to one who does not work, who has faith in the one who declares just the impious, his faith is credited to him as justice. (6) David, too, talks about the happiness of the human being to whom God credits justice without works: (7) "Happy are they whose iniquities have been pardoned and whose sins have been covered up. (8) Happy the human being against whom God will not debit sin."

(9) Now *does* this declaration of happiness *apply* (only) to circumcision, or to uncircumcision as well? After all, we say that faith was credited to Abraham as justice. (10) But how was it credited? After he was circumcised or before? Not with circumcision, but in (a state of) uncircumcision. (11) He received the sign of circumcision as the seal of the justice of faith *that he had* (in the state of) uncircumcision; so that he could be the father of all who have faith in (a state of) uncircumcision and thus have it credited to themselves as justice, (12) as well as the father of circumcision, *i.e.,* of those who not only are circumcised but also follow the trail of faith that was our father Abraham's even in (the state of) uncircumcision.

(13) It wasn't through the law, you see, that the promise (was made) to Abraham and his seed that the world would be his inheritance; it was through the justice of faith. (14) If the inheritance (is due) to the law, then faith is made an empty thing and the promise is nullified. (15) For the law produces wrath. But where there is no law, there is no transgression either. (16) So it is due to faith, that the promise might be a gratuitous gift

guaranteed to all his offspring, not only those of the law but also those of
the faith of Abraham, who is the father of us all— (17) as it is written, "I
have made you the father of many nations"—in the eyes of God, in
whom he had faith as a God who gives life to the dead and who calls into
being what does not have being. (18) Hoping against hope, he had faith,
and so he became the father of many nations as he had been told: "So
shall your offspring be." (19) He did not falter in his faith when he
considered his own body, almost a corpse—he was almost a hundred
years old—and the deadness of Sarah's womb. (20) Insofar as God's
promise (was concerned), he did not lapse into unbelief. He grew strong
in faith, (21) giving glory to God and fully convinced that (God) has the
power to do what he has promised. (22) And so this was credited to him as
justice.

(23) But the "it was credited to him" was not written for his sake alone,
(24) but for our sake also. To us it will be credited, who have faith in the
one who raised from the dead Jesus our Lord, (25) who had been handed
over for our misdeeds and resurrected that we might be declared just.

Romans 4 is one of the most finished chapters of the letter. The artificiality
of chapter divisions is attenuated here by the fact that the chapter begins with
Abraham and never loses sight of that central biblical figure. Moreover, the
content of the chapter is developed more clearly and logically than is usually
the case with Paul. The initial 'then' links the chapter with the principle
enunciated by Paul in the previous chapter. Abraham is the first example and
proof of the principle that springs to Paul's mind.[93]

The argument itself is drawn from the Bible, so logically its purpose would
seem to be to convince the converted Jews of the Christian community in
Rome. Yet it cannot help but surprise us a bit. Paul has just enunciated the
principle that we are declared just by faith, yet his first example is someone who
could not possibly have had faith *in Jesus*. But let us not rush to conclusions
before we analyze the content of this chapter.

I

What does Paul say about Abraham? Basically he says that Abraham
exemplifies what happens with us (see 4:24); and here 'us' refers at the very
least to Christians, whose faith "will be credited . . . as justice." Abraham, in
short, is an example of the principle just enunciated by Paul: God declares just
the human being independently of the works of the Law.

Let us start by noting two implicit aspects or data of Paul's argument that
must be appreciated if we wish to understand him correctly.

(a). Note that Paul presents a biblical proof.[94] His proof is based on the
content of God's word as presented in Scripture, in the Book of Genesis
specifically. That book is particularly venerable because it deals with the
origins of the universe and, even more importantly, of the Chosen People,

whose history begins with Abraham. It is the sort of argument that could be readily employed by an expert in scriptural interpretation such as Paul, who had been educated as a Pharisee under Gamaliel.

Three basic things underpin Paul's biblical argument. First, there is the literal text of a verse in Genesis: "And Abraham *had faith* in God, and *it was credited to him as* justice" (Gn 15:6). Abraham's *faith* in the fulfillment of the divine promise, in other words, was judged by God to be a successful *substitute* for a justice that did not suffice or that Abraham did not have at all.

The second underpinning is the *place* where the verse appears in Genesis: two chapters *before* the account of Abraham's circumcision, which was done to obey Yahweh and to ratify the covenant with him. Since Paul sees circumcision as the sign of one's acceptance of the Law (see Gal 5:3), the moment when Abraham is credited with justice is of crucial symbolic importance, even though the Law will actually arrive with Moses "four hundred and thirty years later" (Gal 3:17). Why? Because it means that the justice granted by God is totally dissociated from the Law and independent of it. In Abraham's case the same holds true with respect to circumcision as a prefiguration of the Law. When Abraham is declared just, he does not belong to the people of the Law. Technically speaking, we can say that he is an uncircumcised person, a pagan.

There is a third datum underlying Paul's presentation. His biblical argument implies that Abraham was credited with justice before God tested his fidelity with a concrete *order,* a minimal dose of 'Law' to obey. Thus Abraham was credited with justice before one of his major 'works': the sacrifice of his son Isaac, which God demanded and then prevented only at the last moment (Gn 22).

This datum is implicit in Paul's argument because Paul is in the habit of likening certain specific *precepts,* used by God to test a person, to the list of precepts contained in the Law. In Romans 5:14, for example, Adam's sin is likened to that of people who have Law. By stressing the *place* of this verse (Gn 15:6) in the story and life of Abraham, Paul may have been anticipating and implicitly refuting possible or actual objections to his argument based on Abraham.

Consider the Letter of James, for example. We cannot pinpoint its chronological place in the New Testament. Some say it antedates Romans; but it seems to contain such an obvious allusion to Paul's principle of 'justification by faith apart from works',[95] that I find it hard to date it before A.D. 57. In any case, the Letter of James offers a very different exegesis of Abraham, and of the very verse in Genesis that we have been considering. To some extent, at least, it is opposed to Paul's.[96]

For James, Abraham won his declaration of justice "when he offered his son Isaac on the altar" (Jas 2:21–22). Abraham may very well have had an attitude of faith in God's promise long before; but his faith clearly reached its apex, its 'perfection', when he agreed to eliminate the only offspring he had or was likely to have. "And the scripture was *fulfilled* that says, 'Abraham had faith in God, and it was credited to him as justice', and he was called God's friend"

(Jas 2:23). For James, faith is the mainspring of (just) works that turn a human being into a friend of God. The "it was credited to him" of Genesis 15:6 does not imply any substitution of faith for works. It is not without grounding in the actual work of Abraham that will bring fulfillment and justificatory value to faith. As James sees it, not without reason, Paul's argument is very different, being based on the total independence of Genesis 15 and Genesis 22 and the two respective moments in Abraham's life.

We know that Paul's mode of biblical exegesis, common in his day, is not what we would call 'scientific' today. That does not really matter here, however, because we are not interested in what actually happened to Abraham but what *Paul* thought had happened to him. And however good or bad his exegesis may be, Paul clearly thought that Abraham was an example of the principle he enunciated at the end of Romans 3.

(b). There is a second tacit assumption or datum we must keep in mind as we try to interpret Romans 4. To some extent it may seem to contradict what I have just said. I am referring to the saga of Abraham's noble and heroic deeds, not as actual history but as narrated by Genesis and accepted by Paul. In the eyes of Paul or any other Jew, Abraham is no shadowy figure in Israel's past. As Paul points out repeatedly, he is talking about *the father* of the Israelite people. Abraham is the (presumed) physical, historical origin of the Chosen People, who are such precisely because Abraham himself was chosen. Paul describes himself as "an Israelite, *of the offspring of Abraham,* of the tribe of Benjamin" (11:1). Not surprisingly, then, the theme of Abraham's justice and faith will occupy a central place in both Romans and Galatians when Paul is trying to explain the Old Testament and its overall relationship to the New Testament. For Abraham is the "person of faith" (see Gal 3:6-29).

This means that every Jew was deeply familiar with the heroic activity of Abraham as recorded in Genesis. Paul's 'historical revisionism', which depicted Abraham as the father of uncircumcised persons of faith, would not have had any impact if his basic picture of Abraham did not match the general view of Father Abraham: the man of faith, considered just by God and treated as God's friend. The Book of Wisdom, on which Paul is somehow dependent,[97] offers this image of Abraham: "[Wisdom]" knew *the just one*, kept him *irreproachable* before God"(Wis 10:5).

It may be of some importance for our purposes here to try to appreciate why and how a legalistic mentality viewed Abraham not only as just but also as 'irreproachable', the latter designation strongly suggesting a comparison between actual works and some norm. Remember, after all, that both the Yahwist writer (Gn 12:10f.) and the Elohist writer (Gn 20: 1f.) depict Abraham acting in a way that seems to go against 'natural law', and that would later be expressly prohibited by the 'positive Law' of Israel. Abraham lies about his relationship to Sarah so as not to be persecuted or killed. She is taken into the harem of the ruler and Abraham is treated well. He is given many presents: "Sheep, cows, male donkeys, male and female servants, female donkeys, and camels" (Gn 12:16).[98]

Here the ancient writers were clearly confronted with a very firm tradition. They could not omit or water down these episodes. Nor could they even combine the two accounts into one, as they did on many other occasions. And even if the biblical writers regarded such behavior as normal and inescapable in the historical circumstances of the day, it is clear that they did not regard it as normal for the *founding forefather of Israel*. In the eyes of the Elohist writer, it was "a great sin" (Gn 20:9). In both versions divine wrath and punishment follow, until the situation is corrected. Incredibly enough, however, they fall upon the poor party that has been deceived by Abraham even though he has acted with "integrity of heart" (Gn 20:6). Innocent as the deceived victim may be, Yahweh is on the side of the deceiver.[99] Abraham is Yahweh's 'prophet' despite everything, and the affliction of the ruler will be lifted only when Abraham prays for him (Gn 20:7).

Perhaps the significance and importance of the statement in the Book of Wisdom will now be clearer. Here we have a deuterocanonical book at the end of the Old Testament, linked to the theology of the Pharisees and apparently known to Paul. It applies the description 'irreproachable before God' to a man who was directly responsible for 'a great sin'.

We do not know whether Paul regarded Abraham as 'irreproachable' or not; but Paul clearly thought that Abraham did not escape the common human condition, that he was and continued to be a *sinner.* In Romans, Paul tells us that all human beings are under Sin and liable to God's judgment (3:9–10). Writing about Abraham in the next chapter, he clearly hints that it is a case of God's declaring just the impious (4:5). And in Romans 5 Paul tells us that Death, the consequence of Sin, reigned from Adam to Moses (5:14). This period takes in the lifetime of Abraham and includes him among *all* who sinned (5:12).

What are we to make of the biblical view of Abraham and Paul's re-examination of it? Permit me to suggest a general hypothesis. Israel seems to feel and act towards Abraham as a small child does towards its father. Every father is permitted to do things that the child is forbidden to do. The child does not judge its father by the norm to which it must be obedient. Though the child may not say so, it believes that its father possesses a *maturity* and wisdom that it does not yet have.[100]

As a general hypothesis, this may be too vague and unsatisfactory insofar as Judaism as a whole is concerned. But it becomes more specific and credible when we try to explain a standpoint such as Paul's, who is critical of the role of the Law.

Paul's unequivocal devotion to Abraham, evident whenever he discusses the theme of the Law in Galatians and Romans, is obviously connected with the 'pre-evangelization'[101] he sees in the heroic saga of Abraham. Recall Paul's view that the Law is typical of the *infantile* stage of life, when the *offspring* and *heir* is not yet aware of owning the paternal property and asks its servants what is permitted and prohibited (see Gal 3:23–4:11; Rom 8:14–16). Abraham, by contrast, has an *adult* filial relationship with God, who makes him a father in turn. Abraham is free to resolve moral cases in terms of the suitability of a course of action, as Paul would have the adult Christian do (see 1 Cor 6:12; 10:23). There is no doubt that Paul displays a nostalgic longing for Abraham's sort of situation, the most *Christian* one before Christ. In Paul's eyes, the transition from that magnificent situation of mature freedom, based on confidence in God, to the observance of commandments is a kind of death (see 7:9).[102]

•

Keeping the above data in mind, let us now analyze the content of Romans 4 and its single, unifying theme: the faith of Abraham. Three points will help us to get a better grasp of Abraham's faith.

(1). In Abraham's faith do we find traces of the opposition that Paul clearly enunciated in his abstract principle at the end of Romans 3? Do we find a contrast between Faith and works of the Law (faith and works being another possible formulation)?

Not surprisingly, we do. Since our present chapter divisions are artificial, it is only natural that Romans 4 would reiterate the formulation that shows up so often in the last ten verses of Romans 3. But in this chapter the formulation centers around a concrete historical personage: Abraham.

At first glance the opposition seems to center around faith versus works: "Because if Abraham was declared just by *works*, he has ground for *glorying*. But *it is* not *so* before God" (4:2).[103] Paul obviously could not write 'works of the Law' here because Abraham belongs to the stage running from Adam to Moses when there was no Law, at least not the external Law that would allow people to 'count' or 'compute' sins and good 'works'. But I said 'at first glance' for a reason. In this chapter Paul seems to disregard a point that he will make in Romans 5 concerning the impossibility of moral 'counting' in the absence of Law. It suddenly becomes obvious that we overlooked one important element when we were examining the precise content of Paul's famous principle as enunciated in Romans 3. That important element crops up again here.

Remember we found three possible terms for the second item in Paul's set of opposites: works of the Law, Law, or simply works. If we look at Romans 3 closely, however, we will notice that the term 'works' never appears *alone* except in one important context: "Where, then, the glorying? It has been ruled out. By what law? By the law of *works*? No, but by the law of faith" (3:27).

As I already indicated, the term 'law' in that verse refers to something like a 'mechanism'; that alone is food for thought. Even more importantly, we must specify more exactly what has been ruled out by the mechanism of faith: not simply 'works' but what might be described 'works that give us grounds for glorying in ourselves'. What has been ruled out, in other words, is 'glorying' in our 'works'. We have every right to conclude that it is not working that is opposed to faith but rather *counting up one's works to present an invoice of them as the basis of a debt owed to us by God.* And since a debt always results from an implicit or explicit *contract,* which must be a law in the case of Abraham's justice, we find once again that 'glorying in works' is synonymous with 'works of the Law'.

The fact is that we have overlooked the importance of the word 'glorying' for Paul's theology and anthropology, even though we have already come across it several times. In describing the sinfulness of the Jews, for example, Paul mentioned 'glorying in God' (2:17) and 'glorying in the Law' (2:23). They came to regard something divine as their *de facto* or *de jure* possession, as something owed to them. That is precisely what has been ruled out for *all* (3:27), and hence for Abraham as well (4:2).[104]

Insofar as any such *contractual* relationship with God is concerned, Paul sees something very different in the case of Abraham. And in the time of Abraham, of course, there had not yet appeared the Law, which would give people some basis for thinking in contractual terms. Paul posits a relationship of 'gratuitous gift' between Abraham and God as the typically Abrahamic one. And precisely because it is gratuitous, a free gift, it paves the way for the universality of the Promise: "So it is due to *faith,* that the promise might be a *gratuitous gift* guaranteed to *all his offspring,* not only those of the Law [Jews] but also those of the Faith of Abraham [pagans]" (4:16).

Unfortunately Paul makes use of a lame image or analogy to get across the idea of a gratuitous gift, and it has led to much exegetical misunderstanding and confusion. He uses the image of a *wage,* which implicitly suggests the idea of a contract. Paul himself admits: "now to one who works, the *wage* is not counted as a gift but as *something due*" (4:4). To move on to the notion of a gratuitous gift, Paul should have dropped the image of a wage. Once having adopted it, however, Paul felt obliged to continue: "But *to one* who *does not work,* who *has faith* in the one who declares just the impious, his faith is credited to him as justice" (4:5).

It is true that a 'wage' is a gift for someone who does not work. But nothing could be more false, more remote from the thinking of Paul, than the notion that Abraham did not work. If there was ever anyone in perpetual motion to carry out the will of Yahweh, it was Abraham. The profession of faith at the end of the Book of Joshua has Yahweh saying: "I took your father Abraham from beyond the River and led him through all the land of Canaan" (Jos 24:3). At the age of seventy-five, Abraham heard the call of God, left his native Mesopotamia, and headed for Canaan. In his interminable wanderings he endured hunger, went down to Egypt and returned, separated amicably from his nephew Lot, fought the four kings, and rescued Lot and his household. All this Abraham had done before the divine promise and his faith in it, as Paul knew from reading the account in Genesis.

To characterize Abraham as 'one who does not work' would be to indulge in senseless literary stupidity, unless the writer is already taking 'work' in the sense of a *contractual* relationship between employer and employee that gives the latter the right to a wage. In Paul's mind, Abraham is the supreme example of someone who works 'by vocation'. He seeks a land and a progeny. In the curious words of Romans 2, he seeks "glory, honor, and incorruption" (2:7).[105] It is worth noting that even the section on the 'covenant'[106] between Yahweh and Abraham (Gn 15:7f.) *follows* the account of the Promise, Abraham's faith in it, and the consequent declaration of justice by Yahweh.

To sum up this point about Paul's view of Abraham, we can say the following. As Paul sees it, Abraham's *faith* is opposed to any and all 'glorying in works', works that would supposedly spawn a right. That would have been possible even before the Law of Moses, though the latter obviously lent itself much more readily to such works. Logically speaking, we can see a growing crescendo of 'glorying' as precepts permit people to visualize and tote up their works and sins.

Thus it is not a correct exegetical interpretation of this passage to say that it positively dissociates God's judgment of Abraham (and his justice) from God's sympathy towards him. It is not correct to say that God's gift is purely arbitrary, that Abraham's way of *working* counts for nothing. Paul says only that Abraham cannot claim any right deriving from his works, that he cannot *glory in them*. Not the same thing![107]

(2). Another basic characteristic of Abrahamic faith becomes clear when we consider *in whom or what* it is placed. The text of Genesis, cited twice in Romans 4, is quite clear: Abraham had faith *in God*. But in Romans 3, Paul clearly linked God's declaration of justice with faith *in Jesus Christ* (see 3:22-26).

Sound exegesis and good faith demand that we not minimize the difference between Abraham's faith in God and the Christian's faith in Jesus Christ, on the grounds that we know Jesus Christ is God. First of all, there is a crucial chronological difference. Abraham lived in the first stage of God's plan, the Christian does not. More importantly, minimizing that difference could put us off the track completely in trying to appreciate Paul's thinking. Judaism as a whole 'believes in God', yet Paul says it is enslaved to Sin and looking in the wrong place for God's declaration of justice. That declaration is granted to one who believes in Jesus Christ, says Paul, apart from any and all works of the Law: "Brothers and sisters, my heart's desire and my prayer to God for them is that they be saved. I testify on their behalf that they *do have zeal for God*, but a zeal not in line with adequate knowledge. *Failing to recognize God's justice* and seeking to establish their own, *they did not submit to God's justice*. Christ, you see, is the end of the Law, for the justification of all who have Faith" (10:1-4; see Gal 2:15-16; 3:4, etc.). Thus there must have been another ingredient in Abraham's faith in God besides Yahwist orthodoxy, which with the passage of time would become Christian orthodoxy.

Clearly people can latch onto all sorts of later theological theories to wipe out the ostensible difference between 'faith in God' and 'faith in Jesus', claiming they both have the same result: God's declaration of justice. But careful exegesis cannot help but point out that the ten verses in which Paul enunciates his principle begin with a solemn *"But now . . . "*(3:21), and

Abraham certainly did not belong to that 'now'. Whatever theological equations one may try to set up, the fact remains that Abraham belongs to a 'before'. Indeed he comes even *before the Law,* as Paul makes clear in some detail in this fourth chapter (see 4:9–12.16).

We must be careful, then, in pinpointing what Paul may have in mind when he equates the 'faith' of Abraham and the 'faith' of Christians insofar as the *effects* are concerned. One problem may be that we are too much inclined to think in terms of some sort of content: e.g., the *creed* of Abraham or that of Christians. We would do better to consider Abraham's *attitude* before God, which is amply described by Paul in Romans 4. It is an attitude centered around gratuitousness in acting (see 4:16). It is also trust or confidence in a seemingly impossible promise (4:21), a "hoping against hope" (4:18), a *gratuitous* hope.

But Paul goes further in his description of Abraham's faith, spelling it out almost in the form of a *creed.* Abraham is "the father of us all . . . in the eyes of God, in whom he had faith as a God *who gives life to the dead* and who calls into being what does not have being" (4:16–17). This creed or belief (which will be realized in Isaac) becomes even more comprehensible when set over against verifiable experience. Abraham "did not falter in his faith when he considered his own body, almost a *corpse* . . . and the deadness of Sarah's womb" (4:19).

Paul's stress is on Abraham's faith in the life that follows death (and hence that arises out of what no longer is). This emphasis cannot be accidental because Paul ends his treatment of Abraham in this chapter on the same note, linking it to what is specifically Christian: "But the 'it was credited to him' was not written for his sake alone, but for *our sake* also. To us it will be credited, who have faith in *the one who raised from the dead* Jesus our Lord, who had been handed over for our misdeeds and resurrected that we might be declared just" (4:23–25). Note the parallelism in the content, all the more so because here God again becomes the one in whom faith is placed, this time by Christians. They have faith, not in Jesus himself, but in the one who raised him from the dead.

Here are further elements to justify the conclusion that *faith,* as discussed by Paul, is an *attitude,* but one implying a *datum* that makes it meaningful. And if the attitude is to be basically the same one in both cases, then the datum must be practically the same: namely, the victory of life over death that God makes possible and promises.

Now *who* can have this sort of faith, from which the declaration of justice follows? Looking solely at Romans 4, we see that the answer is simple. This faith should find its maximum development in Christians because in their case something becomes clear, universal, and certain, that was only a vague, particular, crazy wager in Abraham's case.

Yet that faith *was* there in Abraham. It was a mini-faith, if you will, but enough to evoke God's gift: the declaration of justice. And Paul stresses that it has nothing to do with the Law that would come later. It is something universal for all those who "follow the trail that was our father Abraham's even in (the state of) uncircumcision" (4:12).

Obviously this trail is followed by both pagans and Jews who have converted to authentic Christianity. But was there any possibility of following it between Abraham and Jesus? And even though Abraham is the first *biblical* character who is said to have been declared just by reason of his faith and hence declared *the father* of all, was no one before Abraham able to have that sort of faith, in the first stage of human existence?

Paul takes advantage of a specific biblical verse to ground his principle on a concrete example, but that hardly means he has lost sight of his habitual key, his anthropological key. It is hard to imagine that he pictures Abraham as a unique and miraculous figure preceded and followed by an enormous void. The very idea of 'paternity' suggests some continuity in the future at least. The author of the Letter to the Hebrews, who may have been a disciple of Paul, speaks of faith in pretty much the same terms as Paul; and in so doing, that author points to other biblical figures like Abraham who came before and after him. In the very next chapter of Romans, Paul himself writes about a declaration of justice spread throughout humanity as a whole and equalling or surpassing the scope of Adam's sin (5:16–19).

Hence there is nothing silly about asking what the *minimum content* of this attitude of faith in a human being must be for it to be like the faith of Abraham in its nature and results. Paul, of course, pictures Abraham as an orthodox Yahwist and takes for granted the purity of his faith in Yahweh. He knows nothing of recent exegesis that would view Abraham and the patriarchs as believers in the 'God of our fathers', who would later be identified with Yahweh.[108]

In declaring Abraham 'uncircumcised', however, Paul uses a technical term that links Abraham with religious heterodoxy of any and every sort: with idolatry, for example, or even with what we today would call atheism. The Jews divided humanity into the circumcised and the uncircumcised. Their dividing line was not based on the orthodoxy of a person's creed, as we may be inclined to draw it today. A person might have a perfectly orthodox faith or creed and nevertheless be uncircumcised, which would mean that he did not belong to the people of God.[109] The term 'pagan' or 'Gentile', synonymous with 'uncircumcised', is applied to the justified Abraham by Paul in accordance with the Bible. In itself the term does not imply or rule out in principle the possibility of a religious deformation.

Who, then, shares the faith of Abraham in Paul's view? Without much risk of error we can say: anyone whose actions or works imply that there exists in the universe a power that can give life to the dead and call into being what does not exist. Who is a child of Abraham, 'the man of faith'? Every atheist,[110] pagan, Jew, or Christian who refuses to have a contractual relationship with the Absolute, who trusts in the promise inscribed in the human values offered by existence and fights for them as if death did not render that struggle futile.

To convince ourselves that this is correct, we must examine one further element.

(3). We are still on the same question: Who can be 'children' of uncircumcised Abraham and follow his faith? One tempting and facile hypothesis is that Paul is referring to pagans *who have converted* to Christianity. But that hypothesis will not hold up under any serious exegesis of Romans 4, or of other passages in Romans that we shall consider later.

First of all, as I have already suggested, that hypothesis would make Abraham the object of a special privilege, so special in fact that he would have had no true descendants until the Christian era. His progeny would only be physical. Such a descent would not be salvific, nor would there be a declaration of justice for anyone after him until many centuries had gone by. Such a view clashes with the whole general tone of Romans 4, which is addressed to Jews who saw in Abraham the start of a salvation plan. Paul's presentation does not come down to telling them that there was no such salvation plan; instead he tries to make clear where the plan lay and to whom it extended. Far from putting Abraham down or diminishing him, Paul makes him a sort of positive Adam, almost a pre-Christ.

Second, the hypothesis under consideration thoroughly contradicts what Paul has been saying about God's universal judgment. Recall how Paul stressed the fact that no one enjoys advantages vis-à-vis that judgment. That is the way it should be, Paul insisted, against the contrary opinion of those who thought the Law gave them a new and superior criterion for judging and being judged. Now the oneness of the criterion for all human beings was peculiarly *characteristic* of the stage in which Abraham is found. It is represented and stressed here by Paul with his image of the universal fatherhood of Abraham. Just as the one criterion of judgment is faith (3:30), so the basis of Abraham's universal fatherhood is likewise faith (4:11-16).

Third, if the Christian by definition has the same faith as Abraham, and if that same faith was accessible to the rest of humanity, then Abraham can have all nations as his offspring—in a restricted but real and effective sense. But if we have to jump from Abraham to the faith of the Christian, then we are faced with a new *particularity.* Everything Paul said about the particularity of the Law and the need to get beyond it could be turned against Paul himself. *Faith* must be an attitude accessible to all human beings *always*, just as enslavement to Sin is accessible to them (to say the least).[111]

So we arrive at the conclusion that faith is something very different from a specific act, accessible to human beings specifically situated in history. We see it as a way of being human, as something that moves the human being from infantile timidity to maturity, from action based on petty calculation to action performed in a gratuitous and creative manner.[112] Obviously that implies betting on some transcendent datum, which different people would formulate differently. But at bottom it would be the very same datum, and it would surface clearly in the resurrection of Jesus.[113]

Such a human being, though a sinner, would be an 'irreproachable' co-worker of God. Because there is no contradiction between faith and works, you see. Quite the contrary, only faith makes possible a human way of working.

II

We have seen that Paul sets up a process in three stages: the first is the stage prior to the Law and takes in all human beings; the second runs from the Law to Christ and takes in the Jewish people; the third is from Christ on and will again take in humanity as a whole.

Now if we look for concrete roots of this Pauline conception in the historical message of Jesus, we will obviously be able to verify material relating only to the last stage.[114]

Indeed the essential characteristics of the last stage, especially the 'liberty' brought to humanity by Christ when he stripped the Law of its supposed place above the human being, serve as the backdrop of Paul's effort here. They prompt Paul, who now faces a largely pagan audience, to imagine a universal divine plan that would seek precisely that *result*; and that would dovetail with what both Scripture and experience tell him about the respective situations of the pagan and Jewish world (Romans 1–3).

The thing I want to point up here, and to trace back to its gospel origins, is that the process involves a real *dialectic* in the strictest sense of the word. And if we understand the final stage as the *synthesis*, we see that it is Paul who describes the steps of the dialectic in careful detail in order to pave the way for that synthesis. He demonstrates the ambivalence of each of the preceding stages, pointing up the factor that puts them in conflict and obliges them to move towards Christ. Here, too, *conflict is provoked and decisive.*

Paul describes how the Flesh turns pagan universality into a mistaken, inhuman universality: human passions alone are set free to falsify all human relations. In a parallel way, the Flesh turns Jewish particularity into a mistaken, inhuman particularity: Jewish moral and religious concern, framed in an attitude of fear and business-like contracts, turns the particular into something abominable and counterproductive.

In Paul's setup, the synthesis comes only with Christ. As a *fact*, as a new attitude different from the first two stages, it is verifiable in the prepaschal data of the gospels. But it is not verifiable specifically as a *synthesis* there because the gospels do not discuss the whole anthropological process that interests Paul. We might also note that Paul gives a *name* to that synthesis: faith. Understood as the rich and complex attitude we have been examining, the word could be applied just as well to the attitude that Jesus adopts as an epistemological premise over against the attitude of his opponents, when he debates the proper interpretation of the Law with them (see Volume II).

In Romans 4, Paul tries to show that the very beginning of divine revelation to the Jewish people already implied, prefigured, or proclaimed beforehand the good news of that synthesis. Sometimes Paul even gives the impression that the movement of the process towards its synthesis was unduly delayed or retarded by the excessive development of the antithesis: the religious particularity of the Law. It is almost as if that had to undergo all its development as a negative factor before it could give way to the synthesis (see Gal 3:19; Rom 7:13).

In the distant past, then, there was another key moment when the synthesis could be sensed as near. There was a moment of promised synthesis or *pre-synthesis* embodied in a *pre-Christ*: Abraham.

In his mind Paul may well be preparing the antagonistic parallelism between Sin (Adam) and Grace (Christ) that he will spell out in the next chapter. But in that *anthropological* antagonism there is no evidence of the *special* function of the Jewish people specifically. Their particular function was real (3:2), however, and Paul is writing to a community made up largely of people who had been structured by that particularity. So Paul needed the *pre-synthesis* in his argument, to point up the *functional* peculiarity of the Jewish people as it related to Christ *at the very start*. Who better than Abraham, the father in faith of Jews who came to faith, would serve Paul's purpose?

To ground his interpretation of Abraham, Paul clearly does not look to the gospel message. Instead he uses a type of biblical exegesis that was common in his own day. We would not call it scholarly or scientific today.[115] It is what he learned in his formal education as a Pharisee. It was the only one he had, and it was the most effective way to convince people who had been educated in the same way. Even more importantly, however, its results dovetail with the message of Jesus and represent a vivid reading of that message in the context of real human life.

We have already seen Paul's argument about Abraham, based essentially on the fact that Genesis 15:6 is prior to Genesis 17 and Genesis 22. But why say that Abraham constitutes a *pre-synthesis* in the dialectical process of Sin and Grace? The basic answer, we know, is that Abraham already represents the Faith that wins justification in God's judgment. The synthesis of faith and justification will reach its definitive fulfillment in Jesus, but somehow it is already present in Abraham.

It is also worth noting that the two antagonistic forces, the two main anthropological characters, are already at work in Abraham to some extent. Abraham is *under the reign of death* (5:14) as an offspring of Adam, who introduced sin into the world. So he is *under Sin*, even though it cannot be counted and quantified before the Law appears (5:13). On the other hand Abraham is also *under Grace*. He has been the object of a particular vocation, flowing from a particular promise made to him in person: i.e., that in the future he would constitute a universal blessing having to do with the whole world (4:13). But Abraham, unlike his children, is not given orientation or guidance by the (dangerous) Law of Moses.

It is important to note that Sin and Grace are two constitutive elements of the Promise in Paul's thinking. If Abraham were not a sinner, the blessing would not be the object of a promise, of a gracious gift in advance. And if it were not given as a grace or gift, Abraham could only look forward to the 'mortal' consequences of his sinful way of acting.

Now do we find anything similar to that sort of synthesis in the gospels? Yes we do.

(1). The work/wage/gift relationship immediately reminds us of a teaching given by Jesus in the parable of the workers in the vineyard. The parable talks about workers *contracted* to work a whole day for a fixed wage, perhaps the minimum wage of the day: a denarius. These we can dismiss right away because, for Paul, *they never existed* in the historical reality of God's plan. They are the imaginary product of a misunderstanding; or they might be viewed as a limit-concept designed to highlight, by way of contrast, the real situation of humanity before God.

Now consider the workers of 'the last hour'. They are called to work because they were 'idle' during the rest of the day (Mt 20:3), and no contract is made with them. The most they can have is a promise, and that only if the owner told them the same thing he told the workers of 'the third hour': "I will give you *what is just*" (Mt 20:4).

Now when the workers of the last hour get a denarius, what can be said about them in relation to the owner of the vineyard? Clearly they have been the object of a 'gift' or 'grace'. This is suggested by the reply of the owner to the protest of the workers under contract. The owner can do what he chooses with what is his. The denarius is not a *debt*, something owed as a *wage*. The workers of the last hour worked, to be sure, but their work was not *proportional* to what they received. So Paul might put it, and in fact the Abraham described by Paul fits perfectly into that category.

As we saw in Volume II, Jesus' parable is a piece of political polemics. The workers contracted for a wage represent those protesting against what they see as the injustice of the kingdom of God, which is going to disregard prior merit and come as a gift for the poor and sinners. When we move from a political key to an anthropological key, however, that group of workers disappears: not because their claim is bad, but because no human being was put under contract or received wages from such a contract. The Jews, as depicted by Paul in Romans 2, certainly understood the matter in those terms; but that was because they misunderstood the meaning and function of the Law. In the eyes of God they too, like all human beings, have been 'idle' enough so that they cannot claim a wage from their work.

If Paul were to have reworked Jesus' parable in his anthropological key, he would have had to change it almost completely in order to be faithful to its message. In particular, he would have had to explain one thing that the parable leaves obscure, but that is crucial in his key: What logical *motive* could the workers of the last hour have for working? That would mean Abraham and his children, all those people of faith.

One might be inclined to say that they had *the promise* of the owner that they would receive what is *just*. But in two respects that answer does not mesh either with the parable or with Paul's conception.

First of all, if that were the motivation, the quality and quantity of work would decrease proportionately to the ridiculous size of a *just* wage for so little work. This is often not appreciated by people in affluent countries, who have introjected an obsession for work as an element of human dignity and social prestige. To understand Jesus in his Palestinian context we must abandon presuppositions deriving from a very different world.

Second, if that were the motivation, then the *grace* would be solely in the owner. The workers would take the promise, or the call to work without any promise, as the equivalent of a *contract*. They would have 'faith' in the owner only as 'contractor'. The work would be nothing more than work done under a tacit or assumed contract, and the denarius would amount to nothing more than an extrinsic 'reward' or 'bonus'.

Readers might object that I am asking too much of a parable, and that comparisons don't match completely. But the fact is that the anthropological problem under consideration exists in any case: What are we to hope for or expect from 'historical' work vis-à-vis a 'gratuitous' or 'gracious' God?

When we pose this crucial question to the gospels, we do get an answer. But it comes *outside* the context of the parable, and it is worth noting why that is the case. The labor of a worker under any sort of contract has no intrinsic, personal relationship to the intention or project of the contractor. The latter has one plan or aim, the former has another. Something *extrinsic*—a wage or reward—brings them together, so that the work remunerated by one and done by the other serves the intentions of both. The extrinsic character of the worker's involvement is evident in his prior 'idleness'; and it is evident in the owner insofar as he uses his money 'as he chooses', without any connection to the vineyard itself.

What do we find in the gospel message when we eliminate that sort of mediation, which is extrinsic both to the human being who works and God who gives gifts? We find the attitude that Jesus expects of his disciples, and that he expressed in one of his deepest sayings: "Seek first the kingdom of God . . . " They are to immerse themselves in its dynamism and work *for it*. If we wanted to translate this idea to the parable, we would have to imagine workers who forgot about pay and enthusiastically labored to see the vineyard itself grow and flourish.

Now Jesus himself announced the arrival of the kingdom to the vineyard of Yahweh, "the house of Israel" (Is 5:7). In Paul's case, it is a matter of extending that reign to the very boundaries of the universe, *for the good of humanity.* And that is the attitude of Abraham, whose inheritance is the world (4:13).

That is not all. Not only is there no longer any extrinsic mediation between the motive for working, however faulty the work may be, and the project involved. There is also a Promise with universal content: " . . . and everything else will be given you (free) as well." It is not by way of a wage or miraculous reward, however. The kingdom itself, realized, signifies *what is necessary for all.* To set out on that search, however, one must *believe* in the coming of the kingdom. Only that *faith* can free human beings from their preoccupation with keeping track of their needs day by day and trying to satisfy them on their own.

Thanks to faith, work on behalf of the kingdom, the quest for it in the labyrinth of historical causes, is converted into the *intrinsic* motive of the work itself. Living in a different historical context, Paul talks about the longing of all creation rather than about the kingdom. All creation, he says, is longing to be put in the service of the plan of God and God's children. We shall come back to this later.

Notice that Paul is radically faithful to the historical Jesus, even in his most creative interpretations. Indeed we could almost paraphrase his view of Abraham in gospel terms: Abraham believed that he could seek the blessing of all human beings and that justification would be given him as well. And what he believed, God turned into reality for him—faith collaborating with his works.

(2). We cannot end our examination of the gospel roots of Romans 4 without considering the introduction of two new anthropological characters: death versus life, corruption and uselessness versus incorruption and the power of creation. To put it in a nutshell: *Death* versus *Resurrection*. And all this is clearly found back in Abraham (4:17–19.24–25), the pre-Christ of Paul's theology.

It takes little imagination to figure out the roots of this christological development. It is rooted in the death and resurrection of Jesus, because the experiences of both facts are equally *true* for Paul even though we would place them on different levels of verifiability. As this basic opposition comes to occupy an increasingly central place in Paul's anthropological key, we will be looking more closely at his view of the meaning of Jesus' death and resurrection.

Right now I want to call attention to one important point regarding these two new characters. From the start Paul goes *beyond* a mere physical contrast between death and survival.

We have already seen that Paul applies the term *death* to the uselessness of Abraham's efforts to get offspring at his and Sarah's age. He also applies the term *creation* to the power of God to inject life and existence into that same project (4:17.19). In Paul's thinking, Death and Resurrection vie, not only or mainly for individuals, but for the future of their projects. Let us look at a few passages where this is evident.

In Romans 2, Paul has this to say about God's universal judgment: God "will give to each human being according to its works. To those who *seek* glory, honor, and *incorruption, eternal life*. But for those who are . . . indocile to the truth but docile to injustice, wrath and indignation" (2:6–8). Now 'seeking incorruption' means more than reacting against the fear of personal death. As many Pauline passages indicate, it is characteristic of all *authentic* projects, where truth is not shackled by injustice and bad faith is not the underlying attitude.

Two passages most clearly reveal the spontaneous desires of the human being named Paul. In both we find this demand for life that goes beyond his own individual person. Writing about resurrection in 1 Corinthians he says: "*This* corruptible (_____neuter sg.) must put on *incorruption*, and *this* mortal (_____neuter sg.) must put on immortality" (1 Cor 15:53–54).[116] Here 'this' obviously designates a wider reality than Paul's own body or physical life.

The second passage informs us that Paul seeks immortal, incorruptible life for his 'tent',[117] his whole existence with its values and projects: "We know that if this tent, our earthly dwelling, crumbles into decay, we have an edifice from God: an eternal dwelling in heaven, not made by human hands. So we sigh (anxiously) in this state, ardently desiring to *put on* our heavenly dwelling . . . We who are in this tent . . . do not want to have it *taken off* but to have the other *put on over it*, so that *what is mortal may be absorbed by life*" (2 Cor 5:1.2.4.5). The verb 'put on over it' suggests the same thing as the above quotation: placing a garment over another already existing one.

That is why he depicts *all creation*, rather than individual persons, as subject to uselessness (8:20). The enslavement to *corruption* (8:21) affects human *freedom*, and it will disappear only when that freedom is made manifest. 'This' is what has to undergo resurrection, according to Paul: the corruption or death of human projects.

Paul does a much better job than Peter in Acts of rescuing and bringing out the *problem* of Jesus' death. Jesus preached the coming of the kingdom, not himself. And it is the kingdom, not just Jesus, that has to be resurrected in power (1:4) if the existence of Jesus, as he himself lived it, is to have meaning. His death discredited his message, not his person. Paul's christology, using Abraham as example, points to the kingdom of God dawning in power at Easter, though he uses other names to describe it.

CHAPTER V

Adam, Christ, and Victory

Romans 5:1-20

(1) And so, having been declared just by reason of faith, we are at peace with God through our lord Jesus Christ, (2) through whom we also have gained access with faith to this grace in which we persevere, and we glory in the hope of God's glory. (3) Not only that, we glory even in our afflictions, knowing that affliction produces endurance, (4) endurance maturity, maturity hope; and the hope is not delusory (5) because the love *proceeding* from God has been poured into our hearts by the holy spirit that has been given to us.

(6) When we were still without power, Christ died at the right moment for the impious.— (7) It is hardly conceivable someone would die for a just person, though one might chance it for a good person.— (8) But God proved his love for us, since Christ died for us while we were still sinners. (9) With all the more *reason*, then, we shall be saved by him from the wrath, since we have been declared just by his blood. (10) If we were reconciled with God while still God's enemies by the death of his son, with all the more *reason* we, *already* reconciled, will be saved by his life. (11) Not only that, we glory in God through our lord Jesus Christ, thanks to whom we have now received reconciliation.

(12) So you see, just as sin entered the world through one human being (only), and through sin death, and thus death reached all human beings because all sinned— (13) For sin was *already* in the world before the law and, even though sin was not computed since there was no law, (14) death nevertheless reigned from Adam to Moses, even over those who did not sin the way Adam had, who was a type of the one to come—. . .

(15) But there is no equation between the offense and the gift. Because if by the offense of one (only) the many died, the grace of God and the gratuitous gift of one human (only), Jesus Christ, did much more abound in the many. (16) And there is no equation between the result of the one's aberration and the gift. Because the judgment following from

76

the one (only) *ended in* condemnation, whereas the (work of) grace, following the many offenses, *ended in* a declaration of justice. (17) If by the offense of one (only) death reigned on account of one, much more will those who receive the abundance of grace and the gift of justice reign in life by one (only), Jesus Christ. (18) So you see, as the offense of one (only) *turned out to be cause of* condemnation for all human beings, so the justice of one (only) *turned out to be cause of* justice bringing life for all human beings. (19) As by the disobedience of one (only) the many were made sinful, so by the obedience of one (only) the many will be made just.

(20) *As for* the law, (it) intervened to increase the offense. But where sin abounded, grace abounded even more; with the result that, as sin reigned in death, so grace will reign by means of justice for eternal life, through Jesus Christ our lord.

With the first verse of Romans 5, Paul's thinking moves away from the case of Abraham to explore other themes. The transition actually began in the last verses of the previous chapter, where Paul tells us that justice will be credited to all those who have faith in the God who resurrected Jesus—i.e., to us Christians—just as it was credited to Abraham.

Thus there is no sharp break between Romans 5 and the previous chapter. Romans 5 is linked to that chapter by a logical consequence: i.e., the peace that follows the *reconciliation* between God and the sinful human being. If we follow in the footsteps of Abraham's faith, we too will be transformed from powerless (5:6), sinful (5:8) enemies of God (5:10) into God's friends (see Jas 2:23).

This theme of reconciliation is treated explicitly at some length in the first part of the fifth chapter (5:1-11), where Paul discusses the *moment* and *function* of reconciliation. But the theme also appears in the rest of the chapter (5:12-20) more tacitly, where Paul deals with the *extent* of reconciliation. Let us analyze these two parts.

I

At the outset we must note a difference of level between the fourth and fifth chapters. Paul's line of argument in Romans 4 presupposed the faith of Judaism in its own Scripture. *No less* was needed because a problem concerning the relations between the human being and God could not be resolved without knowing what God thought about it. And the force of Paul's argument lies precisely in the fact that the Law—i.e., what the Jews recognized as God's revelation—spoke of those relations in the case of Abraham. *No more* was needed, however, because Paul did not have to use any specifically Christian argument to draw conclusions from his exegesis.

By contrast, Romans 5 is wholly *based on the Christian faith*. Its force depends on one's acceptance of Christianity. But note: I am not saying that

Romans 5 *refers to Christians*. That is an interesting and perhaps crucial question we will take up later. I am simply saying that Romans 5 *supposes* the Christian faith. Whatever the view of Abraham may be, whether one thinks he was never a weak sinner and enemy of God and hence never needed reconciliation or that he was the object of a 'reconciliation' limited to his own person, Paul certainly thinks that the *great reconciliation* takes place with the death of Jesus Christ. I would not venture to say that Paul understands 'with' in a strictly temporal sense, but I would say that the whole of Romans 5 rests on the Christian faith.

There is another important point to note. In the thematic content of the chapter Paul does not refer to data preceding the reconciliation, data deriving from faith in Jesus or in the God who resurrected him. Paul starts from zero. The explicitly Christian *zero* from which Paul begins his argument about reconciliation is the *reconciliation itself*, thanks to the death (blood) of Jesus.

It is true that Paul has already mentioned the resurrection at the end of the fourth chapter (4:25), which might be regarded as the beginning of this chapter. But when he focuses specifically on reconciliation, he talks about it as a zero-happening. It is as if he were recounting an act of 'creation' that changes us from God's enemies into God's friends, only in this case the agent of creation is not the divine word but the 'blood' of Jesus (5:9).

This should not prompt us to think that Paul would minimize the data referring to the historical Jesus and his fight for the kingdom, or that he would begin with reconciliation in preaching the faith to pagans or Jews. Paul is writing to a community that is already Christian, that has already gone through a process of evangelization and catechesis and is grounded on it. But neither can we evade the fact that the anthropological key chosen by Paul and applied chapter after chapter leads him to the data on Jesus that are likely to have a more directly universal import.[118]

An even more concrete fact is that the first element in his line of argument in Romans that is based explicitly on properly Christian faith is his discussion of the reconciliation won for us by the death of Jesus. One cannot say that his earlier statement about the declaration of justice based on faith in Jesus Christ was such an argument because there Paul did not really offer an argument; he simply laid down a principle without explaining where he got such a conclusion.

In reality, Paul's overall line of argument is subtle, and we have seen it in his treatment of Abraham. There we found an argument based on the Jewish faith but having to do with a pagan. It is an *a fortiori* approach. If, as the Jewish faith maintains, an incipient, vague faith in a God who resurrects the dead was credited as justice to the pagan Abraham, how much more . . . Taking the next step, Paul aims specifically Christian guns at the same target.

(1). The first of these guns, in the theme that occupies the *first part* of Romans 5, is the *moment* when God effects the reconciliation of human beings (Christians?) with God through the death of Jesus. The assumption is, of course, that belief in this reconciliation is part of the faith of a Christian. So let us see how the moment of reconciliation affects the argument.

When God reconciled the human being with God, the situation of that being was *the worst* it could possibly be. It was when we were without power, sinners, enemies of God (5:6.8.10). It was then that God "proved his love for us . . . by the death of his Son" (5:8.10), the greatest and most precious thing God could give us. "With all the more reason, then . . ." (5:9.10), "the one who did not spare even his own beloved Son . . . how will he not gift us with everything besides him?" (8:32). And if with the first "we have been declared just" (5:9), this *total* gift will make sure that we are 'saved' (5:9.10), that the gift perdures and does not fail to achieve its ultimate consequences of grace.[119]

What is Paul trying to prove with this argument? That people who see the world and their own destiny from the standpoint of Christian *faith* cannot fall back into *fear* or *doubt* about salvation, not if they are logical at least. At the most critical and seemingly inappropriate moment, reconciliation signified a gift from God that takes in every other gift, including that of saving justice.

Granted that the Christian who knows this cannot doubt about salvation, one still might ask: But the salvation of whom? That will be the explicit theme of the second half of Romans 5. But even in the first half we find three implicit data on this point that are connected with the *function* of this argument in Paul's letter.

First, Jesus dies *before we can have faith in him.* What was chronologically true of Abraham turns out to be equally true of any and every Christian. We would still be waiting for reconciliation if, to get it, we had had to prove we believed in the God "who raised from the dead Jesus our Lord" (4:24). It was while we were still God's enemies that "we were reconciled with God" (5:10). Moreover, Christ died "for the impious" (5:6), an epithet that hardly suits even Abraham, with his vague faith in the God "who gives life to the dead and who calls into being what does not have being" (4:17). Remember that faith was enough to win him a declaration of justice. It should be obvious, then, that *the greater gift at the worst moment* was given to all human beings without taking into account their faith. Faith could not have been a precondition for the gift. It was a consequence of the gift, included in it.[120]

Second, we cannot simply say that faith was a consequence of the reconciliation-happening. We must add that it was not a secondary or *contingent* consequence that comes *after* human beings have been reconciled and *only now and then,* thus differentiating a group among the reconciled who are going to receive a declaration of justice. Highly significant in this respect is the strict parallelism between Paul's two statements: "We have been declared just *by faith*" (5:1 see 3:21–30; 4:23–24); "We have been declared just *by his [Jesus'] blood*" (5:9).

For Paul, then, faith cannot be a free *act* that can be performed before as a precondition of reconciliation or that can follow after as a possible consequence of reconciliation. And if it is not that, then faith can only be the reconciled being's whole way of being and acting, freed from fear and calculation. That is the proper style of the reconciled being, of Abraham for example.

Every other possible hypothesis is improbable and implicitly denied by Paul. One hypothesis would be that when Abraham proved his faith, God *had to* declare him just; this would turn the free gift back into a wage. The other hypothesis would be that when Abraham proved his faith, God could have *not* declared him just; this would invalidate the principle. The only possible hypothesis is that faith was an attitude which did in fact make Abraham a just person, an attitude of walking with God as a reconciled person. And this was so because faith was a general attitude towards his whole life, dovetailing in its primitive way with the type of humanity demonstrated and endorsed by the message, life, death, and resurrection of Jesus of Nazareth.

The concrete nature of this Abrahamic attitude accessible to every human being is implicitly indicated by Paul at the start of Romans 5. In clearly anthropological terms he spells out the stages of human growth to maturity. When people have faith, the afflictions and challenges of life do not over-whelm them; they produce endurance, which in turn produces maturity in human beings. Hope is an essential component of this maturity. It is a sure bet or wager that never fails or disillusions. And the Christian knows that better than anyone, since the Christian knows about the infallibility of love after having been present in Spirit at the death and resurrection of Jesus (5:3-5).

Every human being who has truly loved at some point has gone through this humanizing process of *faith*, in however precarious a fashion (see 5:1-2).

To sum up: As we move from the abstract principle enunciated in the latter part of Romans 3 to the concrete exemplifications of it in Romans 4 and the first part of Romans 5, we discover that in Paul's thought *faith* does not replace working (or doing) in God's judgment. On the contrary, faith enters into the process of working, transforms it, makes it human and mature, and *thereby* receives God's approval in the form of a declaration of justice. And the justice is real, even though it may be imperfect and compatible with many sins.

(2). The *second part* of Romans 5 simply spells out these two elements of the anthropological dimension that surfaced in the first part of the chapter. It deals explicitly with the *extent* of the reconciliation discussed in the chapter. What human beings were, are, and will be included in the reconciliation, with its corresponding declaration of justice and its resultant salvation? (These terms are but different expressions for the divine gift to us signified by the death of Christ.)

There can hardly be any doubt after what we have seen about the paternity of Abraham and the implied universality of reconciliation for 'the impious'. Reconciliation takes in *all the children of Adam*, i.e., the whole of humanity.[121]

Now suppose we ask: Is this dependent on *faith* or independent of *faith*? Again we must make the crucial distinction we made above. Yes, it is independent of faith insofar as faith is an act, a *particularity* accessible only to some. No, it is *not* independent of faith insofar as faith is a life-attitude that bets on the immortality and infallibility of love—not because that attitude precedes reconciliation but rather because it is part and parcel of reconciliation itself.

At this point mistrust prompts the perennial question: In how many human beings will God find or place the wager that love is *worthwhile*, the hoping in love against all hope? Once again, as if the first part of Romans 5 did not suffice, the second part replies: *in all the children of Adam*. That is what Paul thinks, however strange it may seem to us after all the speculation on the quantification of eternal rewards and punishments.

First, it is worth noting that if Romans 4 goes back to Abraham in discussing the theme of faith and its extent, Romans 5 goes all the way back to Adam in discussing the synonymous theme of victory over Sin. Whereas Paul had to do some abstruse exegesis to show how Abraham took in the whole of humanity, no such exegetical batteries are needed in the case of Adam. By very name Adam is the father of all human beings, at least in the biblical tradition of monogenism available for Paul's consideration.

We now find that Sin, which reigned in the first two stages (Adam to Moses; Moses to Jesus), has been conquered in the third stage, at least insofar as its enslaving power is concerned (see 5:12–14): "Where Sin abounded, grace abounded even more; with the result that as *Sin reigned* in Death, so *Grace will reign* by means of justice for eternal Life, through Jesus Christ our lord" (5:20).

Reading this description of the third stage and its explicit reference to Jesus Christ, we must remember that the third stage once again takes on the universality of the first stage (and the particularity of the second stage, in a dialectical way, i.e., through its failure and culmination). This universality and its full extent show up clearly not only in the verse just cited but in each of Paul's five comparisons between Adam and Christ. *Adam alone* affects all humanity. Likewise, *Jesus alone* affects all of humanity *more* than Adam did, as we shall see.

Paul's saying this may not show up clearly in the literal text of some of the comparisons, which may mislead people unfamiliar with biblical language. In that language 'the many' or 'the multitude' designates totality: everybody. Thus while the mere allusion to Adam might not be enough to indicate this, even though the effects of Adam's action "reached all human beings" (5:12), in two of the five comparisons Paul writes about 'the many' (5:15.19). And to make sure there is no mistaking him, a third comparison refers twice explicitly to 'all human beings' (5:18). Paul expresses himself similarly when he sums up this antithetical parallelism in 1 Corinthians: "As by a human being came death, so by a human being comes the resurrection of the dead. For as in Adam *all* die, so in Christ will *all* be made alive again" (1 Cor 15:21–22).

Second, not only does Paul attribute this complete universality to the influence of Jesus. He also sees in it a 'superiority' over Adam and his influence. There is a 'much more' in the case of Jesus. He is a 'superwinner', and he makes superwinners of those whom he loved (8:37).

It is not easy for Paul to explain what exactly goes into the disproportion in the victory, and that is understandable. Notice that the first time he tries to introduce the point, he leaves his sentence hanging in midair (5:14). And though he goes on to state it three times (5:15–17), he does not demonstrate it clearly. He generally is content to point out the strict parallelism of the antithesis between Adam and Christ: just as, so also . . .

Only one verse clearly indicates the reason for Christ's superiority, which lies in the 'results'. Grace (Jesus) achieves its result, "following the many offenses" (5:16). The disproportion, then, is *qualitative.* Sin cannot end in Death after one single Grace, one single Love, whereas Grace can end in Life and a declaration of justice after all the offenses.

Let me just mention that this qualitative difference will prove to be the key for solving the anthropological problem posed by Paul at the end of Romans 7, where Sin would seem to be the winner by all appearances. But here I want to use it exegetically to move beyond a theologically distorted interpretation of the antithetical parallelism between Adam and Christ. It is obvious that Paul uses the parallelism with Adam to point up the universality of Jesus' contrary influence on humanity. Faced with this picture of universal salvation, classical theology has sought a way to escape it by relying on two artificially connected passages.[122]

We know that Augustine offered a quasi-magical interpretation of Adam's first sin (or original sin). This was largely due to a defective Latin translation of those passages, and of Romans 5:12 especially. Paul wrote: "Death reached all human beings *because* all sinned." The Latin translation interpreted it as: "Death reached all human beings *in the one whom* all sinned," i.e., Adam. [123]

Difficult as it is to conceive this sinning 'in another', except perhaps in terms of abstruse juridical categories, this became the classical explanation for the strange fact that all human beings (hence even children without the use of reason?) were systematically and even biologically sinners.[124]

It is hard to know from this passage what Paul thought about the exact relationship between the offense of Adam and the fact that 'all sinned' (which seems to be the cause of universal death in Paul's view). Paul probably did not have children in mind, so we can assume he likely thought that Adam's offense 'inaugurated' the reign of Sin in the world and that all human beings then contributed to it by their own sins.[125] The fact that Paul considers all human beings to be sinners (3:10) need not have the sin of Adam as the *cause.* Indeed Paul seems more inclined to base his view on real sins such as those described in the diptych of the first two chapters of Romans.[126]

Classical theology, in any case, understood that all human beings had sinned 'in Adam'. Thus one merely had to be born into the human species to contract this truly 'original' sin. Starting from that point, it was extremely difficult to see how Jesus could exert an equally universal influence of the opposite sort with equally *sure* results. If human beings are declared just *by reason of their faith*, their act or overall attitude of faith would have to be a free one. And how could one be as sure of the results of freedom as one might be of nature and its effects?

How, then, could Paul talk about a victory of Grace in *all* human beings? Even though the offer of redemption and faith might be made to all human beings, one would have to assume that not all would accept it. That would throw the parallelism of Adam and Christ out of line, at least insofar as results were concerned, with Adam emerging the clear favorite. Fitting in neatly with this conception was a later passage in the letter where Paul writes of those "destined . . . beforehand [by God] to reflect the image of his Son" (8:29).

Now the idea that God in divine knowledge predetermines those who will and will not accept the redemption and salvation offered to all may seem monstrous. But at first glance, at least, it does seem more logical and sensible than that Paul would venture to predict the use that human beings will make of their liberty in responding to God's gift. Yet the fact remains that Paul ventures to do just that. He not only talks about something 'offered' but also compares the results or consequences it will have for all human beings (5:16).

Only one hypothesis seems logical on the basis of such a prediction. Human beings will make unforeseeable use of their freedom, to be sure; but there is a *qualitative disproportion* in the *necessary mixture* of their works, which are simultaneously influenced by both Sin and Grace. This disproportion, inherent in the work itself, is what permits Paul to foresee the victory *in all*.

Let's look at this another way. Paul has already made it clear that human free will is not such as to move human life solely and completely in one direction. Pagan sinners will have things both to accuse and defend themselves before God's judgment (2:15; see 2:14-16), and so will Jewish sinners (2:28-29; 3:3). In short, that will be the case with every human being. Forecasting the final result, then, can be done only if there is a crucial difference between the opposed elements of the necessary mixture. This difference must be such that all the offenses cannot destroy a single work due to Grace, whereas one single work of Grace is capable of nullifying or destroying the sum total of offenses. In that case the forecast is not based on knowing beforehand how each human being will use free will. It is based on knowing the intrinsic quality of the different elements in the mixture that every human action is. That is what Paul is saying in the parallelism when he states: "And there is no equation between the result of one's aberration and the gift. Because the judgment following from the one only ended in condemnation, whereas the work of *Grace, following the many offenses, ended in a declaration of justice . . .* the many will be made just" (5:16.19). Thus Paul's statement, "Where Sin abounded, Grace abounded even more" (5:20), does not depend on any quantified forecast of the use of free will.[127]

All this reflection, important as it may be, prompts us to take an even closer look at the influence attributed to the two figures in the parallelism. There we find even clearer indications that we are on the right track with our hypothesis.

Third, then, Paul's antithetical parallelism spells out what Adam gave to humanity in inaugurating the reign of Sin, and what Christ gave to humanity in inaugurating the reign of Grace.

In the case of Adam we find three terms in the comparisons: sin, death, condemnation. We also find three terms that describe the work of Grace: declaration of justice, life, justice. If we add the summary parallelism of 1 Corinthians 15:21-22, we find that death is once again attributed to Adam, whereas the Grace of Jesus Christ will be responsible for the resurrection of the dead. And there it explicitly says that such resurrection will reach all human beings.

We should not assume too quickly that we know these terms and, even more importantly, what their mutual connection is.

To begin with, something appears here for the first time and it is significant. Remember that we have been trying to translate the Greek words dealing with justification more accurately as 'declare just' and 'declaration of justice'. In Paul's second comparison between Adam and Christ, where he is talking about divine *judgment*, he says that Adam's influence ends in a sentence of *condemnation* whereas Christ's influence ends in a *declaration of justice* (5:16). Nothing new so far. But then comes a surprising innovation in the third comparison. Paul describes the gift that comes to us from Christ, not as a declaration of justice but as *justice* plain and simple. And the same thing occurs in the fourth comparison (see 5:17-18). In effect, Jesus 'causes justice' (5:18). This is hardly consistent with a mere declaration of justice that would leave the human being a sinner as before (see also 5:20). As if that were not enough, Paul almost seems to forestall any argument that might arise from the use of the verb meaning 'declare just' in his last comparison. There he concludes: "The many [i.e., all] *will be made just*" (5:19).[128]

In other words, Paul spells out, delimits, and makes more realistic the meaning of what faith produces as indicated at the start of the chapter: "And so, having been *declared just by reason of faith*, we are at peace with God through our lord Jesus Christ, through whom we also have gained access *with faith* to this grace in which we persevere, and we glory in the hope of God's glory" (5:1-2).

This will show up even more clearly if we note two sets of connected terms that also appear here for the first time: Sin-Death (5:12.14.15.17.20) and Justice-Life (5:17.18.20).

The first time this shows up in Paul's discussion, it is in relation to Adam. The connection between Sin and Death is a biblical reminiscence of the punishment that followed the first sin (Gn 2:17; 3:3.4.19).[129] With Adam Sin entered the world, "and through Sin Death" (5:12). In the primitive account of the Yahwist, the only connection that can be established between the sin of Adam and death is that of *punishment* for disobeying the only precept imposed in Paradise; not to eat of the tree of the knowledge of good and evil.

In discussing Romans 1, I brought up the difference between a *result* and a *punishment*. The latter represents an interruption in the cause-effect relationship. If a student gets bad grades, the annoyance of his or her parents is a *result*; their refusal to buy the student a promised bicycle would be a *punishment*. Obviously the same holds true for the relationship between a *result* and a *reward*.[130]

Now Paul's use of a biblical reminiscence here should not lead us to assume that Paul sees only a relationship of punishment between Sin and Death, and of reward between Justice and Life (5:18). While this theme will be treated much more extensively and profoundly in the following chapters, we already find two elements in the parallel between Adam and Christ that point to an intrinsic relationship between the terms. We do well to note them here.

First, remember the distinction I made between 'sins' (offenses or transgressions) and 'Sin' (the great force that enslaves human beings and causes them to fall into self-deception and bad faith). I noted that in the case of someone imprisoned in such bondage, sins themselves worked against *Sin*, and all the more when they were big sins. Like the symptoms of a disease, they made self-deception difficult or impossible. They worked against the twisted judgments that clouded a person's vision and enabled him or her to justify inhuman conduct.

Now Paul is very aware that the sin of Adam was the transgression of a precept.[131] The way Adam sinned is more like that of people who consciously break some commandment of a law known to them, except that Adam was faced with only one commandment. Thus Paul seems to face a logical difficulty in trying to say that "Sin *reigned*" from Adam on inclusively. Paul may have thought that Adam was 'entangled in his own reasonings', but the breaking of one precept is not a sufficient sign that *Sin* reigned over him.[132] Undoubtedly that is why Paul moves to the other end of the argument and writes that "Death reigned" (5:14), deducing from that, not *directly* from Adam's disobedience, the proof that Sin already reigned in Adam. Paul's direct assertion of the reign of Sin for the first stage (without the Law) comes from his observation of the mechanisms of Sin operating in the pagans of his own day, since they represent the first stage.

In the last verse of Romans 5 we also have a crucial datum that confirms the direction of Paul's thought. Remember that the second part of the chapter is devoted to the antithetical parallelism between Adam and Christ, to a comparison between the first and third stages of God's universal plan. It compares two universalities: that of Sin and that of Grace. In this context Paul omits any reference to the second stage, that of the Law. With his Jewish audience in mind, however, Paul does not want to end his treatment of the parallelism without indicating what the function of the Law and its stage could have been. He does so in the last verse: "As for the Law, it intervened *to increase the offenses*" (5:20).

Paradoxical as it may seem, Paul assumes that the increase of the 'offense' is a positive factor in the overthrow of Sin *by Grace*. As Paul sees it, this is undoubtedly because it makes the human being despair of what he or she can achieve by personal good works, in accordance with the Law, in order to win credit from God.

The assumption is that human beings must wake up to their mistake and seek another way out. That can only be the way of faith, surrender to Grace, the rejection of a negotiated salvation.

This leads us to the consideration that a life under the enslavement of Sin is a life without hope or meaning for any human course of action guided by some overall purpose. In short, it is a sort of 'death in life', a death to purpose and meaningfulness even while physical life persists. Physical death is merely the logical culmination of the whole situation.

Hence Paul offers the contrary argument about the Life, or *Vitality* if you will, of human beings of *faith* such as Abraham. These are the people who seek 'incorruption' and live trustingly in a Promise. They act gratuitously, motivated by values that they seek and hope to achieve.

Here, then, we have the basis for an argument that will be elaborated later. The argument is that we should not view *Death* and *Life* in terms of punishment and reward. Death is the *result* of a physical life managed by Sin through the counting of 'works of Law'. Life is the result of a physical life structured by Grace in its faith-inspired working.

We can already glimpse the most important features of a point that Paul will explore more deeply in the second half of Romans 7. The 'Death in life' of which we are speaking here is nothing else but the alienation of the slave that was described in the first two or three chapters of Romans.

Human beings who succumb to such self-deception and submit to the power of another (Sin) lose their own works, the result and meaning of their own lives. As is the case with all slaves, what they produce is their master's, not their own. An active and personal life as something their own does not exist. Since they are the instrument of another, they are like functioning dead people or corpses. Existentially speaking, alienation and death are synonymous; and alienation is the concept that can best help us *today* to understand the human slavery of *yesterday*. This will prove to be a crucial theme for Paul's anthropology and christology, and we see it surface here in the intrinsic relationship between enslaving Sin (not sins) and Death. Paul, by the way, is the only New Testament writer to develop the point so much.

Second, another element appears in Romans 5 and points us in the same direction. It is the opposite side of the first element just considered. It concerns the intrinsic unity of such terms as *Justice* and *Life* (resurrection). Their relationship is the same as the opposite relationship between Sin, Death, and Condemnation (see 5:16–19). We definitely lose the force of Paul's argument when we take those terms in the usual, vaguely spiritual sense as applying to the last things, be they positive or negative.

I have already cited 1 Corinthians on the resurrection of the dead. Assuming it postdates Romans, it again picks up and summarizes the parallelism between Adam and Christ: "As by a human being came Death, so by a human being comes *the resurrection of the dead*. For as in Adam *all die*, so in Christ *will all be made alive*" (1 Cor 15:21–22).

If we add these two *results* to those of the parallelism of Romans 5, we once again find Death on the negative side. On the positive side, life in Romans 5 is matched by Life in all its plenitude: *the Resurrection of all the dead*. Readers can see that there is an anthropological realism in Paul that our spiritualizations have lost sight of.

Here we have one of the most original thoughts in Paul's christology. It is original by comparison with the messianic and apocalyptic expectations of his day, which maintained that the resurrection of the dead was a precondition for God's universal judgment. It is original by comparison with the views of the other New Testament authors as well,[133] and it is original even by comparison with theology today. The latter two currents do not go beyond the theology of the Pharisees on this point, a theology already present in some respects in the Book of Wisdom. Indeed the eschatology of the Book of Wisdom almost seems more 'Christian' than that of Paul, for that very reason (see Wis 3:1-8; 4:20-5:16).

Analyzing Romans 8 later on, we shall consider what this resurrection embraces in the human being and its existence. But we already have sufficient data about its cause and extent, according to Paul. The resurrection *of all human beings* is due to the victory of Grace over Sin *in each one*. If Sin came out victorious in a single human being, there would be no *resurrection of all the dead* (5:18; 1 Cor 15:22). In the realism that is Paul's, the alienation of a whole existence is not compatible with life, much less with incorruptible restoration to life.

Thus the fact that Paul places Sin and Death in a strictly causal relationship is crucial and decisive. It is apparent in Romans 5, but even clearer in 1 Corinthians 15. Talking about 'the end', Paul says that Jesus must reign "until he has put all his enemies under his feet. The *last* enemy to be destroyed will be Death" (1 Cor 15:25-26). Then Paul cites Scripture on this total victory: "*Death* has been swallowed up in victory. O Death, where is your victory? O Death, where is your *sting*?" (1 Cor 15:55). He goes on to explain: "The *sting* of Death is *Sin*, and the *power* of Sin, *the Law*" (1 Cor 15:56). The image of a sting is obviously that of a *cause*, not of a punishment. And, as we have already seen, the Law is a mechanism whereby the enslavement of Sin takes on its fuller power, making it possible for people to indulge in a 'revealed' and sacral form of self-deception.

Thus the second element confirms the first. The enslaved human being lives and works as an alienated being. It can be said to *live* a life of its own only if it and all it has done are liberated from their master, even if that be only at the end. Confronted with that Life, the gift of Jesus, Death will have to let go of its prey. The release takes place first invisibly in the interior of the human being, so that it can act *as if* it were child and master. Then the same sort of release must take place exteriorly. The human being must be given back its works and its own physical life, though the latter will now be superior and incorruptible.

Paul presents the universal resurrection of the dead as the universal defeat of Sin *with its causes and effects*. And the importance of this anthropological equation is essential for understanding Paul's idea of the significance of the dead and resurrected Jesus.[134]

II

So far it has been my practice to devote section II of each chapter to the connection between Paul's thought and the life and message of Jesus of

Nazareth. I noted that just as some people intermix the two things improperly, so others separate them too much as if Paul's christology had no connection whatsoever with the historical Jesus.[135] Making clear both the creativity and the fidelity of Paul was central to my aim in this volume: i.e., showing how the same basic historical background of Jesus gives rise to different christologies, different interpretations of his significance for human existence.

From here on, however, I cannot do the same thing in the second section of the chapters: not because Paul ceases to be faithful to Jesus or starts quoting him directly, but because Paul's interpretation now finds its basis in the *paschal happening* of Jesus.

The paschal happening (including the resurrection) is part of the *real* Jesus, to be sure, of what was experienced and transmitted by the witnesses. Paul numbers himself among those witnesses (1 Cor 15:3-8). And of course the first part of the *paschal* happening, the death of Jesus on the cross, was both historical and verifiable. But when it comes to interpretation there is a difference. Jesus' death was immediately absorbed by his resurrection in the process of interpretation, and that was not true of his message and public activity earlier. It is not that easy, you see, to reinterpret Jesus' whole message about the kingdom of God and its arrival in the light of the paschal experiences. But it is easy to disengage his death from that historical whole and insert it into a divine plan in which the resurrection is the desired *result* or, at least, the key to it: i.e., the end of and purpose of his death and its meaning.

Thus the subsequent chapters of Romans will not just be Paul's deepest exploration of the human problematic and Jesus as a response to it. They will also be an explicit reflection on the death and resurrection of Jesus. I will not have to pinpoint hidden connections. Readers will be able to see the connection between the historical message of Jesus and Paul, and to *form their own judgment* about it. We can assume that Paul, like anyone else, gains something and loses something by his approach.

Right here at the start, however, it is fitting to offer several general considerations about Paul's interpretation of Jesus in the light of the paschal happening. In general, we can say that Paul has already shown us that the basic elements of his christology are rooted in the historical Jesus and specific elements of his message. Like the Synoptics, he has every right to base himself on the paschal experiences as well, so that those experiences project their light on everything that went before. We cannot ask Paul, any more than we can ask any other Christian, to prescind from the paschal experiences in formulating the significance of Jesus.

We can demand, of course, that the paschal projection or retrojection be *faithful*. And *the later steps will be faithful* to the extent that they follow *logically* from equally faithful premises or foundations. We have already examined the latter. We are no longer looking for *new* data that are faithful to the historical material of the Synoptics. Instead we are looking for a sound inner logic that will open up the meaning of the paschal happening vis-à-vis the human problematic that Paul is studying in the reality he is analyzing.

Keeping this principle in mind, let us look at the new christological developments that surface in Romans 5 and that will thread their way through subsequent chapters. They are obviously central ones.

(1). The first is not new to us. It is something we saw in Appendix II of Volume II. In all the early Christian Churches we find a shift from the central message of Jesus (the coming of the kingdom of God) to *the person* of Jesus himself (Who is Jesus of Nazareth?). This shift was undoubtedly produced by the dazzling impact of the resurrection, and it led Christians to focus on Jesus' relationship to the divine.

We can see that shift of emphasis in Paul, though his is a fairly well balanced one, at the end of Romans 4. Disregarding whatever factors may have actually led to Jesus' condemnation and death on the basis of his own preaching, Paul presents him as one who "had been *handed over for our misdeeds* and resurrected that we might be declared just" (4:25). As we saw in Appendix II of Volume II, the Lucan account of the first Christian community describes a more extreme shift. They tried to justify their belief in the crucified Jesus by proving he was the promised Messiah of Israel, not a fake. For Paul, on the other hand, the transformations introduced into human life by the resurrected Jesus are of such enormous dimensions that they can hardly be equated with merely human results. I am not saying his argument is in any way opposed to that of the first Christian community. I am simply saying that he never shifts his primary emphasis from the anthropological dimension to the individual person of Jesus.

We have already seen how the *function* of Jesus fulfills and transcends that of the greatest figures of Israel: Abraham, the father of Faith, and Moses, the father of the Law. The reconciliation between God and all of humanity takes place in Jesus, thanks to him, by his blood. With Jesus' death God proved God's love for us. The supreme gift by very name, salvation, comes through him.

All that far surpasses the historical possibilities of a mere human being.[136] Of course it would take centuries to spell out exactly Jesus' relationship with God, especially given the context of fierce monotheism that Christianity inherited from Israelite religion. Yet even in the New Testament we find various images proposed in order to grasp that relationship: Son, image, word, high priest, mediator, God made flesh, and so forth.[137]

The point to remember here is that Paul focuses more on the premises, the transformations introduced into the anthropological drama by Christ, than on any conclusions that might be drawn with regard to his divine nature. Here again we find evidence (or proof) of the balance in Paul's treatment of this matter. Let me verify that point by looking at a central theme which surfaces in Romans 5: the resurrection of Jesus.

The resurrection is obviously and rightly a fundamental datum in all the christologies of the New Testament. After all, christologies are not historiographical works that must stick to universally verifiable data. They are constructions and explicitations of *faith,* of a faith that regards as *equally true* the most trustworthy historical data about Jesus' prepaschal life and the transcendent data about his postpaschal life that can be verified only in the context of a decided 'partiality' for Jesus.

Perhaps stretching the strict sense of the 'appearances of the resurrected one', Paul includes himself among the witnesses to that phenomenon (1 Cor 15:8). The conclusion that Paul draws from the resurrection of Jesus, and undoubtedly from his own encounter with him on the road to Damascus, does relate to *who or what Jesus is;* but even more it stresses what Jesus transforms (thanks to who he is, of course). In the very introduction to Romans, Paul writes of Jesus that "he was constituted Son of God *in power* by his resurrection" (1:4).

Obviously the term 'power' has no meaning in itself here.[138] It is bound up with the project announced by Jesus. Remember that he differentiated his own proclamation and thaumaturgic activity from the complete arrival of the kingdom and talked about a future "coming of the kingdom of God *with power"* (Mk 9:1). Paul simply did not use the Synoptic term, 'kingdom of God', to designate God's plan or project for humanity.

(2). That brings us to the second christological development here in Romans. Recall the most salient feature of the chapters analyzed so far. Paul undertakes an in-depth analysis of human existence and its chief elements, adopting what I have called an *anthropological key.* To comprehend Paul, we must join him in exploring this new territory and appreciate the instruments he uses in his work.

So far those instruments have been notions derived from the teachings of Jesus and translated into personified characters: Sin, Flesh, the Law, Faith, Grace, and so forth. He uses them to understand as Jesus did, but not in the same key. The same basic, overall meaning is transposed from Jesus' political key to an anthropological key.

Now once the paschal experiences come into play, something curious begins to happen. Remember that Jesus himself could not put them into his political key. Now the intention of Jesus' own teachings undergoes a shift to the intrinsic relationship of his person to the divinity. Let me go back to the example I just mentioned above (1:4). Paul implicitly suggests that what the paschal experiences proved about the 'power of the kingdom' can be said just as well about the 'power of the Son of God' to carry out and realize the divine plan. At first glance the shift in key takes place easily enough and has no disconcerting consequences. The installation of the kingdom of God on earth (political key) is translated by Paul as the creation of a *reconciled, justified, and saved* humanity (anthropological key; see 5:9-10.15-19).

The three participles just noted, which sum up the results described in Romans 5, can only be attributed to verbs whose active subject is logically *God.* They can hardly be attributed to the historical acts of the human being named Jesus of Nazareth, unless we endow him with magical powers that are closely bound up with divine intentions and capacities. Thus even in this 'more well balanced' statement of Paul's, we see the historical causality of Christ (and the rest of humanity) giving way to a causality of a very different sort.

Recall Paul's statement in Romans 4:25: ". . . who had been handed over for our misdeeds and resurrected that we might be declared just." A few grammatical observations may help us to grasp the meaning of this twofold statement. In all likelihood we are dealing with a *divine passive* here, a normal grammatical way of avoiding use of the name of God. The active subject of the verbs is really God. There is also a strict parallelism in the original Greek between the two phrases: handed over for *our misdeeds* and resurrected for our *declaration of justice*. In both phrases the Greek preposition is *dia* with the accusative: 'on account of, for the sake of, because of'. Thus we could paraphrase the verse as follows: *God handed over Jesus for (the remission of) our sins and resurrected him for our being declared just.*

Setting aside the exact chronological order of Romans, Galatians, Corinthians, and Philippians, we can say that such a basic statement constitutes a major step in the task of creating christologies, and that it was made possible by trying to answer the question of Jesus' relationship to God.

According to the historical-political key of the Synoptic narratives, for example, Jesus did not die *for anything*. His violent death was the fairly predictable consequence of certain conflictive characteristics inherent in the kingdom of God. His resurrection by God does not prove that the kingdom is *no longer conflictive*. It does not prove that the kingdom is now reconciliatory, or that the things Jesus invested in its service (his person, activity, and life) are stronger than death.

But if we shift to the anthropological-theological key that surfaces in Paul's twofold affirmation above, the perspective changes completely. If Jesus is regarded primarily as the conscious envoy of a divine project, and if he is our focus, then the conflict that caused his death becomes secondary. It becomes the historical *occasion* for the occurrence of his death and resurrection, and for their consequent transformation of humanity's situation vis-à-vis God. Jesus is led to death by God, not by adversaries of the kingdom who are also his adversaries. In dying, Jesus undertakes a task that has to do with the sins of humanity, not with the happiness of the poor and marginalized. And in being resurrected by God, Jesus manifests the declaration of justice won for us rather than the power (*dunamis*) that should inspire us to face up fearlessly to the conflicts that the kingdom will necessarily provoke.

We are so used to this historical short circuit in the more classical and familiar christologies that we are not shocked at all when we read that "Christ died for us" (5:8; see 5:6–7). Yet we know by heart from our reading of the Synoptics[139] what the *historical* causes of his death were.

Here I would differentiate between *historical* causes and *real* causes of Jesus' death because we cannot rule out *a priori* the possibility that the verifiable historical causes might coincide with others on a different plane that are real even though not objectively verifiable in the same way.

Right from the start of Volume II, I pointed out that there is no good reason why a christology 'from above' has to contradict or oppose a christology 'from below'. Ordinarily they should dovetail with each other and ultimately comple-

ment one another. But in the process of constructing a christology, it is difficult
not to sacrifice one or the other, and we must now see whether or not that is
what happens in the case of Paul.

I am now compelled to go back to Romans 3 and bring up a point that I chose
to bypass earlier. Back in that chapter, you see, Paul already inverted the order
of intentions and causalities. Here is the pertinent text: "All have sinned and
lack the glory of God, being declared just by the gift of his grace through the
redemption accomplished by Christ Jesus, whom God destined to be, in his
own *blood, expiation* through faith . . ." (3:23-25).

Here we have the most important metaphorical elements of the imaginative
scheme designed to explain and justify the death of Jesus. They are framed in a
new key, of course: the *cultic-legal* key. We could also call it a legal key, realizing
that once such a key is applied to the peculiar relationship between creature and
Creator, it necessarily becomes cultic as well.

The universal sinfulness of human beings placed all in a permanent state of
enmity with God, thereby necessitating a reconciliation. So far we do not seem
to have gone beyond the anthropological plane of attitudes and their logic.
Using the vocabulary of the Synoptics, we could say that conversion (*meta-
noia*) would be the basic factor in such a reconciliation and sufficient to effect
it. But if we introduced a legal framework here, particularly as understood by
primitive peoples when they thought of justice, we would have to 'buy' the
pardon that would effect our reconciliation. Paying the price or 'ransom' for
our offense, we would be offering expiation and thereby propitiating the one
offended.

Disregarding the metaphysical arguments used centuries later by St. Anselm
to systematize this judicial process from a *theological-legal* standpoint, we can
put it this way. The offender buys back (*apolutrosis*, 'redemption') the relationship lost by the offense by paying a price (*lutron,* 'ransom'), as if a friendly
relationship were a hostage in the power of the offended party. From the
theological -cultic standpoint, the expiatory ransom for an offense against God
is always the *blood* (i.e., the life) of a victim offered in sacrifice in place of the
offender.[140] As the Letter to the Hebrews puts it: "Without the shedding of
blood there is no remission" (Heb 9:22). Moreover, when the sin in question is
that of all humanity (as Paul indicates), only a 'blood' intimately associated
with the Divinity could make ransom and win redemption. But even though all
the preparations may have been made by God, the victim has to be offered
from within humanity since it serves as expiation for the latter. The author of
the Letter to the Hebrews is an expert on that sort of cultic legalism, demon-
strating point by point that this is precisely what happened with Jesus Christ
(Heb 5; 9:11-14; etc.).

Since this is not the only occasion where elements of that christological
scheme appear, some basic observations are in order.

I think it is crucial that we distinguish two things here. One is the matter of a
christology 'from above'. The other is the cultic-legal key. Of course both have
been habitually associated in classical theology, especially since the Middle

Ages.[141] But the fact is that a christology 'from above' need not use the cultic-legal key. Thus the fourth gospel and Johannine theology in general must be viewed as a christology from above, but the central event in them is the Incarnation rather than Jesus' death and resurrection viewed as a ransom for sin.[142] I shall come back to the whole matter of christologies from above, but one important principle should be clear: though such christologies have a dangerous tendency to minimize the prepaschal history of Jesus, in and of themselves they do not represent a negation or denial of christologies from below, i.e., christologies starting off from the historical Jesus.

Thus it is the *cultic-legal key* that is the issue for us here. With some justification we might ask to what extent Paul *believes* in that key when he uses it. We need only note, however, that people may have different attitudes towards a particular set of symbols and the proper way to use them. Some may adopt them in a strict, almost literal way while others may take them in a very broad sense.

Consider two examples. Paul tells us that "Christ died for us" and that "by the obedience of one only the many will be made just." Here we have a symbolic scheme that attempts to explain two simple acts: (1) the *physical* act of dying; (2) the *moral* act of intention in Christ's death for us out of obedience to the Father. In both cases the symbolic scheme is the same: *cultic-legal*.

We can take the symbolism in a stricter, more realistic, and more literal sense. In that case we might imagine a courtroom where a defendant has been convicted of Sin. The judge asks: Has Christ died yet? If the answer is no, the defendant continues to be declared convicted because he or she has not paid for Sin. If the answer is yes, the defendant is declared innocent or just (pardoned). The death of Christ, in other words, was the precondition and the decisive, immediate, sufficient factor for our reconciliation with God.

Using the same symbolic scheme, however, we can come up with a looser interpretation of the fact that Christ died for us. When Christ consented to die for love of us while we were still God's enemies, he freed us radically from our moral fears and thus opened up a whole new possibility for us. Despite all our human limitations, we can now forget our own destiny compromised by Sin and move out creatively and freely to build the kingdom of God insofar as the latter depends on us. Or, to use a Pauline synonym for the kingdom of God, we might say that our task now is to effect the real humanization of the human world.[143] Note that the symbolism is still framed in the juridical scheme. The fear that would be ours if Christ's death had not freed us is metaphorically that of a sinful defendant standing before the most just of judges.

The difference between the two 'interpretations' of the symbolism is very great, however. In the strict interpretation Christ's death is viewed not only as necessary but also as the *direct cause* of the sentence that declares just a sinful human being. In the looser interpretation Christ's death proves to be a suitable way to affect our behavior *indirectly*. By altering our attitude so that we have greater confidence and liberty, it prompts a different way of acting and working in people who had been shackled by fear of the Law. And it is our new way of working that God will evaluate in God's just judgment of us.

The same comments apply just as well to the second Pauline expression noted above, so there is no need to add anything here. Given these two basic types of interpretation, I argue here that Paul uses the cultic-legal scheme in the broad or loose sense rather than in any strict sense.

My *first* argument is of a more general nature. A literal use or interpretation of the cultic-legal key would nullify the whole anthropological analysis that Paul has been offering up to this point. In chapter X of Volume II, I discussed the possible use of imminent eschatology as a key to the Synoptics. I argued that the use of such a key was incompatible with the political key that I had put to the test and verified. I see the same sort of incompatibility here in the strict or literal use of the cultic-legal key to interpret Paul.

If my analysis so far has been correct, up to now Paul has been trying to show how certain basic human attitudes, deriving essentially from the prepaschal message of Jesus, modify human existence in an intrinsic way. With a logic that is consistent, though subtle and complicated, they impart new possibilities and a new maturity to human existence. If we take the cultic-legal key in a strict or literal sense, on the other hand, the anthropological causality at work in the loose interpretation is immediately replaced by a very different causality that would operate miraculously and from outside[144] to change the relationship between God and the human being, thanks to Jesus' death.

Please note that I am not denying that Paul uses the cultic-legal key. It is clear that in some places Paul does seem to attribute magical or miraculous power to faith in Jesus Christ, as if some extrinsic factor won a saving declaration of justice for human beings even though they remained what they had been before. All I am saying here is that Paul's use of this key does not tell us automatically how he interprets it. And when we view his use in terms of everything that has gone before in Romans, it seems to me we are forced to conclude that he uses it in a broad, indirect sense. In short, the cultic-legal key is subordinate to the anthropological key that pervades and integrates Paul's christological conceptions in Romans.

Obviously the validity of this argument depends on the validity of my interpretation of Romans throughout this volume, both in the previous pages and the ones to come. My readers will ultimately have to pass judgment on that.

My *second* argument for Paul's loose use of the cultic-legal scheme is based on the importance of the *resurrection* in Paul's christological system. It gradually assumes more and more importance in his treatment until it comes to occupy a central place. This is already obvious in the second half of Romans 5, which deals with the antithetical parallelism between Adam and Christ. Well, the fact is that *the resurrection does not play any crucial role in the cultic-legal scheme*. The price of our redemption is paid with the *death* of Christ. Victims thus offered as ransom do not rise again, nor are they restored to their former owners (a possible metaphorical sense of 'resurrection'). The resurrection or non-resurrection of Jesus adds nothing to the procedures required for reconciliation in legal or cultic terms. With the death of Jesus (the redemptive payment), the sentence of absolution comes from God, who now looks with favor on humanity.

Even if we assume that the resurrection of Jesus might serve as 'notification' of the justifying sentence, that fact means little by comparison with the crucial fact that we have been declared just and, whether we have been informed or not, this justice has been truly credited to us as it was to Abraham. In other words, the resurrection is not a cause within the context of the whole process and its outcome. At best it is merely an accompanying fact that carries the whole matter to its culmination.[145]

Let's look at this again from another angle. Recall the twofold affirmation of Paul at the end of Romans 4, framed in the cultic-legal scheme and paraphrased by me as follows: "God handed over Jesus for (the remission of) our sins and resurrected him *for* our justification." The latter statement, that the resurrection of Jesus took place for our justification, does not jibe with the symbolism of the cultic-legal scheme. This was tacitly realized by the theological tradition that has always preferred to use his death as the connecting link. In the cultic-legal key, the latter statement should read something like this: "and resurrected him for (the purpose of *notifying us* of) our justification."

But *whether we accept or reject that implied remark*, we are logically compelled to give a broad and indirect sense to the causal relationship between resurrection and justification. That broad sense, in turn, points to the corroboration of *faith* and the transcendent datum of the resurrection it offers us. Once again, you see, we are led back to the main lines of the anthropological key.

Going back a bit further in Romans, we find testimony to this fact in the third chapter. Paul alludes to "the *redemption* accomplished by Jesus Christ" (3:24). And he describes the divine plan and Jesus' role in it as follows: "whom God destined to be, in his own *blood*, expiation *through faith* . . ." (3:25). Notice here again how the cultic-legal key is interrupted. It would logically seem to move towards the word 'blood', to end with Jesus' death. But then there is the phrase 'through faith', an allusion to that basic change of outlook or attitude in the human being. I think that clearly shows us that Paul uses the cultic-legal key in a broad sense, and that it is always framed within the contours of his anthropological key. Within the latter, human attitudes will always be the crucial and decisive factor.

(3). That brings us to the third and final christological development we must note here in Romans 5. It has to do with the source of Paul's conception of the Adam-Christ parallelism. As I have already indicated, the parallelism clearly arose out of Paul's interpretation of the paschal experiences, which certainly represent the point of convergence for 'low' and 'high' christologies or those two aspects of one and the same christology. I said that the connection was very well balanced in Paul's thought, and that it naturally shows up right here.

I would remind readers of my remarks on the literary genre of the Synoptic resurrection accounts (Volume II, Appendix I). We saw that those accounts clearly suggested that the resurrection should not be interpreted as just another event within the chain of history. It was a momentary, tangential glimpse of the *eschatological* reality. The testimony of Stephen may well be our best example of this: "I see *the heavens opened* and the Son of man *standing at God's right hand*" (Acts 7:56). In Volume II (Appendix II) we also saw that focusing on the question of Jesus' identity and his exact relationship with the Divinity *could* lead people to devaluate or undervaluate what Jesus himself preached and did before his death and resurrection. According to the Synoptic documents, the historical Jesus proclaimed the coming of the *kingdom of God*.

Now let us look at the steps whereby Paul recovers this evangelical dimension of the resurrection. Here I shall merely outline them, since we shall find more such elements of great importance in the following chapters of Romans.

Almost all our witnesses tell us that the eschatological breakthough embodied in the paschal happening of Easter led to an understanding of the new and definitive *power* of Jesus.[146] After Paul, it is Mark in particular who uses a clearly postpaschal prediction to equate that power with the realization of the divine *project* announced and prepared for by Jesus: i.e., the arrival of the kingdom of God (Mk 9:1).[147]

Paul does not use that term for God's project. He translates it into his own key. In the political key used by Jesus in Israel, the kingdom or reign of God meant that God was coming to Israel to combat the infrahuman situation affecting the lives of the poor, the helpless, and the marginalized. The kingdom would restore them to the condition of human beings. It would humanize them by destroying the power of the 'strong one' who was dehumanizing them: Satan.

In a different key Paul also sees God's project as a battle, coextensive with humanity itself, against the infrahuman condition of human beings. But in Paul's context and his anthropological key the people in this infrahuman situation are all those, pagans or Jews, who suffer from infantilism and bad faith because they are under the bondage of Sin. He is talking about all those who have not achieved human maturity, the freedom of faith that propels human beings towards untrammeled and unreserved creative activity out of love for their brother and sister humans.

But there is much more ground to cover here. In Paul's treatment, the resurrection of Jesus 'with power' (and its eschatological world) is intimately and primarily related to the *universal* resurrection of the dead. That relationship is so basic for Paul that one would make no sense without the other. In 1 Corinthians 15:13, for example, Paul begins his argument in a really strange way: "If there is no resurrection of the dead, then neither was Christ resurrected."[148] For such an argument to have any weight, and not be brushed aside by appeal to a unique privilege enjoyed by Jesus as the Holy One of God (Lk 4:34; Acts 2:27), Paul must be assuming that some Corinthians not only don't believe such a resurrection would take place but also think it is impossible or contradictory (1 Cor 15:35f.).

Of course Paul tries to knock down the reasons alleged for that position, which he regards as 'senseless' (1 Cor 15:36). But his main argument against any such supposed contradiction or impossibility is *a fact*, to which he himself was a witness after many others: i.e., the undeniable resurrection of Jesus (1 Cor 15:5–8.20). The point of his remark in 1 Corinthians 15:13 might be paraphrased more clearly as a contrary-to-fact condition: "If the dead could not be resurrected, then neither would Christ have been resurrected." Paul, however, chooses to leave the question of possibility aside. Taking a turn of one hundred and eighty degrees, Paul makes this deduction instead: If Christ was resurrected, that implies the future fact of the resurrection of all the dead as well. Paul cannot conceive the fate of Jesus himself as separated from that of Jesus' humanizing project: "Christ was raised from the dead as the first fruits of *those who have fallen asleep*. For as by a human being came *death*, so by a human being comes *the resurrection of the dead*. For as in Adam *all* die, so in Christ will *all* be made alive again" (1 Cor 15:20–22).

Note that the (sole) resurrection of Jesus prompts Paul to spell out, more briefly but in almost the same terms, a parallel between Adam and Christ that is identical with the one we have been analyzing in Romans 5. Surely this is a good indication that we are on the right track with our exegesis. The resurrection of Jesus is a visible projection in the present of something that will take place *visibly* only in the ultimate future but that already is having its effect on the existence of all human beings: "And when *this*[149] corruptible puts on incorruptibility and *this* mortal puts on immortality, then will the word of Scripture be fulfilled: '*Death* has been swallowed up in *victory*. O Death, where is your victory? O Death, where is your sting?' The sting of Death is *Sin*, and the power of Sin, *the Law*. But thanks be to God who gives us the victory through our lord Jesus Christ!" (1 Cor 15:54–57).

We have not given due theological and christological importance to a fact that distinguishes Paul from all the other New Testament writers.[150] For Paul, the universal resurrection of the dead is a *victory* for Christ. It is not a matter of some characteristic proper to the human being, such as the immortality of the soul assumed by Greek philosophy. Nor is it even a matter of a final action by God designed to defend and justify God for the lack of justice in history (theodicy). It is not as if God was somehow obliged to resurrect the good and the wicked to give them another life that accorded with their works, although that was the view of a good segment of theology in Jesus' own day: e.g., that of the Pharisees (see Wis 1–5).

The *universal* resurrection is a victory of Jesus over the three great anthropological adversaries: *the Law, Sin,* and *Death*. The obsessive power of the Law carried Sin to its peak. The inhuman and enslaving power of Sin, acting like a sting (not a punishment), produced a death that starts in our life here and now and that culminates in physical Death. One by one the slaves lost their own projects in a preliminary and anticipatory death; they were alienated from their own projects. In 1 Corinthians, then, Paul immediately draws the anthropological conclusion from the universal resurrection that can be foreseen in the resurrection of Jesus as its first fruits. And it is the very same conclusion we shall find further on in Romans: "So, my beloved brothers and sisters, be steadfast and persevering . . . knowing that *your labor is not in vain . . .*" (1 Cor 15:58).

To track down the source of the parallelism between the human being who springs from Adam and the human being who springs from Christ, we need only notice that the very same anthropological enemies are conquered in Romans by the 'more' universal *power* of Christ (5:15.16.20). Here, too, the Law is conquered by Grace (5:20), hence Sin by Justice (5:18-19), and consequently Death by Life (5:17-18).

The resurrection of Jesus, as an eschatological experience, thus enables Paul to see how the realization of the kingdom in power is to be translated in his own anthropological key. It must be translated as a *resurrection*: the victory in all human beings of life, of the grace received in faith, and of an effective freedom that proves to be creative in love for others.

The following chapters of Romans will flesh out this basic scheme outlined in Romans 5, fully revealing Paul's fidelity to the preaching of Jesus and his creativity in transposing his christology to a new context.

CHAPTER VI

The New Life of the Christian

Romans 6:1–7:13

6   (1) So what *are we* to say? That we should continue in sin so that grace may increase? (2) Never! How could we, who have died to sin, still live in it? (3) Do you not realize that all of us who have been baptized in Christ Jesus have been baptized in his death? (4) We have been buried with him by baptism in death so that, as Christ was resurrected from the dead by the glory of the father, we too might operate in the newness of life. (5) For if we have been assimilated to the form of his death, so we will be to the form of the resurrection, (6) knowing this: that our old humanity was crucified with him so that the body of sin might be destroyed and we might not be slaves to sin any longer. (7) Because one who is dead is declared just of sin.

(8) If we have died with Christ, we believe we shall also live with him, (9) knowing that Christ, once resurrected from the dead, will never die again and (that) death no longer has dominion over him. (10) Dying, he died to sin once and for all; living, he lives for God. (11) So you too should count yourselves dead to sin, but alive for God in Christ Jesus.

(12) Don't let sin reign in your mortal body, so that you obey its cravings (13) or offer your members to sin as weapons of injustice; offer yourselves to God as alive from the dead, and your members to God as the weapons of justice. (14) For sin will no longer have dominion in you, since you are no longer under the law but under grace.

(15) What then? Are we going to sin because we are not under the law but under grace? Never! (16) Don't you realize that to whomever you offer your obedience as slaves, you become that one's slaves: either of sin, toward death; or of obedience, toward justice? (17) But, thank God, you who were slaves to sin have wholeheartedly obeyed the standard of teaching to which you have been transferred (18) and, liberated from sin, you have made yourselves slaves of justice—I speak in human terms because of the weakness of the flesh *in* you—. (19) Just as you offered

your members (as) slaves to impurity and iniquity, to *live in* iniquity; so now offer your members (as) slaves to justice, to *live in* sanctification. (20) When you were slaves to sin, you were free of justice. (21) What fruit did you reap then? (Things) of which you are now ashamed, since their end is death. (22) But now, having been liberated from sin and made slaves of God, the fruit you have is sanctification, and the end is eternal life. (23) For the wage of sin (is) death, whereas the gift of God (is) eternal life in our lord Jesus Christ.

7   (1) Don't you know, brothers,—I am speaking to *people* who know about *laws*—that law has dominion over a human being only so long as that being lives? (2) A married woman, for example, is bound to her husband (while he is) alive; but if the husband dies, she is free of the husband law. (3) While her husband is alive, she will be treated as an adulteress if she becomes another man's ; but if her husband dies, she becomes free of the husband law, so that she does not commit adultery if she becomes another man's. (4) In like manner, my brothers, you have died to the law, by the body of Christ, to become another's—the one who was resurrected from the dead—and to bear fruit for God. (5) When we were in the flesh, the passions of sins *roused* by the law were at work in our members, so that we bore fruit for death. (6) Now, on the other hand, we have been liberated from the law, having died to what bound us, so that *we can* serve in the newness of the spirit, not in the oldness of the letter.

(7) What shall we say, then? That the law is sin? Never! Admittedly, I did not know sin except through the law. I would not *have come* to know *what* covetousness *was*, if the law had not said: "Thou shalt not covet." (8) But sin, seizing its opportunity, by means of the precept aroused in men every *kind of* covetousness. Without law, you see, sin (is) dead. (9) Once upon a time I was alive without law. Then the precept came and sin began to live. (10) I, on the other hand, died. And the result for me was that the very precept given for life served for death. (11) Sin, seizing its opportunity, by means of the precept deceived me and thereby killed me.

(12) So, now, the law itself is holy and the precept holy, just, and good. (13) If that is the case, did the good turn into death for me? Never! But sin, to be manifestly clear as sin, produced death in me by means of something good; so that sin, by means of the precept, might turn into something exaggeratedly sinful.

Romans 4 dealt with Abraham, the father in a certain way of all humanity divided religiously by the Law, on the basis of data of the Jewish faith recorded in the Bible. Romans 5 dealt with all humanity, not as children of Abraham but as children of Adam, on the basis of data deriving from Christian faith. Both chapters, of course, were elaborations and exemplifications of the abstract principle enunciated near the end of Romans 3.

The sixth and seventh chapters consider the situation of Christians in the light of the same principle. They focus on those 'baptized in the name of Jesus'. So it is strange to see that the general order of these chapters is messy. Indeed, of the first eight chapters of Romans they may well be the most disconnected, hesitant, and fragile.[151] Considering that Paul has come to a situation where he can truly be regarded as an expert, we would expect these chapters to reflect a special mastery, as the result of his own unique experience among other things. That is not the case.

We notice this and simultaneously make an important discovery when we pinpoint the question where Paul runs into difficulty: Are Christians, those who believe in Jesus Christ, freer from Sin than the rest of humanity?

It would seem that Paul would be afraid to answer *no*. If the answer is no, why be a Christian? What saving and liberating value would there be in faith in Jesus Christ? But we can assume that Paul would be equally afraid to answer *yes*. If his answer is yes, he would be reintroducing a privilege when his major concern has been to prove that all human beings find themselves on equal terms when they face God's judgment.

In any case, it is clear that the sixth and seventh chapters form a fairly well defined unit up to Romans 7:14. Baptism is the doorway into the community of Jesus for converted Jews and pagans alike. Paul makes clear that this Baptism aims at liberation from Sin. To put it more exactly, he says that Baptism signifies a 'death' that liberates from Sin and the Law. Liberation from Sin is the predominant theme of Romans 6, which is addressed primarily to converted pagans. Liberation from the Law, which is the 'power' of Sin (1 Cor 15:56), is the predominant theme of the first half of Romans 7, which is addressed primarily to converted pagans.

What about the latter half of Romans 7: verses 14–25? Although some ambiguity and indecisiveness remains, I would say that from 7:14 on Paul clearly opts for a *no* answer to the question we are considering. Paul situates the human being as such vis-à-vis Sin and analyzes the mechanisms that induce human beings to become slaves of Sin whether they be pagans, Jews, or Christians. Paul thus comes up with statements of much greater daring and depth, but he has to pay a price for that. He is forced to devote a whole chapter (Romans 8) to reexamining and reworking the theme of authentic liberation. This should help to explain the setup and division of my treatment in this chapter and the two following ones. So let us begin with Romans 6.

The present division of chapters rightly sees that Paul broaches a new topic in 6:1. The sureness of victory conveyed by the Adam-Christ parallelism of Romans 5 might prompt some people to conclude that it is worth staying in sinfulness or even increasing it so as to add to the luster of the victory. Paul's answer is: "Never!" (6:2). And the reason is undoubtedly that Grace is all the more victorious, the more it liberates human life and work from enslavement to Sin.

Paul's argument now enters new terrain. He lays hold of a new instrument specific to the Christian community: *Baptism*, the rite of initiation into membership in that community. Once converted, both pagans and Jews go through that rite.

Today the rite of Baptism suggests to us a purifying or cleansing bath reduced to a few drops of water sprinkled on the head. In the ancient world, and particularly in the mystery religions of the Hellenistic period, there were two important differences. First, water was regarded as the source and origin of life. Second, the rite entailed total immersion of the body, suggesting a symbolic death and burial and then emergence to a new life. Thus while baptism may have been used by John the Baptist and the earliest Christian community in Jerusalem (Acts 2:28) to symbolize purification from sins, and by Judaism to signify the new ritual purity of proselytes,[152] in Paul's Christian communities it served as a suitable sign of the great happening and the distinctive transcendent datum of Christian faith: Jesus put to death and then resurrected by God to a new and higher life (6:4). In Baptism catechumens embraced that happening, grounded their own lives in it, and 'assimilated' themselves to its two aspects: death and resurrection (6:5).

Logically enough, this assimilation should transform the human being who goes through it, just as Jesus himself was transformed, from what we know of his disciples' experience of him. And if there is a transformation, then there is something 'old' that disappears and something 'new' that arrives (6:6). The 'old human being' that disappears, that 'dies' in Baptism, is the 'slave to Sin'. The new human being born in Baptism is the one 'declared just of Sin' (6:7). The 'death' in Baptism symbolizes the new life that defeats Death in the resurrection (6:8.11).

At this point Paul divides his argument, addressing himself first to converted *pagans* (6:12-23) and then to converted *Jews* (7:1-13) in the Roman community.

(1). The first part of Paul's argument considers how the death and resurrection of Jesus, signified in Christian Baptism, affect and liberate the human being. There is practically no mention of the Law, except in 6:14-15. Paul stresses the factor that induces human beings to indulge in self-deception, get entangled in idolatry, and thus come under bondage to Sin and "hold truth shackled in injustice" (1:18). It is the same factor we saw in Romans 1: strong desires or 'cravings' (6:12)

The new life would consist in not obeying those cravings, something which should be possible. If it were simply a matter of a juridically imputed justice, we should logically expect Paul to urge Christians here to *preserve* and defend their faith. That would seem to be the logical conclusion to be drawn from the principle enunciated in Romans 3. Some might argue that this exhortation to faith is made implicitly in Romans 6, but that only lends further weight to my hypothesis. For I would maintain that he is talking of *faith* throughout Romans 6 when he insists on *a new way of behaving that was not possible before but is now*: "Don't let Sin reign in your mortal body,[153] so that you obey its cravings or offer your members to sin as weapons of injustice; offer yourselves to God as alive from the dead, and your members to God as weapons of justice. For Sin will no longer have dominion in you . . ." (6:12–14).

At the start of this chapter I indicated that Paul seems to have doubts about our victory over Sin. Yet his future tense (6:14) suggests certainty of liberation from it for Christians. Let us see first what lends support to this future certainty, and then what raises a question mark about it.

The text just cited is the clearest indication that in Paul's thinking continued enslavement to Sin is incompatible with Baptism. How could human beings continue to be slaves to Sin once their faith in Jesus has led them to Baptism! The text also brings out Paul's central concern with the new way of acting or working that is possible *from then on*: "so that . . . we too might operate in the newness of life" (6:4).

There are further arguments in this vein. In this chapter Paul compares two existential situations differentiated precisely by a different use of the more direct instruments a human being has to work with. In both this chapter and the next one he calls those instruments 'members' (6:13.19; 7:23).

I would insist that in Paul's thinking this graphic term is really a synonym for the realm of *instrumentality* in general. Why? Because it always surfaces as something mediating between human intention and human performance. And that is not exclusive to the bodily members. In Romans 6, they are described as "weapons of" twice: i.e., instruments placed in the service of some intention or project. In two other places in the same chapter we find that the 'members' are in the service of impurity or justice. Paul adds the words 'as slaves'. Whether that refers to the members or the person who possesses them, it is clear that the members are the cause of the alienable feature in human activity. The 'I' cannot be sold or hired out, but its accompanying instruments can be.

So we find a type of independence where there should be subordination in the relationship between intended project and realization of it. This will be brought out even more clearly in Romans 7, where we find that the 'members' should obey two distinct imperatives or laws but actually only serve one of them. One of the laws comes from 'outside' the self or 'I' with its freedom. The other comes from the 'inner humanity' of which the instruments are members.

The latter law, however, is a kind of utopia belied by reality. It imagines a free being who has the universe at its disposal to carry out its projects. But the *fact* of the matter is that those members or instruments have their own law imposed on them by nature rather than by their supposed master. It is nature that dictates how one is to use a hammer because the characteristics and limitations of its activity are part of its essence and independent of the user for the most part. Thus what Paul calls the 'law of the members' is, in the strict sense, the mute opposition posed by any sort of instrument to the free intentions of a person.

As I said, this means that the term 'members' takes in much more than the instruments inherent in the *body* itself. Law of the members also includes the mechanisms that regulate social relations. Those mechanisms prevent the human being from making use of them, and end up using the human being to consolidate their own position and power. Paul repeatedly alludes to these fixed and seemingly inexorable patterns of behavior that regulate specific relationships and determine what they should be: between man and woman, slave and free man, Jew and pagan (10:12; and especially 1 Cor 12:13–14; Gal 3:28; Col 3:11). Thus they pose a challenge to human freedom and creativity.

According to Paul, something fundamentally new is a correlate of Baptism and what it signifies: i.e., *the possibility of snatching human instrumentality from the service of injustice and putting it in the service of truth*, of the *just* intentions of the human being (6:13–19).

It is worth noting that Paul, recalling the earlier situation, confirms my proffered hypothesis about the intrinsic relationship between Sin and Death. Speaking of a time when instrumentality was in the service of injustice, he asks his readers: "What fruit did you reap then?" His answer is: "(Things) of which you are now *ashamed*, since their end is Death" (6:21). This being *ashamed* of one's actions is closely bound up with what we today would call *alienation*. It is the attitude of attempting to disown what one has done so that others will take responsibility. In other words, one puts *distance* between the free 'I' and the work performed. If we keep piling up these distances, these disavowals of our own work, we end up with an empty life: Death.

In the very terms Paul uses to establish this close relationship between Sin and Death we find a new argument for his realism in considering the possibility of a new justice. I have maintained that Paul is far from being uninterested in the quality and result of human work, that in fact he seems to *measure* faith by the qualitative result of such work rather than relying on a gratuitous declaration of merely forensic justice. Now the term 'fruit' used in 6:21 is nothing else but a metaphor for the word 'result'; and when the partial results or fruits are added together, we get the *end* result that is long-term and definitive. In Greek, the word *karpos* designates the immediate result and the word *telos* designates the mediate and definitive result. And we find that Paul differentiates the Christian *now* and the time *before* on the basis of their respective *fruits* and *ends*: "When you were slaves of Sin, you were free of Justice. What *fruit* did you reap *then*? Things of which you are now ashamed, since their *end* is Death. But *now*, having been liberated from Sin and made slaves of God, the *fruit* you have is sanctification,[154] and the *end* is eternal Life" (6:20–22).[155]

Note that both Death and eternal Life are seen once again to be *consequences* of working. Faith is not mentioned explicitly; but if Baptism is its sign, then faith must consist in a *way of working* that falls under this *final* alternative. I think this confirms my hypothesis that Paul never regards *faith* as a substitute for human action. Instead he sees faith as a bold, creative, gratuitous way of acting: the same way of acting that characterized Abraham and the only one which, by its *intrinsic* anthropological makeup, is destined for resurrection and eternal Life rather than alienation and Death.

Even granting all the above, however, we cannot deny that this first part of Romans 6 also contains contrary arguments suggesting that not even the baptized are free from Sin; that they, too, are or can become *slaves* of Sin.

These first eight chapters of Romans are Paul's theological letter of introduction to a community he supposedly does not know personally. Logically enough, their basic style is expository. So we are surprised to find that Romans 6 becomes largely *exhortatory*. To be sure, his future tense of 6:14 declares: "Sin will no longer have dominion in you, since you are no longer under the Law but under Grace." But it is surrounded by imperatives in verses 11–19 that suggest this outcome is not certain or inevitable: "Don't let Sin reign . . ." (6:12).

In fact, we do have good reason to think that this liberation is not certain and inevitable on the basis of other Pauline texts. Remember that the theme of liberation from the Law, Sin, and Death shows up in Galatians and 1 Corinthians as well. It is in Romans that Paul switches the order in which that liberation is considered: Sin, the Law, Death.

In the previous chapter (p. 97), I cited the passage in 1 Corinthians 15 where Paul indicates that the resurrection signifies a victory over Death (the final enemy), hence over its 'sting' (Sin) and its 'power' (the Law). Taking the process from the other end, it would seem logical to start with liberation from the Law, move on to liberation from Sin, and end with liberation from Death. That, in fact, is the order Paul follows in 1 Corinthians. He tells his readers to liberate themselves from the Law by ceasing to worry about what is or is not licit and focusing on what is suitable. Everything is licit; suitability is the criterion. But since Sin can still deceive human beings even when stripped of its power (the Law), Paul adds that he will not allow himself to be dominated or enslaved by anything (1 Cor 6:12). And his example is precisely one of those 'cravings' of the human heart which, even without Law, prompt human beings to fall into self-deception and enslavement to Sin (1 Cor 6:13–14).

He follows the same order in Galatians. The Law was our pedagogue until Christ came. Now we are no longer under the pedagogue because Christ has liberated us so that we can be truly free (Gal 3:24–25). Further on he adds this admonition: ". . . only do not turn this freedom into a pretext for the flesh" (Gal 5:13). The Flesh is the point of origin of desires or cravings (Rom 13:14; Gal 5:16.24). Even deprived of its power (the Law), Sin can still seduce human beings and enslave them. So Paul moves on to discuss liberation from Sin after he has discussed liberation from the Law.

In Romans 6:1–7:13, by contrast, Paul follows the order dictated by his earlier chapters, where he first established the enslavement of pagans without Law to Sin and then the enslavement of Jews to Sin under the Law. He thus reverses the order of the first two items as they appear in the other two letters, which probably reflect better the order Paul envisioned in treating the theme of liberation. His desire in Romans to explain the three stages of God's plan for humanity may also have prompted him to make the reversal.

The point here is that by not beginning with liberation from the Law, Paul probably found it even more difficult to make clear how faith assuredly liberates humanity from Sin at the Christian level. Remember that Paul uses the term 'faith' in opposition to 'works of *the Law*'. And even though faith was operative in Abraham the pagan, Paul does not demonstrate that in anthropological terms; he simply states the fact on the basis of a biblical verse. Once we get to Romans 6, we find only one place where Paul expresses certainty about our liberation. And it happens to be the only one that mentions the Law: "Sin will no longer have dominion in you, *since you are no longer under the Law* but under Grace" (6:14).[156]

Even allowing for all that, we can still ask: Is the process of liberation certain and irreversible? His Letter to the Galatians clearly answers no: "Foolish Galatians! Who has bewitched you, before whose eyes Jesus Christ crucified was publicly portrayed? . . . Having begun with the Spirit, are you now ending in the Flesh?" (Gal 3:1.3). Further on he explains: "It is I, Paul, who tell you: if you let yourselves be circumcised, Christ will be of no advantage to you . . . All of you who seek justice in the Law have broken with Christ, have fallen from Grace" (Gal 5:2.4).[157]

Paul seems to be convinced that the Law aggravates or at least brings out a tendency already inherent in human Flesh to become enslaved to Sin, insofar as human beings cannot bear the burden of behavior based on gratuitousness and freedom.

Getting back to Romans 6, we must admit that Paul's exhortations seem to allow for the possibility of enslavement to Sin even among Christians. Without the support of the Law, Sin loses its compulsive power; and the whole logic and symbolism of Baptism point to liberation from Sin. But it is up to Christians to decide whether they will return to the bondage of Sin or not, and they must realize that: "Don't you realize that to whomever you offer your obedience as slaves, you become that one's slaves: either of Sin, toward Death; or of Obedience, toward Justice?" (6:16). Right at the start of his letter, Paul had mentioned '*the obedience of Faith*' (1:5). Here in Romans 6 he seems to spell out its content and say he knows which choice the Christians of Rome have actually made: "Thank God, you who were slaves to sin have wholeheartedly *obeyed* the standard of *teaching* to which you have been transferred" (6:17).

In the teaching that sees the life, death, and resurrection of Jesus as the standard or model of all human existence, Christians apparently find clearer reasons and more explicit data for the radical wager—obedience to faith—that could be made by any human being in any set of circumstances. It was made by the pagan, Abraham, after all. And that wager is to see oneself "as alive from the dead" (6:13) and act accordingly. Or, to put the same thing another way: to believe or have faith in a God "who gives life to the dead" (4:17).

As Paul sees it, then, the plan of God is to lead human beings "from faith to faith" (1:17) to justice. That is a bird's-eye view of the whole process, which starts with a universal 'thesis', proceeds to a particular 'antithesis', and then reaches its 'synthesis' in the recovery of universality that is embodied in the *singularity* of Jesus Christ.

Attributing such dialectical subtleties to Paul might seem pedantic and offbase, and it probably is if we insist on the technical triad of thesis, antithesis, synthesis. But in my opinion that only proves that dialectical thinking is much older than Hegel, that it is in fact a normal human way of envisioning processes. Indeed I challenge any exegete to present a non-dialectical explanation of the role played in Romans by God's granting of the Law and the stage that begins and ends with it. This is proved, I think, by Paul's argument in Romans 6. Since the Law is the 'power' of Sin, his argument lacks 'power' because his study of the import of Christian faith starts off with liberation from Sin instead of liberation from the Law.

In short, we seem to have backtracked from the certainty that marked Romans 5 with its parallel between Adam and Christ. Contrary to what we supposedly get from Adam, what we get from Christ is apparently going to depend on the use of free will by human beings, Christians included. That rules out a unanimous, universal response.

(2). The second part of Paul's argument (7:1-13) deals with the liberation of the Christian from the Law, thanks to Christ. Though the treatment is far from being clearcut, we notice at once that there is no room for doubt about this liberation, at least in theory.

The Law and its obligation are something external and juridical, so proving we are no longer under its dominion should be easier than proving we are no longer subject to the cravings of our heart. Paul makes use of a juridical argument here, while continuing to use Christian Baptism as a basic theme. Since it embodies a *death* to the old situation, it also frees us from legal commitments. This is obvious in many instances of societal life, and Paul uses marriage as an example (7:1-3). He compares the situation of the wife under Roman law (i.e., the husband law) to that of the Christian.

Jesus subjected himself to the Law and died on account of it (Gal 4:4; 3:13-14; 2:19). He thus dragged it along with him to death and freed human beings from it, provided they submit to a death like Christ's in and through Baptism. They, too, must boldly accept the curse of the Law rather than seeking servile approbation in it.

Despite the possible confusion of Paul's example and symbolism, his basic argument is very clear and conclusive. Christians must regard themselves as dead to the Law (7:4), free from it as the widow is from the 'husband law' (7:3). God has freed us from the Law (7:6), as the passive construction indicates.

But here is where our difficulties begin. We are in the third stage of a dialectical process, so that elements of the positive and negative sides of the previous stage remain. What if the cravings of our heart are in connivance with the Law?

Remember that Paul never denies that God spoke God's will in the Law, even if through a mediator (Gal 3:19). To what extent, then, have we been liberated from the Law? Insofar as it was necessary so that "we can serve in the newness of the Spirit, not in the oldness of the Letter" (7:6).

We now owe nothing to the Law. We are no longer under its bewitching power (Gal 3:1). But Paul indicates that we must differentiate between its "letter that kills, and the Spirit that gives life" (2 Cor 3:6). Now whether we use 'Spirit' here with a small or capital 's'—and the capital does seem more appropriate since it is a life-giving force—it is obvious that it has some relationship with the Law and that even Christians must have a 'spiritual' relationship with the Law. As Paul will tell us in Romans 7:14, the Law is 'spiritual'; and our relationship with that 'spiritual' Law is made more difficult by the fact that we are 'fleshly'.

It is time for us to get a clearer picture of what Paul means by his antithesis between Flesh and Spirit, an antithesis he sometimes puts in terms of Body versus Spirit.[158] In much of the Old Testament, the term 'flesh' is a synonym for *creature*, the creature in its *totality*, whereas 'Spirit' normally designates God at work with God's power: creating, guiding history, giving the breath (= spirit) of life to everything that breathes on earth (Ps 104:29). Thus the antithesis between Flesh and Spirit does not basically refer to two elements that go to make up human nature; it is not akin to our talk about body and soul.

It is also clear, however, that in the Old Testament 'flesh' does not exist alone. It exists and lives because the Spirit of Yahweh acts and dwells in it as a life-giving breath. Without that, human beings and all living things would return to dust and nothingness. So although the Spirit is not a *part* of the human being, we can say that it is what makes a human being to be such. First it gives human beings the more general and important capabilities: existence, cognition, will. But to the Spirit are also attributed the peculiar characteristics that bring out those basic qualities even more: original talents and extraordinary abilities. All that is the work of Yahweh and therefore is to be attributed to Yahweh's Spirit.

In later biblical literature we find that 'flesh' continues to designate the whole creature. But now the focus is on the creature as dependent on Yahweh and by itself incapable of anything important. In the sapiential literature the creature or 'flesh' is overwhelmed by the terrible chasm between the transcendent Creator and the creature.[159]

Getting back to Paul, we find that this notion has greatly influenced him. At the same time we find that he greatly depreciates any relationship with God based on the 'flesh', i.e., on the reverential fear of the creature. He sees 'fleshly' fear at work in the Galatians (Gal 3:3), for example. After having been liberated from the Law, they are driven by that fear to seek security in subjection to the Law once again. Any 'fleshly' reading of the Law will seek false security vis-à-vis the transcendent by focusing on the 'letter' or literal tenor of the Law.

We may now consider the antithesis between letter and Spirit in terms of the above remarks. We could substitute 'flesh' for 'letter', and then write 'Spirit' with a capital or small 's'. Thus 'spirit' would refer to the meaning and usefulness of the Law, which is never grasped or ventured by the 'flesh' on its own. And since human 'flesh' on its own would reject that 'spirit' for the sake of security, 'Spirit' would signify the power that God gives human beings to overcome fleshly fear by faith and discover the true purport of the Law.

This has relevance for us here. The presence of the Spirit of God in the Christian community is an *experience* resembling and continuing the one in which the Spirit resurrected Jesus from the dead (8:1f.; 1:4; Gal 3:2–5). But

Christians continue to be creatures ('flesh'), tempted to overcome their fear by seeking support in anything that seems to offer them security vis-à-vis God (1 Cor 3:1-4).[160] So although liberation from the Law is a fact seemingly even more clearcut than that of liberation from Sin, we end up with a certain ambiguity in both cases. We need the Spirit to obtain life and peace (8:6), to discover the *spirit* of the Law and let go of its *letter*. To some extent Paul has already indicated what the *spirit* of the Law is in the preceding chapters on *faith*, that basic attitude whereby the human being is freed from the obsession of bargaining with God to obtain salvation through 'works' based on the letter of the Law. Faith frees human beings to be their own masters in their activities rather than continuing to be slaves.

Now let us assume we have such a human being, free of enslavement to its own 'cravings' and the 'letter' of the Law. As Paul would wish, it focuses on doing what is 'suitable'. But there is no point in asking Paul: suitable *for what*? The question is superfluous, because it has to do with the *meaning* or 'spirit' of the Law that Paul describes later in Romans in the following terms: "Have no debt with anyone except that of mutual love. The one who loves neighbor has fulfilled the Law. You see, the precepts, 'Thou shalt not commit adultery, Thou shalt not murder, Thou shalt not steal, Thou shalt not covet', and all the other precepts are summed up in this formula: 'Thou shalt love your neighbor as yourself'. Love does no wrong to the neighbor. Hence love is the Law in its fullness" (13:8-10). Here we have the basis of the attitude of *faith* whose *work* is love (Gal 5:6).[161]

Once again we find that even though liberation from the Law is an irreversible fact for Paul, it is not so in the concrete life of the Christian. Nor can it be, so long as Christians are 'in the flesh' and the forces that besiege every human being are operative in them. We are threading our way through a needle, as it were. On one side are the cravings of the heart in general; on the other side is the specific craving for security. We fear insecurity even though that is the price of freedom.

That brings us to a second point about Paul's treatment of the Law in Romans 7:1-13, and the possible return of the antithesis that we thought overcome. Even before his analysis of the divided human being in Romans 7:14-25, we find his treatment of the relationship between Law and Sin to be somewhat odd. The content is puzzling. So is the place he puts his treatment and the personal 'I' that he uses. Perhaps his ongoing dialogue with his interlocutors prompts him to raise such questions and answer them, even though he is thereby distracted from the plan that is being carried through.

In any case, Paul speaks in the first person amd makes one last effort to show how the Law constitutes a temptation for *the human being*. He makes no explicit mention of the Jew, and his arguments here become more and more anthropological.

"Sin, seizing its opportunity, by means of the precept deceived me and thereby killed me" (7:11). This could be Paul's conclusion about the relationship between Sin and the Law. If we ask him what the precept of the Law did concretely to deceive him, Paul replies: "I did not know Sin except through the Law" (7:7). Yet the deception must lie elsewhere because the essential purpose of the Law in God's plan is precisely that just indicated: "Since with the Law comes knowledge of Sin" (3:20).

How could self-deception creep into this knowledge provided by God? Let us stay with Paul's concrete example. "I would not have come to know what *covetousness* was, if the Law had not said: 'Thou shalt not covet' " (7:7). While that may not be perfectly clear, it is entirely consistent with the notion that knowledge of Sin comes with the Law. To pinpoint the place of self-deception, however, we must remember certain things about the biblical decalog that Paul alludes to here. Paul seems to cite a precept that is one of the central matters in God's will insofar as human action is concerned.[162] Yet he surely knows that no such precept is to be found in any of the Old Testament decalogs. Moreover, the term translated as 'covetousness' by us is the Greek word for 'strong desire' or 'craving', which we have seen already.[163]

Two points deserve to be noted. First, what the Bible prohibits here is 'desire' that becomes a *quest*: a *social* interaction that does not respect the property of another person. The fact is that the biblical decalogs never prohibit *interior* attitudes. Indeed the novelty of Jesus' reading of the Law lies precisely in his shift from external *act* to internal *attitude*. In Matthew's gospel we find six illustrative examples in the Sermon on the Mount (e.g., Mt 5:27–28).

Second, in using this example that associates desire or craving with respect for property, Paul is establishing an obvious link with what he has already pinpointed as the mainspring of pagan enslavement to Sin: i.e., the *cravings* of the heart. It seems clear that Paul's focus remains fixed on the *universal* judgment of God, so he deliberately chooses a supposed precept of the decalog that will enable him to prove that Sin, with or without the Law, takes control over the human being by making use of the same basic mainspring.

But this process operates by way of deceit or self-deception, and we must try to figure out what that means. How can Paul say that without the precept he *would not have known what covetousness was*? Or, to put it another way, how can he say that without a precept against craving he would not have known what 'craving' was (see 2:15 for a different view)?

The normal, logical explanation, which is even suggested by the context, is that Paul means that he would not have known the attractiveness, extent, and power of the craving without the precept. One way of explaining this is the old saw about the special allure of forbidden fruit. The very existence of a prohibition prompts a *rebellious* reaction against it on the part of human beings. Readers who have followed Paul's thinking so far will realize that such an explanation won't do at all. Sin's way of entangling human beings in self-deception and thereby enslaving them has nothing to do with the active rebelliousness of a Lucifer. The Law 'bewitches' human beings by offering them security and an easy way out. It is the *lack of audacity* in human beings, their reluctance to act in a gratuitous manner, that prompts them to focus on 'the works of the Law' as opposed to 'Faith'.[164]

We must look for another explanation. Remember that here Paul is talking about *liberation* vis-à-vis the Law. In this part of Romans 7 he is addressing himself specifically to Christians converted from Judaism, so in all likelihood he is making use of his own experiences as a Pharisee educated in the interpretation of the Law. When he writes about *enslavement to the letter of the Law*— another argument against the explanation that rebelliousness is the key—he probably has in mind a problem encountered in his own training. Any *letter* of the Law that purports to be a moral code accompanying a person from morning to night (Dt 11:19) is incapable of taking into account the infinite variety of circumstances in which it has to be applied. Indeed one precept will often come in conflict with another. If you do not kill the letter, it will kill you. How?

If you take the letter seriously, as the Pharisees certainly did, you must get involved in intricate casuistry to apply the Law. A person focused primarily on a personal project will be waylaid by covetousness now and again. But a person scrupulously concerned to anticipate all the possible traps of covetousness will find it everywhere in countless, varied forms. This discovery will not trigger unrestrained covetousness.[165] On the contrary, it will engender fear of falling into the traps; and fear will paralyze the human being, making it impossible for him or her to fulfill the *intention* of the Law. The slave of the Law is a 'dead' person (7:11), deceived and enslaved by Sin as well.[166]

●

Let me sum up briefly what we have seen in Romans 6:1–7:13, where Paul is talking to baptized Christians. Curious as it may seem, he offers a rehash of the first two chapters of Romans, where he noted the *de facto* enslavement of both pagans and Jews to Sin. And even though he grants the possibility of liberation from that enslavement, he shows that the same mechanisms are still around, capable of enslaving even those who have accompanied Jesus in his death and resurrection.

But something has changed. Paul is drawing closer to a key point: the unification of the mechanisms into one, single mechanism. Because the Christian continues to be 'flesh', *its human condition* is such that it tends to fall into enslavement, hence Death, with or without Law. That leads Paul to his final, definitive analysis of the divided human being in Romans 7:14–25.[167]

As I have already indicated, I no longer propose to trace Paul's thought back to its possible source in the historical Jesus as I did in the early chapters. But I cannot end this chapter without indicating its general relationship with the *historical cause* of the death of Jesus of Nazareth. Jesus was killed because he was born under the Law (7:4; Gal 4:4) and the *letter* of the Law condemned him to death. The accusation of blasphemy that permitted the Sanhedrin to condemn him was not the underlying factor. It was something that goes much deeper. Jesus was condemned to death because he had attacked the literal interpretation of the Law, *thereby* attacking the craving for secular power in the religious authorities of Israel. They condemned him for undermining their *security*.

Thus the historical death of Jesus proves the great anthropological argument that Paul has been elaborating: the connivance between the religious *letter* of the Law and the secular *cravings* of the human being. Both tendencies come down to one that eventually dehumanizes the human being, alienates it, and turns it into a being enslaved to Sin and subject to Death.

It is this historical convergence of the secular and religious mechanisms of Sin that explains the necessity Paul feels for a final overall analysis of human existence in Romans 7:14–25.

CHAPTER VII

The Divided Human Being

Romans 7:14–25

(14) We know that the law is spiritual, but I am fleshly, made a slave *of the power* of sin. (15) I do not recognize what I accomplish because I do not perform what I want to do, I perform what I hate. (16) Now if I perform what I don't want to do, I am in agreement with the law that it is good. (17) But if that is the case, then it is not I who accomplish *that*, but sin that dwells in me. (18) For I know that the good does not dwell in me, i.e., in my flesh, since wanting it is within my capacity but accomplishing good is not. (19) I do not perform the good I want to do; I perform the evil I don't want to do. (20) But if I perform *precisely* what I don't want, then it is no longer I who accomplish it but sin that dwells in me.

(21) So I discover the law: wanting to do good, I find it is evil that is within my capacity. (22) I am delighted with the law of God in my inner humanity, (23) but I observe another law in my members warring against the law of my mind and making me prisoner of the law of sin that is in my members. (24) Wretched human that I am! Who will deliver me from this body of death? (25) Thanks be to God, through Jesus Christ our Lord! So with the mind I myself serve the law of God, but with the flesh I serve the law of sin.

In setting aside these verses of Romans 7 for separate treatment, I am trying to correct an arbitrary division of chapters that does not give due credit to the specific theme treated in these verses. But any division of a letter written as such remains artificial, of course, even mine. I divide the chapter at verse 13, for example, but other interpreters of Paul have noted that he begins to use the first person 'I' in 7:7. And this grammatical practice continues to the end of the chapter.

To this grammatical usage we must add a more important and deep-seated feature, however. It is the *pessimism* of Paul, his own peculiar pessimism, which reaches its peak in Romans 7:14–25. And this from a man who seems to

113

be a cockeyed optimist when he is talking about God's overall plan and the *now* as opposed to the *before*. As soon as he begins to write in the first person singular, he seems to lose all his assurance and grant all the possibilities still open to Law, Sin, and Death!

Exegetes have performed all sorts of acrobatics to prove that the 'I' in question could not possibly mean Paul the Christian.[168] I say nonsense. There is not the slightest doubt that Paul is referring to himself and to every other human being in the world, Christian or no.

My simplest argument is this: Anyone who does not feel described in Paul's portrait is free to search for another hypothesis. Those who feel that Paul's analysis hits home, be they Christian or not, might admit that Paul is here analyzing the situation of every human being.

There is also a weighty exegetical argument: the overall context of the letter. Let's go back over it. In Romans 1-2, Paul described the enslavement of all human beings, pagans and Jews, to Sin. At the end of Romans 3, he sets forth the criterion of salvation for all that God will use: faith. In the following chapters he offers concrete cases where such faith has produced salvific results. Moving 'from faith to faith', in Romans 6:1-7:13 Paul uses data from Christian belief to consider the situation of the baptized. And here is where the difficulty arises. Christians should be free from the Law, Sin, and Death. But if that did happen automatically and magically, it would constitute an 'advantage' of Baptism akin to the dangerous 'advantage' of the Law in the second stage of God's plan. If Christians must struggle like all other human beings to avoid enslavements, on the other hand, where is the superiority of faith in Jesus Christ?

Paul never expresses any doubt about the criterion behind God's judgment. It is *faith*, or *faith at work in love*. Lack of faith means turning one's back on the summons to free, human maturity and its risks. And in his new Christian communities Paul sees evidence of the two types of self-deception he noticed in pagans and Jews respectively, both types ultimately rooted in the cravings of the human heart. That should not surprise us too much, since he is dealing with a basic, anthropological level. We might consider it pessimism by contrast with the triumphal tone of earlier chapters. But when we ponder the constants of our own human existence, not to mention twenty centuries of Christian history, we might do better to call it realism.

Following Paul, we find that the Christian, like any other human, is a *divided being*. In Romans 7:14-25, Paul analyzes this dividedness. In Romans 8, he considers the meaning and significance of Jesus of Nazareth vis-à-vis the problem.

Paul's general statement of the problem in anthropological terms is summed up in these words: "I do not recognize what I accomplish by work" (7:15).[169] And he discovers that human life is ruled by *two opposed mechanisms* or laws (7:21.23). So we have two basic questions to consider in this chapter: Where exactly does the conflict between the two laws lie? What is the result of this conflict that divides the human being from its work?

(1). The locus of the conflict. Let us begin by considering the different terms Paul uses to analyze the divided human being. We find four basic types of opposition:

  (a). Between 'I' and what 'dwells in me', be it Sin or Evil (7:17.18.20.21).
  (b). Between 'wanting,' which the 'I' can do, and 'performing' or 'accomplishing', which escapes it (7:15–21).
  (c). Between the 'spiritual law' that is 'good' or 'the good,' and 'the evil' or 'Sin' (7:14.16.19.22.23.25).
  (d). Between the person's 'inner humanity' and 'law of the mind', whose will is in accord with the law of God, and 'the members' or 'law of the members' obedient to Sin (7:22–23).

If we can frame these four basic oppositions in a coherent scheme, that should shed light on several others which also surface in these verses: e.g., fleshly/spiritual (7:14); body of death (7:24); mind/flesh (7:25).

In the first opposition we have a real subject and an impersonal, mythical subject at odds. The 'I' of the human being wants and does not want (7:15.16.18.19.20.21). But there is a part of the human being that is not controlled by the 'I'. It is opposed to the decisions of the 'I', at least in the sense that it ignores them and hinders their performance. Paul refers to it as something 'that dwells in me', either Sin (7:17.20.23) or Evil (7:21).

This first opposition is a bit unbalanced, since there is only one personal subject. The second opposition between *verbs* indicates what sort of action is to be attributed to the 'I' and what 'dwells in me'. We find that the 'I' is credited with the *beginning* of the action, whereas what 'dwells in me' is credited with the actual *result* of the action in reality. The 'I' can want, decide, evaluate, project (7:15.16.18.19), but the Sin or Evil that 'dwells in me' has control over the concrete performance or accomplishment (7:15.17.18.19.20).

Paul clearly equates the 'I' with the innermost center of the human being, its authentic, inner humanity endowed with freedom (7:22). But in moving into action and accomplishing work, the human being must travel from inside to outside itself. And in this process, says Paul, impersonal forces take control of human action. So we have a divided human being, described summarily by Paul in these terms: "I know that the good does not dwell in me . . . since *wanting* it is within my capacity but *accomplishing* it is not" (7:18).

This shows up even more clearly when we consider the fourth opposition, which deals with the means or *instruments* of action. The 'I' as such seems to lack instruments. To carry out its intentions, decisions, or projects, it has to have recourse to 'what dwells in me'. The instruments are simultaneously 'mine' and 'not mine'. Paul refers to this instrumental realm as the 'members' or the 'law of the members'. He is not referring to the body alone, though the opposition is perceived more clearly and close at hand there. Between the intentions of the 'I'[170] and what we manage to accomplish or perform with the body there lies an area of opaqueness and viscosity, of something that escapes our liberty because it has its own laws. That is what Paul calls the 'law of the members'. To offer a silly but indicative example: I decide to drive a nail into the wall with a hammer, but the physical (and even psychic) laws governing my arm and hand cause me to hit my finger instead.

This is what seems to have caught Paul's attention. On the journey of human freedom from plan to performance, there necessarily seems to be some deviation; and it is due to the fact that every instrument, no matter how close it may be to the 'I', is already endowed ahead of time with *its own law*. It always proves easier to let oneself be dragged down by the law of the instrument than to impose one's own intentions on it, and in the long run it seems to be inevitable. The human being is a helpless 'creator' in a world already made behind its back, in an alien world that seems to operate more rapidly and effectively when freedom does not intervene. So when the human 'creator' takes stock of its work, it does not recognize its 'creation' in the finished reality. That is not what it wanted *to do*.

But let us move on to the third opposition, for which Paul reserves his biggest surprises and his most profound observations. *What* does the 'I' want on the one hand, and *what* is accomplished by that which 'dwells in me' on the other hand?

Contrary to our normal way of considering such a question, *good* and *evil* are not to be found equally in the two phases. Paul distributes them separately between the two verbs. The human being wants good and accomplishes evil. As Paul sees it, the human being is not free to accomplish the good (7:18). What the 'I' wants, you see, lacks the corresponding power over that which 'dwells in me'. All my powers of performance or accomplishment, strangely enough, seem to be under the control of Evil or Sin (7:17.19).

Why do I say *strangely*? Because Paul seems to give no place at all to two possibilities that would occur to anyone, and that are part and parcel of our customary anthropology: (1) that the 'I' might want Evil; (2) that the intention of 'doing good' is carried out, sometimes at least. And the most likely explanation for this omission is that Paul does not even regard them as possibilities. For him, the label 'good' is an essential component of intention and the label 'evil' is an essential component of actual performance.

We have two proofs that Paul is totally unconcerned about the possibility that the 'I' might choose Evil. One is indirect, the other more direct and explicit.

Let's begin with the *indirect* proof. If we read these verses hurriedly, and particularly if we fail to keep in mind the basic distinction in Paul between *Sin* in the singular and *sins* in the plural, we cannot help but notice that Paul never says that the performances or accomplishments are *sins*. He does say that they are alienated, in the power of Another, shackled (as was truth in the first two chapters), hence subject to Sin (7:25). Paul is far more afraid of the distance that *Sin* puts between intention and performance than of the possibility—if there is such a possibility—that the 'I' may want or choose *sinning*. His greatest fear, in other words, is that the human being may not be *free*: that its actions, no matter what the end result, may be dragged down by forces alien to its innermost choice. For Paul, freedom does not consist in choosing between good and evil. Freedom is, or would be, being able to carry out or accomplish what one has chosen. It is as if he were saying: If human beings could recognize their initial intention in their actual performance, then their performance would be necessarily *good* because it would be also free. And vice versa.

This conception of freedom as necessarily and positively moral[171] would seem to be cockeyed optimism if it were not immediately counterbalanced by Paul's pessimism. For he tells us that it is impossible for us to perform or accomplish what we want or choose. More of that later.

The point here is that Paul seems to have no concern about the moral orientation of the intentions of the 'I' or our 'inner humanity'. Indeed this lack of concern is a fundamental datum of his anthropology and it shows up elsewhere. It is what he calls Christian freedom, the new reality introduced by Jesus; or its result, if you prefer.

Paul alludes to it earlier in this same chapter of Romans when he describes himself as alive in the period preceding the Law (7:9). It surfaces even more clearly in his first letter to the Corinthians, where he urges his readers to change their approach to moral issues in a radical way. They should stop worrying about what is licit and illicit and start asking themselves whether a given course of action is suitable or not. To talk about suitability is to imply the existence of some project. Licit and illicit may be absolute terms. But one can determine suitability only when one *relates* a project to the means at one's disposal for carrying it out. It is typical of Paul that he does not move on to specify which projects might be licit for Christians; indeed this trait has probably kept him on the sidelines insofar as manuals of so-called 'Christian morality' are concerned. He does indicate from time to time that love is the *ultimate* criterion of what is 'suitable', as if to suggest that the projects of the Christian could not be otherwise (1 Cor 10:23-24; Rom 13:8). But he seems to identify this love with any and every project that is truly free: "I will not let myself be enslaved by anything" (1 Cor 6:12). If someone were to ask him whether that principle might not serve as a pretext for egotism, I think he would reply that egotism arises *only when we let ourselves be dominated or enslaved by mechanisms that oppose their law of least effort to the original intention of our 'I'* (see Gal 5:13).

We also have a *direct* proof of Paul's identification of the 'I' and its choice with *the good*. It is his repeated affirmation that our 'I', our 'inner humanity', is in agreement with, and *only* with, the law that is spiritual (7:14), good (7:16), God's (7:22); in short, with 'the good' (7:18.19.21; see 7:12).

Of course we are a bit surprised to see *the Law* reappear in positive terms after his negative description of it in 7:1-13 (especially 7:11-13). We must not try to evade the contrast by the simple trick of writing 'law' in small letters here. But neither can we deny or overlook the fact that Paul uses the term 'law' in at least three different senses in these verses:

(a). in about the same sense at the Law of Moses, except that here he uses the term in a *positive* way;

(b). in the sense of the *overall structure of existence,* as when he writes: "So I discover *the law*: wanting to do good, I find it is evil that is within my capacity" (7:21);

(c). in the sense of *partial structures* or mechanisms associated with one or another of the human dimensions that is being compared or contrasted. Thus 'the law *of the mind*' (7:23.25) seems to obey 'the law of God' (7:25), whereas 'the law *of the members*' (7:23) seems to subject the human being to 'the law of Sin' (7:23.25).

It is the first usage of 'law', with or without capitals, that is the disconcerting one. After all he has written so far, how can Paul say that the law "is spiritual" (7:14)?

In the previous chapter we considered the basic meaning of Paul's contrast between Flesh and Spirit. If the law is spiritual, then, he must be talking about 'the law of God' (7:22.25); for the Spirit is the agent of God's works. It is a *norm* or principle of discernment (2:18) given by God to the Jews in particular, just as God has given the breath of life to 'all flesh'. And the receiver of the gift is 'fleshly' (7:14), is a weak, fragile, insecure creature.

That does not solve our perplexity, however. For even the Law of God, as mediated to us by Moses (Gal 3:19), was not capable of giving life (Gal 3:21). The *letter* of that Law is like 'flesh' as opposed to Spirit. It kills, because the 'fleshly' human being gives way to fear in the face of it and becomes its slave, thus alienating its human works (7:5). That situation has changed, however, as Paul tells us in the very same chapter. Clearly speaking from his own situation as a Christian, he writes: "Now . . . we have been liberated from the Law . . . so that we can *serve in the newness of the Spirit,* not in the oldness of the letter" (7:6). Thus the Law (of Sinai), like any human being or creature, seems to be a composite of 'flesh' (or 'letter') and 'Spirit' (or 'spirit'). As 'flesh', its letter is in cahoots with the tendencies of Sin and Death; hence it cannot give life, but it can *kill* (7:11).

Now, then, what might the Law be as 'spirit' or 'spiritual law'? Here we find two basic interpretations that are worth considering in some detail.

The first interpretation associates the presence of the Spirit in the Law with the presence of the Spirit (and its charismatic phenomena) in the Christian community. The latter experience is attested by practically all the New Testament writers. This presence of the Spirit, in turn, is linked up with the promise of the Old Testament prophets that the Spirit would be poured out in abundance on the whole Chosen People, not just on specific persons. Jeremiah, in particular, associates this eschatological promise with a *new covenant,* different from the one embodied in the Law of Moses that was systematically violated by Israel: "I will plant my Law *deep within them,* I will write it on their hearts . . . There will be no further necessity of neighbor teaching neighbor, saying 'Come to know Yahweh', since *all* of them will know me, from the least to the greatest . . . when I forgive their guilt and remember their sin no more" (Jer 31:33-34; see Heb 8:8, 10:16).

Here we find an allusion to a (utopian?) Law without *letter*, hence without any temptation for *the flesh*. This Law would go directly from heart to heart and hence would be fulfilled spontaneously (Jer 31:32.34).[172] Many exegetes claim that Paul is referring to this new covenant and this new *modus operandi* of 'the Law'. That is why he can write in the next chapter: "God sent his own Son in the likeness of a flesh of Sin and, with respect to Sin, condemned Sin *in the flesh . . . so that the just precept of the Law might be fulfilled in us*, who walk *not according to the flesh but according to the Spirit*" (8:3-4).

This optimistic and enticing hypothesis has more than one flaw, however.[173] The most crucial one should be obvious from my analysis of Romans 7. In those verses Paul says *exactly the opposite*. Even though the Law may be spiritual and the Spirit may effect the inner agreement of our 'I' with it, that in no way ensures *the possibility of performing the good,* or of liberating ourselves once and for all from Sin. Paul states this bluntly in 7:14 and, as if that were not enough, reasserts it in 7:25.

Not unfamiliar with the prophecy of Jeremiah and the use that might be made of it, Paul is much more subtle and complex in his anthropological analysis. Remember that Paul is primarily concerned with the humanization of the human being, with its struggle towards maturity and creativity. He is far less concerned about violations of the Law. Indeed he thinks such violations may be positive in effect. Nor does Paul share Jeremiah's optimism about the possibility of a spontaneous fulfillment of the precepts of the Law. So we are forced to look for a better hypothesis to explain this new and curious notion of 'spiritual Law' in Paul.

Even with the first hypothesis it was clear that this 'spiritual' Law has to do with the Christian *now*. But it is not because the precepts of the ancient Law automatically take on some allure they did not have before. Rather, the point is that through the Spirit of God we discover in Jesus the 'spirit' of the Law: i.e., something opposed to its 'letter'. Here Paul joins up with the great current that runs through the New Testament. That current makes clear that the Law of the Old Testament points toward (Mt 25:31f.), reduces to (Jn 13:34; 15:12.17), finds fulfillment in (Rom 13:8.10), or is 'recapitulated' in (Rom 13:9), one thing: *love* turned into reality in the mutual relations between human beings. For it is in those relations that we find the measuring rod of any alleged love for God (1 Jn 4:12.20).

We should note immediately that our word 'recapitulate' is an unsatisfactory rendition of the Greek word *anakefalaiosis* and its cognate verb, which literally means 'to put a head on', i.e., 'to give meaning to' something. When Paul writes about the 'recapitulation' of the universe in Christ at the end of the world (Eph 1:10), for example, he is obviously not suggesting that the universe is going to be 'summed up' or 'abridged' in Christ. And when he writes here in Romans about the 'recapitulation' of the precepts of the Law, he is writing about that which gives them their true sense and value, that which is the true gauge of their normativeness. He is talking about human maturity, which does not come from 'summing up' the Law but from knowing and understanding the when, why, and wherefore of each of its elements.

That is the 'spirit' of the Law. And since it turns the Law into a living thing in the human being—as opposed to the deadening effect of the 'letter'—it must be communicated by the life-giving 'Spirit'. Only such a Law deserves to be called the 'Law of God' or 'Good', and only such a communication of meaningfulness serves as the basis for the overall agreement of our 'inner humanity' with the 'spiritual law'. Following this spirit/Spirit, the 'I' experiences its unique personal and creative vocation in self-giving love and, in the face of *all the laws or mechanisms* of reality, seeks out what might be 'suitable' for achieving its vocation or project.

But, alas, another surprise awaits us. Even this 'spiritual Law', however much it may be in tune with the 'I', cannot be put into practice as a general rule! Here is where Paul parts company with the optimistic perspectives of the new covenant as proclaimed by Jeremiah. And it is here that his anthropological analysis goes much deeper and sounds far more persuasive.

The accord between the 'spiritual Law' (the project of creative love) and our 'inner humanity' or true 'I' touches only *one level* of human activity. The level of the members or instruments remains subject to another 'law'. This other law is not evil *in itself* or particularly attracted to moral evil; but it *is* made up of *the mechanisms of an already created world,* of a world that is ignorant of the creative freedom of the human being. Yet the free human being needs that world and its instruments to achieve its projects.

Creative freedom or liberty, then, is the meaning and worth of the human being. Seen in that perspective, which is Paul's, Evil and Sin are not this or that result of human action measured by some extrinsic gauge; rather, they are *the distance* that separates intention from actual performance and accomplishment, whatever the latter may be.

We begin to see why Paul uses the word 'law' in several different senses, even though all of them except 'the spiritual Law' come down to one: i.e., the opposition of what is already made and done, of the route already traced out, to human freedom. To discover a 'law' in whatever area of human behavior is to discover our freedom or 'inner humanity' is not the master of that behavior. Our behavior is dominated by the repetition of what is easy, and it finds mathematical expression in *statistics.*

Moreover, the term 'law of the members' is a way of expressing the lure that 'dwells' in human 'flesh', in the human condition. We are tempted to renounce our innermost projects by virtue of self-deception, to let ourselves be carried along by the law of least effort and then give excuses to ourselves and others for that course.

This lure is not rooted solely in the body, not by a long shot. It is also buried in our psyche, with its congenital and acquired mechanisms; in our society, with its customs, ideologies, and prejudices[174]; in the revealed Law itself insofar as it remains a merely external *letter* in the Bible and hence an external psychosocial authority. All of these are part of 'the law of the members'. And it is worth noting Paul's insistence on creatively bypassing the socioreligious categories that divide human beings and ultimately turn them as groups into mere tools: "There is no longer Jew nor Greek, slave nor free, male nor female . . ." (Gal 3:28; see Rom 10:12; 1 Cor 12:13; Col 3:11).[175]

The realm of the already created takes in both our first nature and the second nature of culture. To the extent that the mechanisms of that realm take control of our work and lead us down the easy way, our whole 'flesh' is headed for death. We are destined to become one more thing among many things, one more cog in a mechanism. We will pass by as if we had never been here at all. That is what compels Paul to exclaim: "Who will deliver me from this body [flesh] of death?" (7:24).

All this, in my opinion, confirms the validity of our second interpretation of the sense and import of the 'spiritual Law' as used by Paul. Indeed it is the only one that is consistent with Paul's thinking and logic as argued in Romans.[176]

(2). The result of the conflict. Paul writes: "I do not recognize what I accomplish because I do not perform what I want to do, I perform what I hate" (7:15).[177] Is that situation ultimately modified by the Christ-happening or not?

Here we find something very strange if we take the last two verses of Romans 7 in conjunction with Romans 8:1. The 'so' of the latter indicates that there is no break in continuity between it and the preceding verses. Yet we find four statements that alternately seem to point us in two different directions. Reflecting on the situation he has just described, Paul writes:

(a). "Wretched human that I am! Who will deliver me from this body of death?"

(b). "Thanks be to God, through Jesus Christ our Lord!"

(c). "So with the mind I serve the law of God, but with the flesh I serve the law of Sin."

(d). "So there is no longer any condemnation for those who are in Christ Jesus." (7:24–8:1)

The contradiction is obvious. Phrases (a) and (c) clearly sum up the situation of the irreparably divided human being, trapped between intention and actual performance and hence subjected to Sin and Death. Phrases (b) and (d), on the other hand, allude to a mysterious liberation effected in Christ. I say 'mysterious' because in this key passage he makes no effort at all to explain the manner, extent, or concrete effects of that liberation vis-à-vis the situation he is analyzing. Moreover, the antithetical verses alternate with each other in a surprising way.[178] We must frankly admit that these verses simply do not provide us with any clearcut answer to the anguishing issue of dividedness in the human being, and we could find many other texts of Paul to support either alternative: ultimate victory or defeat.

Now if the four verses under consideration here indicate indecision, we might ask ourselves whether that derives from Paul's own thinking or from the reality he is analyzing.[179] If the latter is the case, we might be able to get a little further with our exegesis, formulating an hypothesis to be verified or falsified by Romans 8.

The basic hypothesis itself can be stated simply: Suppose we are dealing *simultaneously with a victory and a defeat, but on different levels.* Take Jesus himself, the model or 'standard of teaching' (6:17) for what Paul is trying to get across here. Do we not find in him two seemingly contradictory aspects, which are nevertheless compatible when situated on different levels? On one level we have a *verifiable* defeat, on another level we have an *unverifiable* but experienced victory. Living a life consistent with his *faith*, doesn't Jesus of Nazareth disclose the hidden side of reality, the *transcendent datum* that is the key to understanding the situation we face?

Some might object that there is not one shred of textual support for this hypothesis in these verses. Even if that were true, and I don't think it is, we have the previous chapters of Romans and the Synoptic material we saw in Voume II. I would maintain that the inner logic of all that material points us in the same direction.

Moreover, I would also maintain that the four verses under discussion here are not as chaotic and contradictory as they might first appear, when we look at them in terms of my suggested hypothesis. Perhaps we have been too hasty in assuming that Paul's first summary of the divided human condition (7:14–15) coincides with his final summary (7:25). In the former Paul says: "The Law is spiritual, but I am fleshly, made a slave of the power of Sin. I do not recognize what I accomplish by work because I do not perform what I want to do, I perform what I hate." In Romans 7:25 Paul sums up the final situation *after* giving thanks to God for Jesus Christ and his liberation: "*So* with the mind I myself serve the Law of God, but with the flesh I serve the law of Sin."

One element certainly remains the same. The human being, as flesh, remains the slave of Sin. But what about the 'spiritual Law' or 'Law of God'? In his first statement Paul seems to take for granted that nothing can be expected of the human being since its fleshly component remains active and dominant right to the end of the passage. He goes no further than to affirm the *ineffectual* accord of the 'I' or 'inner humanity' with the Law of God, thanks to some mechanism that covers only the 'mind'. But in his final statment (7:25), it seems that the 'law of the mind' has the human being *serving* the Law of God.

Now in Greek the verb 'serve' (*douleuein*) is even stronger than our term, which may mean little more than 'be of use to'. It implies being *wholly and totally in the service of* someone or something. That is much more than mere inner delight (7:22), agreement (7:16), or ineffectual wanting. Here, then, we have a key point for our hypothesis: the final antithesis or opposition in 7:25 is not between *wanting-in-principle* and *serving-in-reality*, but between *two real services*. And the fact that human beings are somehow rendering real service to God would justify and explain his conclusion in 8:1: "So there is no longer any condemnation . . ."

That would certainly make the four assertions in Romans 7:24–8:1 a little less chaotic and incomprehensible. First, Paul sums up his whole analysis of the divided human being with an expression of pain and anguish (7:24). But this is followed by three assertions deriving from faith, three transcendent data that really come down to one and that are not verifiable in an external or impartial way. He gives thanks to God for Jesus Christ. He indicates that even though he visibly continues to serve Sin with the 'flesh', the 'mind' is now capable of rendering real service to love as the 'recapitulation' of the Law of God. And since one who loves has fulfilled the Law (13:8), both revealed and written in the heart, then obviously "there is no longer any condemnation" (8:1).

That is about as far as we can go with our hypothesis for the moment. We have tried to establish its plausibility, hoping that Romans 8 will confirm its general drift and thereby help us to understand Paul's curious balancing of two 'laws' that inflict mutual victory and defeat on each other.

One thing further we can do here is consider the criteria that would logically permit us to make this verification in Romans 8. As the text itself suggests, I am of the opinion that the end result of Paul's existential analysis coincides with a reflection on the significance of the resurrected Jesus. And the resurrection of Jesus, first-fruit and guarantee of the resurrection of all human beings at the end of history, was an *eschatological experience*. So the criteria for verifying our hypothesis have to do with certain distinctive features of Paul's eschatology.

(a). We must assume that new reflections on the meaning of Jesus' resurrection led Paul to a gradual but thoroughgoing transformation of his earlier conception of eschatology. The imminent second coming of Jesus, a central theme in his letters to the Thessalonians, did not entail any complicated anthropology, even though it may not have been as oversimplified as the anthropology implied in the eschatology of John the Baptist. In these chapters of Romans, by contrast, we find a rich and complex anthropology. We must assume that a new element has entered the picture for Paul, an element not easily incorporated into the eschatological viewpoint: i.e., the meaning and importance of history, a long history that serves as the arena of human activity and that is the one and only dimension in which the human being can become a creator. Thus Paul gradually came to recover the balance between history and religion that characterized Jesus himself, who struggled and died to construct the kingdom. I shall now use that term from here on, even though we know that Paul preferred to use other expressions for various good reasons.

(b). We must assume that the resurrection of Jesus does not mean that the kingdom has finally arrived, or that it is about to arrive at any moment. Nor does it entail the structure of 'already and not yet' used by some theologians to describe a victory already won whose results are yet to surface. The point, you see, is that it is not simply a matter of knowing what God alone did or did not do. The kingdom of God, or whatever term Paul might use as its equivalent, is a common work of Jesus *and* his disciples, of God *and* God's collaborators (*synergoi*). Its dependence on the work of such collaborators must form a part of eschatology. Thus something must remain pending in human history without that in any way diminishing God's glory, since the Father wills the creative freedom of his children. In his reflection, therefore, Paul ponders how the resurrection of Jesus discloses the power of the kingdom in the working of human beings.

(c). Following the same thread, we must also assume certain things about Jesus of Nazareth, the model or 'standard of teaching' for his co-workers. Despite his resurrection, he visibly left his kingdom at the mercy of the powers that corrupt human projects, *as if* his, too, had been a 'flesh of Sin'. Otherwise he would have no further need of collaborators, and human beings would be mere spectators of his victory today or at the end of history. This is confirmed by Paul's analysis of human work, Christian work included. Believers in Jesus must realize that they, even with the help of the Spirit, cannot construct a kingdom different from the one intended and constructed by Jesus of Nazareth. No matter how many *signs* of its power may be firmly planted in history, there will always be a verifiable distance between embodiments of the kingdom and the kingdom itself. The laws of the easy way in an already created world will always be at work against the kingdom. And even though there may be interludes of success that are our 'earnest money' from the Spirit, those laws will always defeat the kingdom insofar as any attempt at verification can tell. Thus the task of constructing the kingdom with God, of taking the next step forward, will continue in all its radicalness from one generation to the next, challenging every individual and generation to display the full creativity of their love.

(d). We must assume that only those projects that face up to this resistance to love and overcome it *as effectively as possible* will constitute a definitive service to the plan of God, even though they may seem to be buried under the weight of reality and statistics. To put it another way: only a creative love that realistically fights against the mechanisms of nature and society and continues to hope against hope will have access to the definitive. That is what is made clear by the resurrection. We will never be able to use the resurrection as an excuse for not planning, or for planning in a totally romantic and utopian way. Every attempt to escape from realism—and the indiscriminate fight against any and all absolutizations is precisely that—is condemned to unreality in the end. In the building up of God's kingdom, not even God will supply the results that were not procured in a creative, realistic way by God's co-workers seeking to be *as effective as they could be.*

(e). We must assume that there is a *qualitative* disproportion or imbalance, associated with the power of the kingdom, that enables us to determine where the real, definitive victory lies. Indeed the resurrection of Jesus, combined with that of all human beings, bears witness to it. Only love is constructive, and constructive forever. Objectively speaking, we can say that egotism is nothing else but the recapture of human work by the impersonal mechanisms of nature and society. Hence it exercises its action only on impersonal results. So long as the project of love is not supplanted subjectively by the temptation of the easy way, by such things as facile irenicism, romantic unrealism, and utopian waiting, its constructions will endure even though that love may not be pure and unalloyed. Yet that will remain tentative and unverifiable until the end when, thanks to God's gift, the best and most precious part of us will be revealed: our freedom.

So there we have our hypothesis and our criteria of verification. Let us move on to Romans 8 and see what it has to offer us.

CHAPTER VIII

Death Defeated

Romans 8:1-39

(1) So there is no longer any condemnation for those who are in Christ Jesus, (2) since the law of the spirit of life has liberated you in Christ Jesus from the law of sin and death. (3) For God sent his own son in the likeness of a flesh of sin and, with respect to sin, condemned sin in the flesh— something the law was incapable of doing, because weak on account of the flesh— (4) so that the just precept of the law might be fulfilled in us, who walk not according to the flesh but according to the spirit.

(5) Those who live according to the flesh focus on the things of the flesh; those who (live) according to the spirit (focus on) the things of the spirit. (6) The mentality of the flesh is death; the mentality of the spirit, on the other hand, (is) life and peace. (7) Hence the mentality of the flesh is enmity with God because it is not subject to the law of God, nor indeed is it capable of that, (8) and those who are in the flesh cannot please God. (9) But you are not in the flesh; (you are) in the spirit, since the spirit of God dwells in you.—If one does not have the spirit of Christ, one is not Christ's.— (10) Now if Christ is in you, the body (is) dead because of sin, to be sure, but the spirit lives because of justice. (11) And if the spirit of the one who resurrected Jesus from the dead dwells in you, the one who resurrected Christ Jesus from the dead is going to bring to life your mortal bodies as well by his spirit dwelling in you.

(12) So, my brothers, we are not debtors to the flesh that we *have to* live according to the flesh. (13) If you live according to the flesh, you will die; but if with the spirit you put to death the praxis of the body, you will live.

(14) You see, all who are guided by the spirit of God are children of God. (15) You did not receive a spirit of slavery, to *fall back* into fear again. You received a spirit of adoption *as child*, by which we cry out: Abba, Papa! (16) The spirit itself joins in to testify with our spirit that we are children of God; (17) and if children, heirs as well, heirs of God and

joint heirs with Christ, assuming that we suffer with him so that we may also be glorified with him. (18) Because I think the sufferings of the present moment are not worth considering vis-à-vis the coming glory to be revealed in us.

(19) For the anxious expectation of creation yearns for the manifestation of God's children, (20) since creation was subjected to uselessness not by *its own* will, but on account of the one who subjected it, with the hope (21) that creation itself would be liberated from the slavery of corruption to *pass to* the freedom of the glory of God's children. (22) We know that all creation together is groaning and in travail up to now. (23) But not only it. We ourselves also, possessing the first-fruits of the spirit, groan within ourselves as we long for adoption, i.e., the redemption of our body. (24) *It was* in hope we were saved. But a hope seen is not hope. Why hope for what one already sees? (25) But if we hope for what we do not see, we do so with patient yearning.

(26) In the same way the spirit, too, helps our weakness. We do not even know what we should pray for, but the spirit itself intercedes *for us* with unspeakable groanings. (27) The one who scrutinizes hearts knows the intention of the spirit, and that it is interceding for the saints in accordance with God.

(28) We know that everything works together for the good of those who love God, those who were called in accordance with his resolve. (29) For those whom he knew beforehand, he also destined them beforehand to reflect the image of his son so that the latter might be the firstborn of many brothers and sisters. (30) Those he destined beforehand, he also called; and those he called, he also declared just; and those he declared just, he also glorified.

(31) What shall we say after all that? If God (is) for us, who (will be) against us? (32) The one who did not spare even his own beloved son, but handed him over for all of us—how will he not gift us with everything besides him? (33) Who will be the accuser of God's chosen ones? When God declares just, (34) who will accuse (them)? It is Jesus Christ, who died, or rather who was resurrected, who is at the right hand of God and who is also interceding for us. (35) Who will separate us from the love Christ *has for us*? Affliction or anxiety or persecution or hunger or nakedness or danger or the sword? (36) As it is written: "For your sake we are being put to death all day long, we are counted as sheep (for) slaughter." (37) But in all these things we come out superwinners, through him who loved us. (38) I am convinced that neither death nor life nor angels nor principalities nor present nor future nor powers (39) nor height nor depth nor any other creature will be able to separate us from the love of God (that is) in Christ Jesus, our lord.

Our first impression as we cross the threshold of Romans 8 is that Paul loses the guiding thread of the argument he was presenting in the latter half of

Romans 7. Indeed the basic reason for setting off Romans 8 as a separate chapter is the tone of victory in it, and it marks the end of his attempt to elaborate a christology in this letter. In Romans 9–11, Paul will consider the destiny of Israel; and in the concluding chapters he will offer various exhortations to the Roman community.

The thematic unity of the first eight chapters is quite clear, and it is accepted by the majority of exegetes. Thus Romans 8 is Paul's final and complete response to the whole set of problems that he has been considering from the very start of his letter.

Within the general tone of victory that gives unity to Romans 8, we find various themes mentioned. It might be noted in passing that we find confirmation of the supposition that the year 57, in which Paul wrote letters to the Romans, Galatians, and Corinthians, was a key year in the 'missionary' theology of Paul; for in them we see him working out a christology that will dovetail with his 'mission'. We find great theological unity in the letters of that year. At the same time, however, we must acknowledge a certain lack of logical continuity in them, particularly in their christological development. Whether this is a characteristic of Paul's style or not, we do not find the connections that typify the orderly exposition of a theme in a clear, comprehensible way.

As commentator, it is up to me to introduce a bit of clarity. The best way to begin, I think, is to enumerate the various themes of Romans 8:

  (a). the Law is fulfilled, thanks to the Spirit (8:1–4);
  (b). the resurrection is a sign and guarantee of the Spirit (8:5–13);
  (c). fear is to be replaced by the experience of adoption (8:4–18);
  (d). the status and destiny of the created universe (8:19–27);
  (e). the divine plan of adoption and universal brotherhood and sister-
        hood (8:28–30);
  (f). the victory of Christ (8:31–39).

In my opinion, we need only read the chapter with this thematic division in mind to grasp something that is exegetically basic and essential: the whole chapter deals with the relationship between the (historically) visible and the eschatological, between what can be ascertained by analysis and what *will be manifested* in the end (8:17–18.18–21). Paul explicitly emphasizes the difference between what is *seen* and what is *hoped for* (8:24–25).

In dealing with Romans 7 and its obscure final verses, I proposed an hypothesis to resolve the seeming antithesis between victory and defeat that Paul posed there. I suggested that it was not a matter of 'this *or* that' but rather of 'this *and* that' on two different levels, one level being clarified by the eschatological light emanating from the experience of Jesus' resurrection. Would it be so strange, then, if the historically *verifiable* were to constitute one of these levels, and the *unverifiable* (except by way of eschatological manifestation) were to constitute the other level? Suppose we are not dealing with a contradiction but rather with the rich profundity of a dialectic that takes both into account!

(1). Let us begin by examining the response, *unverifiable* in our daily working, that Paul gives to the issue he raised in Romans 7. He begins Romans 8 as follows: "So there is no longer any condemnation for those who are in Christ Jesus, since the law of the Spirit of Life has liberated you . . . from the law of Sin and Death . . . so that the just precept of the Law might be fulfilled in us, who walk not according to the Flesh but according to the Spirit" (8:1.2.4).

Thus there is no condemnation for those who have received liberation, thanks to Christ. Note that this is not due to some external declaration or to divine forgetfulness. It is due to the fact that the precept of the Law, understood in its authentic sense and spirit, has been fulfilled in the human being.[180]

It is a matter of force, power, or strength. The Spirit, the *power* of God, has overcome the weakness of the Flesh (8:3-4). At the end of Romans 7, Paul gives thanks for this victory. At the same time (7:25) he suggests that the human being remains divided insofar as this strength is concerned. While the Spirit does seem to win in some respects, the Flesh seems to win in other respects. What are we to make of this?

Recall that Sin, for Paul, represents the *distance* that separates human intention and project from actual performance and accomplishment. Now if we assume that this continues to be the case with the Christian, then the victory of the Spirit must logically have the features we noted at the end of the last chapter. Two are of particular importance and pretty much sum up all the rest:

(a). on certain occasions or at certain moments the (Sinful) *distance* must be eliminated or so reduced that the human being can experience something of its works as truly its own;

(b). even though these moments are exceptional and objectively unverifiable by comparison with the many works human beings cannot recognize as their own, there must be a *qualitative disproportion* here akin to that we noted in our analysis of Romans 5. It permits us to give the victory to something that seems to suffer defeat insofar as merely quantitative verification is concerned: e.g., Life versus Death.

Let us dwell on the first characteristic for a moment. When we think of two mechanisms or laws fighting for control of human work, we might be inclined to think of a straight opposition or antithesis between them. Thus the result, conceived in dualistic terms, would be either completely good or completely evil. We serve either Sin or Grace. Paul is much more realistic. He talks about the *mixture* of Sin and Grace in every human action, the combination of egotism and love, self-determined intention and alienated result.

This human tendency toward dualistic thinking is no figment of my imagination. With the exception of Paul, almost all the New Testament images of God's judgment of human beings are dualisitc, *literally dualistic*. Consider the picture of the last judgment in Matthew 25:31f., where human beings will be judged in terms of their willingness or refusal to help others in need. The only criterion is mutual love effectively offered to even the least. Now if Paul had written that parable, he might well have apologized for speaking in simplistic human terms. After all, what gigantic computer would be capable of deciding between the two extreme alternatives, since the life of any human being is an interwoven mixture of love and egotism, of help offered and help refused? Indeed how would it be possible to differentiate love from egotism in any single act performed in the real world, since giving help to one person means denying it to others?[181]

As I just said, Paul is the only New Testament writer to suggest a vision of divine judgment that takes into account the mixed nature of human action. We find his picture in his first letter to the Corinthians: "Let everyone be careful how they build . . . For no one can lay any other foundation than . . . Jesus Christ himself. And whether one builds on it with gold or silver or precious stones, or with wood or hay or straw, the work of each one will be made manifest. The day will make it manifest, appearing with fire, and fire will test the quality of each person's work. If a person's work, built on the foundation, stands the test, the person will receive recompense. But the person whose work is burned up will suffer the loss. Nevertheless that person will be saved, but as one passing through fire" (1 Cor 3:10-15).[182]

Let us note a few elements in this passage that are of major importance for our theme here. The *first* element is Paul's explicit reference to God's universal, eschatological judgment. He uses the classical biblical term 'the day', an accepted shorthand version of 'the day of Yahweh'. That term expresses Israel's growing hope in a universal divine judgment that will restore the justice not evident in the visible events of history (see Job, Ecclesiastes, Wisdom). To this we must add the metaphorical term that is always associated with divine judgment: fire, which consumes everything worthless (see Mt 3:10-12).

The *second* element may seem to be a common New Testament image of divine judgment at first glance: the criterion of judgment is applied to the totality of a human being's activity. Paul uses the term 'work' in the singular to designate that totality. But there is a marked difference between the other New Testament writers and Paul here. In the case of the former, the *human being* is the object of divine judgment and its good or bad result, even though an examination of his or her work is part of that judgment. In the case of Paul, however, emphasis shifts from the human being to his or her *work*. It is the work that is judged, that will stand the test or be destroyed. Fire is not a means of punishment, as in other New Testament images, but a means of testing. Human beings will suffer or not, according to the ultimate destiny of their work.[183] Thus any notion of reward or punishment is ruled out as an incentive for working; the crucial emphasis is on the causal result of a human being's way of acting, even though it will become visible only in metahistory on the basis of divine judgment.

The *third* element is provided by the surrounding context in 1 Corinthians, and it has to do with something crucial in Paul's version of morality. In deciding what is 'suitable', human beings must consider what 'builds up' their brothers and sisters (1 Cor 10:23-24; Rom 14:19-20). Love consists in collaborating with God in the work of building or constructing a human existence for human beings. Hence the importance of this *work*: it is—partially and secondarily, to be sure—the work of God himself (14:20) on behalf of humanity, and we are cooperators and joint workers (*sunergoi*; see 1 Cor 3:9) in it.[184]

The *fourth* element has to do with the crucial nature of human *work* in the singular, as opposed to human *works* in the plural, insofar as it is intimately connected with the declaration of justice granted to the human being by God on the basis of *faith*. Note that if Paul meant the same thing by *work* and *works*, his picture in 1 Corinthians would directly contradict his principle in Romans 3:21f. That is not the case, however. By *works* Paul means acts that can be counted on the basis of the *letter* of the Law; they are products of *the Flesh* and its fear-ridden, dickering mentality. By *work* in the singular Paul means the free prolongation of the human being in reality through the one and only project that is truly free: i.e., that which unites the human being with God in real, effective love of brother and sister humans. *Faith* is necessary for us to forget self, our natural fears as creatures, and our sterile accounting approach to our own salvation. By faith we put our trust in the gracious gift of the promise. Giving up self-preoccupation, which makes us an easy prey for natural and societal mechanisms, we concentrate all our energies on the project we hold in our hands. In short, as we have already seen in the case of Abraham, *faith* is not opposed to *work*. On the contrary, *only faith makes possible human work*: i.e., free work that bears the stamp of the human being and defies death.

The *fifth* element is the most obvious one in the picture drawn by Paul. The work of the human being, done in conjunction with God, is a building made up of *a mixture of materials of diverse quality and resistance*. Paul lists six in a descending order based on the physics of his own day. The image of fire testing the total work of the human being provides another symbolic clue. Throughout my analysis in this volume we have seen that Paul keeps stressing the *causal* link between Sin and Death. In this passage of 1 Corinthians, the quality tested by fire is resistance. But resistance to what? Obviously to the destruction and death that fire brings to the combustible material in the edifice. The degree of resistance found in the latter will measure the degree of freedom vis-à-vis Sin. For it is Sin that enslaves human beings, alienates their works, and hence destroys them as works of their own. In the working of the human being, "everything that does not proceed from *faith* is Sin" (14:23). So the human being will bring to the definitive stage only that dose of "faith working through love" (Gal 5:6) that God finds in him or her.

And that brings us back to Romans 8. As we have seen, so long as history lasts, the human being will remain divided between its projects and its actual accomplishments; the victory of the Spirit will not be achieved in any Manichean way. Now and then, imperceptibly, the distance between intention and performance in a project of love will almost disappear. It is not a matter of minute 'verifications' but rather of glimpses of a reality that will be made manifest only later in another dimension: the transcendent dimension. In the realm of the verifiable, our projects will continue to appear under 'the slavery of corruption' (8:21) due to 'the Flesh', which is what is verifiable in us (7:25).

Analyzing history, we see that progress turns on and against humanity. Even the most humanitarian and promising revolutions go astray. Social consensus, the pledge and jewelpiece of any democracy, has buried within it a crushing mass force. The ideologies of liberty, brotherhood, and love become sclerotic and bureaucratic. The martyrs are lost in the mists of incomprehension and forgetfulness. The sacrifices, in the long run, are made in vain.

Now what is this if not a meditation on the 'verifiable' destiny of Jesus himself and his project: the *kingdom of God*? It is no accident that the visible and verifiable aspect of that destiny is the fact that God sent God's own Son "in the likeness of a Flesh of Sin" (8:3). What does Paul mean by that? Certainly not that the 'flesh' of Jesus is an illusion. What he means is that the fleshly element, what is visible and verifiable in the life of Jesus and his project, is 'like' a destiny dominated by Sin. Not because Jesus appears to have broken the Law, but quite the reverse: 'the Law' appears to have gained control over his project, causing it to succumb to incomprehension, false expectations of the multitude, and the mechanisms of envy first and triumphalism later. The Son of God himself *could not extricate it from that law*. His death on the cross is disconcerting because it seems to hand over his project to corruption, disenchantment, and death as if it were under the dominion of Sin.[185] Indeed his very resurrection, when stripped of its simultaneously eschatological and historical character, seems to be more like a sorry religious revenge that has forgotten the kingdom.

Only the *unverifiable and eschatological* aspect of the paschal experiences makes clear that God "condemned Sin in the Flesh" (8:3), not to reward Jesus with individual power but to provide his project of the kingdom with the power needed to turn it into a reality.[186] The real victory of Jesus does not change the 'appearance' of defeat on the verifiable level. It operates on a deeper level, in which we must believe as we believe in his resurrection, the first-fruit and pledge of our own resurrection and that of all human beings.

We could sum it up this way: although the Spirit gives human beings the ability to build up the definitive despite all 'external' resistances, the Flesh continues to make sure that this upbuilding cannot be verified. And since it cannot be verified, human beings cannot calculate it and thereby use it to bargain with God on a sure footing. Thus Paul's eschatology tells us two things are equally certain: thanks to Christ, the world changes radically for the human being, and the world has not changed one bit with Christ; the kingdom has already arrived with power, and the kingdom will never arrive with power in history.[187]

What are we to say then about Christ's *victory* over the condition of the divided human being? As we have seen, it is a *transcendent datum* concerning what we can hope for with respect to our existence (8:24-25). From Volume I we know two things about transcendent data. They are coherent extrapolations, based on the work of reason, of our verifiable experiences that give them a more universal dimension. And they are also logically necessary suppositions or premises if the values that attract us are to be capable of realization and hence reasonable.

The latter aspect applies to what we have just been considering. There is an inescapable division in the human condition, since the *creative* freedom of the human being must operate in an *already created* world. Hence the values to which Jesus of Nazareth bore concrete testimony in his message and life can be realized only if the 'I' of each person has the power to accomplish a project that is both personal and definitive; and if it is indeed a free project, it must be that of self-giving love. Without that 'spiritual' power, the anthropological faith placed in Jesus of Nazareth would be meaningless, irrational, and contradictory.

What experience can Paul extrapolate to give a foundation to this hope? Clearly the experience of Jesus' resurrection. He says so in Romans 8: "And if the Spirit of the one who resurrected Jesus from the dead dwells in you, the one who resurrected Christ Jesus from the dead is going to bring to life your mortal bodies as well by his Spirit dwelling in you" (8:11). The experience, then, it twofold: Paul's own experience of Jesus' resurrection and the experience that Christians have of the presence of the Spirit in them. We shall consider Paul's experience here, leaving the other experience for section (2) of this chapter.

Why does Paul extrapolate his own experience of Jesus' resurrection and view it as a universal victory over the Law, Sin, and Death? The answer is really simple. Even though Paul does not generally use the term 'kingdom of God', he in fact centers the message of Jesus around it once again. For Paul it is the *Promise*, akin to that which long ago served as the mainspring behind Abraham's life and activity. Paul correctly interprets the kingdom as God's intention to lead *homo* to full and total humanization, to complete maturity as a free, creative person dedicated to cooperating with the creator God (Gal 3:23–4:7). That is why Paul locates the crucial human quality not so much in love (the *result*) as in the inner mechanism that is capable of directing all the energies of the human being into the creative project of love: i.e., *Faith* (Gal 5:6).[188] Paul's pre-eschatological experience of Jesus' resurrection is thus linked up with the project that was the center of Jesus' life and message. Christ could not possibly be victorious unless the project for which he gave up his life was victorious as well. Hence the Spirit, the power of God, snatches from the dominion of Death not only Jesus but also his and God's project of full humanization for the human being.[189] Christ could not be resurrected by the Spirit without the latter also resurrecting 'the mortal bodies' of all human beings.[190]

How does this universal victory take place? Paul's response is richer and more complex than the usual exegesis would indicate. It is certainly far richer than the classic image offered us by tradition of 'the resurrection of the dead'. That image is not only an oversimplification but also an infantilization, tailored to serve the consoling rites offered by the Church to friends and relatives of a deceased person.

The notion of the 'resurrection of the *body*' is a Hebrew one. Hebrew thought never separated the *soul* from the body and focused on the former's immortality. In the prevailing eschatology of Jesus' day, the resurrection of the body was to be the means used by God to bring all human beings before God's tribunal and render a judgment that would restore the justice missing on earth. But the Greek idea of the substantive immortality of the soul served that purpose just as well, and so the notion of a total resurrection ended up as a dogma without much meaning (see 1 Cor 15:12f.). It was used almost exclusively to console bereaved relatives.

At first glance it might *seem* that Paul goes no further when he asserts that our mortal *bodies*, too, will be resurrected (8:11) or redeemed (8:23).[191] But what does Paul mean by the word 'body'? We do well to recall two things. First, when he complains about the gap between human project and actual accomplishments in 7:24, it is clear that 'this *body of death*' refers to the whole human condition. And the weakness that produces this condition stems from 'the Flesh', another term that designates the totality of the human being in both the Old and New Testaments (see 7:14.18.25; 8:3). Second, Paul's use of the Greek word for 'body' is clearly influenced and toned by the Hebrew biblical term 'flesh' (see 8:13 specifically and 8:5–13 in general). We know that Paul derived the term 'flesh' from the Old Testament, where it referred to the totality of a being as creature, of the human being as creature in particular. Moreover, in ancient literary usage it went beyond the limits of the individual and included all the emotional components of human existence.[192] Thus it took in spouse, relatives, friends, and fellow countrymen (see 2 Sm 19:13; Jgs 9:2; etc.).

We now can understand how Paul concretely envisions his hope of resurrection, and in fact we have seen it already in an earlier chapter. It is his vision of Christ's victory over the Law, Sin, and Death.[193] In 1 Corinthians he tells us that this whole corruptible reality must *put on* immortality.[194] And in 2 Corinthians he tells us that he seeks and expects immortality for his whole existence with its values and projects.[195] The whole 'tent' of our earthly reality, of human life with all its relationships and projects, is to have immortality put on 'over' it.[196] At present this injection of life seems to be invisible, but it is not totally so because God has given us the Spirit as a *pledge* of it (2 Cor 5:5). That is the way an experience, which is not scientifically and impartially verifiable (see Acts 2:13) but is an experience nevertheless, becomes a reasonable basis and support for hope. And the hope, in turn, thereby ceases to be a mere wish, becoming instead a premise that gives structure to one's existence.

(2). But Romans 8 does not end with Paul's conception of Jesus' resurrection as the basic *transcendent datum* in his christology and as his response to the problem posed in the latter half of Romans 7. In the rest of Romans 8, and to some extent in the first part also, he touches upon various themes that do not seem to be closely connected at first glance. To be sure, in all of them we find the same tone of victory, which suggests that Paul sees them as *reinforcing* the response he has already given. Since that response had to do with the *transcendent datum* of a resurrection interpreted in connection with history, we can reasonably assume that the reinforcing themes also deal with history in some way.

How does one reinforce a transcendent datum? The answer is simple: with other transcendent data. Arrived at in the same way, these data must dovetail rationally with the first datum so that they constitute what Proust might call 'hostages'. Either they all perish together or they all are saved together. And we get a tradition when it is possible to collate various transcendent data so that they form a reasonable and trustworthy complex.[197]

The communities addressed by Paul found themselves within two traditions. First, there was their own specifically Christian tradition. They transmitted to each other various interpreted experiences that served as ontological and epistemological premises for their structured life. Thus they reflected on such experiences as the resurrection of Jesus, the incarnation of God, and the mission of the Son, with all the implications they had for the life and thought of the nascent Church. There was a second important tradition, however. Even in communities that were largely of pagan origin, Paul never dissociated himself from Jewish tradition as a basic frame of reference. He reinterpreted it, stripping it of its oppressive content so that its rich data might shed clearer light on the significance of Jesus of Nazareth.

Speaking broadly, we can say that two transcendent data were used to reinforce and guarantee the central one (the resurrection of Jesus): the datum of *adoption as children of God* and the datum of *brotherhood and sisterhood* in relation to Jesus.

Let us look at adoption. Every transcendent datum extrapolates experiences. Paul tells us that the Spirit of the one who raised Jesus *is dwelling* in Christians (8:11). In this Spirit Christians have a guarantee and *pledge* of resurrection (2 Cor 5:5). Both terms allude to existential experiences of the early Christian communities. And Paul goes on to indicate the content of those experiences: "All who are guided by the Spirit of God are *children of God*" (8:14).

There is nothing magical or merely legalistic about this. The existential content of this experience is quite clear. We are liberated from a relationship with God ruled by fear and submission to the bookkeeping of the Law. Now that relationship is to be one of absolute trust and confidence: "You did not receive a spirit of slavery, to fall back into fear again. You received a spirit of adoption as child, by which we cry out: Abba, Papa! The Spirit itself joins in to testify with our spirit that we are children of God" (8:15-16).

In and of itself the universal paternity of God is not a new idea for the biblical tradition of the Old Testament. But Paul stresses two elements that are indeed fundamental and new. In both of them *Faith* will surface implicitly once again as the crucial attitude. First, the special confidence[198] mentioned by Paul and urged upon Christians does not have to do with any old kind of adoption. It has to do specifically with the coming to *maturity* of a true child and heir.[199] The passage just cited above mirrors another passage (Gal 4:1-7) where the attitude of the son as *child* (subject to his servants and unaware that he is 'master of all') is contrasted with that of the *mature* son who receives his inheritance in a real, conscious way. This mature child and heir owes nothing to anyone except 'mutual love' (13:8), and all things are at its disposal in carrying out that debt (1 Cor 3:21-22). Second, however, this adoption as child is not verifiable, manifest, or glorious as a spiritual experience. It is not visible, as is 'fleshly' affiliation with Abraham. To the term 'child' Paul adds the term 'heir'. Contemporary exegesis tends to disregard the connection, as if it did not need any clarification. But what human being, Christian or no, has the experience of being able to act as if it were heir of the world and master of everything?

What might it mean *in the concrete* to be the heir of God, in line with Jesus (whose limited historical life we have already explored in Volume II), in the dominion of the world? Father and child have a relationship of likeness and continuity. When God is involved, this relationship must be bound up with a divine plan that begins with creation. The Father is a *creator*. The child and heir can be a creator only in a restricted and metaphorical sense, but a real sense nevertheless. What reality in the human being-child can somehow be likened to the idea of 'creation'? The reality of *freedom* as Paul understands and stresses it throughout his christology.[200] He does not regard it as a pendulum oscillating between good and evil. Paul sees freedom as the ability to carry out the projects that the 'I' chooses to perform. In the first phase at least, when they arise in the personal 'inner humanity' of a person, those projects have to do with collaborating in God's 'construction' or 'cultivation' work. This is Paul's way of expressing God's plan to humanize humanity that is called the 'kingdom of God' in the Synoptic gospels.

Here again we are dealing with an eschatological reality, but it is eschatology as Paul understands the term. For him it has to do with actions in history that are building something lasting and definitive even though they may seem to be going astray and heading for corruption and death. The definitive reality will not come about without the creative freedom of God's children; but only at the end will we see its *manifestation*, its full positive visibility or *glory*.

As is his habit, Paul invents a new personification. This time it is all *creation* that "yearns for the *manifestation* of God's *children*" (8:19). What characteristic is to be manifested eschatologically? Paul tells us that it is *"the freedom of the glory* of God's children" (8:21). If that freedom and its likeness to the creator Father are to be glorious or manifest, then the projects that the human being wanted to etch into the universe must be "liberated from the slavery of corruption" (8:21).[201] They must be liberated from Death (corruption), Sin, and the Law, from all the mechanisms that render them alienated and force them to serve alien interests.

Wherein lies the reasonableness of this transcendent datum (i.e., the revelation of human beings as the children and heirs of the creator God)? It lies in its logical connection with something that can be extrapolated from the actual experience of human beings in family life, friendship, and love. Here is where our 'hostage' shows up. If this transcendent datum were false, then God would lose the only paternity he could possibly have vis-à-vis human beings. Authentic *personal* love is always characterized by the fact that it accords crucial importance to the freedom of the loved one, so that our own happiness and fulfillment depend on that person's free decisions. This, in turn, assumes two things: (1) that we leave something crucial and unfinished to the other's freedom; (2) that we consider the riskiness and pain of the inconclusive and unfinished to be better for the other party and ourselves, even though we must depend on the other's decisions. Something finished, painless, or indifferent cannot be crucial and decisive. The best of all possible worlds would mean that our own lives lost all meaning and value.[202]

Our 'hostage', then, is the fate of God's whole creation. Being 'heir' does not mean inheriting something already acquired. It means inheriting something immensely worthwhile *to do*. And we know that creation remains something to be done because we know that all creation is groaning in the pains of labor up to now (8:22). That is why the children of God must be manifested in all the glory of their freedom. Otherwise all the mechanisms of the created universe would keep spinning their way toward *uselessness*.

We can see how crucial and definitive in Paul's thought are the 'co-working' of God's children and the necessity of their creative cooperation. That this fundamental datum is expressed in mythical or poetic form matters little. The point is certain and clear: "Creation was subjected to *uselessness* not by its own will, but on account of the one who subjected it,[203] with the hope that *creation itself would be liberated* from the slavery of corruption to pass to the freedom of the glory of God's children" (8:20–21).

Thus we hold a strange *hostage* to the resurrection of our projects of love and humanization: "the *sufferings* of the present moment" (8:18). God himself would have created a world *in vain*, a world that does not honor him directly, if the human being did not turn this suffering into the meaning and mainspring of its freedom, of what can still be called 'creation' in an already created world: the appearance of a new being, the building up of brother and sister, the 'birth' that gives meaning to labor pains. If human freedom never managed to stamp the seal of its unique, personal intention on its performances, then God himself would be a failure.

But there is something more here, if we pay close attention to the logic of Paul's argument. He seems to be attempting nothing else but to prove that it is 'incomparably' worthwhile to endure the apparent defeat and death of our projects "vis-à-vis the coming glory to be revealed *in us*" (8:18). Yet that implies something else that we have already seen in other passages of Romans and other Pauline letters of the same period: i.e., the rediscovery of the theme of the *kingdom of God* being turned into a reality in its *historical* dimension.

Efforts have been made to set up an opposition between historical importance on the one hand and eschatology on the other. It is the argument of Marx against religion in general and Christianity in particular, to cite just one example. In Volume II we considered that problem in terms of the historical

Jesus. In this volume Paul's change of key poses the problem to us once again, since his anthropological key seems to be less historical, on the surface at least. But Paul's eschatological response to the problem posed in Romans 7 contains a revaluation of the historical. Indeed his is the only kind of eschatology that can reinforce committed involvement with the problems of causality and effectiveness in time. Why? Because, as Paul sees it, eschatology is not the suppression of human freedom or a replacement for it, but rather the manifestation of it.

Readers might be inclined to object that if the manifestation took place *at the same time* as action in history, the importance of the latter would be even more evident. But that is not so, at least on the plane of logic. If universal entropy (the majority tendency towards degradation and corruption) did not appear to be handing over the humanizing projects of the human being to deviation and death, then in the course of history the human being would find itself facing increasingly superficial and negligible problems. Creation would be standing on its feet and reaching its fulfillment at the expense of the significance of humanity and the decisive importance of human history.

Is that thought present in Paul more or less consciously? We do not know, but it certainly fits in as a component of the transcendent datum having to do with creative adoption as children of God, on which the sense and 'usefulness' of the universe depends.

The *second* transcendent datum is that of universal brotherhood and sisterhood. Paul alludes to a divine plan or 'resolve' (8:28) that is closely bound up with that of adoption: to make human beings *real* brothers and sisters of Jesus. It is not to be a merely legal relationship. They are to "reflect the image of his Son" so that he who was formed first as the model, irregardless of the arrow of time, will be "the firstborn of many brothers and sisters" (8:29). And since 'many' in biblical usage refers to all, he is to be firstborn of *all* brother and sister human beings.

This plan or resolve is seen as already worked out among all "those who love God" (8:28). But it is also depicted in terms of its logical stages, from its start in the divine mind to its manifestation in the eschatological reality: "For those whom he knew beforehand, he also destined them beforehand to reflect the image of his Son . . . Those he destined beforehand, he also called; and those he called, he also declared just; and those he declared just, he also glorified" (8:29-30).

In themselves the stages are clear enough. The first stage is to be included in the divine project. Then comes the historical accomplishment of the divine project through a call or 'vocation'. If one responds affirmatively to this call, then the declaration of justice comes in the present[204] and is followed by the manifestation or glory of that (still hidden) justice in the eschatological reality.

But two questions merit consideration here. What exactly is the divine project in question? Who are included in its realization?

At first glance the answer to the first question would seem to lead us back to the theme of adoption as children of God. It is a matter of making human beings who 'reflect the image of his Son', who behave like him and hence act as his children in turn. That would take us back to the theme of being 'heir' of creation and master of a universe that God has left unfinished. Human beings are to imprint their own free, original, creative projects on it.

It is clear that the two projects come down to one, when all is said and done; but here Paul stresses the community life of brothers and sisters. Just as the passage on adoption probably confronts humanity with its historical dimension, so the passage on brotherhood and sisterhood confronts humanity with its social dimension.

We must admit quite frankly that Paul does not show anything like the keen sensitivity of Jesus of Nazareth to the injustice and oppression embodied in sociopolitical structures. It may be by default or by design, but it is a fact. Yet on the anthropological plane that is Paul's own turf, we have seen one theme surfacing repeatedly and it really is connected with the social realm. Paul stresses the danger inherent in all 'religion', which uses supposedly 'sacred' instruments: it may marginalize human beings in the name of the deity.

As we have seen, Paul lays down a principle that is paradoxical for a *religion*, one that wants to be competitive and that therefore has its own peculiar advantages and limitations: "There is no partiality on God's part" (2:11). That is why Paul shows a clear preference for the human situation in the first stage, when God judged every human being by the same criterion. That is why he makes the accusation he does against Judaism and its interpretation of the Law. And that is why he returns, by way of Faith, to a single, universal criterion.

For Paul, moreover, the basic oneness of human beings in God's eyes is replete with concrete consequences. It entails the abolition of all more or less religious criteria that give some human beings an excuse to place themselves above other human beings. All Paul's letters of this period bear witness to the same concern, which is a central point of his christology: "There is no longer Jew nor Greek, slave nor free, male nor female; for you are all *one* in Christ Jesus" (Gal 3:28; see also Rom 10:12; 1 Cor 12:13; Col 3:11).

It is also a crucial point because its acceptance depends on *Faith* and the renunciation of security and privilege. Rejection of it, on the other hand, is the opposite of Faith: i.e., 'glorying' (2:3) in something that seems to be divine but is merely human (see Gal 6:13; 1 Cor 3:21; 2 Cor *passim*).[205] The crucial nature of this issue can be seen in the fact that it may arise even in Christian communities which have accepted the abolition of the Law as a principle of privilege and separation. Even the human elements or instruments of the Christian faith, once embodied in communities with their own distinctive traits, may almost automatically be turned into new excuses for privilege, separation, and discord. Paul is forced to see and attack it, for example, in a Christian community of converted pagans founded by himself (1 Cor 1:10–11; 3:3–4).

So it is totally incorrect to say that Paul is not aware of the possible and even probable use of religion as an ideology by some human beings to exploit other human beings.

That brings us to our second question: Who are included in this plan for brotherhood and sisterhood centered around Christ as the firstborn of many brothers and sisters? Two answers seem possible.[206]

One answer would be that here Paul prescinds from the *quantitative* aspect of the plan, merely outlining the stages of its realization. *Nothing in his text* contradicts the possibility that if he were asked directly who were included in the plan, he would say that it included all humanity.

Important elements in the text incline us toward that position. One of the stages in the divine plan is that of being 'declared just' (8:30). From the victory of Jesus over Adam we know that the 'many' (i.e., 'all') will be made just (5:19; see 5:16–18). Hence those 'predestined' to be declared just are, quantitatively, all the children of Adam.

We also know that Abraham, by virtue of his attitude of Faith (not faith in Jesus Christ specifically), was declared just and the father of all believers, be they circumcised or uncircumcised. Now if Abraham is brought into God's plan, what principle could Paul invoke to restrict the entry of any human being into it, so long as that person had an attitude like that of Abraham?

If pagans prior to Jesus and all the children of Adam are involved in *one* of the stages, the crucial one involving God's declaration of justice, then we have a right to suppose that *all humanity* is part of the total project of brotherhood and sisterhood centered around Jesus, even though all human beings may not have been involved in all of the stages of God's plan.

That brings us to our second possible answer to the question: even though all human beings may be involved in one of the stages of the process, the process as a whole is to be found among the members of the Christian community.

In line with this possibility, it is worth noting that *all* the passages about the abolition of barriers, especially religious barriers, between human beings occur when Paul is speaking directly and explicitly to the Christian community. In his letter to the Galatians, for example, the passage is immediately preceded by a reference to "all the baptized in Christ" (Gal 3:27). In 1 Corinthians, it is preceded by the statement: "in one Spirit we all have been baptized . . ." (1 Cor 12:13). In Romans, the passage is preceded by a significant statement which some exegetes regard as a basic formula of faith used by Christian communities[207]: "If with your lips you confess that Jesus is Lord and believe in your heart that God resurrected him from the dead, you will be saved. For with the heart one believes to obtain justice, and with the lips one confesses to obtain salvation" (10:9–10).

Another argument is more grammatical in nature: the use of the Greek aorist tense to indicate past, *completed* action. Paul uses it to say that those included in God's plan, "he also *glorified*" (8:30). Some exegetes argue that Paul is not really talking about the past here but about the certainty of the eschatological future based on 'God's already decided purpose' (Zerwick: 349). I disagree. It seems much more likely that Paul is indeed referring to something that has already occurred. And where might we see this resplendent glory of those who have been declared just already? Obviously, in the glorification of the resurrected Jesus. What is experienced in the resurrection somehow takes what has already been glimpsed in its basic reality and turns it into something past.

Looking at all the factors, I would say that the second hypothesis is the more likely one and I would put it this way: in speaking of the overall process involved in God's plan for brotherhood and sisterhood, Paul is referring specifically but not exclusively to Christians insofar as they have reached the ultimate stage in their own present experience. Now what human experience, extrapolated beyond the bounds of the verifiable, serves as the basis for the transcendent datum of universal brotherhood and sisterhood willed by God? For Paul, it seems to me, it is the visible brotherhood and sisterhood of the Christian community, of the Church, at least of those churches founded by Paul. His extrapolation is based on the overcoming of all divisions within the Church—above all, of divisions attributed to God.

It is no easy matter to see to it that in a divided world a particular community reflect universal brotherhood and sisterhood in a meaningful way. First of all, the dissolution of barriers must be fully experienced and lived within the community.[208] The Christian of pagan origin must be accorded the same rights as the Christian of Jewish origin, and indeed Paul's whole letter to the Romans deals with that issue.[209] The slave must be treated like the free person (Philemon 16). As a 'freed person of the Lord' (1 Cor 7:22), the slave must profit from this new status even though it does not reach beyond the bounds of the Christian community. And even though there are major differences of opinion between his churches and the church of Jerusalem, Paul feels that a central task of his ministry is to make sure that his churches share their resources with the mother church in Jerusalem (2 Cor 8–9).

Paul also insists that the Christian community avoid hasty judgments and remain open as a convivial space for both the weak in faith (14:1–15:2) and the strong in faith. Moreover, this brotherhood and sisterhood is to be lived in the midst of humanity, not in some desert area, even though it may entail risks for those who are weaker (1 Cor 5:9–13).

On the other hand meaningful universality cannot be effective unless it drastically excludes from the Christian community anything and everything that is incompatible with its function of building up a humanity that is mature in its love. That is why Paul is so severe with those who would make the name of brother and sister 'hateful' (1 Cor 5:11), who would reduplicate the sin of Judaism in causing the name of God to be blasphemed. That is why he is so severe with those in the Christian community who marginalize others on account of their poverty, even in the very remembrance of the Lord's passion and death (1 Cor 11:19–22.27–32). And that is why he is so severe with those who would marginalize others on the basis of some 'fleshly' religious trait such as circumcision (Gal 1:8–9; 5:12).

Here we have our second *hostage*. The main work of a Church dedicated to the service of universal brotherhood and sisterhood in Jesus Christ the firstborn would be meaningless, would crumble into uselessness and nothingness, if in the course of history God did not somehow give the dignity and function of 'brother' or 'sister' to every human being. Even though this reality may be lived with special clarity and guarantees in the Church, it is a transcendent datum that touches every human being as such.

In the light of these transcendent data we can see why all the components of the 'law of the members' have lost their intrinsic, crucial power, even though they may remain powerful on the visible, extrinsic level. This holds true for all those elements that come between the human intention of love and actual accomplishment: "Affliction or anxiety or persecution or hunger or nakedness or danger or the sword" (8:35). All the objects of our fear, which detour us into the byways of security and the easy way out, have been defeated at their very roots. And this is true no matter how much we may try to hallow them religiously by placing them above human beings and giving them high-sounding names and superhuman attributes: death, life, angels, principalities, present, future, powers, height, depth . . . (8:38–39).

•

One final matter deserves mention before we end our consideration of Romans 8. It has to do with an apparent gap in Romans 8 insofar as the latter is supposed to offer an answer to the issue raised in the latter half of Romans 7. We find a curious lapse in Paul's curiosity. As we saw earlier, Paul seems to *pose* certain questions in terms of the 'human being' as such (2:6–16; 5:6–10; etc.). When he uses such terms as 'I', 'inner humanity', and the like, they also seem to refer to human beings as such. And his general *anthropological key* also suggests that his formulations of problems have to do with human beings of all ages and creeds. Such is not the case, however, with the *solutions* he offers to the problems. With the curious exception of Abraham, those solutions are framed in terms of the Christian *now*. One might well assume, therefore, that the solutions apply only to those situated in that now. Hence the question arises in our minds: If a problem is truly anthropological, how can it be solved for all human beings *in* one specific era or *starting from* then?

Reading Paul, readers may well be tempted to assume that whatever the fate of human beings before Christ may have been, the problem of the human condition is solved for *all humans* once all humanity is made Christian. As if earlier humans had not existed; or as if Paul did not realize that many of his contemporaries and future human beings would reject faith or the Christian community for good reasons, for mistaken but guiltless reasons, or simply for lack of information.

Some exegetes do not hesitate to offer a reason for Paul's lack of concern with this issue. They say it has to do with a basic stance taken by Paul either unconsciously or consciously, superficially or thoughtfully. For him, they say, the whole system of grace and salvation bound up with a declaration of justice *begins to operate with Jesus Christ*. Only from there on is it applicable, and normally to those who believe in Jesus Christ. There might be an exceptional case here and there, as was Abraham in the past.

If that were the deeper, unconscious thought of Paul, then obviously my whole exegesis of these chapters is mistaken. I have tried to point up the inner logic of his thought, to show how the pieces of the mosaic fit together as a coherent line of thinking. If his deeper line of thought is different, I am wrong.

Now the fact is that Paul himself does not fit all of the pieces into the mosaic. And one of the pieces he neglects to deal with is the issue that concerns us here. How exactly does God's declaration of justice operate, and to whom exactly does it apply? What about the multitude of human beings in history who never did or never will have any knowledge of, or association with, Jesus of Nazareth?

One way of handling this would be to pretend we are interviewing Paul and that he did have a direct answer to this latter question. Thus we would ask him whether salvation was possible for those who refused to adhere to the Christian faith and join the Chrisian community.[210] We must be careful here, however. When we get a specific answer to a question that a particular person did not raise specifically in his or her own line of thought, it is possible that the answer does not really fit in with the logic of their thinking and other relevant data in their viewpoint. Hence it is *possible* that Paul would answer 'no' to our question (see Acts 2:47; 4:12; 16:30–31; 1 Cor 1:18–21).[211] Yet that simple 'no' might not fit in with the deeper reaches of his thinking.

My own opinion is that Paul would not proffer a simple 'no' answer to the question, at least not by the time he had gotten around to writing to the Romans. I don't see how the question would not trigger associations in his mind with such central data as the parallelism between Adam and Christ, for example. Yet the crucial point remains the logical connection of his answer, whatever it might be, with the rest of his thinking. In short, the real question is how Paul would have answered the question *if he posed it in the same depth as other issues he confronted in Romans.* And at that deep level, it seems to me, neither a simple 'yes' nor a simple 'no' would be completely satisfactory. If we look at the internal logic of Paul's thought, we will find that a more complex answer is called for.

In talking about plans *of God*, we must remember that the literary genre of myths, like that of dreams, is not subject to the temporal order.[212] To take just one example, consider the two plans attributed to God in Romans 8. Both depict Jesus as their basic model: the model of adoption as children of God and the model of other brothers and sisters (8:14.17.29).

Following a temporal order, we know that the mold or model could begin to operate only from the time of Jesus on. In that case Paul's anthropological analyses would cease to be truly anthropological. We could have a human species with certain basic characteristics before Jesus, and with very different characteristics after Jesus. On the other hand, Romans 8:29 suggests that the model has to do with the 'image' that God used to fashion the human being *from the very beginning.* Jesus is called the 'firstborn' of many brothers and

sisters. And while that could apply to human beings after the historical
existence of Jesus, we have seen that it does seem to have something to do with
God's declaration of justice long before Jesus was born (4:5.11.12). Jesus is the
mold out of which Abraham himself was fashioned.

With regard to adoption Paul writes: "All who are guided by the Spirit of
God *are children* of God" (8:14). Again that could refer to the period from
Jesus on, but it is very unlikely. Again there is an implicit reference to Abraham, and Paul would hardly be unaware of all the biblical figures who had
been 'guided by the Spirit'. Jesus' function as model seems to work back into
the past as well as forward into the future.

Many people also loved God before Jesus, and Paul writes: "We know that
everything works together for the good of those who love God . . . He also
destined them beforehand to reflect the image of his Son . . ." (8:28-29).

The resurrection of *all* human beings, not just of dead Christians, is another
datum among many that proves the seriousness of Paul in using an anthropological key. Once again Jesus is loosened from his fixed place in history, shifted
to the remote past to serve as the model for all human beings from Adam on,
and then shifted to the furthest reaches of the future to serve as the life-giving
goal of all humanity (5:15-17; 1 Cor 15:21-22).

So why does Paul take something that includes all humanity and link it up
with Christian faith and Baptism? Because at a certain point in the process,
already operative and effective through the good faith, hope, and love of
human beings, God's plan *is revealed* in all its magnitude. Jesus defines the
significance of the human being *of all times*, but that definition is made visible
and guaranteed by the experience of his resurrection as seen in the light of his
tradition, his life, his message, his fight, and his death.[213]

The difference between the *before* and the *now* is great, and it simply must be
made visible in the conduct of those who believe in that transcendent datum.
They cannot logically behave as if that transcendent datum were not a part of
their faith. But no *anthropological* change has taken place. Human beings are
not made just by it, nor is it any easier for them to do good. As is the case with
any meaningful knowledge, their behavior should take on new forms and new
responsibilities. Knowing God's plan should help to enlighten them, and make
it easier for them to carry on the humanization of humanity in history.[214]

Remember, I am not claiming that Paul thought *all this* out in a conscious,
explicit way; but I do think he would have said most of this if he had been
pushed to clarify his thinking on this issue. In the light of his own christology he
would have said something like that, though he would have put it much better.

CHAPTER IX

Conclusions:
Christ and the Human Being

Step by step we have followed the twists and turns of Paul's thinking in the first eight chapters of Romans, which are central to any effort to trace out his christology. Using similarity and contrast, I hope that I have gradually been able to shed some light on the key anthropological terms of that christology: e.g., Flesh, Spirit, Law, idolatry, works, works of the Law, inner humanity, law of the members, Sin, Grace, and Faith.

I have also tried to make clear that Paul, in his work of fashioning a christology, is profoundly faithful to what the historical Jesus expressed about the kingdom of God in his deeds and his message. The only thing is that Paul, like all the other New Testament writers, sees the historical Jesus as the latter could not see himself: i.e., already illuminated by the decisive datum conveyed by the paschal experiences.

The relationship between Paul's anthropological characters is an intricate one, however, and Paul often adds his own twist by changing the meaning of words when his argument requires it. So by now many readers might find it hard to frame all that we have seen so far in a coherent whole. That is hardly surprising. When we are dealing with Paul, we have no reason to assume that his first readers understood clearly what seems abstruse and complicated to us.

A general overview and summary now seems to be in order. And in these eight chapters I think there are *two terms*, two anthropological personifications, that can serve as our guiding thread. Not only do they occupy the whole development of Paul's thought in Romans 1–8. They also contest human existence as a whole, to the point where Paul can offer this curt summary later: "Everything that does not proceed from *Faith* is *Sin*" (14:23). Faith and Sin, then, will serve as our guides for this concluding summary.

After following the many twists and turns and seeming contradictions of Paul's development, we may justifiably conclude that Sin and Faith seem to measure *the gap or distance* that is always there between what a human being

145

intends and what he or she *actually performs or accomplishes*. It is the distance between the human project that arises in our 'inner humanity' and the project we actually accomplish, given that our project must go by the way of 'the law of the members' to become a reality. The effect of Sin[215] is to put *greater* distance between the two, so that human beings find their own actions incomprehensible and unrecognizable. The effect of Faith is to put *less* distance between the two, so that the works and deeds of human beings are somehow restored to them as their own, at least to some extent.

Looking back, we notice that the theme of Sin reigned undisputed from the start of Romans 1 to the middle of Romans 3. Up to that point Paul's aim was to pound home the accusation "that we all, Jews and Greeks [i.e., all humanity], are under Sin" (3:9). Far from overcoming it, the Law only reveals its essence and its universal extension, "because all sinned" (5:12).

From the middle of Romans 3, Paul presents an opposed reality: Faith. First he lays down a rather abstract principle, then he depicts its early realization in Abraham, then its full realization in Christ (as opposed to Adam), and finally its realization in the Christian.

This shift of focus does not do away with the theme of Sin, however. Instead it presents Sin as something that has been defeated as an enslaving power over the human being: defeated in all the descendants of Adam, defeated in Christian Baptism, and defeated as a power than can impose itself on those who believe in Christ.

Yet Paul returns to it again, considering an even more radical aspect. He shows how Sin, even in the Christian, renders human actions incomprehensible and unrecognizable to their performer. Sin 'dwells' in the human being, imperceptibly distorting the good intention of our 'inner humanity' as we try to turn it into reality in the outside world. That is the 'Flesh', our human condition. And that is why Paul says: ". . . with the Flesh I serve the law of Sin" (7:25). To our surprise, however, Romans 8 once again depicts Christians, those under the influence of Christ in and through Faith, "liberated . . . from the law of Sin . . ." (8:2). Thus Sin disappears from the scene of Romans 1–8, apparently defeated again and once and for all.

Now let us note how the theme of Faith implicitly and explicitly fills the interstices left by the theme of Sin in Romans 1–8. This should tell us something. Near the very start of his letter Paul, who is very likely thinking of the progression from Abraham to Christ, brings up the term 'Faith' or its equivalent no less than four times: "I am not ashamed of the gospel. For it is the saving power of God for *everyone who believes* [i.e., has *Faith*], for the Jew first and also for the Greek. Because in it the justice that proceeds from God is being revealed from *Faith* to *Faith*, as it is written: 'The one who is just by *Faith* will live' " (1:16–17).[216]

The theme of Faith then disappears until the middle of Romans 3, where it moves to center stage and remains until Romans 5. As an explicit theme, it then remains submerged through chapters 6, 7, and 8.[217] Yet it should be noted that the whole of Romans 8, dealing with victory over Sin, is an implicit descriptive definition of Faith.

In the following sections of this chapter I shall consider Paul's treatment of Sin, of Faith, of the human existence that arises from their interaction, and of new elements that Paul's christology may offer us for our human existence today.

I

Sin *dwells* in the human being in a total way. That is not true of *sins*, the specific acts that represent the visible fragments of Sin. Indeed sins as such, precisely because they are visible, can constitute a force opposed to Sin. The latter power, Sin, is not the innermost humanity of the person; but its mechanisms are not external either. Sin and its mechanisms are part of the human condition as such.

When Sin first appears in Romans, Paul concentrates on its scope and extent. Its dominion is universal. It is easy enough for anyone to show that the pagan world is under its enslavement; but from the very start Paul also wants to make clear that *the same is true* of the Jewish people, who received God's authentic, normative revelation in the Law and who are, at least on the surface, a cut above the moral standards of Greco-Roman paganism. Thus Paul is compelled from the very start to make sure that his readers *comprehend* the basic concept of Sin and what it entails.

Paul sees Sin as an enslaving element throughout the first eight chapters of Romans. Human beings are slaves, compelled to hand over their works to another, who has power over them. From the very start, then, we are confronted with the negative quality that will be brought out clearly in Romans 7: the gap or distance that Sin creates between the decisions of our inner humanity and our actual deeds or accomplishments.

To achieve this enslaving and alienating power, Sin must rely on some complicity in the human beings. Something *in* the human being, very close to the source of its acts, lends itself to this enslavement and benefits from it. According to Romans 1, the accomplice is the 'desires' or 'cravings' of the heart, very akin to what we today would call instincts. It seems that these 'cravings of the heart', close as they are to our inner humanity and our authentic 'I', obey a law that ignores the dictates of our inner humanity. In that sense they are like nature in general, which also ignores those dictates. Nature seems to be endowed with its own laws and mechanisms, and even in the human being they seem to operate as if human freedom did not exist.[218]

How is this basic, ongoing conflict resolved in most instances, and in whose favor? It is resolved through a mechanism of 'bad faith', a modern term for Paul's description of human beings who "have become entangled in their own reasonings" and whose "uncomprehending hearts have been darkened" (1:21). The cravings of the heart trigger a process of lying whereby human beings deceive themselves and end up in the tangled web of their own self-deception. The result is that Sin reigns, creating the maximum possible separation between the basic orientation of our inner humanity and the actual realization of our intended projects.

It is important to note that Paul demonstrates our enslavement to Sin in this way, rather than on the basis of serious, conscious faults. Such faults might alarm us and help to wean us from our self-deception. But bad faith remains impervious to the gradual degradation of all human relationships. Dehumanizing injustice does not attract our attention because our inner truth has been neutralized and shackled.

Paul adds a highly significant example of this confusion in the moral reasoning of human beings: idolatry. Human understanding shifts from a natural and perhaps historical knowledge of the Absolute to a non-existent focus that uses religion to justify and endorse inhuman conduct. Thus idolatry becomes a crucial instrument in the darkening of the human heart.[219]

Given these mechanisms, we could hardly expect any radical change in the human situation with the promulgation of a divine Law, a normative revelation to the Chosen People of Israel. As Paul sees it, even the seemingly *positive* feature of the Law noticed first soon proves to be a *negative* thing. The Law is a principle of 'discernment'.[220] It raises the ethical coefficient of human existence in those who acknowledge it. A preoccupation with morality is heightened and refined in their lives. Through prescriptions covering every area of life, the Law permits people to 'know Sin'. But the Law gives direction and orders to the human being *from outside*, as Paul stresses repeatedly. This is a crucial, negative feature that must be appreciated if we are to understand the final result. God cannot, or in fact does not, give direction to human beings from within themselves. The Law must be 'mediated' to human beings. It becomes visible in a 'letter' that grows old and outdated as soon as the circumstances in which it was promulgated for people change. It is not 'life' and 'power' that strengthens and reinforces the options of people's inner humanity.

Not surprisingly, then, the appearance and multiplication of precepts ends up in the impossibility of carrying them out. This 'multiplication of the offense' is the first result of a Law that squanders the energy of human beings in a futile way, especially when they are convinced that fulfilling the Law will guarantee their justice and hence their salvation. Paul is very clear about his own view of the matter: No one will be declared just by the works of the Law.

Moreover, an external Law leaves untouched the structure of human existence. The same 'cravings' that make their way in the pagan by darkening the heart also take control of the Law and make it serve the same end: i.e., the dehumanization of human relationships. The only difference is that in the latter case twisted reasoning may not be necessary to achieve the effect. The anxiety of the human being to find security in something absolutely firm and solid may suffice. In the letter of the Law human beings find the supreme guarantees they are seeking for their behavior. They need not take the relatively difficult step into idolatrous *heterodoxy*. Instead idolatry becomes their way of living *orthodoxy* itself.

The inhumanity resulting from such behavior is no less than that of pagans. Both pagans and Jews use a god that does not exist to defend themselves from the God who wills that human beings be fully human. But there is a difference. The inhumanity is less barefaced and more subtle in this Jewish use of the Law, as is their conversion of theoretical orthodoxy into practical idolatry by way of the Law. It is more subtle and more thoroughgoing: more subtle because the forms of idolatry and the offenses produced by it are not so apparent; more profound and thoroughgoing because this other kind of dehumanization is more difficult to uproot. It is marked by the haughty pride and bad faith of resting securely in a privilege that bears the seal of divine approval, that excuses people from their responsibility of loving, that leads them to despise other human beings and relate to them with disdain.

Here again, and especially here, the human being who wills the good inwardly but relies on the letter of the Law for its accomplishment finds that his or her works are truly 'indocile to the truth but docile to injustice'. Indeed, so terrible and awesome is their dehumanizing content that they cause God's name to be blasphemed.

On the other hand a second, seemingly *negative* feature of the Law turns out to be more *positive* and hope-giving upon closer inspection. It is the useless preoccupation of the human being to negotiate with God by fulfilling the prescripts of the Law as if they were clauses in a contract. By multiplying human offenses, this should lead human beings to such desperation and insecurity that they are open to the possibility of a very different attitude. It is the attitude that Christ proposes to us with his life and message, and that Paul sums up in the term *Faith*.

Insofar as Sin is concerned, however, Paul would not have us think that those who have made an act of faith in Jesus Christ and entered the Christian community are in a totally different situation from that of other human beings who share the same human condition (the same 'Flesh') but not the same *creed*.

First of all, we know they are threatened by the temptation to rekindle, even within the Christian community, an attitude of fear and bargaining with God. They are tempted to return to the yoke of the Law. And, as the Jews did with their Law, they are tempted to use the religious structures incorporated in the Church to indulge in 'glorying'. They may use those religious structures to feel personally at ease and to pass judgment on others, regarding salvation as a 'wage' which is admittedly hard to earn but to which they do have a right.[221]

Second, even after announcing how a life oriented by Faith in Christ transforms the task of achieving human maturity, Paul applies to himself a new and even more profound description of Sin and its 'reign'. And since this description covers elements common to the existence of all human beings, we must assume that these mechanisms continue to operate even after the arrival of Faith.

In his brief and touching analysis of the divided human being, Paul makes

Sin explicitly responsible for the loss of freedom: i.e., for the incomprehensible distance between the work performed by human beings and the initial intentions of their inner humanity. They cannot see their original, authentic intention in what they actually accomplish. Here again, the inauthenticity and bad faith of the human being is logically implied in the process whereby actual performance unconsciously slips through their fingers and escapes them.

Thus Sin inexorably wipes out the works of human beings. They pass through the universe as if they had never been there as free, creative persons. Death gets a controlling grip on their lives long before they actually die.

Paul adds a new and certainly central element to this explanation of bad faith and the *de facto* loss of human freedom. As a being with freedom, the human person attempts to bend a world with its own laws and mechanisms to human purposes and projects. The 'members' of the human being, its instruments for the carrying out of its projects, already possess their own dynamisms deriving from our first physical nature or our second sociocultural nature. The law of least effort, in a universe where sources of energy are counted, always prevails in the end. A 'corruption' or 'death' lies hidden in the world, and somehow or other it always separates human intention from human performance to some extent.

If the human creature were no more than this, no more than 'Flesh', it would pass by as if it had never existed as a human person vis-à-vis the natural mechanisms of an already created world with its own laws. Death would simply continue to lay its fatal grip on all human actions, whether or not they conformed to the precepts of the Law.

This process of 'corruption' and 'death' in life would be more rapid and fatal, the more the human being focused on self, forgot other human beings, and tried to find security in sacred guarantees. No womb is more secure than the womb of nature and its laws, particularly when we attribute a divine character to those laws and subordinate our freedom to them.

To be carried along that far, of course, human beings must silence their innermost voice, justify their surrender with tangled rationalizations that darken their judgment, and ultimately appeal to a non-existent god (the idol of bad faith) and worship the inhuman.

II

At first glance there does not seem to be a neat opposition between Sin and Faith, even though they seem to alternate as the main themes of Romans 1–8. In our modern languages we would expect Sin to be opposed to Virtue or some other noun of the same sort. Even in Paul's presentation, the more logical opposition would seem to be between Sin as the characteristic of the human being's action and Grace as the characteristic of God's action. Or, in more classical biblical terms, the opposition would seem to be between Sin and Justice as the two basic options facing the human being.

Remember also that in the elaboration of his thought Paul seems to be more concerned with the role of *attitudes*. In terms of the anthropological key he uses, what he calls Sin is a *universal* concept that covers a multitude of particular attitudes. Faith on the other hand, no matter how rich and complex may be the content Paul gives it, remains a *particular* attitude. Now we could say that Sin goes against the will of God because it represents a form of egotism, whatever its object may be. And if that is the case, why not set it over against the attitude that sums up the very will of God, according to both Paul and the gospels: i.e., love?

The point, you see, is that Paul is contrasting *two* basic, anthropological *processes*. And whereas he labels one in terms of its *result* (Sin), he labels the other in terms of its *origin* (Faith). That is the clear meaning of his statement cited earlier in this chapter: "Everything that does not proceed from Faith [origin] is Sin [result]."

In terms of our own modern usage, then, the opposition is perfect. At the origin of the process that produces enslavement to Sin is a crucial factor that we today would call '*bad* faith'. And, not surprisingly, at the origin of the process that leads to Justice is what we would call '*good* Faith'.

What exactly is this thing that Paul calls Faith?[222] Clearly we cannot answer by extracting some definition from a philosophical or theological treatise on the subject. Nor did I take into account the Greek and Pauline use of the term when I tried in Volume I to redefine faith vis-à-vis ideologies through a phenomenological analysis. We shall see that my definition and the ancient use of the term do not coincide neatly.

Philology is not of much help to us here either. Both the Greek noun for faith (*pistis*) and the corresponding verb (*pisteuō*) take in a wide range of attitudes: e.g., accepting things as true that one cannot personally verify (belief), entrusting one's goods or even one's life to another (trust or confidence), and giving up favorable prospects for an unknown future (hope).

We can keep these possibilities in mind, of course, as we seek to understand Paul. But the best course is to pay close attention to his own explanations and applications of the term 'Faith'. Even then we must be careful not to jump to conclusions. As we saw earlier, the latter half of Romans 3 presents Faith in *abstract* terms as opposed to three things, which may or may not come down to the same thing: the Law, works, and works of the Law. There can be no doubt that Faith is opposed to the Law and works of the Law in Paul's eyes. But there is good reason to doubt that Paul sees Faith as opposed to works in general. From other passages we know that Paul sees God passing judgment on the 'work' or 'works' of the human being. The same point is made in the Synoptic Gospels, and that datum undoubtedly goes back to the historical Jesus.[223] So we have good reason to suspect that when Paul opposes Faith to 'works', he is implying 'works of the Law'. In other words, he is referring to *works that are counted up* in order to obtain a legalistic kind of justice.[224] Elsewhere we find explicit passages where Paul, without denying the merciful and gracious nature of God's judgment, has that judgment focusing on the work or works of the human being that were done out of love.

As I noted earlier, however, it is a methodological mistake to begin analyzing Paul's understanding of Faith in those passages where he speaks of it in abstract terms. As is often the case, it is the *concrete* example that best introduces us to the real content of the concept. Paul's example is Abraham, neither Christian nor Jew but a simple human being. The whole of Romans 4 is dedicated to this character, the father of the Israelite people. It is quite clear that Paul is not simply using him to resort to a biblical text for proof that one human being who had 'Faith' was given credit *as if* it were justice, and that this is an isolated example of a particular and special moment. First, Abraham's faith is explicitly defined as *hope* by Paul. Second, it is a hope placed in *a future,* a future that overcomes death. Third, this gratuitous future is not promised to Abraham as a reward or a wage. It is the complete *fulfillment* of his human project, which had been threatened by death: to have descendants and give them the earth as their inheritance. Fourth, death would annul that promise if there did not exist Someone who was capable of calling the human being and its project out of nothingness at the start, and even more importantly, at the finish.

Leaving aside any evaluation of Paul's mode of biblical exegesis in modern terms, we find the example of Abraham to be valuable because it conveys Paul's understanding of *Faith* in a case that has nothing to do with the Law or with any christological content. We are presented with Abraham's Faith as an attitude that was possible before Christ. And insofar as the *result* of that attitude is concerned, Paul situates it in any and all human beings before Christ "whose iniquities have been pardoned and whose sins have been covered up" (4:7).

In my commentary I have already given the reasons for the exegetical alternative I chose.[225] I mentioned Paul's anthropological key, his other writings of the same period, and the gospel roots of his christology. All those things suggest that the content of Faith, as understood by Paul, is compatible with the situation of any and every human being both before and after Christ.

Going back to the faith of Abraham and its concrete content, we see in it what I have chosen to call a *transcendent datum.* This one is clearly tailored to fit the average human being. It is imprecise and far from fully worked out, particularly in terms of its foundations and guarantees. Expressed in general terms, it is the assertion that *loving is worthwhile,* whatever it may cost in self-giving and even death. By the same token, it is not worthwhile to live in constant anxiety about death and keep worrying about oneself.

It is a 'hope against all hope', wagering on a future that verifiable experience seems to belie. Such a future can only come from Someone who values, more than anything else in the universe, the hostages created by love's projects and works, by true self-giving no matter how imperfect it may be. Here we have all the components that Paul includes in the *Faith* of Abraham.

Now we are in a position to move from Paul's concrete example to his abstract use of the expression 'Faith in Jesus Christ'. We find that the content of the latter is the very same *transcendent datum,* accessible to all humans from the very start but this time spelled out in terms of the message, life, death, and resurrection of Jesus of Nazareth.

The very beginning of Romans 5 focuses on what the Christian alone *knows* and how this is to have an impact on behavior: "Having been declared just by reason of Faith . . . we glory even in our afflictions, *knowing* that . . . the hope is not delusory . . ." (5:1-5).[226] It is not without reason that Romans 4, dedicated mainly to Abraham, ends with a reference to 'us Christians', "who have Faith in the One who raised from the dead Jesus our Lord" (4:24).

Moreover, the guarantee for this transcendent datum does not lie solely in the eschatological triumph of love that was lived in the paschal experiences. Even more importantly, it lies in taking cognizance of the *moment* when the hostage mechanism began to operate historically: "If we were reconciled with God while still God's enemies by the death of his Son . . ." (5:10). It is crucially important, you see, that the transcendent datum take into account the point made clear in Romans 7: even Christians cannot wholly escape the mechanisms of Sin. Some might logically think that this weakens the force of the transcendent datum, that our sins can therefore invalidate the redemption that has been promised and realized. Not so, argues Paul. The great Promise was made and carried out while human beings were under the bondage of Sin. Thus the price paid by the hostage includes any human sin whatsoever.

It is precisely after Paul has explored the mechanisms of Sin still operative in the Christian (7:14-25) that he moves on in Romans 8 to examine the content and impact of the transcendent datum as it is explicitated and reaffirmed in the Christian Faith. Note, however, that he does not explicitly mention the term 'Faith' in this treatment.

(1). Paul adds two new reasons to reinforce his transcendent datum. They increase the value of the hostage, guarantee its liberation, and thereby guarantee the infallibility of our hope.

Paul's first argument is that if Sin managed to alienate all human works, then nothing less than the entire universe would fail to achieve its intrinsic purpose. It would be a total failure in itself and for God, and all its mechanisms would have functioned in vain. Nothing would remain but the mute pangs of a birth that was stillborn. Death in the fullest sense would prevail. All the projects of life would sink into corruption and uselessness. Death would wipe out humanity and its works; and God, the Creator, would end up a failure.[227]

Paul's second argument, closely related to the first, expresses God's plan in a different way. The infallibility of the hope placed in love is linked in a different way with the success of the divine plan. What God 'decided in advance' was that Jesus, God's Son, was to be 'the firstborn of many [i.e., all] brothers and sisters', so that the latter would 'reflect the image of his Son'. Now Paul himself may not have had in mind the image of the Son creating the universe, but the 'reflection' in question must include what it did in the case of Abraham: i.e., actually inheriting the world. The human being is to be 'lord of everything'. So God's plan for the universe cannot be successful until his children are manifested as such, until 'the freedom . . . of God's children' is made manifest. And in Paul's eyes this freedom, which is not simply free will, will not exist so long as any *de facto* separation between intention and performance systematically alienates all human creation in favor of an impersonal universe.

(2). A transcendent datum already present in humanity is thus made explicit in Christ, and this explicitation alters the force of the datum in each and every human being.[228] Both before and after Christ this force or power was a gift of God: Grace. Paul gives it the classical biblical name of *Spirit*. To be sure, humanity was never abandoned to its *Flesh*, its purely human condition. But with Christ the gift becomes a conscious, reasoned force or power, crossing the threshold of reflection.

That is why the anthropological fruit of the Spirit is 'joy and peace'. In the deeper logic of existence that is what follows from the basic transcendent datum as reaffirmed in Christ. In 'living according to the Spirit', we avoid the mistaken path of egocentric 'fear' for our own salvation and the waste of energy involved in keeping a moral scorecard of our actions. We thus can concentrate the power of our 'inner humanity' on its projects, investing in them some of the 'desires' or 'cravings' that would otherwise fall prey to the 'law of the members' and the easy way out. This helps to prevent them from undermining the creative freedom of the human being and putting distance between human intention and actual accomplishment.

Of course we cannot expect the Spirit to supplant the Flesh. Faith does not and cannot effect a perfect match between intention and performance. Only the Creator succeeds in doing that with a world evoked out of nothingness— which is another way of saying *the Creator's* world. Thanks to Faith, the power of the Spirit reduces the distance between human intention and human performance. Through 'hope' rather than actual sight, the human being knows that some part of its works belongs to it; that it has built something that has stood the test of fire and will bear its name and stamp in the definitive creation; that this something would not be there if it were not for his or her effort, and it is now forever free from corruption and the frustration of uselessness.[229]

III

What, then, is the final picture of human existence that Paul paints in the light of Christ?

The *first* problem, one to which we have already alluded, has to do with the situation of human beings who apparently are not under the light of Christ: human beings separated from Christ by insuperable barriers of time (those living in the past before Christ) or barriers to comprehension (those living in the present or the future).

We know that Paul's analysis of the human being was done in the light of the Christ event, even though his key was certainly anthropological. He is interested in human existence as it is affected by knowledge of the events centered around the earthly and eschatological life of Jesus. So if we want to know something about the possibilities and realities of human existence when it has no apparent or conscious relationship with those events, we must explore the *implicit* thinking of Paul. And we must focus especially on Romans 4, 5, and 8.

Abraham, Christ's victory over Adam, and the usefulness of all creation as something recovered by human freedom are key elements. They tell us of a possibility, gratuitous but not for that reason rare, open to the gift given by God to *all* Christ's brothers and sisters. In its 'consequences' it will win out over the consequences of Sin in all the descendants of Adam. But Paul is not so clear in spelling out the how and when of this gift.

The antithetical parallel between Adam and Christ seems to offer us the solution we are looking for. Adam affected all human beings *when* he sinned and *because* he sinned; Christ affected all human beings *when* and *because* he obeyed the Father by giving his life for human beings. Other Pauline passages suggest the same thing.

I have already indicated the difficulty we moderns have with this picture. The legendary figure, Adam, is supposed to have had a causal impact on all his descendants, but such causality has to be of the magical and mythical sort. Paul seems to have noticed the difficulty to some extent. The effect of Adam's sin is depicted by him as *inaugural* rather than causal. After Adam "all sinned," says Paul, undoubtedly on their own.

But however magical and mythical Adam's influence may seem to be, it is exercised in the right direction at least. It affects those human beings who come after him in the course of time and biological causality. Such is not the case with Christ's causality. To be equated with Adam's causality, that of Christ must work *backwards* to a large extent. The parallelism would not exist, much less favor Christ, unless it were certain that from Adam to Jesus "where Sin abounded, Grace abounded even more" (5:20). So if Adam's influence on his natural successors seems magical, Christ's influence on his predecessors is even more magical in nature.

In principle, of course, we cannot deny God the possibility of bypassing the laws God himself inscribed in the bosom of the universe. But in an age when the miraculous was taken much more for granted in religious thinking, Paul himself was very cautious about appealing to God for direct explanations that explain nothing, that merely attribute what has to be explained to some mysterious divine action. His anthropological key may have urged such caution on him, at least to some extent.[230]

On the other hand Paul could not get beyond certain limitations in the thinking of his day, particularly its fixist view of the universe and creation. The prevailing conception of an instantaneous creation, effected once and for all, weighs heavily on Paul's anthropology. It forces him, for example, to place on Adam the responsibility for a human condition (a Flesh) that could not possibly have come that way from the hands of the Creator. Yet, as we have seen, Paul is not wholly insensitive to the lack of categories that might express his thinking more suitably. Indeed his treatment of the relationship between the 'sin' of Adam and that of 'all his successors' is much more fluid and complex than the treatment to be found in the vast majority of Christian theologians who have come after him.

The same basic problem shows up even more clearly with regard to his treatment of Christ's influence. Christ's reach is at least as universal as that of Adam. That means that Jesus should have been the first human being and, in fact, Paul says he was! Paul knows very well that God "did not spare even his own beloved Son, but handed him over for all of us" at a specific moment in history. Yet he does not hesitate to state that the Son of God is "the firstborn of many [all] brothers and sisters."

Today we possess some of the categories that might be more suitable for the expression of Paul's thought. One important thought category is that of an *evolutionary* creation. It enables us to appreciate Paul's tour de force in attributing *two different times* of existence and causality to one and the same reality, Christ: the time of absolute beginning and the time of a specific irruption into history.

Insofar as the first time is concerned, our present-day category of evolutionary creation enables us to say that the human being came on the scene, from the very first moment of its existence, with the 'Flesh' that always characterizes it. By the same token, however, that category also obliges us to say that the human being, as a being destined to be brother or sister of the Son of God, came on the scene with the 'Spirit'. In some primordial form that Spirit, from the very beginning, made possible the saving and liberating attitude known as Faith. The witness to this fact is Abraham, although the transcendent datum involved here would be spelled out and confirmed in a specific historical event at a later date.[231]

That brings us to our *second* problem. Even if we assume the complete adhesion of the human being to Faith in the correct Christian sense, wherein lies Christ's victory over Sin insofar as concrete human existence is concerned?

Everything that has gone before should prepare us for a complex answer from Paul. Indeed it is in the complexity of his answer that we find his greatest originality and profundity as a thinker.[232]

Gradually the simplistic eschatology that first structured Paul's thinking about Christ came to be transformed from within, although Paul himself may not always have noticed this from the outside. It became a complex eschatology crying out for evolutionary categories, which of course were not available at that time. In this respect it is quite likely, in my opinion, that the process undergone by Paul was akin to that which Jesus himself went through in his awareness of the coming of the kingdom of God. Both began by focusing on the imminent arrival of that moment, sharing the common expectations of their milieu. But on a deeper level both creatively laid the bases for a far more complex, long-term understanding of history and its function in their eschatology.

In any case we are at the limits of Paul's explicit thinking. All we can do now is pull together disparate elements and see how they work in terms of their own inner logic. That logic is sufficiently clear, I think, to guarantee the fidelity of any conclusions we may draw.

At various points in Romans, and particularly in Romans 8, we notice that

Paul takes things from two different planes of reality and categorizes them all as 'real'. The two planes, of course, are that of the *invisible* and that of the *manifest*.

Faith, Paul tells us, is an attitude of 'hope'; and we 'cannot see' what we are hoping for. If our attitude is one of hope, it is precisely because of the invisibility of what we affirm and stake our lives on. Paul uses many different formulations to express what we are hoping for, but they all dovetail by analogy with what we saw to be the content of Faith in Abraham.

This means we cannot *see* our status as 'children of God' and hence 'inheritors of the world'. We cannot see the effective achievements of our freedom putting an end to the impersonality, Death, and 'uselessness' of the universe. Nor can we see any assurance of the final, victorious unity of our 'inner humanity' and 'the law of the members'.

Even after Christ, the plane of the *manifest* continues to operate 'against all hope'. All we have to go on is the *transcendent datum* on the ultimate possibilities of human existence that was revealed and corroborated in Jesus. It gives us the 'joy and peace' that on certain occasions enables us to suspect that our human work can resist the onslaughts of Sin better than we might think.

What is needed, then, is another plane that is equally dynamic but also positive. This plane is characterized by the 'manifestation' of that which was hidden and invisible on the other plane: i.e., of the 'glory', not of the children of God, but of 'the *freedom* of the children of God'. Thanks to God's judgment, our work of 'cooperating' in 'God's building up' will be tested by the 'quality' of its own inner dynamism and will successfully pass to the plane of the visible.

This 'becoming visible' is eschatological, so it has to do directly with metahistory. But it has to do equally with the hidden dimension of history here and now. The 'manifestation' should not be taken to mean that we are going to exchange historical reality for another, non-historical reality. Instead it means that we are going to see how suprahistorical life is ultimately injected into what has been accomplished *in history*. As Paul puts it, we do not want to be stripped of this life but to have something put on over it, "so that what is mortal may be absorbed by life" (2 Cor 5:5).

The glory of God and the defense of the Absolute do not entail relativizing historical reality in order to make room for the irruption of God alone.[233] The glory of God means seriously making human beings sharers in a joint construction project and giving them all they need to offer this cooperation, without which God alone will do nothing. The personal, creative stamp of each one of these human cooperators (*synergoi* in Greek) with God will be tested and verified in love, in 'mutual service'. Then it will be inserted in the definitive reality, in the only way that a finite freedom can do that: i.e., by hammering away, like the chisel of a sculptor, at the stubborn solidity of the resistant materials, but with the invisible hope that those materials will be overcome and to some extent turned into God's new heaven and humanity's new earth, the new creation as the joint work of Father and children.

IV

Can we go further still in Paul's christology without going beyond the period in which Romans was written? Can we find any additional new elements in that letter concerning the significance that Paul attributes to Jesus insofar as human existence is concerned?

The answer would have to be 'no', if going further means adopting the frequent procedure of 'christologies' and adding data from other christological efforts in the New Testament or elsewhere. Let me reiterate my reasons for not adopting that approach, which have nothing to do with mere 'Pauline purism' or a reluctance to mix different thoughts and sources for purely historical reasons. I am interested *solely* in Paul and his view of the Christ event for two basic and closely related reasons.

The first reason was brought up in my General Introduction at the start of Volume II. Such efforts to mix data implicitly or explicitly aim at *completing and ending* the interpretation of Jesus, however humbly they may go about their task. Christologies tend to bring together all that was thought and said about Jesus in the most authoritative sources or, within the Scriptures, in the New Testament.

By contrast with that sort of christological effort and intent, I described my own effort as an *anti-christology*. My aim has been to lay bare the mechanics of a couple of christologies, to learn a creative methodology, to learn how to do christology today. Of no use to us for this purpose are intermingled christologies which provide only data, in which we cannot see the original way in which the data were arrived at.[234]

The second reason is less pragmatic, but it is more relevant with regard to accurate knowledge of christological materials. The mixing of data from different christologies, each with its own key, does not contribute to the task of interpreting the significance that Jesus of Nazareth had, and can have today, for the human being. Quite the contrary, it reduces that significance.

As I have indicated earlier, not everything in the New Testament is of equal depth and balance. The conclusions drawn from Jesus' resurrection in the Acts of the Apostles are historically important, but they are less balanced and profound than the conclusions which Paul drew from the very same paschal experiences. A christology from above was imposed too quickly in Acts. However justified it may be in principle, it invaded to excess the christology from below that had been lived before Easter and that centered around the project of Jesus rather than his own person. So if we were to combine christological data from Paul's central period with data from the Jerusalem Church in Acts, our resultant christology would be impoverished rather than enriched.

An even better example, I think, is intermixing the Pauline and Johannine conceptions of the resurrection. John's profound view of Jesus' resurrection is undoubtedly superior to the reaction provided by the Acts of the Apostles. So why not add to Paul's view such Johannine statements as the following: "I am the resurrection and the life. One who believes in me, even if he or she dies, will come to life. And everyone who is alive and believes in me will never die at all" (Jn 11:25–26).

The point here is that Johannine thought has its own proper logic, which follows from its own proper key.[235] It is consistently apparent in the opposition, somehow connected with Platonic culture, between the false and fleeting world offered to our senses and the immobile, eternal, 'true' world of ideas and the divine. Thus, when Jesus says 'I am the resurrection and the life', he is saying something about a divine world present in himself. In Johannine thought that conception, far from dovetailing with Paul's christology and directly enriching it, is undermining something crucial and central in it: i.e., the relationship between resurrection and victory over Sin *in history*.

Going further in the thought of Paul, then, does not mean going outside his own thought. My concern is to see other ideas that might be undeveloped or merely implicit in his thinking, and to work them out a bit.

I have already suggested that some of the implicitness is due, not to Paul's anthropological key and the need for other keys to unlock him, but to the limitations of his own era. Until very recent years, as even contemporary existentialism proves, almost all analyses of human existence have stressed the strange and unique place of human beings and their destiny in the panoply of nature.[236] Moreover, the fuller implications of Paul's thought will be brought out more clearly in Volume V, where they properly belong. So the following remarks may be regarded as hints and suggestions.

Paul situates human existence on two planes: one visible and dominated by Sin, in which there is a greater distance between human intention and human accomplishment; the other invisible and lived by Faith, where the distance between intention and accomplishment is narrowed. Faith sees what we ourselves cannot see. In short, Faith represents a change in our *epistemological premises*, in the way we see, know, and interpret the sequence of events in our own history.[237]

How does Paul view this sequence insofar as it embodies a progressive development in human existence? He sees it as a battlefield, on which an *accumulation* of one sort fights unsuccessfully against an *emergence* of another sort. Paul pictures human existence without illusions. Even after Christ and Faith, the vast majority of our works follow the 'natural' course toward the easy way out. They are caught in the mechanisms that separate intention from performance.

Yet how can Paul or we ourselves close our eyes to the other side of the picture? In our own lives, in the lives of a few outstanding figures, and perhaps even in the life of every human being if we knew the whole picture, there *emerges* something that is profoundly human and personal, that marks a meaningful investment of giving oneself and one's life. If Paul is correct in saying that 'mutual service' is the mark of freedom, which reduces the distance between intention and performance, how can we fail to recognize it when it surfaces in countless different forms and degrees?

Now if both antithetical things were on the same plane, the majority preponderance of the former would clearly end up winning out over the latter. In that case our verdict of victory would have to go to that which escapes human control, to that which Paul calls Sin. Mutual service, self-giving, and love might seem to win momentary victories, but soon it would become apparent that the law of the members was at work to ensure corruption and death instead of victory. We could have sworn that the world would never be the same, yet the impersonal seems to move in and take over once again.

But the *transcendent datum* spelled out to us by Paul in countless ways, all of them based on the significance of Jesus of Nazareth as he sees it, is the paradoxical one that the reasons of our heart are, in fact, reasonable and right. What accumulates, in fact, is what is emerging. And if that is the case, then where, O Death, is your victory?

Paul makes clear to us that accumulation and emergence *are not on the same plane*. The plane of the definitive accumulates *only* what is free: i.e., love. That which accumulates impersonally and seems to destroy love fails to do so and ends up destroying itself. Our hope is not delusory because a single act of love wins out over the multitude (i.e., totality) of Sin. This explains the 'more' in Christ's victory over Adam.

Here, then, we have the plan of God in Jesus as at least implied in Paul's thinking. Let us stop for a moment and ask ourselves how *we* would have planned things. Without thinking for a moment, we would find it easy to improve God's plan and correct God's world! But we should stop and consider certain things.

Only an unfinished world, entrusted to humanity in a way that entails suffering and death, can give irreplaceable and definitive value to human responsibility, to the human hands that are completing creation as they fight against all the painful elements that affect God himself. Only thus can we all bear in our hands the destiny of all, including the destiny of God himself who chose to fraternize with us.

Only a world in which Sin can accumulate and become Law, as meaningless in itself as Death is, can prevent the accomplishments of one generation from diminishing the importance and decisive character of the next generation. If Sin were quantitatively overcome as humanity advanced in history, then human beings would become useless and wander in vain about the world. We need a world in which creation, love, and life triumph qualitatively, transforming reality irreversibly without ever escaping the quantitative victory of Sin. Only such a world can make human existence worthwhile, can put Faith in the human heart as energy concentrated on its committed involvement in history, and all the power of God in its inner creativity as child of God.

If we let these elements take on their true, deeper dimensions within us, then we should be able to grasp the essentials of Paul's 'gospel', the 'good news' he wishes to share with us in his interpretation of the meaning and significance of Jesus.

Paul's Key and Latin America Today

I do not intend to go back over my reasons for choosing the anthropological key to interpret Paul's christology. Readers have sufficient data now to make their own judgment. When all is said and done, the most reliable test of a 'key' is precisely what it opens, its capacity to explain, not what is easy, but what is difficult. And surely Paul's thought is difficult.

I am not unsympathetic to many serious arguments presented by Krister Stendhal for a different key in Paul, one based on Paul's concern to ground his own mission, to justify his admission of converted pagans to full membership in the Christian community on the basis of Faith alone. But I would reject the extreme conclusions drawn from this hypothesis: i.e., that Paul's existential analysis is merely the result of the Occidental penchant for introspection.

Introspection is not something that has been stuck on Paul from outside, of course. It is clearly present in him. Moreover, there is no good reason to deny that it was largely inspired by his missionary intention. At the same time we must not forget that the right of converted pagans to membership in the Christian community was not a mere question of lawful right. It presupposed a whole christology, without which it could not be established. In short, we are still left with the problem of knowing what key Paul used to interpret the significance of Jesus of Nazareth, whether or not his ultimate aim was to defend the access of pagans to Christianity.

In this appendix my concern is with a twofold problem that is intimately bound up with a creative christology. I want to consider the limitations and the timeliness of an anthropological key in trying to do christology, both in general and in terms of a particular context such as that of Latin America. The first aspect of the problem entails a comparison with Volume II, where we examined the history of Jesus of Nazareth with a political key. The second aspect has to do with situating Paul's anthropological key in terms of our own present-day circumstances.

I

Need I repeat again that the application of a political key to the historical life of Jesus in no way is meant to detract from his possible character as revelation

161

from God? I am simply specifying the kind of language or idiom, meant in the broad sense, that he used for that revelation.

In examining the life of Jesus we can take into account two things: the values-system he chose to reveal as forming part of the heart of his God and Father, and of the latter's plan for humanity; and the theoretical and practical *means* Jesus used to posit those values in the concrete, visible reality of Palestine during his lifetime. If we take those two things into account, then the life of Jesus shows up in all its meaning, the meaning which Jesus himself gave it, but also in *all its limitedness*.

Viewed by itself, apart from Old Testament tradition, that life comes across to us as a beautiful and tragic human adventure, but no more than that. It hardly seems to be the greatest or the only one of its kind.

Like any language forced to use elements from human experience, the one dealing with the historical deeds of Jesus is limited. Note that it has nothing to do with the fact that we interpreted those deeds and events in a political key. If I am not mistaken, the historical Jesus himself wanted to be interpreted in that key; and any other key would have posed the same problem. To be informative and meaningful for us, it would have to tell us something limited, something important in some specific sector of our existence and relative to a fixed context.

I have already had occasion to show that all efforts to forget such limitations are fallacious. Far from giving more importance and significance to Jesus, they strip him of substance and render him even more defenseless before the onslaughts of time.

We are told, for example, that Jesus is 'the man for others', the supreme example of altruism and its possibilities. Wittingly or unwittingly, such a statement is nothing more than a fatal misunderstanding.

Let me prove this with an example that might seem ridiculous, if not downright irreverent, but that does throw a lot of light on the question. If we are talking about the supreme example of 'the man for others', then Immanuel Kant would surpass Jesus Christ. His philosophy is concerned with all human beings equally. His categorical imperative is the same for all human beings of whatever religion, race, or culture. His prohibition against using any person as a mere means demonstrates how far a thinker can go in positive regard for *all* other humans.

I can hear indignant voices being raised to remind me that there is no real comparison possible between the prodigal beneficent activity of Jesus and the methodical coldness of Kant. And of course we must admit that Kant did not die for the sake of those human beings whom his thought sought to defend.

At the same time it must be noted that we cannot thereby verify the *subjective* seriousness of these two commitments. Methodical and cold as it was, Kant's commitment might still have been total. He might well have been ready to give up his life for his humanitarian thought but found no one ready to kill him for it.

It is on the *objective* plane that the comparison can and should be made. If

Kant did not die for his ideas, the reason was that his ideas did not upset anyone enought to get him assassinated for them. If on the other hand Jesus *was* politically tried and condemned to death, the reason was in inverse proportion to the 'universality' or 'unlimitedness' of his message. He was assassinated for taking sides in a real, effective way. He was for some and against others. His options were limited and hence conflictive. Jesus was 'the man of Israel for the poor of Israel'. In short, his divine revelation has an impact on us because of the *ideology* that incarnates it, that puts limited, three-dimensional human *flesh* on it.[238]

This implies two things that run counter to our usual and routine thinking. (1) Even for the Christian, the words and deeds of Christ are not *values* in themselves but *means* to signify and realize values; and as means, they must be judged *in terms of a specific context*, in terms of their historically situated effectiveness. If someone were to do 'the same thing' that Jesus did in a different context, he or she would be seriously mistaken to think that the action was thereby guided by the significance and import of Jesus' life. In that sense we can say that a Christian is not someone who *generalizes* the means used by Jesus to fight for the poor and marginalized of Israel. (2) The relevance and uniqueness of Jesus are not rooted in the perennial or immutable nature of his concrete ideology. And that is not so merely because we interpreted him in a *political* key on the basis of the documents we possess. Any key would have brought out the same ideological component.

It is obvious that our fund of knowledge about the effectiveness of the means at our disposal in nature or society can keep growing indefinitely. Since the time of Jesus there is bound to have been new means and more exact and complex information about the way certain means operate. So it makes no sense to try to prove the perduring superiority of Jesus of Nazareth in political matters, or in any other key used to express the significance of his message and life; and the point holds even if one tries to prove his superiority by appealing to his divinity. It is not just that any person today can know more about how to realize similar values. On the basis of our present fund of knowledge, somebody today could reasonably claim that he or she could have acted more effectively on behalf of those values *in Jesus' own context*. Just as a surgeon today, for example, could say that he or she could have saved the lives of many appendicitis victims in Jesus' day.

There is no irreverence in such comparisons. What *is* irreverent is refusing to make such comparisons, absolutizing the means used by Jesus, and thereby stripping them of all historical substance. For Jesus implemented certain means to flesh out in history certain values, values that revealed God's view and judgmental evaluation of what was going on.[239]

The above remarks should hold true for Paul's christology as well, but let us go back over them insofar as Paul's thought involves a change of key.

We get the impression that the key used by Paul largely overcomes the limitations of the political key used by the historical Jesus. Jesus' key forced him to get involved in conflicts dividing groups of human beings and to use means (ideologies) that framed his activity in a context specified by those conflicts. While this heightened his concrete significance, it also undermined its universality. The opposite seems to be true of Paul's anthropological key. It comes across as something valid for every human being in any context.

To some extent at least, this is true. Notice the way Paul addresses himself to slaves within the Christian community. Because slaves are *human beings*, the humanitarian and humanizing revolution proposed by Paul's christology is open to them. Maturity, anthropological freedom, and the gifts of the Spirit that transform a person into a new being are all within the reach of the slave as well as the free person in Greco-Roman society. The *significance* of Jesus Christ has thoroughly demolished the wall separating human beings in terms of the societal antithesis between slave and free.

Framing his ideas in terms of concrete history, we gain a better understanding of one point that has made it harder for people to appreciate Paul's thought. Indeed his view of the issue seems to put him poles apart from Jesus' commitment to the poor. Paul counsels slaves to remain such![240]: "Everyone should remain in the condition God's call found them. Were you a slave when you were called? *Don't let that bother you.* Even if you could gain your freedom, *make the most of your condition as slave instead.* For a person who received the Lord's call while a slave, is a *freed person of the Lord . . .*" (1 Cor 7:20–22).

The first thing we begin to realize is that the anthropological key is not a device to separate the significance of Jesus from its 'ideological' limitations. Paul is faced with a problem of efficacy, a concrete, limited option, an energy calculus. If the 'preoccupation' of the slave is to win civil liberation and he or she invests energy in doing that, Paul thinks that the cost is too high in terms of humanization.

We may tend to be blinded by the context of Jesus, where people were waiting for the kingdom of God and where the social structures corresponded to a specific religious interpretation. We may fail to see that the context has changed in Paul's case, and that the *power* at Jesus' disposal has pretty much disappeared. To *copy* or mimic what Jesus said to the poor of Israel in talking to the slaves of the Roman Empire would be to commit a sin of 'idealism'. Paul, too, makes a choice; and of course his choice has its limitations. Taking into account the transforming instruments that are really at his disposal, Paul opts to humanize the slave from within, with a conception of his or her human existence [241] that already provides the slave with all the freedom and maturity compatible with that social condition. We must also realize that his dictum, 'in Christ there is neither slave nor free person', was not merely a short-term consolation for a situation that could not be changed. In medium and long-range terms it marked the establishment of an ideal that would reach to the very structures of society and change them, so that they would accord with the principle practiced within the Christian community. I shall return to this point when I compare different possible christological keys for the specific problems of Latin America.

The second thing we now begin to realize is that the different keys, assuming they are faithful to the message and original data of Jesus of Nazareth, do not exclude or negate each other.

Paul's advice to slaves does not negate the commitment of Jesus and his disciples to cooperate with God in the coming of a kingdom that will do away with the inhuman situation of the poor. Paul's advice is not an endorsement of slavery, nor is it even neutral vis-à-vis slavery. If Christian freedom lies in loving service to each other, if in Christ there is no longer any difference between slave and free person, if each is to live and act on behalf of others and not put *obstacles* of any sort in their way, then all that *virtually* implies the abolition of slavery as a societal structure.

Some readers might say that Paul postpones indefinitely commitment to the concrete sociopolitical cause, but the qualifier 'indefinitely' is unsatisfactory. He does indeed postpone it in fact, in the circumstances that he faces and that he cannot change. He postpones it, it seems certain to me, after doing some calculation; and in that calculation he considers the means available or not available to him on the one hand, and the values he seeks to realize on the other. Every key needs an *ideology*, a calculated system of efficacy.

The third thing we begin to realize is that Paul's anthropological key only *seems* to be less limited than the political key of Jesus of Nazareth. Limitedness, you see, is not peculiarly characteristic of the political realm, as is mistakenly thought by those who try to minimize the political key of Jesus' history *in the name of the universal and unlimited nature of his message*. To put it in terms we often hear today, they mistakenly want to *free the interpretation of Jesus from ideologies*.

The fact is that no key can free a message transmitted in history from its ideological limitations. The key can only point up where those limitations are most visible.

As we have already seen, Paul's limitations show up in the instruments available to him for his analysis. He lacks certain ones that would have been useful in analyzing the process of human life, its mechanisms and tendencies, and the impact that Jesus' revelation could or should have on all that.

I don't think there is any doubt that among the New Testament writers John shows his age more than Paul. Nor is there any solid doubt about certain characteristics of John's christological key. However much the origin and roots of his thinking are to be found in the Hebrew world and the Old Testament, as we see in the analogous case of Philo, it seems obvious that John is trying to address himself to adversaries or interlocutors who are Greek, and whose cultural level is higher than those to whom the letters of Paul are addressed. This prompts the Johannine writer to introduce into his key presuppositions that are more or less directly Platonic in origin.

Now if anything has grown dated as an instrument of understanding certainly the categories of Platonic philosophy have. I might also add that insofar as Christian circles today preserve, read, enjoy, and believe they understand the fourth gospel, it is in inverse proportion to their knowledge of its real key, or at least of major elements in that key.

Paul has enjoyed more good fortune, if you will. But as I have already suggested, it would be a false good fortune if people assumed that the survival of many of his categories turned his christology into an atemporal system, hence a *timely and up-to-date* interpretation of Jesus for today that dispensed us from the creative work of fashioning our own christologies.

Leaving aside that extreme, we can say that Paul stands the test of time very well, despite his many obscurities. This is certainly true of the letters of his major period. Once we get beyond the barriers of a language that seems strange at first sight, and a logic that is confusing until we recognize its dialectical character, Paul's analysis of human existence proves to be extraordinarily modern. That is no small achievement for a man whose letters were written almost two thousand years ago.

It is quite likely, for example, that many readers have noticed the similarity of certain Pauline themes to central themes of psychoanalysis that touch upon the anthropological level.[242] Often in the course of my commentary I have resisted the temptation to establish clearcut tie-ins between Pauline notions (the Law, inner humanity, cravings, Sin, Death and Life, etc.) and others that are part of our common culture today in the realm of individual and social psychology (ego, superego, instinctive unconscious, repression, death instinct, Eros, etc.).

This curious *modernity* of Paul calls for two basic comments, two warnings against two possible misunderstandings that would undo the work of this volume.

First, we must not base the value of Paul's christology on any false enthusiasm aroused by its seeming tie-ins with modern *ideologies* on the anthropological level.

It is obvious, to begin with, that psychoanalysis is not one coherent bloc. Its scientific status is debated, at least in terms of its scope and extent. Not all its schools, particularly the more 'orthodox' ones, would agree with the principal elements of Paul's anaylsis. The point to remember here is that Freud began with a therapeutic practice and from there attempted to systematize the corresponding anthropological, metapsychological conceptions. If that provided room for a certain encounter with Paul, it did so in the more ambivalent and fluctuating realms of Freudian thought: i.e., in the looser and more or less heterodox Freudianism of people like Fromm, Marcuse, and Ricoeur.

Now there is nothing to indicate that in any encounter between Freudianism and Paul's thought, the latter will come off well. Even if believers regard Paul's presentation as a 'divine revelation', this does not mean that it will come away with the prize. Categories more precise and subtle than Paul's may come along to provide us with more complete and satisfying elements of analysis. We may come up with practical methodologies that are more effective in the struggle for freer and more mature human beings.

Back in Volume I we saw that it was a mistake to assume that our politics did not need Marx or any other ideology because we already possessed Jesus and the gospel message. The same point holds true here. It is a mistake to assume that Christians do not need Freud or the psychological ideology known as psychoanalysis because they have Paul.

Second, we must make sure we know where the value of Paul's christology lies. Paul must be placed once again *within the process of learning to learn* that is embodied in the Judeo-Christian biblical tradition. We then see that his prime importance does not lie in the possibility that even after two thousand years he can outdo any ideology competing or dovetailing with the key used by him. Instead it lies in the fact that Paul, with his key and his place in the biblical process, offers us invaluable transcendent data for living the anthropological faith that has been handed down to us by the chain of witnesses.

It is not a matter of creating a psychoanalytic therapy based on Paul, though we cannot say such a thing is impossible in principle. That is not where Paul's specific contribution lies. Both in its therapeutic and its anthropological versions, psychoanalysis is an ideology that explores the inner, non-individual world of the human being in the pursuit of psychic health. But psychic health itself is conceived in as many different ways as the various transcendent data held, usually tacitly, by psychoanalytic practitioners.

It is here that Paul's christological thought becomes important, even though his analysis may be regarded as obsolete by comparison with that of others. His christology as such will not be applied to evaluate the achievements of psychoanalytic therapy. The task is instead a creative one. Taking advantage of the opening on both sides—the anthropological thought of psychoanalysis and the affinity of certain Pauline categories—we can proceed to evaluate both and let them enrich each other.

Of course therapeutic findings need not be directly tied to the transcendent data of a 'spiritual tradition' (Machoveč's term for this process of learning to learn). But since no objective investigation of reality is neutral, neither can such findings be closed off *a priori* from such transcendent data. At the very least people must be open to discussing the transcendent data that they have already accepted, perhaps unconsciously, in the course of their 'scientific' investigation. And the mutual enrichment will not come by repeating Paul in his categories of two thousand years ago, or by reducing him to a 'pre-Freud'.

In short, we cannot 'rest' in Paul, as he claimed his adversaries were 'resting' in the Law. Nor can we 'glory' in Paul. He himself would be the first to warn us that his thought is 'human', hence subject to the erosion of time and the ambiguity of the cultures that incarnate his thinking.

I hope readers will pardon me for repeating points that I made at the start of Volume II. But I feel that, by comparison with the apparent *soberness* of the historical Jesus, the soaring and seemingly atemporal anthropology of Paul's treatment of Jesus justified these reminders.

II

There is no great temptation to take Paul's christological key as the only valid one. We are tempted to do just the opposite, to discard it because it does not respond to the authentic questions of human beings living in Latin America. I have no desire to conceal the fact that this work was thought out in dialogue with specific human beings long before it was put in writing.

As my readers know, this book is not meant to be a book of *theology*. Indeed I see a terrible mistake and misunderstanding in a fact that is taken for granted in our culture: i.e., the fact that the significance of Jesus of Nazareth *for humanity* has become the monopoly of esoteric experts in religion, as if theology and its apparatus were the only or chief way to arrive at Jesus' significance. But even granting that should not be the case, we cannot disregard the *fait accompli* and its consequences. One such consequence has to do with the situation in Latin America today. The christology concerned with studying and making known the human significance of Jesus of Nazareth is intimately bound up with *theology*, more specifically with the theology directly involved with the critical reality of our continent that has come to be known as the *theology of liberation*.

This is not the place for a full, formal exposition of liberation theology. Here I simply want to touch upon those aspects that can shed light on the way the significance of Christ is conveyed to Latin Americans by liberation theology, as opposed to the ways theology used in the past to transmit christology to our continent. To put it in a nutshell: liberation theology is closely bound up with the keys used in these volumes to unlock the meaning of the historical Jesus and Paul's christology. Indeed liberation theology may go so far as to pass judgment on those keys.

Past theology, mislabelled 'classical', placed the emphasis on ultramundane salvation. Liberation theology has shifted the emphasis back to history and tasks of humanization. In its view the liberation of human beings from an infrahuman condition, at least on the Latin American continent, must come to grips with the most crucial factor accounting for that condition: national and international political structures. Thus there has been an ever increasing tendency, not always well balanced, to cast in *political* molds the content of theology, including theology dealing with Jesus.

The age-old mechanics of theology, an esoteric discipline to most lay people, required that this shift of emphasis be justified. Naturally enough, this justification adopted two lines of argument: historical reasoning and the Bible.

The first argument noted the growing interdependence of humanity insofar as communications, economics, and politics had taken on a planetary scale. Given this situation, and apart from any explicit biblical data, the one Christian commandment of love simply had to be implemented *more and more* through political mediations, if it was to be real and effective. Moreover, theology as interpretation of the faith could not disregard this inevitable transformation by simply repeating formulas from the past (formulas drawn from a much more private, intimate, 'spiritual' context) and linking faith to the same sort of problems associated with it in the New Testament, for example.[243]

The second argument, based on the Bible, looked back at the start of the Old Testament. It noticed that the discovery and establishment of the Yahwist faith in Israel had political liberation as one of its dimensions. It also involved the creation of just, liberative social structures in the society that Yahweh had chosen as Yahweh's own. Thus the Israelite Exodus from Egypt became the undisputed theological paradigm for liberation theology, at least on the level of popularization. Claims were made that it was the key to reading the whole Bible, even the most seemingly apolitical parts of the Bible such as the New Testament in general and Paul's letters in particular. If the Jesus transmitted by the Synoptics seemed to be scandalously insensitive to the political problematic posed by the structures of the Roman Empire,[244] Paul seemed to go even further in the wrong direction. His apolitical conception resulted in clearly conservative pointers,[245] undoubtedly because his main focus was on an inner transformation of the human being in Christ.

What are we to say about these two arguments? In principle, the first is irrefutable. Although Vatican II admitted the *political* implications of the faith in theory,[246] it is extraordinarily hard for the Church to follow through on this admission even though it has no difficulty in stepping into other areas to guide them according to the demands of the gospel message: e.g., such areas as individual behavior, family life, and socioeconomic issues. It is not hard to pinpoint the reason for this surprising refusal to draw out the concrete, practical consequences of the faith in the realm of politics, where the fundamental decisions on the societal destiny of human beings are being made. It definitely is not that these political decisions are especially slippery and ambiguous. One need only scratch the surface to realize that the Church is afraid of the coercive means in the hands of political authorities and their potential impact on the conduct of the masses in the religious realm.[247]

Thus the deprivatization of the theological realm (which wrongly has been given exclusive control over the task of exploring the meaningfulness of Jesus for today's humanity) must be accepted in principle. But, as we shall see, that does not mean that any and every way of perceiving and drawing out the implications is correct.

What about the biblical argument? I find it paradoxical that such a freshly politicized theology has gone on reading the gospel for so long, or perhaps *not* reading the gospel, without perceiving in it the political key that is needed to interpret the public life of Jesus in a serious, logical way. Only very recently has this possibility been noticed and stressed.[248] And exegetes associated with this theological current still refuse to see the Jesus of history as a 'politician', undoubtedly because they are caught in the mistaken ideas I noted in Volume II.[249]

In my opinion, however, this negative attitude is not as basically dangerous as is the way in which the affirmative attitude is often presented. While scholarship is often allergic to the political key in relation to Jesus, "in many theological confabs this view is accepted as a dogma" (Konings).

That is true. When people discover that the political key and its conflict-filled support of the poor shed much more light on the historically reliable words and deeds of Jesus of Nazareth, they are all too ready to turn it into a *dogma*. The concrete fact is converted into an abstract, atemporal theory. Only the political interpretation of Jesus, they say, can do justice to his real significance. Paul's interpretation is disqualified because it is not political but anthropological, devoting far less attention to the sociopolitical factors involved in dehumanization.

Now although the choice of a key cannot derive from any atemporal dogma, neither is it an arbitary matter of little importance. This is evident from the New Testament itself, in which the different keys used are closely bound up with the needs of different Churches.

In the process of learning to learn, it is most important for people to focus on the area where the crises of growth are occurring, where the various formulations of the problem acquire relevance. In Latin America the vast majority of people live amid inhuman conditions, although our continent has borne the label 'Christian' for more than four centuries. This bears clear witness to the long-standing use of erroneous keys to interpret the significance of Jesus for human beings. It is not so much that the keys are erroneous in themselves, but that they have been applied erroneously to contexts where his significance should be obvious and pertinent.

In Latin America, in other words, we have to be suspicious of any christological key that does not issue in political consequences as concrete and conflictive as those that Jesus himself dared to draw from his conception of God. We must suspect that such keys constitute culpable evasion and escapism. The dimensions of Sin are too obvious to pass unnoticed, to excuse those who emphasize something else.

On the other hand one also detects a tendency towards *Manicheanism* in the cultural realm. Vague borderline areas where there is no perceptible break in continuity are turned into clearcut alternatives and drastic antitheses. Marxism, for example, feels compelled to discredit psychoanalysis by making a sharp distinction between social explication and individual explication. The same can be said of many other oppositions of the same sort: reformism versus revolution, social and charitable aid versus consciousness-raising efforts, structural change versus conversion of the heart, evolution versus dialectics, etc.

Now something in reality does justify these oppositions as authentic alternatives, particularly when polarization becomes acute. They are not completely arbitrary. Excessive stress on differences is often better than leaving matters in murky ambiguity and allowing people to evade the issues. While Manicheanism may be a distorted exaggeration, far worse is the tendency to wipe out the distinction between good and evil.

Nevertheless the excessive division of culture into separate areas or compartments tends to destroy the human ecology, first in the mind and then in the real world, as we saw in Volume I. The division of culture into compartments that are falsely assumed to be watertight often leads, unwittingly and indirectly, to an escalation of means that destroys the complex balance we know as a culture.

One consequence relates to my discussion in this appendix. The fundamental indivisibility of a culture means that the human being, defined as a 'political animal' from ancient times on, is political in all its dimensions and activities. Human beings cannot help but be political, no matter how many declarations of neutrality they may make or how many different instruments they may need to express their political reality when the term 'politics' is restricted to the use of means more *directly* aimed at the takeover, exercise, or maintenance of government power. *In the long run* at least, both the creation of a new language and passive acceptance of the partisan destruction of the existing language are examples of political acts, whether one perceives the consequences or not. The education that a child or adolescent receives at home or in school is intrinsically political, even if no explicit mention is made of such topics as political parties, revolutions, and voting rights. Sooner or later it will have political implications. A healthy balance between enthusiasm and criticism is not just a problem of mental hygiene for the individual, as Bateson makes clear. It is also a crucial factor in the formation of the political agent, and it will have an impact on the structures of the *polis* even though the agent in question may never hold an 'influential' position in government decision-making.

It may well be that the Latin American brand of liberation theology has been too readily inclined to make this sort of sharp separation, restricting 'politics' to direct relationships between the individual and the State and regarding them as the only key that can provide a valid understanding of Jesus for our continent.[250]

A more balanced response to the issue might lie, at least in principle, in seeing the Bible as a process of learning to learn, of deutero-learning. Liberation theology has tended to focus selectively on certain parts of the Bible and to slight other parts as being almost incompatible. This tendency is due largely to the fact that liberation theology, like European theology, continues to regard the Bible as a process of proto-learning. It assumes we are to glean readymade answers from the Bible. And since those answers vary in the Bible, we must of course choose between them.

A process of deutero-learning, on the other hand, must maintain a difficult balance between two of its basic elements. First, the enrichment and maturity we expect to gain as a result depend on our going through *multiple* experiences that will broaden our horizon beyond what we can reach by our own individual experience. Only in that way can history be called 'the teacher of life', and herein lies the crucial importance of iconic language. Such language helps us greatly to re-create contexts that are not our own, and to do so in a living way. We thus can experience as our own the crises faced by other human beings, and truly feel the impact of solutions that were liberating and humanizing in very different circumstances. We acquire a reservoir of existential factors. At a given moment they may be recalled, re-created, or corrected to form part of a solution to some crisis that we cannot even imagine today.

Second, the whole process would not evoke faith from us if we did not feel that one or more links in the whole chain affected our lives here and now in our present context. The anthropological faith stirred in us by the chain of witnesses must somehow open a concrete way out for us, an opening to a more mature and happy human life for us in our present situation. If that encounter does not take place, then the whole process will pass us by as just another one of those 'spiritual traditions' that we cannot appreciate because they do not speak to us and our existential situation.

Now liberation theology in Latin America has clearly favored the second aspect of this process and neglected the first. It has stressed the undeniable importance of fashioning a theology that is meaningful for *praxis*. That brings us back to the heart of our problem in this volume and this appendix. Given the present context of Latin America, does it make sense to engage in a reading of Paul's christology once we detect his shift from the political key of the historical Jesus to an anthropological key?

III

Latin American theology of liberation has not steered clear of superficiality and oversimplification. That is not surprising because no theology manages to avoid those things. In the case of liberation theology, one such oversimplification is the notion that it 'arises' out of *praxis*.

The fact that theology is essentially practice, not just partially such, and certainly not a 'science' or theory of the divine, should not surprise anyone, particularly those who have read Volume I of this work.

There is no doubt that some praxis or practice[251] always precedes human reflection about the overall meaning of existence, and even about the meaning of that practical activity itself, which first appears to be spontaneous and instinctive. But it is not a simple matter to carry that precedence over to theology or any group discussion of the significance of Jesus of Nazareth.

It is true that *reflection* is always a second act. But it is also true that experiences preceding us in time take on a certain *precedence* insofar as they constitute a totality with its own intrinsic unity that is independent of our own practice here and now. We cannot simply detach isolated fragments of that totality and try to digest them as they attract our attention in the course of our own activity. Every important historical complex requires a certain gratuitousness of us. We must put aside our own pragmatic urgencies for the time it takes to grasp the overall significance and importance of that historical complex by examining its various elements.

I am not denying that only questions raised by our own set of problems can guide our hermeneutic, which will never be neutral. In that sense our problematic always begins by being practice.[252] While the significance of Jesus does not *arise* out of praxis, it is necessarily connected with praxis whether we realize it or not; and of course our interpretation will be better if we are aware of that relationship. But the fact that classical theology has forgotten the *practical* and even political vector of the old christological discussions should not lead us to the opposite extreme today. We should not go looking for an immediate pragmatic connection between the problems arising on our practical horizon and the solutions offered to us by the life or message of Jesus.[253]

In the previous section I noted that two elements had to be kept in balance in any process of learning to learn: the connection of a given tradition with the context in which our own praxis is unfolding; and the richness and autonomy of the tradition itself, which without us has tried different keys, with their advantages and limitations, to comprehend the significance of the historical person known as Jesus of Nazareth. Now the interpretation carried out in this Volume III was not a scholarly exercise or a laboratory experiment on Paul's christology. It was, in fact, a reading undertaken by a concrete group of human beings in the context of today's Latin America. The group was aware of the limitations and particularities involved. By considering that experience here, we may be able to assess the importance that should be given to the key Paul used to interpret Jesus and thus meet the requirements spelled out in the previous section.

From the start it should be made clear that the group's interpretive experience took place in a situation where two basic things were obvious and keenly felt: (1) the power of what has come to be called 'structural sin' and its stranglehold on our societies; (2) the absence or lack of the usual political instruments that were used in the recent past to combat that structural sin.[254]

Comparing the relatively recent past with the present-day situation, the group also noticed a tendency to let ourselves be controlled to a large extent by an external factor: i.e., what we were permitted to do. In an earlier day political freedom, commitment, and activity often led to an activism devoid of reflection, of serious reflection at least. The theoretical level was marked by hastiness, pragmatism, and superficiality. Subsequent political repression, on the other hand, brought a return to reflection; but it was a reflection without hands. Means of acting seemed to have disappeared, so our thinking was limited to refurbishing our criticism with new arguments. While that criticism may have been regarded as a sign of our own innocence, it was also characterized by ineffectiveness. We were waiting for change to come.

Was this a sign of greater commitment, or perhaps of the only commitment possible? Or was it an escapist justification for our passivity, our lack of imagination, and our own 'structural' Sin as a group?

In short, a radical suspicion began to grow in our minds. Was this the real state of affairs between us and Sin? We had seen Jesus operating in the political key, but what good news or what call to conversion would he bring to us today? It is hard to imagine Jesus being silent in the face of the reality we must live through today, but it is equally difficult to picture him challenging the established power over us in a totally unrealistic way and merely for the sake of principle. If he did that today, even his own passion and death might not be 'martyrdom' in the strict sense of the term because he would not have had enough time to win listeners and acquire the means to transmit his message to them.

It took only a glance at the New Testament to realize that Paul was the author whose situation was more like ours, and whose message assumed many of the contextual features just mentioned. So even though it was not easy to approach the thought of Paul, we found ourselves drawn closer to it *from politics*.

We came to the reading of Paul with an hypothesis that was hermeneutically crucial: i.e., that structural Sin was not just *outside* us. Despite our protests of innocence, structural Sin also was 'dwelling' inside us. Somehow we were part of it; we were its accomplices. Our ineffective criticism, like political suicide, was a sneaky way of escaping from freedom, of evading our own responsibilities.

Mistrusting our own criticism did not mean repudiating it or its underlying arguments. It meant balancing that criticism with a creative project. We had to draw strength from weakness and begin by destroying the watertight compartment of politics that seemed closed to us. We had to realize that everything in the human being is virtually political; that in each one of us there are latent possibilities, much more real and radical than habit and custom permitted us to see and exercise.

With this key hermeneutic premise we drew closer to Paul because his christology, insofar as it replaced politics with anthropology, was pointing in the very direction our own praxis had to go.

This step did not open all doors at once, nor was everything made clear right away. It was very difficult to follow the twists and turns of Paul's complicated thought, to get used to a vocabulary that was not our own. That should be evident to readers of this volume. But gradually we began to detect a piece of *good news* as we proceeded, something important that opened up new avenues of hope and personal creative responsibility.

Some specific points of this reading deserve mention here, even though I may be repeating earlier remarks about Paul's christological interpretation. It cannot be helped, you see, because those points do not 'arise' out of our praxis even though they may be closely connected with it; nor do they arise, as such, from the words or deeds of Jesus. Their origin and derivation is Paul's *interpretation* of the significance of Jesus of Nazareth for humanity.

Knowing that, we can proceed to reread Paul in his *spirit*, not in his letter, just as he himself teaches us to do with the rest of biblical revelation. That 'spirit' is given to us only in terms of the practical context in which we find ourselves rooted and involved. Clearly it is a political context, as we saw in the previous section. Only in that broad sense can we say that our interpretation of Paul (and of Christ based on Paul) 'arises' out of our praxis, out of our overall set of problems vis-à-vis history.

(1). Contrary to what is assumed and taken for granted by many people elsewhere, there is an ever growing awareness in our region of the inhuman and enslaving mechanisms at work on both the supraindividual and the supranational levels. To go back no further than the past few decades, spanning one whole generation, we have found an ever growing gap between the modest, balanced ideals sketched for our societies and the possibility of implementing them in reality, in *our* reality.

It seems that everything has been tried, every possible approach used, yet the result is the same. By some inflexible law, more keenly felt as time passes, we find it impossible to be even partially free, to choose the kind of societal life we want, to even discuss it much less fight for it. Every day we see a road closing to us that seemed open the day before. Since we are not completely stupid or naïve, we witness this phenomenon with open mouths and constricted hearts. We are discovering the logic that links all forms of power, all tactics, and their users, in one single purpose and one single brand of efficacy.

We have not invented a new sin when we talk about sinful sociopolitical structures or structural sin. We are not attributing a specific sin, properly applicable only to individuals, to abstract, impersonal structures or systems. It is Paul who has taught us to escape the political trap of equating *Sin* as enslaving, dehumanizing structure with the specific *sins* that human beings commit in the toils of the Flesh.

In short, Paul has helped us to see the central problem of our human condition today: the creation and maintenance of structures and power-centers that are bound to block all effective forms of loving our neighbors and our fellow human beings in either the public or the private sector. The crucial issue is not the existence of individual *sins* of frailty, even those involving conscious exploitation, which will ultimately be forgiven and forgotten. The crucial problem is the idol that has been erected above and against everything human, the global power that has been set up to endure, to enslave human beings, to strip them of their freedom to create, to make them useless and kill them. Sometimes it does actually kill them physically. Most of the time it kills their projects that are designed to offer hope and meaningfulness.

(2). The second step in our reading of Paul led us to consider the mechanisms that had turned us into unwitting co-authors of this Sin. This question hit home with particular force because our claim as Christians was that the anthropological message of Jesus was relevant to the 'ontological and epistemological premises' we used in perceiving and evaluating the historical events affecting our reality. It was terribly mysterious to us that the groups in closest contact with the tradition that came by way of Jesus of Nazareth and Paul of Tarsus were among the blindest and most offbase when it came to evaluating Sin and sins respectively. They seemed to have a hard time striking a proper balance between the mechanisms of enslavement and bad faith, with their enormous death-dealing power, and individual frailties or explosions of passion.

Despite his seeming apoliticalness, it was Paul once again who offered us a 'political' discovery. On two superimposed planes there was an additional element to be reckoned with, an element that was crucial to the distortion of our value judgments, and hence to our structural slavery: i.e., *Law*.

There is, you see, a moral Law operative in the individual and the social realms. Let us call it a 'secular' Law to avoid the debate surrounding the term 'natural' Law. This Law is designed to check our destructive instincts, which seemingly are incapable of self-regulation. Over and above our person and our personal projects—*superego*—society transmits to us an already established *duty* through its members who are closest and most important to us. That duty is basically expressed in negative, repressive terms: don't do this or that. Long before we know or decide for ourselves the why and wherefore of our life and activity, we already know what is definitely not to be done. There is an enormous disproportion between the clarity and effectiveness of the information we are given by way of prohibition, and the kind of information education provides us about possible creative projects and ways to transform existing reality.

The process of growing to maturity should raise some critical doubts about the values embodied in this negative, absolutized Law; but in most instances we find it much more convenient to stay within its norms. Our native language, with its readymade definitions, offers us many seemingly decisive arguments that prove how well founded those duties are.

On this plane of education in general, there is sometimes imposed another one with a *Law* in the religious sense. Its norm, considered to be of divine origin, reinforces, amplifies, and sanctions the aforementioned secular Law.

Some might well object here that this is not the picture presented to us by Christianity. Paul, and Jesus himself before Paul, warned us about any such distorted conception of God and what human beings should make of themselves. Indeed it would seem completely mystifying that Sin could have made its way safe and sound through communitites that have been obliged to keep rereading the radical critique found in Paul and the gospel message.

The matter becomes more understandable if we remember two points: one historical, the other anthropological. Paul could not have known the first point, so he dwelt on the second.

Even the first crucial element can be found virtually in Paul, if we relate our reading of him to the historical insight we now possess. Liberation from Law, even religious Law, is a central factor in maturity. The Law is not above human beings but in their service. When we realize that fact and achieve such liberation, we have crossed the threshold of the stage known as maturity. Such a step is essentially a 'minority' one, however; everything of a 'mass' nature functions outside that stage. Consider, then, the peculiar historical circumstances in which Christianity had to operate in the West after the collapse of the Roman Empire. The vacuum forced Christianity to become once again the 'pedagogue' of human masses, to step in and create a civic morality of the 'infantile' type. In the name of the *Christian* religion there was a return to something that Christianity, by definition, had surpassed: i.e., the biblical decalog, which had served as the basis for Israel's civic morality. And most exegetes tell us that the decalog was originally drawn up in the form of basic prohibitions, of negative precepts.

Now however detailed a Law may be, it is effective only insofar as it enables people to classify actions in clearcut terms, no matter what the circumstances may be. And since all Law is coercive, its negative formulations with accompanying *sanctions* will always come across more clearly than any positive actions it may enjoin.

Thus the commandment to honor father and mother does not possess the same normative efficacy as the commandments not to kill or steal. Honoring one's father and mother may signify many things and cover a wide range of complex consequences and evasions. Such a commandment will have little concrete impact on conduct unless it is rephrased in its older, negative form: "You shall not curse your father or mother; one who curses father or mother will die." Here we again have a negative formulation and an accompanying sanction.

The problem is that such a prohibition, linked with a sanction, distracts our attention from actions or omissions that will indirectly but inevitably produce even greater evils. The prohibition against murder, for example, tells us nothing about our active or passive connivance in the death of many people, including people close to us. They may have had to die simply because we lacked courage, critical judgment, historical sensitivity, or creative imagination. We offer reasons to excuse ourselves, and those reasons are all the more effective, deceiving, and enslaving insofar as we convince ourselves that our rejection of killing will, by way of religion, put us on solid good terms with the Absolute.

Now it is true that in our religious and liturgical language we do detect some recognition of this sin that slips through the filter of prohibitions. We hear of the sin of *omission*. As such, intimately bound up with the domain of Law, sins of omission cannot be tallied on a moral computer. They cannot be 'added up' like the other sins because they have no limits. The only possible way to combat sins of omission is to leave the domain of Law, move out into the open, and face the whole panorama of human suffering.

(3). Our third step in reading Paul showed us that 'omission' was a rather superficial label for a structure of Sin that was not only outside but also inside us. It took in mechanisms that play a crucial role deep within our very selves.

Reading Paul, we discovered that even admission of our failure to combat evil effectively when it took the form of what ought not be done did not restore to us the meaningfulness and effectivenss of a political commitment bound up with our faith. We could sense the terrifying power of 'omission', resulting from immature subordination to secular or religious Law. While we could not find reasons to kill, we could find countless reasons for *letting people be killed*, for remaining inactive while others killed, and worse still, for allowing thousands and millions to die even though no one had made a conscious decision to kill anyone.

And what did we offer by way of opposition to this power of Sin, of dehumanizing deceit? A ready tendency to glory in our own irreproachable purity. We put ourselves outside Sin through our criticism and said 'no' to what was going on. Although our 'no' was incapable of changing anything, it enabled us to relax in the certitude of our own innocence. We could see ourselves as 'guides for the blind', though only in theory of course. But our reading of Paul and his treatment of the divided human being put an end to any such mistaken notion of pure, monolithic opposition to Sin. Our criticism could well be the innermost expression of what we think and want, yet everything that moves from there toward execution in the outside world was ending up in the toils of the system, in the enslaving structures of Sin, and serving the latter.

Our members, and their extension in the instruments of our culture and our societal activity, revealed our irremediable connivance with Sin. When carried into practice, the final result of our intentions was unrecognizable. Our reading of Paul was a painful but healthy lesson in the subtlety and invincible power of the mechanisms dwelling inside us, as well as in the futility of our escapist attempts to free ourselves from them.

One of these forms of escapism is to cut back or even mutilate our outside activity, our attempts to accomplish something. We do not use our members so as not to succumb to their law. Our social activity becomes paralyzed, since we restrict it to the private expression of our negative criticism and our hope for change.

Quite apart from the ineffectivenss of this quest for our own 'justice' by way of escapism and 'omission', it proves impossible for us to carry it through in many cases. One of the clearest examples is the inescapable problem of educating the younger generation. For the sake of clarity I will oversimplify the matter here. Leaving aside the repressive impact of the reigning government and system on family life and the whole educational system, let us pretend that the educational milieu of the family is amenable to the creativity of parents.[255] How can they communicate a critical attitude to their children? How can they provide their children with a values-system that is diametrically opposed to the one forced on them by society at large?

One frequent answer is the escapist sort noted above. Parents tend to *carry over their criticism* to the education of their children. The results do not match their expectations, however, and the reason is simple enough. While adults may be able to tolerate intense doses or periods of criticism, the same dosage proves to be counterproductive and even destructive in an educational process. You see, a goodly portion of the *critical base* in adults, of the energy equation that enables them to expend costly energy in criticism, is provided by the store of cheap energy embodied in their patriotism. They are 'pitiless' critics, in other words, because they are 'pious' patriots, because they are viscerally and uncritically devoted to their native land. This means that the social instruments designed to evoke such an attitude had a profound impact on them when they were young. Such instruments would include the emotional feelings associated with symbols like the flag and the national anthem.

The adults see that the same instruments are now being used on their children to introject emotional solidarity with an order of which they do not approve. The easiest way for them to react to the 'bad educator' is to convey their criticism to the children being educated, to relativize the same national symbols or even show disgust for them. But the ability to dissociate symbols (and their content) from the use being made of them is a characteristic capacity of adults, not of children. Where this capacity is not present, that approach will clash with the youngster's basic need for emotional security and solidarity.

The results of this clash prove to be disconcerting to the parent educators. Their children may react by rebelling against the parental criticism and adopting conservative attitudes. They may get around the criticism in all sorts of ways. Or they may accept the criticism on the conscious, rational level but experience all sorts of psychological conflict that seem to have no direct connection with the matter. Excessive anxiety leads to a state of confusion and disequilibrium.

There is another clear example of the same tendency toward personal renunciation in the face of Sin and its power. In a completely unreal way people set up a force opposed to Sin, *Anti-Sin*, and then identify themselves with it. It is a way of seeking protection by going back to the womb. This force or power is given the task of safeguarding their hope against the onslaughts of reality. It must also assume the riskier task of discerning the *effective ideologies* that will prove to be victorious sooner or later. In the end we will find that our anxieties and doubts stemmed solely from our own intellectual reflection done in despite of Party, Church, Class, or whatever the authentic historical force for liberation is assumed to be.[256]

In short, people look for some supposedly *qualitative* power which, by virtue of its equally *quantitative* character, will eventually be able to turn the tables on the apparently disproportionate strength of all merely quantitative factors. It presumably will halt the process of 'corruption' that seems to affect human projects in the political realm.

This unrealistic and paralyzing utopia has crept into liberation theology itself, to cite one example. Because Paul is said to be apolitical, liberation theology has refused to undertake a close reading of his thought. Instead it has erected its own image of a simultaneously qualitative and quantitative power: 'the People', or more specifically, 'the Poor'.[257]

It seems to me that this, not secularism or atheism, is the real danger of Marxist premises or similar ones when they are not evaluated in terms of Christian transcendent data. Needless to say, I am not attacking this tendency because it 'degenerates' into class conflict or turns the proletariat (by another name) into the privileged agent of history. My problem with it is its simplistic, mistaken eschatology, which raises false hopes and hence in the long run will only intensify people's desperation and despair.

(4) That brings me to the fourth step in our reading of Paul. We discovered the complexity of his eschatology and its fidelity to the thrust of Jesus of Nazareth and his message. Confused at first, we were slow to realize that such an eschatology is the only kind capable of giving real meaning to human history, and to the dialectic of freedom that has to be incorporated into that history.[258]

Paul taught us to give up the idealistic and unreal task of inverting the power ratio, in terms of energy, between quality and quantity—in politics as in every other area of culture. We learned to accept the fact that only quantity accumulates in the course of history and dominates human instrumentality as the law of the members. We learned that *true and definitive* efficacy, which neither promises victories nor promotes triumphalism, is rooted in creativity placed in the service of love and humanization. Therein lies the only meaningful destiny for freedom. In Paul, then, we found a broader and more ecologically sound vision of the political realm. We saw that it was more deeply rooted in, and dependent on, the rest of culture.

This opened up for us a humanizing political realm that no repression could control or render useless. Our customary political mechanisms were terribly important, to be sure, and they were now in the implacable grip of the government. But they were, after all, of fairly recent vintage in human history and its efforts to fashion societies for beings becoming more and more human.

It is impossible to convey an adequate idea of the implications we saw in Paul's vision for the whole concrete realm that was thus opened up, a realm dependent on the possibilities of each and every individual. Notice, for example, that the effort to transform *language* in a creative way is a political act once our culture is involved. Giving full, coherent expression to Paul's statement about oneness in Jesus Christ is such a political act: "There is no longer Jew nor Greek, slave nor free, male nor female; for you are all one in Christ Jesus" (Gal 3:28).

Paul was not escaping from that realm to the 'private' sector when he gave priority to human maturity in addressing himself to slaves. In his own context he was simply stressing that the dehumanizing *status* of slaves need not prevent them from attaining human maturity. They could do so by adhering to anthropological or religious *faith* in Jesus and the *transcendent data* brought by him.

We are not injecting a political dimension into Paul when we view him as laying a political foundation, within the framework imposed by his own context, that would eventually lead to the abolition of slavery in the social system.[259] We are simply stressing a political dimension that he probably glimpsed in only a vague, remote way. Our added stress is not infidelity to Paul. The simple fact is that the political dimension poses priority problems to us today, so it has guided our reading as people who want to know Paul's teachings about love, freedom, and humanization.

We are not fooling ourselves, or trying to fool anyone else, about the context in which we are reading Paul. We know it is our own context, and we know it is a limited one. But it is precisely in that context that our reading of Paul has proved to be an enriching and liberating experience.

This narrative account of our concrete experience with Paul's christology ought not mislead readers about several crucial points. I discussed them in Volume I, so here I shall touch upon them only insofar as they relate to the last section.

(1). My *account* of our experience with Paul is not enough to appraise the *change* produced by that experience. I have described it in brief, abstract, 'digital' terms, which can hardly capture the concrete, human results. That will always be the case when we transcribe or transmit the experience of other people with a transcendent datum. What they do with it, how they live it, always depends on a world of values and possibilities associated with groups or individuals.

Consider, for example, the transcendent datum I mentioned in Chapter VI of Volume I (p. 157): " . . . don't ever expect any help, or a hand, or a favor." It can be used to justify superficial and wholly unnecessary frustrations, or it can be transformed into a profound work of art or a tragic personal destiny. Another example is the resurrection of Jesus and what it *signifies*. As we have noted in these volumes, it could only be perceived and appreciated by those who adhered to his person and his values from the start. Confronted with his death, they had to ask themselves what ultimate chance those values had to become reality. In itself, the resurrection is irrelevant.

Now it would not be strange, indeed it would be perfectly normal, if our experience in reading Paul should seem equally irrelevant to people who come to it from a different horizon of values. It might also seem irrelevant to people who share our horizon but simply *read* our experience, since the latter was undertaken, not to be read, but to be pondered and lived over a long period of time.

(2). Living in a specific political context, we have shown how people can undertake a reading of the christological data that Paul offers us in an anthropological key. This may prompt some readers to false comparisons.[260] Careless readers might assume that the result of our reading is a specific 'politics' or political line, a specific political ideology that could and should bear comparison with other political ideologies. A word of warning is therefore in order.

Our reading will certainly influence the process of discernment whereby we distinguish and choose between the range of ideologies that propose to deal with our situation. But our reading of Paul itself *is not* one ideology among many others. Those who go through the process do indeed feel compelled to create or use ideologies in order to transform reality, but we should make clear what we mean by that. The process gives them tools for evaluating ideologies in terms of what we can or cannot *ultimately* expect from reality.[261] But it does not possess the criteria to decide once and for all whether the objective, scientific data of a given system of political efficacy are true, or whether they are the only data to be considered in trying to flesh out certain values in history.

To put it another way, every ideology must be judged in terms of two complementary viewpoints or dimensions: the values we are trying to achieve, and the objective truth about the efficacy of the means we are using towards that end. Our process of judgment is a complicated one, and no digital formulation can reduce it to a simple formula. Two examples will suffice here.

(a). Suppose someone thinks that it is worth destroying half the planet in order to invert the congenital weakness of quality vis-à-vis quantity, which accounts for the 'corruption' of our political projects. Our reading of Paul would pass negative judgment on that *ideology*. Not because there is anything wrong with the physics equation to produce nuclear explosions. Not because we accept *slogans* that reduce the biblical process of deutero-learning to supposedly transcendent data: e.g., 'violence is not Christian'; 'violence always provokes greater violence'. But because our reading has relocated the irreversible weakness of the qualitative in a coherent image of reality, dependent on faith to be sure, where it is now synonymous with final victory rather than defeat.

Obviously this does not mean we will cease to look for what is qualitatively better in terms of efficacy. Nor does it mean we will neglect the quantitative dimension and the opportunities it cannot help but offer to quality (i.e., love in this case).

(b). My second example is closely related to the first, but it comes from the discipline created to investigate the significance of Jesus' life and message for humanity: i.e., *theology*.

I have already mentioned the tendency, born of desperation, to unload on 'the People' the task of creating the only ideologies that could possibly liberate them. Pursuing this line of thought, some have gone so far as to say that there will be no authentic theology of liberation until it is created by 'the People'(?), until 'the *whole* People' or 'the lowliest of the Poor' gain their own voice, become subjects of history, and act as conscious protagonists of their own liberation; and this has to take place in the interpretation of Jesus as well as in every other field.[262]

Those who have followed our reading of Paul and agree with its thrust will suspect an *ideological* trap in the notion or hope of a 'totally conscious People'. For that would represent an empirical inversion of quality and quantity, which hardly seems to be a sound basis for an effective system of liberation.

I need hardly point out that this final section is not a futile effort to replace an experience of anthropological or religious faith with a description of its valid 'results'. It is merely a warning to those, all too numerous in Latin America, who think that the crucial thing in reading the Bible is to adopt the *best* key, and that the best one for our type of human oppression is the *political* key.

Offering a proof I consider valid, I have simply tried to show that human reality is in much more lively intercommunication than is assumed by all too prevalent notions of that sort.

Notes

Introduction

1. With the exception of the words said over the bread and wine at the Last Supper (see 1 Cor 11:23f.).

2. True if the John-Mark of Acts 13:5 and 15:36–39 (see 2 Tm 4:11) is the author of the second gospel, and if "the brother whose fame in connection with the gospel has spread through all the churches" (2 Cor 8:18) is Luke (see Col 4:14; 2 Tm 4:11).

3. It has been ascertained, for example, that the typical internal structure of Matthew's gospel points specifically to this catechetical function. On this matter see X. Léon-Dufour, *Les Évangiles,* p. 157.

4. This is what many christologies do without taking the proper hermeneutic precautions, including that of Jon Sobrino *(Christology at the Crossroads).* Moreover, the very idea of *one* christology assumes that such addition is possible and necessarily leads to a sneaky, shamefaced christology 'from above'. I repeat again that Volume II was not an effort to construct *one christology,* which might be called the christology of the Synoptic gospels. That is an impossible task, considering the gap between the christology of Matthew and the christology of Luke, for example. My effort in Volume II was to get to the most reliable data about the history of Jesus of Nazareth, dislodging those data from the different christologies in which they are imbedded.

5. Unanimity is hard to come by, even with regard to this central nucleus. The *date* of the Letter to the Galatians depends on the exact meaning of the geographical term, Galatia. Some exegetes also have doubts about Paul's authorship of Colossians.

6. On the other hand there is near unanimity in not attributing the Letter to the Hebrews to Paul, though it bore his name for centuries. Given the many differing opinions, it is much harder to say what writings of the New Testament show traces of Paul's close influence. Besides the Letter to the Hebrews itself, some exegetes see the same sort of influence in 1 Peter.

7. A similar claim for the Letter of James must explain how it could allude to the Pauline doctrine of justification by faith without works of the law. All indications are that this doctrine was still being elaborated in the following period when Paul was writing to the Galatians and Romans.

8. To these we could add echoes of postpaschal data later recorded in the gospels and Acts: e.g., the resurrection (1 Thes 1:10; 4:14), the gift of the Spirit (1 Thes 4:8), and the imminent second coming of Jesus from heaven (the central theme of both letters to the Thessalonians).

9. Particularly when we realize that evangelization, at that point in time at least, began in the synagogues. Only afterwards, when it met with rejection from the synagogue, was it extended to other groups who presumably were somewhat open, if not attached, to the Jewish religion (see Acts 13:43f.; 17:1–4).

10. According to Luke, this was also the content of Paul's (truncated) discourse to

the Athenians in the same period. That discourse is the first example we have of a group evangelization that substantially prescinds from the synagogue approach (see Acts 17:22-34), a step that Paul personally took in Athens (see Acts 17:17).

11. Hence the notorious fluctuation between words of terror and words of joy and thanksgiving. As we saw in Volume II, the replacement of 'the poor and sinners' with Christians as the object of the kingdom's happiness shows up in Luke's redaction of the beatitudes (Lk 6:20-23). The equating of 'salvation' with membership in the community of those who believe in Jesus can be found in Luke's own comment on the numerical growth of the Church near the beginning of Acts: "Every day the Lord was adding to the community those who were to be saved" (Acts 2:47).

12. Sometimes the greater length means little insofar as our purposes here are concerned. 2 Corinthians is an example. The kinds of problems treated there have to do mainly with personal relations between Paul and the Corinthian community. And then there are problems with regard to the coherence of the text, possible transpositions and interpolations.

13. The term is all too convenient for us. 'Old' and 'New' Testament (Covenant) are the products of a later christology, permitting us to shut our eyes to the problems of the time that the first Christian communities had to face and solve.

14. As we know, Pliny the Younger wrote from Asia Minor to Emperor Trajan (much later) that in those regions Christians sang hymns to Jesus *as God*. We may have backup for his testimony in Philippians 2:6-11, Colossians 1:15-20, Ephesians 1:3-14, and such fragments as Ephesians 5:14 and 1 Timothy 3:16, if Philippi (Macedonia) is included in the same cultural (if not geographical) region where that practice was characteristic enough to be mentioned explicitly to the emperor. I might add here that some exegetes attribute the same origin to the Prologue of the fourth gospel, claiming it is a hymn from the same area: Ephesus, in this case.

15. The term 'kingdom' or 'kingdom of heaven' is not totally absent in this period of Paul's writing. But with the exception of 1 Cor 15:24, its use seems to be bound up with moral exhortations. Thus it has lost its dynamic character as something moving and arriving: Rom 14:17; 1 Cor 4:20; 6:9-10; Gal 5:21.

16. This may seem to be an exaggeration, especially for those who grant that Philippians belongs to the same period as Romans, Galatians, and Corinthians. In that case Phil 2:6-11 would represent an awakening curiosity in Paul (or in a community founded by him, if it is a citation). That curiosity, lasting centuries from Easter to Chalcedon and beyond, led Christians to ask *who* brought the message of the kingdom and what exactly his ontic *status* was, so to speak.

17. Remember that even when we were examining the Synoptics in Volume II, we did not analyze their specifically christological elements. If I did happen to touch upon some such element, it was to extract some datum of historical value that was relevant to our purposes.

18. There is no mention of the destruction of Jerusalem as a sign, which had not yet occurred when Paul was writing. That would confirm its postpaschal character as a prophecy after the fact. But Paul does mention the great temptation to apostasy that is associated with the Antichrist (see 2 Thes 2:1-12).

19. I do not claim that my division is hermeneutically innocent. But there is no such thing as hermeneutic innocence anyway.

20. Verse-by-verse exegesis has many disadvantages. First, it allows for a false levelling. Not everything in Paul's text has the same importance or interpretive decisiveness, especially when it is read from a different context such as our own. Second, there is an even more serious disadvantage. When we try to clarify each verse by itself or in

conjunction with its immediate neighbors, we find it hard to resist the temptation to turn each verse into a definitive *thesis* and then accommodate the following verses to it. We thus lose *the dialectic* that is so obvious in the process of Paul's creative thinking.

21. In the most unexpected places, and *not precisely* in those places where we think we see it: e.g., in his recommendations to obey authorities or in his advice to slaves that they remain such.

22. Faced with all these exegetical questions, I certainly had no thought of introducing my readers to the vast scholarly literature on them that has accumulated over the centuries. I did not want to weigh down this volume with material not directly relevant to its purposes. At the same time I wanted to do something that would substantiate my assertions in the eyes of exegetes and other readers interested in checking them out. On all such questions my decision was to appeal to a long tradition of biblical exegesis embodied in *The International Critical Commentary.* In 1895, W. Sanday and A. C. Headlam published their commentary on Romans in that series (ICC 1). For eighty years it remained a much used and highly respected work, particularly because it presented differing exegetical opinions before opting for its own. In 1975, C. E. B. Cranfield published a new commentary on Romans in the same series (ICC 2), retaining all the valuable features of the approach used in the earlier edition. On almost all exegetical questions I will refer my readers to those two volumes, citing them as ICC 1 and ICC 2 and then indicating the relevant page numbers. See note 24 also.

23. When *grammar* calls for it in the translation, I add words in parentheses. When *logical sense* seems to call for it, I add words in italics. Obviously there is no neat division between the two in all cases. The basic point is that I don't want my readers to attribute words to the original Greek text that are not there explicitly. This full text may be handled more briefly in my chapter commentary.

24. When scholars and readers disagree on *scholarly* grounds with the interpretation offered in my text, they should direct their complaints and criticisms to the ICC commentators (see note 22). If I depart from their commentary, I will indicate my reasons for doing so.

Chapter I

25. Actually this general conclusion continues to be elaborated in the third chapter (see Rom 3:11–18. 23 and the singular 'human being' in 3:28).

Since this is the first note of the present chapter, let me call the attention of my readers to a typographical abnormality that they will come across often in this volume. Everyone should know that the earliest manuscripts we have found of the original Greek New Testament are 'uncial', i.e., written entirely in capital letters (majuscules), and without our modern punctuation marks. This situation lasts until the tenth century at least. It has certain consequences, even for our translations of the Synoptic gospels. But this is even more true in a discourse such as that of Paul with long, complex sentences. Two examples will suffice to indicate some of the difficulties faced by translators. One has to do with the problem of capital letters (majuscules) versus small letters (miniscules). Paul writes: "THE SPIRIT BEARS WITNESS TO OUR SPIRIT" (8:16). Faced with a manuscript written entirely in capital letters, we can only assume that the first SPIRIT should be written with a capital 'S' because in context it must refer to the Holy Spirit; and that the use of OUR means that the second SPIRIT should be written with a small 's'. In short, the capitals and small letters of translations are products of exegetical hypotheses, some of them more obvious than others. My second example has to do with the problem of punctuation. Paul writes: "creation was subjected to uselessness by the one who *subjected it with* the hope that creation too would be liberated . . ." (Rom 8:20–21). There could be a comma between 'it' and 'with', but the manuscript indicates nothing about the matter to us. If we insert a comma, then 'with the hope' complements 'creation was subjected'; hope is attributed to creation. Without the comma, 'with the hope' modifies 'the one who subjected it', indicating that the latter subjected creation to uselessness provisionally and entertained the hope of the later liberation of creation. Only in the latter case, without the comma inserted, is it possible for us to identify 'the one who'. With the comma, the hope is attributed to creation itself and there is no real possibility of identifying 'the one who'.

In the face of such problems we could adopt the possibly scholarly but impracticable solution of 'imitating' the early manuscripts and writing our translations completely in capital letters without punctuation. Here I have opted for a half-way solution. I put punctuation where it seems to go obviously; when it seems necessary, I discuss the different possible punctuations of a given phrase. With regard to capitals and small letters, I have opted for the following compromise. *In my translations of Paul's text of Romans at the beginning of each chapter (gathered together in one place at the end of the book),* I reserve initial capitals for proper names (Jesus, Jerusalem, etc.) and the word 'God'. Other common nouns, even those that could designate persons, are put in small letters. I assume readers will realize that it is for exegesis to decide whether an initial capital is more appropriate. *In the text of my chapter,* however, I use initial capitals and small letters on the basis of which seems to fit better in a given context by prior determination. Thus 'Sin' is something very different from the 'sin of lying'. For Paul, Sin is a personification of a certain anthropological force, to which he attributes 'personal' acts such as enslaving, killing, and so forth. Other personifications may also be capitalized consistently (e.g., the Law), but this is not necessary in some cases. Use of the uncapitalized noun may be clear enough, but I may capitalize it at times to remind readers that Paul sees it as a personified force. The interplay, I hope, will help to awaken readers to the meaning of the terms in the biblical text and Paul's thinking.

26. To what is Paul referring when he says that at least some pagans naturally do what is commanded by the Law? Our commentators cite Mark Pattison here, indicating how Christian theologians have interpreted the passage: "In accordance with this view they interpreted the passages in St. Paul which speak of the religion of the heathen: e.g., Rom 2:14. Since the time of Augustine (*De Spir. et Lit.* §27) the orthodox interpretation has applied this verse, either to the Gentile converts, or to the favoured few among the heathen who had extraordinary divine assistance. The Protestant expositors, to whom the words 'do by nature the things contained in the law' could never bear their literal force, sedulously preserved the Augustinian explanation. . . . The rationalists, however, find the expression 'by nature', in its literal sense, exactly conformable to their own views . . . and have no difficulty in supposing the acceptableness of those works, and the salvation of those who do them" (ICC 1:60; see ibid., 106). If we disregard the theologically pejorative and positive terms, 'rationalists' and 'orthodox', the commentary makes clear the obvious and logical sense of the verse. If one interprets 'Gentiles' as those already converted to Christianity, for theological reasons alien to the text itself (ICC 2:156), one loses the thread of Paul's whole second chapter, not to mention his first chapter, since both chapters are obviously referring to pre-Christian pagans and Jews. Moreover, it is hard to see how 'fulfilling the law' could be of any use, as Paul affirms it is, to people who are already under a system where the human being is justified 'without the works of the law'.

27. It is true that we do come across the phrase, "full of . . . murder." But both the context and the force of the adjective ('full') tell us right away that Paul is talking about

the rage that incites the desire to kill, not saying that pagans continually commit murders. It is instructive to compare this list of Romans 1 with another list of sins depicted by Paul as incompatible with possession of the kingdom: ". . . the impure, idolaters, adulterers, the effeminate, homosexuals, thieves, the greedy, drunkards, insulters, the rapacious . . ." (1 Cor 6:9–10). Despite some coincidences, we find in the list of 1 Corinthians a 'materiality' and a direct opposition to the law that is missing in the list of Romans. This suggests that the two lists are pointing in different directions. Indeed the attention of exegetes has been alerted by the strange gap in the list of Rom 1:28–31, namely, the fact that there is no mention of sexual sins (see ICC 2:130). As I shall indicate in this chapter, the gap is not filled by Paul's passage on homosexuality (Rom 1:26–27).

28. Today 'anti-natural' and 'highly immoral' have become synonyms, particularly on the level of language reflecting emotional reactions. We could say that on the rational level this synonymity is alien to the thinking of Paul. For Paul, the human being is lord of the universe, and all its forces and powers, because Christ's liberty frees the human being for love. But it is also obvious that this responsibility to build up love must take into account what is and is not 'suitable' for the task (see 1 Cor 6:12; 10:23). Knowing nature and its laws or mechanisms should help people discern what is and is not suitable for an effective project of love. Significantly, in this first chapter Paul calls these homosexual relations 'the unsuitable' (1:28). His rational soberness here contrasts with the 'moral repugnance' for everything violating 'nature' that has been incorporated into the Christian outlook even though it is not Christian. For Paul, as for Jesus, nature does not furnish morality readymade: it has an indirect influence on morality insofar as it helps us to judge the effectiveness and sincerity of our projects.

29. Readers will recall my remarks on the meaning and import of Satan's 'possession' of a human being in the Synoptic gospels (see Volume II, Chapter IX, section II).

30. Paul supports this statement as follows: "What is knowable of God is manifest in their midst, because God has made it manifest to them. The fact is that since the creation of the world the invisible (____pl.) of his are seen intellectually by means of (his) works, both his eternal power and divinity, so that they have no excuse . . ." (1:19–20). On the possible interpretations of this correct knowledge of God that is attributed to pagans (before they corrupt it and go astray), see note 38.

31. Some exegetes, who want to diminish divine responsibility in this 'handing over' maintain that it is to be interpreted in a judicial sense as a sentence in the most impersonal sense, i.e., as a mechanism that operates automatically (see ICC 1:45). Another interpretation of this 'handing over' takes into account the Pauline context of a vast historical plan of God and thus has more likelihood: "We suggest then that Paul's meaning is neither that these men fell out of the hands of God, as Dodd seems to think, nor that God washed His hands of them; but rather that this delivering them up was a deliberate act of judgment and mercy on the part of the God who smites in order to heal (Is 19:22)" (ICC 2:121). But I think it is even more likely that Paul is using a mythical language in which 'God' here anthropologically represents the function performed by authentic knowledge of the Absolute in the human being. In that sense Dodd could be right. See pp. 19f.

32. In other places Paul certainly does talk about the wrath or indignation of God, and we must not forget that the language about God is fashioned to enlighten the human being: "For indignation against wickedness is surely an essential element of human goodness in a world in which moral evil is always present. A man who knows, for example, about the injustice and cruelty of *apartheid* and is not angry at such wickedness cannot be a thoroughly good man" (ICC 2:109). We should also keep in mind the

excellent observation of Bultmann about biblical language and the intention of the biblical authors: qualities or attitudes that are attributed to God and seem to be atemporal attributes of God's essence constitute references to divine *acts* that somehow alter human destiny. Thus God's 'grace' or 'wrath' allude more to saving acts or divine judgment than to 'atemporal' qualities (see Bultmann, *Theology of the New Testament,* I, 288f.).

33. Actually Paul, like Jesus himself, talks about a divine 'punishment' when God withdraws a responsibility that has not been carried out well from a person, group, or people. Thus God withdraws the 'privileges' that Israel regards as its own (see 11:20–21; Mk 4:11–12).

34. Nor is it evident why God would attribute such great importance to a merely formal orthodoxy since Romans 2 does not say that the Jews have been 'handed over' by God to the desires of their hearts, despite the fact of their impenitence and hardness of heart or the ways in which they have contributed to the blaspheming of God's name. But there are some exegetes who claim that the sins of 'injustice' are to be derived from the sins of 'impiety'. They remind us that one of the deuterocanonical books of the Old Testament that seems to have influenced Paul is the Book of Wisdom (see ICC 1:51–52), in which we read: "The invention of idols was the beginning of fornication" (Wis 14:12). But there seems to be no doubt that such exegetes have failed to ponder a fact rightly noted by the *Jerusalem Bible:* i.e., that here the word 'fornication' already has its classic metaphorical sense (like the word 'adultery') of Israel's infidelity to her God, i.e., idolatry, not its literal sense of sexual sin. This could not have escaped Paul.

35. This phrase has an almost exact parallel—in its curious opposition—in another phrase of the second half of the diptych that covers the Jews (less likely, all human beings): ". . . egotists, indocile to the *truth* but docile to *injustice*" (2:8). By comparison with the phrase in Romans 1, this phrase has the advantage of clarity. The basic mainspring of sin is not sinning against the truth (by changing gods) but being freed for injustice (in human relationships).

36. Exegetes offer different explanations for this sort of disappearance of 'impiety' in favor of 'injustice'. Here is an example: "According to some interpreters, *asebeia* ['impiety'] and *adikia* ['injustice'] here denote two distinct categories of sinfulness, namely, those covered by the first four of the Ten Commandments and by the last six, respectively. But, in view of the fact that the single *pasan* ['every'] embraces both *asebeian* and *adikian,* and the fact that in the participial clause *adikia* by itself is apparently meant to represent the double expression, it is more probable that they are here used as two names for the same thing. . . . That, by using at this point *adikia* by itself, Paul meant to indicate that impiety has its ultimate source in immorality (in the wider sense of the word), is quite unlikely" (ICC 2:111–112 and footnote 3). Readers can see that this alleged unlikelihood is not based on any exegetical reason whatsoever. On the contrary, its basis is theological: the sin against God could not have the sin against the human being as its basis. Thus the reason will have to be debated on that level since the most logical *literary* reason for the disappearance of 'impiety' in the main phrase would *in and of itself* lead us to that hypothesis (see ICC 2:134).

37. Of course it is possible to strip this passage of its apparent anthropological profundity: "In the present verse it is perhaps rather more satisfactory to understand by 'the truth of God' the reality consisting of God Himself and His self-revelation, and by 'the lie' the whole futility of idolatry . . ." (ICC 2:123). But then one loses sight of Paul's description of the process of 'the lie', i.e., of bad faith, in 1:21: "They . . . have become entangled in their own [justificatory] reasonings and their uncomprehending

hearts have been darkened." One also loses sight of the indirect relationship of this 'lie' with the 'uselessness' of the universe in 8:20–21.

38. 'Since' the creation of the world, not 'by means of' or 'because of' (see ICC 1:42; ICC 2:114). And if one accepts the view that the better translation is "in their midst," not "within them" (see ICC 2:113), then the thought shifts from what might seem a 'natural theology' (as opposed to 'revealed' theology) based on creation towards a knowledge of God in God's historical activity (that could exist outside Israel as well). It would be a mere tautology to say that the works of God have become visible only since creation. It would seem more logical to think that, ever since the world began, human beings, who have always attributed events in one way or another to God or some supernatural power, can know, from the characteristics of God's way of acting, what values are represented and imposed by the true God. Hence idolatry would be due to a more or less conscious will to evade the responsibility of cultivating those values. To introduce an argument of theodicy here would be an exception to Paul's whole thinking in Romans, although Acts reports a frustrated attempt at that approach in Paul's discourse to the Athenians. Some commentators, seeking to rule out this sort of 'natural theology', come close to this view insofar as creation by itself would be incapable of producing the recognition due to the Creator, but "a real self-disclosure of God has indeed taken place and is always occurring" (ICC 2:116). For our commentator, however, this sort of revelation outside Scripture seems to remain more associated with the act of creation than with happenings in history.

39. This pessimistic conception of the human being or of what is 'within it', given the frailty of the human condition (of its 'flesh'), grows ever clearer in Paul's presentation and culminates in Romans 7:14–25. It is hard to decide to what extent he depends on a theology of 'original sin', which would logically be already present in his thinking. To begin with, it is exegetically very difficult to attribute to Paul what can indeed be attributed to a later theology: namely, that the 'dogma' of original sin enables one to exonerate God for such things as the fact that *since creation* 'the cravings of the human heart' tend on their own towards injustice and the infrahuman.

40. In both cases the harmony with God is rooted in the innermost part of the human being. But as we move away from that innermost area, even that which 'dwells' in the human being takes charge of its intentions, insensibly detours them towards easiness and, through the self-deception I have been mentioning, prompts human thinking to forge some justification for this deviation (see 7:17.20.22–23; 1:18).

41. This active translation, 'haters of God', seems more probable to exegetes than the passive translation, people 'hated by God' *(Deo odibiles)*. See ICC 2:131 and the entries under the names Bauer and Zerwick in the Reference Bibliography.

42. If one continues to assume some influence of Wisdom 12–14 on the thought of Paul (see note 34), then it is even more surprising to note the absence here of any allusion to idolatrous worship of the heavenly bodies—except within the framework of my hypothesis. We read in Wisdom 13:1–2 the following: "They were unable from the good things that are seen to know him who exists, nor did they recognize the craftsman while paying heed to his works; but they supposed that either fire or wind or swift air, or the circle of the stars, or turbulent water, or the *luminaries of heaven* were the gods that rule the world" (RSV). Only in Wisdom 13:13 do we find a reference to idolatrous worship of the image of the human being or "some worthless animal." Apart from that specific issue, another place one may note the alleged influence of the Book of Wisdom on Paul is in the list of sins, very similar to that of Paul, in Wisdom 14:25–26.

43. Of course some readers could say that my search is pointless since Paul himself

indicates later on where he finds the bridge between what applies to Jews and what applies to pagans: i.e., in Abraham (see Romans 4).

44. Note, for example, how insistently Paul talks about this enslavement or alludes to it in almost all the verses of Romans 6 (see verses 6, 12–14, 16–17, 19–20, 22).

45. This shift from the physical to the existential would situate Paul's teaching on a more 'spiritual' and less 'material' plane than that of the Synoptic gospels. One of the results, as we shall see, is that situations characterized in 'material' terms, such as poverty and marginalization, do not get the same emphasis in Paul that they get in the historical preaching of Jesus. In principle at least, that does not imply infidelity but rather a complementary extension.

46. The relationship between this and a distortion of judgment, already unconscious and only partly perceived, is evident in the Synoptics. It is not without reason that 'hardness of heart' and 'hypocrisy' are key terms in those gospels.

47. We do not know for sure how trustworthy is Matthew's testimony that Jesus described his adversaries as an *'adulterous* generation'. In biblical terminology that is a metaphor for 'idolatry', not an allusion to a sexual sin. Certainly Jesus criticized their mistaken way of interpreting the true God in the harshest terms. To put it bluntly, this meant that they were following a god that did not exist. Even though they continued to identify their deity as Yahweh, it was actually an idol, a (verbal) image with no reality behind it.

48. The fantasies of amateurish exegetes to the contrary notwithstanding, the Yahwist account of the first sin already exemplifies the terrible consequences of worshipping the serpent (one form of the Canaanite deities) in the quest for knowledge of good and evil—i.e., for universal magical powers.

49. Hence the Prophets of this period often denounce a type of practical or implicit idolatry. They suggest that certain things done in Yahweh's name are not recognized as such by Yahweh (see Jer 7:4–15; 22:1–9). But it seems that it is Yahweh who likens these practices to idolatry, or to the gravity of idolatry. It is not clear that they *are* idolatry or that they *lead* to it.

50. I say 'more apparent than real' because, insofar as we envision idolatry as a gratuitous practical negation of natural theology (made evident in creation), we break its relationship with the second chapter and also obscure the connection between idolatry and *injustice,* which Paul stresses so much.

51. Though this goes back to the first period of his letters, it is interesting to note a certain duplicity in Paul vis-à-vis the idolatry of the Athenians—the same sort of duplicity Paul could not endure in Peter's attitude towards the Judaizers of Antioch. On the one hand: "While Paul was waiting for them at Athens, his spirit was provoked within him as he saw that the city was full of idols" (Acts 17:16; RSV). On the other hand, he tells the Athenians: "Men of Athens, I perceive that in every way you are very religious" (Acts 17:22; RSV).

52. To use terminology from Volume I: the ontological and epistemological premises used to *read* some alleged divine declaration are more crucial than the later *letter* which records that revelation, when it comes down to knowing God.

53. Here I mean 'largely' in quantitative terms, and also in terms of the problems that come to the fore in those particular communities.

54. Paul makes the same accusation of religious 'infantilism' against the Galatians, who were letting themselves be seduced by Judaizers, and treats them as 'minors' by their own choice (Gal 4:1f.; 3:24). They had failed or were unwilling to grasp the fact that they were 'owners of all' (Gal 4:1), and to act accordingly. The same applies to the Corinthians, who did not appreciate the fact that all things were theirs (1 Cor 3:21).

55. Images relating to these different levels of *sub*ordination are persistent and crucial in Paul. Compare, for example, 1 Corinthians 3:21 with Galatians 3:22-25; 4:2-5; 5:1.

56. Here I offer two recent Spanish translations of the New Testament, one Catholic and one Protestant, as examples. 1 Corinthians 3:3 has: "you are *fleshly.*" De Fuenterrabía, *Nuevo Testamento,* translates it: "weak in the faith." The version, *Dios llega al hombre,* translates it: "purely human." Romans 7:25 has: "with the *flesh* I serve the law of sin." De Fuenterrabía translates it: "purely natural state." *Dios llega al hombre* translates it: "human nature."

Chapter II

57. If the mechanism of Sin ('holding God's truth shackled in injustice') leads to the same sort of idolatry among both pagans and Jews, and if we assume that the same mechanism continues to be operative in Christians since it is bound up with human 'flesh', then we cannot read Romans 2 as a chapter referring merely to the past. "So we understand these verses as the revelation of the gospel's judgment of all men, which lays bare not only the idolatry of ancient and modern paganism but also the idolatry ensconced in Israel, in the Church, and in the life of each believer" (ICC 2:106). We certainly do have to be careful because our deep-rooted tendency is to view Paul's portrait of the Jewish world much as the Jews might have viewed his portrait of the pagan world: i.e., passing judgment from an illusory standpoint of privileged superiority. Romans 2 has to do with us too because in many instances we, instead of inheriting 'filiation' in Christ, have inherited from Judaism a new, more complete and more privileged edition of the Law of Moses.

58. Hence the importance of the opening phrase, "for all that" (2:1), which covers the whole of 1:18-32. Its importance lies in the fact that it suggests that the *practical* idolatry discussed in Romans 2 cannot excuse itself on the basis of its *theoretical* 'orthodoxy'. Here is one more reason for concluding that the argument from 'God's works' in Romans 1 is not an attack on pagan lack of orthodoxy (piety/impiety) but on pagan failures in the area of orthopraxis (justice/injustice).

59. No matter which hypothesis one adopts, it is not easy to see the sense or purpose of the three examples adduced by Paul. "Some commentators, therefore, feeling the need for an interpretation of *klépteis, moicheúeis,* and *hierosuleîs,* which makes them true of all Jews, have understood them to refer to what the Jews as a whole had done with regard to Jesus Christ and were doing with regard to His followers. Others have explained—and this seems more probable—that Paul is thinking in terms of a radical understanding of the law, cf. Mt 5:21-48" (ICC 2:168-169). Thus the ICC commentator suggests that adultery be understood in the sense of Mt 5:27-32 (as adultery of intention), not as a reference to the religious sense of adultery (i.e., idolatry as in Hos 1-3; Jer 3; Ez 16, etc.). Either way, however, the parallelism between the two chapters or diptychs is lost. Moreover, the ICC commentator doubts that it is a matter of concrete sins against the law, because there does not seem to have been idolatry in Israel at that time nor widespread sacrileges against pagan temples by stealing or use of stolen goods. "Again, we may take him to be thinking not only of behaviour which is obviously sacrilegious, but also of less obvious and more subtle forms of sacrilege" (ICC 2:170). But what exactly might those sins be, and how could the Romans identify them precisely without knowing Paul or having more information?

60. Or that *the whole world* presents itself "guilty before God" (3:19).

61. The difference from the similar expression in Romans 2 is further explained by

the same factor that differentiates the Jew from the pagan. The former, unlike the latter, does not possess a law that arises from inside the self and that must be suffocated or shackled in order to give free rein to one's cravings. Jews possess a truth *taught* by God: i.e., the Law. They cannot suffocate it or fail to hear it; they can only be *indocile* to it through hardness of heart.

62. That is why the *three distinctive sins* attributed to them by Paul lose all importance and significance. They could be mere abstract examples of the way bad faith operates by focusing on the mote in someone else's eye and neglecting the beam in one's own eye. What takes on crucial importance is the fact that Paul, at the very start of Romans 3, can prove that the Jews "do the very same things" as the pagans once this process of self-deception has run its course.

63. Even when we note slight differences, that can be attributed to two reasons. First, in addressing himself to the Jews, Paul cites the Greek translation of the Old Testament known as the Septuagint. Since it was an established text, he could not make any major change in it. To describe pagan conduct, on the other hand, Paul makes use of everyday, vernacular Greek, which is less stereotyped and richer in connotations. Second, in his description of Jewish conduct as dehumanized, there is no extended treatment of homosexuality as there is in Romans 1. This is undoubtedly a sociological trait that Paul could use in the case of pagans but could not apply similarly to the Jews. And there is the further fact that no biblical texts speak of that sin as a generalized one in Israel.

64. This knowledge of Sin, transmitted to all humanity by the testimony of a people who fulfilled the Law, must have been God's original plan for the Law, with all humanity in mind. Because it is all humanity that Paul has in mind when he undertakes this description of the anthropological mechanisms of Sin. To achieve this aim, however, there was need of a people who would demonstrate in their own persons the meaning and spirit of that Law: i.e., its usefulness as a *humanizing* agent. But what the rest of humanity sees in the Law, as embodied in the distorted version of the Jewish people, causes them to blaspheme the God of Israel. Instead of uniting humanity, it separates them religiously. As we shall see, this theme is central to Paul. Equally central to him is the question: How do we prevent the same thing from happening in the case of Christianity?

65. Although in this case Paul describes the self-deception more in terms of pride and insensitivity: "hardness and impenitence of heart" (2:5).

66. Paul's argument here is summed up in his statement: "Circumcision is certainly useful if you fulfill the Law" (2:25). Knowing what he says further on about the Law, we can assume this is mainly an *ad hominem* argument. It is as if Paul were saying: I assume that if you are glorying in the Law it is because you have fulfilled it, because that is the function of all law. It is within the context of this argument, posed in his opponent's terms even though they be false, that Paul asserts: "Those who have sinned without law will perish without law, and those who have sinned in the system of the law *will be judged by the criterion of the law*" (2:12). But at the end of Romans 3, Paul will deny that God's judgment takes into account the difference signified by the Law (see 3:30).

67. This change of people is seen by Paul as the price that had to be paid for the universalization of (the system of) Grace (see 11:11-12).

68. In connection with this 'glorying', remember how Paul criticizes the Corinthians for glorying 'in the human' while pretending to glory in the religious. His remark about being a "guide for the blind" (2:19) seems to allude to a responsibility. But the irony of his remarks suggests the behavior of a privileged person who poses as a model for others

without actively assuming the responsibility of helping them to improve.

69. The word used here in Greek is *epithumia,* which means 'strong or passionate desires', 'cravings', is translated as 'concupiscences' in the Latin Vulgate. It introduces us to a new character in Paul's anthropological analysis: *the Flesh.* That character plays a major role in the behavior of the Galatians and the Corinthians, as we have noted. In Paul's system, the Flesh is the seat and source of the strong, root desires of the human body, its cravings, which are really akin to what Freud calls 'instincts' in his psychology.

70. Jesus tries to prevent this by means of the so-called 'messianic secret', which we examined in Volume II.

71. Here one might wonder about the 'natural' faith discussed in Romans 1, whereby human beings can know God through God's works. Would that faith put up greater resistance to the anthropological mechanism we see operative in 'revealed' religions? There is nothing to suggest that such is the case. Here again we have another reason for adopting the hypothesis that sees *injustice* as the anthropological source and origin of *idolatry.* If one chooses the other hypothesis, then one must say something like this: once human beings make the *culpable* shift from natural revelation to the adoration of "the corruptible human being, birds, quadrupeds, and reptiles" (1:23), then the whole realm of religion (now twice removed from human values) is set up for human beings to *use* it to support their tendency to practice *injustice* vis-à-vis other human beings.

72. If we do not interpret Paul in this way, then these verses directly contradict what he says near the very end of the third chapter: "So if God is one and only, it is God who will declare just circumcision in accordance with faith, and uncircumcision by means of faith" (3:30).

Chapter III

73. According to Mt 5:17, Jesus says that he has come to give 'completion', which probably means 'culmination' to the Law and the Prophets; i.e., to everything in the Old Testament. Mt 5:18 should undoubtedly be interpreted the same way, although his reference to 'one iota of the law' seems to allude solely to the *normative* divine message in the Pentateuch. The next verse (Mt 5:19) clearly moves on to talk about *commandments,* the Sinai decalog, rather than God's saving events in history. Insofar as giving 'culmination' to the Law is concerned, note the significant difference between the 'more' demanded by Jesus in Matthew (5:20–48) and the 'something different' he demands in Luke (6:27–35). In Mark (7:19) Jesus seems to explicitly abolish at least one section of the Law: that having to do with foods.

74. Paul uses the term 'law' in a wide variety of senses. My translation and those of other people cannot neatly differentiate all of them, since we cannot do full justice to all the shadings of Greek and its use of the definite article. To put a little order into the matter, it is said that generally 'law' with the definite article 'the' refers to the Law given by Moses, without the definite article it refers to 'law' in general terms (see, for example, 2:12–14; 3:20f.; 4:15; 5:13). But a second meaning of 'law' without the definite article must be noted: "There is yet a third usage where *nómos* without article really means the Law of Moses, but the absence of the article calls attention to it not as proceeding from Moses, but in its quality *as law* . . . St. Paul regards the Pre-Messianic period as essentially a period of Law, both for Jew and for Gentile . . . his main point is that they were under 'a legal system' " (ICC 1:58). This grammatical view is generally correct, but it overlooks several important things. First, 'the law' also designates the Pentateuch, not just as a legal system, but also as interpretation, prediction, and prophecy of salvific

events. It thus can designate Scripture as a whole (see 3:19). Second, in the context of the Christian message 'the law' is *fulfilled* or brought to its culmination in a way that cannot simply be identified with the law 'of Moses'. Third, it is a gross oversimplification to say that the pre-messianic period was under a 'legal' system (see 7:9; 4:10; 5:12; etc.). Paul takes great pains to bring out certain points. (1) Individual pagans of that period had 'faith', a saving faith, starting with Father Abraham. (2) The Mosaic Law introduced a new element or system that affected only the Jews and hence had a specific function, both positive and negative; its function was dialectical, in short, so that a liberation from 'the law of Sin' might be conceivable and possible with the arrival of the messianic period. This one example should make it clear that philology cannot supply the theological interpretation, particularly when we are dealing with an original line of thought such as Paul's. Following and working out the logical development of his thought, doing theological interpretation, is another task.

75. Thus Paul indicates that the *real* labels of 'pagan' and 'Jew', of 'uncircumcised' and 'circumcised', will often change places before the judgment seat of God (see 2:25–29). The force of this assertion by Paul is much stronger than it might seem at first glance. Remember that the *totality* of humanity is covered by the contrasting terms he uses. Paul is saying that at least some Jews are pagans and idolaters inwardly, which is what God will judge. On the other hand pagans who become Jews inwardly by their inner attitude, by an inner circumcision, can fulfill something of the true spirit and purpose of the Law, no matter how difficult or rare such an occurrence may be. Contrary to what some commentators have claimed, Paul cannot be referring to pagans who have now converted to Christianity. That would annul his argument. Even more importantly, such a view clashes completely with the thinking of Paul, for whom circumcision ends with Christianity. For the contrary view, see ICC 2:172.

76. In his Letter to the Galatians, who were Jewish converts to Christianity for the most part, Paul does not concern himself so directly with pagans. So rather than viewing the Law as an unfair privilege, he views it as the negation of the Promise. Thus in the same verse he goes on to say: ". . . in order that the promise might be granted to believers through faith in Jesus Christ." But in Romans, in a much broader context, Paul presents Abraham as the prototype of those who lived by the Promise rather than by the Law. Abraham obviously did not have faith in Jesus Christ, and the Promise made to him was that he would be *the father of all human beings* who walk by faith, uncircumcised and circumcised. The meaning of faith in Jesus Christ will be examined in a later chapter.

77. Over against this general image of the diptych, which depicts all *equally* under Sin, Paul seems to present another one that shares only one feature: *equally*. It occurs in Romans 2, when he writes that "some Gentiles, without having law, naturally do what is commanded by the law" (2:14). Verse 15 seems to end in a break, or anacoluthon, when he writes "witness being provided by their own conscience and their inner thoughts, which will accuse *and even defend them*. . . ." Verse 16 adds a temporal or eschatological specification: "on the day when God will judge . . ."

What exactly might this defense before God's judgment be, particularly since Paul seems to suggest that it will be overpowered by the accusation? One hypothesis would omit or displace verses 7–15, so that verse 16 would be the natural continuation of verses 5–6: "the just judgment of God, who will give to each human being according to its works/ on the day when God will judge the secrets of human beings through Christ Jesus, as per my good news." In that case the accusing or defending thoughts could not have any connection with God's final judgment, which follows upon verse 6. This interpretation is not supported by the texts as we have them, but it is particularly alluring to some commentators (see ICC 1:62) because it enables them to maintain that outside faith, faith *in Christ* (see verse 16), there can be no defense for the sinner.

I think that another possible interpretation is more coherent and balanced. Rather than relying on a distortion of the text, it relies on a difference that Paul himself always would acknowledge: the difference between *Sin* and *sins*. To be under subjection to Sin does not mean that a person simply commits sins. And the fact that even pagans frequently do what is right is an *ad hominem* argument against those Jews who think that possession of the Law permits them to pass negative judgment on everybody else.

78. Paul's assertion that he was blameless vis-à-vis the *justice* demanded by the Law (Phil 3:6) directly contradicts my statement here and the whole picture that Paul presents in Romans 2–3:20. It is all the more interesting if, as many exegetes think, the Letter to the Philippians dates from his imprisonment in Ephesus, approximately a year before he wrote the Letter to the Romans. It could mean that a profound theological deepening took place in Paul during that time with regard to the import and power of Sin.

We find interpretations swinging from one end of the spectrum to the other in order to resolve the apparent contradiction. At one end we have a very interesting Protestant exegesis from Krister Stendahl in his fine book, *Paul Among Jews and Gentiles*. Stendahl fully accepts Paul's statement in Philippians. Paul was a man of 'robust' conscience (p. 80), nothing like the *simul justus et peccator* figure seen in him by Augustine, Luther, and the introspective plague of the West (p. 14). The only sin Paul would acknowledge in himself, says Stendahl, was that of having persecuted the nascent Church. At the other end of the spectrum, other commentators would reject Paul's assertion in Philippians or say that it was merely an *ad hominem* argument against those who denied his status as a faithful expositor of the Jewish faith. My interpretation further on falls somewhere between those two extremes, and it is connected with what I said in the previous note. Paul could be blameless vis-à-vis the supposed justice stemming from *literal* fulfillment of the Law, and still be under the dominion of Sin. It was precisely that enslavement that closed his heart to recognition of Jesus as the culmination of the Law and turned him into a persecutor of Christianity (see note 166).

79. To be more precise, we would have to exclude Adam from the first stage. According to Paul, in Eden Adam received a sort of *minimum* 'Law', so his situation there was somewhat akin to the later situation of the Jews. So let us say that the first stage begins after Adam's sin (see 5:14). Readers might also note that Paul does not conceptually equate 'paganism' or 'gentileness' with idolatry or offbase religion, even though such an equation may turn out to be true in practice. Paganism and gentileness are characterized by the lack of the revealed Law, and hence the *sign* of obedience to that Law becomes the distinguishing feature. Thus pagans are the uncircumcised, as Abraham was (see 2:25–28; 4:10–13.16).

80. Having the law written in one's heart rather than in some external document, as Paul says to be true of some pagans at least, also constitutes an eschatological promise (see Jer 31:33). Hence some commentators feel that if this were true of some pagans, it would be a contradictory sign that the promise had been fulfilled even before Christ (see ICC 2:158–159). But the eschatological promise is a promise of completeness and fulfillment. The fact that faith might be present in people's hearts in some initial way says nothing against the superabundant fulfillment reserved for the eschatological promise that is somehow realized in Christ.

81. See the magnificent studies of Von Rad (e.g., *Estudios sobre el Antiguo Testa-*

mento, pp. 283f.) on the Deuteronomic Law to appreciate the positive evaluation of that Law when understood in a way far different from that attacked by Jesus. His articles also indicate how the process of interpreting the Law in a distorted way got started.

82. As I indicated earlier, I do not use the translations 'justify' and 'justification'. I use 'declare just' and 'declaration of justice'. The usual procedure is to use the first set of terms, *even though the translator realizes that the real meaning of the words is the second one.* Such is the case with our ICC commentator: ". . . there seems to us to be no doubt that *dikaioûn,* as used by Paul, means simply 'acquit', 'confer a righteous status on', and does not in itself contain any reference to moral transformation. This conclusion is surely forced upon us by the linguistic evidence. It would also seem to be borne out by the structure of Paul's argument in Romans" (ICC 2:95). Euthymus Zigabenus interprets both 4:5 and 4:25 as 'to *make* righteous', insofar as the verb is concerned. Our ICC commentator does not accept that authority here, though he cites him often to clarify questions of Greek grammar and usage. And his reason for rejecting the witness of a Greek expert here is clearly theological in nature: "The evidence is too decisive (p. 30 f. *sup.*) that *dikaioûn* = not 'to make righteous' but 'to declare righteous as a judge' . . . The Greek theologians had not a clear conception of the doctrine of justification" (ICC 1:101).

Such strong statements of a general nature, applied to all of Paul, call us up short even though they may be correct in most instances. What about the 'make just' of 5:19, for example? As generalizations, they sacrifice too much to a specific theological viewpoint. They preclude the exegetical possibility of examining the use of the terms *in each case,* which is a very important consideration when we are dealing with a writer like Paul and his creative use of language.

83. Unless one adopts the extreme hypothesis of Krister Stendahl, which is not without some real merit. Stendahl has wrought a Copernican revolution in the exegesis of Paul, explaining why there was no real consideration of any possible justification by faith during the first three centuries of church history. Such consideration had to wait for Augustine because earlier 'justification' was not interpreted as God's salvific judgment. It was interpreted as God's judgment of converted pagans, whereby they were admitted into the Christian community as honorary Jews (see *Paul Among Jews and Gentiles*, p. 5, and Romans 2:15–16). In short, God *justified them* as true heirs of the divine promises to Israel. I do think this is a dominant concern in Paul, but not to the point of annuling his anthropological analyses and the central role of justification in those analyses.

84. Paul was well aware of the danger of misunderstandings here, as his repeated allusion to questions that might be asked of him indicate (3:31; 6:1.15): "St. Paul was accused (no doubt by actual opponents) of Antinomianism. what he said was, 'The state of righteousness is not to be attained through legal works; it is the gift of God'. He was represented as saying 'therefore it does not matter what a man does'—an inference which he repudiates indignantly, not only here but in 6:1f; 6:15f" (ICC 1:74). We should not assume right off that Paul's indignation is perfectly understandable. Instead we should wait to see exactly how he frames his arguments to preclude misunderstandings. Because if it is true that human actions do not matter to God because the gift is given equally, that God does carry out the salvation plan without any causal cooperation on the part of human beings, then Paul's statements on the importance of human actions are little more than pious, demagogic rhetoric.

85. Notice that the two elements in this formula of faith are the two preconditions for becoming a member of the Christian community. And according to Luke, the first

community in Jerusalem thought that salvation depended on such membership: "Day by day the Lord was adding to the community *those who were to be saved*" (Acts 2:47). So even though Paul has a less magical and more complex line of thought, he does use this primitive 'formula of faith' as an argument in his argument against the Jews. But he never employs it in the first eight chapters of Romans, where we find his christology.

86. When Paul says that glorying has been ruled out and then asks by what 'law', it seems obvious to me that 'law' here refers to the mechanism which rules out glorying. Hence 'the law of works' is not a fourth complex opposed to faith, nor is it an inverted synonym for 'works of the law'. And unlike the three terms mentioned above, the expression 'law of works' does not crop up again in Paul.

87. The exception was the law inscribed in the hearts of pagans during the first stage of the divine plan. But it is an exaggeration to say that this law proves that human beings found themselves under a *legal* system during that first period (see ICC 1:58).

88. Here I must give due weight and respect to the fine, pointed observations and arguments of Stendahl, which seek to show that Paul's main concern was to prove that *faith* gave pagans *the same right* as Jews to become part of the successor community of the people of Israel.

89. Besides the difficulties Paul has in attributing some value and function to the Law in God's plan, there is the difficulty of the word itself. In this chapter 'law' has at least three different meanings. Particularly when linked with 'the Prophets', it means God's revelation in the Old Testament. It may also refer to the explicitly normative part of that revelation and its 'theological' elaboration in the history of Israel. In this second sense it is a central element of Israelite 'religion'. Finally, 'law' has the 'secular' sense of *mechanism* or explanation. It is in that sense Paul uses the term when he discusses why 'glorying' has been ruled out.

90. An attitude very different from the strain of gaiety and joyousness that characterized the message and preaching of Jesus of Nazareth about the kingdom.

91. The basic argument holds good today too, because we do not float away cleanly from our teachers when we reach adulthood. But we must realize that the metaphor was even richer in Paul's day because the *paidagōgos* was a slave entrusted with the education of a boy and had a certain amount of authority over him. When the boy grew up and took charge of his father's estate, the slave took on new functions *under* his own student. Here it matters little whether the slave actually taught the boy or merely led him to school. In either case he watched over the boy's conduct and gave him orders.

92. Paul is not exaggerating. Remember that Mark draws the same conclusion from the preaching of Jesus (Mk 7:19). Even if the comment on pure and impure foods is postpaschal, the fact that it is included as a conclusion proves its connection with the teaching of Jesus: i.e., that nothing from outside a person, not even some supposed Law of God in the Bible, can put a moral label on things *in themselves* (see the universal formulation of this in Romans 14:14). The fact that the application is solely to food in Mark undoubtedly is due to the influence of the term 'mouth' in the 'parable'.

Chapter IV

93. This indirectly confirms my argument in the previous chapter that Paul was referring to the Law of Moses when he ruled out 'the works of the law' as the reason behind the declaration of justice. In other words, the negative part of the principle in question applied exclusively and formally to the descendants of Abraham. What Paul

does, however, is to turn Abraham the Jew into Abraham the human being, stripping him of ethnicity.

94. In short, it is based on the Law insofar as that term may designate the Pentateuch and the whole Old Testament: "If, as we must needs think, ch. 4 contains the proof of the proposition laid down in this verse, *nómon* must = ultimately and virtually the Pentateuch. But it = the Pentateuch not as an isolated Book but as the most conspicuous and representative expression of that great system of Law which prevailed everywhere until the coming of Christ. The Jew looked at the O.T., and he saw there Law, Obedience to Law or Works, Circumcision, Descent from Abraham. St. Paul said, Look again and look deeper, and you will see—not Law but Promise, not works but Faith—of which Circumcision is only the seal, not literal descent from Abraham but spiritual descent" (ICC 1:96). But the ICC commentator forgets that 3:31 is not an isolated assertion, and that it is not the only one to talk about a possible fulfillment of the law. In 8:4 Paul makes it clear that he is not dealing solely with promises contained in the Law or the books of the Law, but also with fulfillment of 'the just precept of the Law' or 'the justice of the Law'. Thus there is a way of fulfilling the Law, of working in accordance with it, that is compatible with faith. In formulating it with the subtlety and profundity required, we come to see and appreciate the difficulty, complexity, and richness of Paul's anthropological analysis.

95. It is worth noting that James's argument holds for the opposition between *faith* and *works,* not for the much more strictly Pauline opposition between *faith* and *works of the Law* (see Jas 2:14.17–18.20–22.24–26).

96. But I do not think that they are opposed in their *conclusions.* I would say that James interprets Paul in a strictly 'Lutheran' sense and tries to refute his argument in that precise sense. Luther himself saw it thus. If we can get a less magical interpretation of Paul's principle, then Paul and James may be saying the same thing. See Volume I of this series, *Faith and Ideologies,* pp. 123–126, as well as what follows here.

97. See note 34.

98. *The Jerusalem Bible* (JB) feels compelled to offer this comment on Abraham in Egypt as narrated in Genesis 12: "The story reflects a stage of moral development when a lie was still considered lawful under certain circumstances and when the husband's life meant more than his wife's honour. God was leading man to an appreciation of the moral law but this appreciation was gradual" (comment e).

99. The Elohist writer (see Gn 20:12) clearly tries to excuse Abraham. Abraham used a mental reservation! Sarah was his sister on his father's side, but not on his mother's side. The Yahwist ignores that sort of excuse.

100. To borrow a phrase from fiction writers and movie directors, however much their work may be based on real events, I would say here that any similarity between this hypothesis of mine and psychoanalysis is purely accidental.

101. Paul coins this word in Greek and uses it only once in relation to Abraham, whose attitude of *Faith* is the model of what will bring justification to the Gentiles (see Gal 3:8, *proeuēngelisato tō Abraam).* It has nothing to do with making 'an act of faith'. Rather, it means 'living by faith', so that one's general behavior is based on faith (see Gal 3:9).

102. Further on, in 7:9–11, "St. Paul uses a vivid figurative expression . . . He is describing the state prior to Law primarily in himself as a child before the consciousness of law has taken hold upon him; but he uses this experience as typical of that both of individuals and nations before they are restrained by express command. The 'natural man' flourishes; he does freely and without hesitation all that he has a mind to do; he puts forth all his vitality, unembarrassed by the checks and thwartings of conscience"

(ICC 1:180). The last sentence is a beautiful description of how Paul sees Abraham.

Two very different observations might be made here. First, it is hard to fathom the why and wherefore of a divine Law being introduced into such a paradise-like situation. Second, I would say that we are dealing with a description, not of any 'natural man', but of a human being grounded in faith in the broadest sense of the term. This is what faith effects in a human being, even a pagan human being, as the example of Abraham proves (Romans 4). Greater grounding and force is provided by the message of Jesus, which provides the 'reasons', the 'transcendent data', for operating in that way.

103. The final part of the phrase reads: ". . . but not before God." Does that imply that he can glory before others? Undoubtedly no, because that declaration of justice is not known by others, historically speaking, and Abraham lives by a promise whose fulfillment is as yet invisible. That is why it seemed better to follow some exegetes and supply the implied words: ". . . but *it is* not *so* before God." Since Abraham cannot feel any temptation to 'glory' before others, another solution would be that the impossibility of glorying thus is to be taken in the figurative or exemplary sense of (e.g.) 3:27.

104. The importance of the term (see Bultmann, I, 242f.) is brought out by other key texts such as Galatians 6:13–14 and 1 Corinthians 3:21. The latter is all the more significant in that Paul must confront people trying to 'glory' in the use of 'Christian' religious instruments: evangelization or baptism by one or another person. So the temptation goes far beyond the presence or absence of the Law of Moses, and it is likely that Paul is thinking of it when he says that the declaration of justice comes 'independently of the works of the Law'.

105. For this statement of Romans 2 to make sense, some relationship must exist between this *active* 'seeking' and what is *received,* even though the latter is not a 'wage'. Now if we are thinking of a judgment that would give a truly universal dimension to that positive relationship, so far we have only two passages to consider; but they are most important. In the first, Paul says that "God . . . will give to *each human being* according to its *works.* To those who seek glory, honor, and incorruption, God will give eternal life . . . glory, honor, and peace . . . for everyone who *works good*" (2:6–7.10). In the second, Paul says: "So if God is one and only, it is God who will declare just *circumcision* in accordance with *faith,* and *uncircumcision* by means of *faith*" (3:30). Obviously if those two passages are to be consistent with each other, they cannot pose an alternative between faith and works. Here is what one ICC commentator has to say about Romans 2: "We are now in a position to look at vv. 6–11 as a whole and to try to decide how the passage is to be understood. The difficulty which faces us here will confront us again in vv. 12–16 and 25–29; and in each of these three closely-related passages it is what we may call the positive element which is specially problematic (i.e. vv. 7 and 10; vv. 13b and 14a; and v. 26)" (ICC 2:151). It is worth noting this clear acceptance of the fact that here we meet a Paul who does not fit into the canons of a definite theology, one that is centered around a few verses. I think it is worth bringing together here the verses that stand in the way of any such theology with a one-sided view of Paul's thinking: "To those who seek glory, honor, and incorruption, God will give eternal life . . . glory, honor, and peace . . . for everyone who *works good,* for the Jew first and also for the Greek . . . only those who *practice [the law]* will be declared just. For . . . some Gentiles, without having law, *naturally do what is commanded by the law* . . . If uncircumcision *keeps the just precepts of the law,* will not that uncircumcision be reckoned as circumcision?" (2:7.10.13.14.26).

106. Exegetes of the caliber of Von Rad warn us against the idea that the biblical notion of 'covenant' implies a certain equality between the parties involved and rules

out the notion of gratuitousness. But even though such relative equality does not exist as a precondition for the covenant, it is somehow created (gratuitously on Yahweh's part) by the covenant itself. Therein lies the danger of any 'covenant': that it will be lived out as a 'contract' between equals and thereby seem to be the opposite of gratuitousness.

107. To say there is no relationship between the work of the human being and the judgment of God is to profoundly dehumanize human existence. In that case Paul would be the creator of a 'system' of salvation in which efficacy was divorced from sense and meaning. "Under the old system the only way laid down for man to attain to righteousness was by the strict performance of the Mosaic Law; now that heavy obligation is removed and a shorter but at the same time more effective method is substituted, the method of attachment to a Divine Person" (ICC 1:83). It is awfully hard to believe that Paul went to so much trouble exploring and analyzing human existence to explain something as simple, elemental, extrinsic, and a-human as the view attributed to him by that ICC commentator. That view would also seem to be very cold-blooded and devastating for the two million years of humanity that preceded the manifestation of the 'Divine Person'. They would appear to be greatly out of favor with a God who, according to Paul, does not show favoritism to anyone. It is hardly a point in Paul's favor that he shortens the time when humanity was subjected to the 'old system' and its 'heavy obligation' to four thousand years, in accordance with the biblical data.

108. In their nomadic wanderings through the land of Canaan, the patriarchs do not seem to have had any difficulty in practicing syncretism, combining their own cult with that of the local area when they saw no incompatibility. That seems to be the case in the relationship between Abraham and Melchizedek, priest of 'God Most High' (Gn 14:17–20).

109. That was the case with the 'God-fearing' people or 'worshippers of God' coming from paganism (see Acts 10:2.22.35; 13:16.26.43.50; 16:14; 17:4.17; 18:7).

110. We know, of course, that *atheism* was not a biblical category. The people who say "there is no God" in the Psalms (10:4; 14:1) are not atheists, strictly speaking. They are saying that God's justice does not get involved in history (see Ps 58:12). It is hard to say when atheism surfaced as a perceptible social phenomenon—aside from isolated cases among Greek philosophers, for example. Paul does not take it into account. He divides all humanity religiously into Jews and Greeks, circumcised and uncircumcised. But we can extrapolate his remarks and apply them to the atheist, remembering what GS had to say: i.e., one of the sources of atheism is the false face of God presented by believers. And certainly one of those false faces is that of a god with whom one dickers for salvation.

111. Here I must briefly allude to the antithetical parallelism between Adam and Christ which Paul sets up in the next chapter. In this chapter Abraham appears in both terms: as a *new Adam* or *post*-Adam on the one hand, as a *pre-Christ* on the other. In short, Abraham has an anthropological dimension that combines features of the two poles of humanity. Note, for example, that Abraham receives 'good news in advance' (Gal 3:8) that has universal content: 'all nations'.

112. Hence the importance of making clear that the opposition which does justice to Paul's *whole* thought is not faith versus works, but faith versus *works-of-the-law;* and that 'law'—some kind of calculator for relations between God and the human being—is implied whenever Paul talks of *works* (plural) in similar contexts. It should be noted that Paul speaks differently of human 'working' and 'work' (singular). Note also that sometimes (in 2:6 for example) the plural 'works' is merely distributive: all human beings will be judged by their works, each by his or her 'work' (see 1 Cor 3:13). Paul is

bound by a citation from Psalm 62:12. When he gets away from that, he prefers to use a verbal phrase: 'to work good'.

113. The author of the Letter to the Hebrews, somehow related to Paul, describes Christians drawing closer to the eschatological, through the resurrection of Jesus, and thereby clinching the transcendent datum they possess. The description is given in the context of the difficulty apostates face in repenting, once they have fallen away from the Christian experience. As Christians, they "were once enlightened . . . savored the heavenly gift . . . were made partakers of the Holy Spirit . . . *savored* the *good word of God and the marvelous powers of the world to come* . . ." (Heb 6:4–5).

114. This is really the last chapter where I shall try to trace the thought of Paul back to the historical message of Jesus in section II. From here on, Paul begins to ponder the fact of the death and resurrection of Jesus and the consequences for the human being. This twofold happening took place without words.

115. Paul's exegetical method, more than ever in this chapter perhaps, seems artificial to us today; but it was the ordinary one in the milieu where Paul was educated, well educated, as a Pharisee. Indeed there was no other, at least with respect to the possibility and obligation we feel today to frame every passage in its historical context. Obviously the author of Genesis 15 did not entertain a specific theory of justification. There is an even more important point to remember in connection with most of the chapters of Romans under discussion here. What was called 'Law' in Paul's day depended on the exegesis of his day, in which context was not operative enough as a factor to shed clear light on the original meaning. Set in their original context, the various catalogs of laws in Exodus, Deuteronomy, and Leviticus are much more like civil *constitutions* in our sense—given by Yahweh at various times as Israel moved through different phases—than one, unique moral law designed to regulate the intimate, personal behavior of the human being (see Von Rad, *Old Testament Theology*, I, 190f.). Even Jesus' 'correction' of that 'Law', brought out especially by Matthew, followed the same exegetical method of his day. Hence it was unfair or unjust to some extent, insofar as it sought to correct the Law as a *moral* law.

116. It is worth noting the repeated presence of the word 'this' *(touto)* in the Greek text. Some Bibles unfortunately translate it as 'this being', 'this nature', or similarly. But here Paul is not being metaphysical; he is being graphic. To translate the expression correctly, we must imagine the gesture accompanying it. It is one of those expressions akin to our own, as when we say: "I've had it up to *here* with your complaining!" We can assume that the 'body' of 8:23 implies the same content as the 'this' of the other cited passages; that it does not indicate solely the *body* of Paul. Some translations, incorrect in my view, give the impression that Paul wants to be 'liberated from the body' rather than 'liberated from his own body'. The latter would seem to be much more connected with the possibility of easily handling the 'law of the members' (7:25), which has to do, not with the body, but with the coherence and carrying out of a human being's *projects*.

117. Note the same broad sense in the Prologue of John's gospel (1:14), where 'flesh' and 'tent' are used as synonyms.

Chapter V

118. "The existence of Jesus Christ does not only determine the existence of believers; it is also the innermost secret of the life of every man" (ICC 2:269).

119. There is a crucial parallelism between verses 9 and 10, i.e., between *"we shall be saved by him . . .* since we have been *declared just* by his *blood"* (v. 9) and *"we were*

reconciled with God . . . by the *death* of his son . . . [and] we, already reconciled, *will be saved* . . .*" (v. 10). This parallelism clearly indicates that 'declaration of justice' and 'reconciliation' are synonymous for Paul (see Bultmann, I, 285f.). Our commentator, however, sees an essential difference between the two verses: "No clearer passage can be quoted for distinguishing the sphere of justification and sanctification than this verse and the next—the one an objective fact accomplished without us, the other a change operated within us" (ICC 1:129). Leaving aside the fact that 'reconciliation' is not synonymous with 'sanctification' (which does not appear here), we may ask: If the declaration of justice occurs *without us,* where does that leave the "by reason of faith"? Even if we assume the impossibility of grasping an immediate effect *in us* of the declaration of justice, his argument won't hold because verses 9 and 10 are identical in this respect. Both set forth an *objective* fact introduced into us by God; and like everything God introduces into us, it must also become a *subjective* fact, at least at the Christian level.

120. Our ICC commentator argues with Lightfoot as to whether 'reconciliation' means a *subjective* change in our mind toward God or an *objective* modification of our relationship with God. For Lightfoot, "the active rather than the passive sense . . . is required by the context, which (as commonly in the N.T.) speaks of the sinner as reconciled to God, not of God as reconciled to the sinner . . . It is the mind of man, not the mind of God, which must undergo a change . . ." (ICC 1:129). A *subjective* change, in other words. Our commentator disagrees, explaining that most commentators do not agree with Lightfoot on this point: "We infer that the natural explanation of the passages which speak of enmity and reconciliation between God and man is that they are not on one side only, but are mutual" (ICC 1:30). Hence, objective. I would simply point out to my readers that this invalidates his argument that verse 9 refers to something objective and verse 10 to something subjective, thereby also invalidating his attempted proof of a real distinction between justification and sanctification. More subtle is the phrasing of the later ICC commentator: "The reconciliation Paul is speaking of is not to be understood as simply identical with justification (the two terms being understood as different metaphors denoting the same thing), nor yet as a consequence of justification, a result following afterwards" (ICC 2:256). The phrasing is cryptic and leaves us in doubt between identity and difference. But I think it tends to prove that in both cases we are dealing with a change that does not intrinsically alter the beneficiary.

121. Recall the citation in note 118: "The existence of Jesus Christ does not only determine the existence of believers; it is also the innermost secret of the life of every man" (ICC 2:269). This recognition of the *fully anthropological* significance of Jesus of Nazareth should also shed light on the earlier verses and logically lead us to find in the life of every human being some real sense for my statement made in the text. Along with unconditional reconciliation, every human being must receive some sort of inchoative faith or *pre*-faith, though already justifying, that becomes explicit and complete only in Jesus. In my terminology, by faith I mean the necessity of living a system of values on the basis of transcendent data.

122. Both Catholic and Protestant. After the rediscovery of Paul's theology in Romans by Luther, it was Calvin, following Augustine of course, who posed the terrible problem of predestination to eternal damnation. How can that be compatible with the antithetical parallel between Adam and Christ (which Luther's theology did not stress)? That is the question I tackle here. Once the incompatibility is established, we have no recourse but to reject it as a false problem that simply does not fit in with Paul's logic.

123. The Latin translation, *'in quo',* inclined people to understand 'in whom' rather

than 'because', although the latter is the correct rendering of the original Greek.

124. "The Greek commentators for the most part supply nothing, but take *hēmarton* in its usual sense: 'all sinned in their own persons, and on their own initiative'. So Euthym. Zigabenus . . . The objection to this is that it destroys the parallelism between Adam and Christ" (ICC 1:134). This argument holds only if, as the commentator obviously assumes, the justice conferred by Christ is merely 'imputed', not real, just as the sin transmitted by Adam to all his descendants (even children who have never chosen to sin) is 'imputed' rather than personal. If we do not assume that theology, which is precisely what I am arguing against here, then the parallelism is confirmed, not destroyed.

125. "What a contrast does this last description suggest between the Fall of Adam and the justifying Work of Christ! There is indeed parallelism as well as contrast. For it is true that as Christ brought righteousness and life, so Adam's Fall brought sin and death. If death prevailed throughout the pre-Mosaic period, that could not be due solely to the acts of those who died. Death is the punishment of sin; but they had not sinned against law as Adam had. The true cause was not their own sin, but Adam's: whose fall thus had consequences extending beyond itself, like the redeeming act of Christ" (ICC 1:130–131; and see p. 132 also). This commentary would suggest many reservations if it had been written after the discussions about *demythologization,* because it is obviously a mythical interpretation. Even taking chronology into account, however, we should not downplay the fact that its magical aspect is bound up with a theological interpretation. That theological interpretation was profound in its study of sin, but magical and extrinsicist in its interpretation of the justification that saves human beings and gives them their true final destiny. The same commentator baldly states: "There is something sufficiently startling in this. The Christian life is made to have its beginning in a fiction. No wonder that the fact is questioned, and that another sense is given to the words—that *dikaioûsthai* is taken to imply not the attribution of righteousness in idea but an imparting of actual righteousness. The facts of language, however, are inexorable: we have seen that *dikaioûn, dikaioûsthai,* have the first sense and not the second; that they are rightly said to be 'forensic'; that they have reference to a judicial verdict, and to nothing beyond" (ICC 1:36).

126. Our commentator speaks against this: "There is an under-current all through the passage, showing how there was something else at work besides the guilt of individuals. That 'something' is the effect of Adam's Fall" (ICC 1:134; see also p. 135). In my opinion, the alleged 'under-current' is nothing but a theological presupposition: along with a declaration of justice made without us by God there is a corresponding transmission of sin effected equally without us. Moreover, the basic difficulty in admitting a sin without an express law derives even more obviously from theological presuppositions. It comes from an unwillingness to admit, despite clear passages of Paul (2:7.14, for example), that pagans could fulfill the law written in their hearts, at least to some extent and without ceasing to be slaves of Sin.

127. An appropriate citation here comes from Schubert M. Ogden (p. 227): "Christian faith does not claim, to be sure, that God's love can in any way coerce man's free response of faith and in that sense overcome sin. It always belongs to man as the free and responsible creature he is to refuse to accept God's acceptance and to continue in the life of unfaith and bondage to sin. God's love, being love, has both the strange power of love and its strange weakness; and it can never compel man to acknowledge it and live in its light and power." These words are right on target and, at that level, the only ones that accord properly with Pauline passages such as Romans 6:16f. Nevertheless they still

assume that faith, love, grace, and life on the one hand, and law, sin, and death on the other, are fighting on equal ground for the choice of the human being. Thus victory would never be sure for either side, and certainly not for grace if we assume the magical effect of Adam's sin. But if the freedom of the human being is capable of carrying out what it chooses and, thanks be to God, chooses the good, one single performance of the good means more than all the abhorrent 'alien' stuff that has accumulated in that human life. Thus love wins by covering the totality of sins, not by magic or the absence of liberty but rather by the very anthropological and theological makeup of the human being. And if that is the case, then there is nothing to prevent Paul from proclaiming with total certainty (because of the superabundance of liberty) the victory of grace over sin in each and all human beings (see 5:20).

128. Of course one can always deny the force of these terms by adding adverbial modifiers that suggest exteriority or the glance of God, which comes down to the same thing. As if God saw the justice of Jesus and then viewed as really just people who continued to be the same sinners as before. I respect such interpretations insofar as I admit that there can be no interpretation without presuppositions. My interpretation is that everything we have seen so far suggests that the faith of which Paul speaks is the only human attitude that can provide the human being with a real, though limited, justice. And since that justice derives from faith it can never be claimed as merit.

129. It is not exegetically clear that the Yahwist regards the necessity of dying as a punishment for the sin of Adam. Rather, the Yahwist writes of the difficulties of human life right up until the human being returns to the dust from which it came. On another occasion (Gn 6:3) the Yahwist offers a similar reason.

130. Here, of course, Paul introduces a subdivision. If it is not a matter of a reward, then the result can be one of two things. It may be a *debt:* e.g., a wage (4:4). Or it may be the result itself, *plain and simple,* when one acts *gratuitously* for no other intention than that intrinsic to the work itself.

131. Paul does not call the sin of Adam a 'sin', undoubtedly because the required singular might be confused with enslaving Sin. He calls it an 'offense' or 'transgression', since it violates a divine precept. Yet it is very likely that the data in Genesis on the self-deception of our first parents were what led Paul to say that with that 'transgression' Sin was introduced into the world. And Sin, as I have said, is not something a human being *commits;* it is something that enslaves the human being.

132. What Paul says of the stage that runs from Adam to Moses probably applies to Adam also: "Sin was not computed since there was no law" (5:13). Some translations prefer, 'was not imputed'. This does not fit, since it is as if sin were committed but then it was not known who had committed it. Paul is not denying responsibility or guilt but the possibility of counting up sinful deeds without law, of making that the central preoccupation. Our commentator paraphrases it thus: "*ellogeîtai,* 'brought into account' (Gifford) as of an entry made in a ledger" (ICC 1:135).

133. Including John, who seems undecided on the question. Sometimes he goes beyond the ordinary eschatological hope (see Jn 5:21–25; 6:39–40.47–51. 58; 8:52; 11:25–26), attributing the resurrection to faith in the Son of God. But on at least one occasion he attributes the resurrection to the need for God to pass judgment on the good and the *wicked:* the former will rise to life, the latter for *condemnation* or *judgment* (Jn 5:29). There does not seem to be any contradiction between the two series of statements because only the former is directly related to the resurrection of Jesus (glorious and triumphant life). But in also accepting the common eschatological idea of a general resurrection for judgment, John had to employ related ideas that are far removed from

Paul's conception, in my opinion: e.g., the idea of a 'second death' (Rev 2:11; 20:6; 21:8).

134. Despite repeated readings of Paul, it will cost Christian theology a great deal to draw the obvious consequences of the antithetical parallelism between Adam and Christ. To accept the universal victory of Grace, theology would have to abandon its *ideological* role as a support for a civic morality based on rewards and punishments.

135. This is obviously the case with Bultmann, who writes of Paul: "After his conversion he made no effort toward contact with Jesus' disciples or the Jerusalem Church for instruction concerning Jesus and his ministry. On the contrary, he vehemently protests his independence from them in Gal 1-2. And, in fact, his letters barely show traces of the influence of Palestinian tradition concerning the history and preaching of Jesus. All that is important for him in the story of Jesus is the fact that Jesus was born a Jew and lived under the law (Gal 4:4) and that he had been crucified (Gal 3:1; 1 Cor 2:2; Phil 2:5f., etc.). When he refers to Christ as an example, he is thinking not of the historical but of the pre-existent Jesus (Phil 2:5f.; 2 Cor 8:9; Rom 15:3). He quotes 'words of the Lord' only at 1 Cor 7:10f. and 9:14, and in both cases they are regulations for church life" (I, 188).

So far I have dedicated section II of every chapter in this volume to prove that this is not the case at all. Despite all the debate aroused by Bultmann's use of Heidegger's phenomenology, it seems to me that Bultmann seriously failed to explore or use the data of an existential phenomenology. His method was more like that of a computer operator. He compared Paul's use of each term with others but he never explored, and sometimes did not even notice, the anthropological problematic of each particular context. I think that explains why he saw a total separation between the Paul of this period and the Synoptics.

136. We could say that these Pauline considerations have gospel and prepaschal roots. Jesus may not have proclaimed himself as Messiah or God; but, as Pannenberg (p. 53f.) stresses, he did indirectly make divine 'claims' in his prepaschal life and message.

137. On the growth of this tendency in Paul's third period see the Introduction to this volume. For its continuation to the dogmatic formulations of Nicea and Chalcedon see Chapter I of Volume IV.

138. At least in the major letters of this period. We find a difference in Philippians 2:9-11, where the power of Jesus seems to have no other purpose than to make every knee bend in heaven, on earth, and everywhere else. Thus his power seems designed to win recognition of Jesus' divine character, of Jesus as Lord, though that does not wholly rule out the aim of fulfilling and completing a cosmic process (see 1 Cor 15:27-28).

139. In Mk 10:45 we do find this statement by Jesus: "For the Son of man did not come to be served either, but to serve and *to give his life as a ransom for many* [= all]" (see Mt 20:28, which undoubtedly depends on Mark; Lk 22:24-27 omits the part of the *logion* on mutual service). The isolated nature of the last part of the *logion* within the overall teaching of Jesus and the prophecy, already interpreted in the context of a later christology, clearly indicate both the postpaschal and probably post-Pauline origin of the part added to Jesus' remark on serving.

140. This is the most likely meaning of the postpaschal Markan statement cited in note 139 that Jesus came to give his life as a ransom *(lutron)* for *(in place of)* many. The 'many', of course, are all his fellow human beings.

141. A crucial point in making this distinction was the medieval controversy between the Thomists and the Scotists: Would God have become incarnate if Adam had not sinned and thus made sinners out of all human beings? Basically the position of John

Duns Scotus gave privileged place to the *Incarnation* as the central event in God's plan, whereas the position of Thomas Aquinas gave that place to the *Redemption*. Both were christologies 'from above'. But insofar as the Thomist position gained sway, christology from above seemed to fit in naturally with the cultic-legal key and its emphasis on *Redemption*.

142. Only on two occasions (1 Jn 2:2; 4:10) does Johannine theology employ one of the basic terms of the cultic-legal key, and it is a term that has a broader sense: *hilasmos,* 'a means of appeasing'. By contrast, following exegesis such as that of Dodd, we find that the whole Johannine narrative in the fourth gospel is an explicitation of the Incarnation, Jesus' death and resurrection included.

143. In the Reformation period Martin Butzer seems to have been moving in that direction, according to Emile G. Léonard. He borrowed from Luther for his first treatise: *That Nobody Should Live for Self Alone, but for His Neighbor* (1523). But whereas Luther started from the problem of the individual's salvation, Butzer began with concern for one's neighbor. We human beings can stop worrying about ourselves, said Butzer, because we can be sure that God our Father is concerned about us as his beloved children.

144. In the controversy sparked by Luther people talked about 'forensic' justice, an allusion to the recognized meaning of the Greek term meaning to 'declare just', as in a court of law. Dealing with this debate, Trent said that through Baptism "we are renewed in the spirit of our mind, and we are not only *declared just* but also called *just and really are just*" (DS 799).

145. In the decade of the fifties an innovative work by F. X. Durrwell *(The Resurrection)* created a stir in theology. His aim, he said, was to take serious note of three Pauline passages: 1 Cor 15:17; 2 Cor 5:15; Rom 4:25. Since the first two passages could easily be interpreted in another sense, the crucial passage is obviously the one that concerns us here: 'resurrected *for* our justification' (4:25). Durrwell's work is theologically rich, but on the exegetical level he does not notice the different keys existing in the New Testament as a whole and even in Paul. Thus he fails to distinguish between the (secondary) cultic-legal key and the (primary) anthropological key used by Paul. In the cultic-legal key, for example, it is difficult to attribute any *causality* for the result to the resurrection of the victim offered up in sacrifice. Yet the transcendent datum of the resurrection occupies a central place in the faith, and hence in the redemptive liberation that Christ brings us. Durrwell himself was aware of this difficulty.

146. See Mt 28:18; Rom 1:4; and, in a clear but more implicit way, Acts 2:24.33–36; 7:56.

147. Without employing the term 'kingdom of God', Luke shows how the 'power' granted to the resurrected Jesus is to be passed on to those who continue his work (see Lk 24:49; Acts 1:8; 4:38). Moreover, the effects of this (eschatological) power are described in the proclamation of the first Christian community. Its description uses terms associated with a new notion of the kingdom on the one hand, and with certain aspects of Paul's thinking on the other, as we shall see. Thus it talks about the author of life or leader to life (Acts 3:15), the restoration of all things (Acts 3:21), the forgiveness of sins (Acts 3:19.26), and salvation (Acts 4:12). Here I cannot consider whether such an interpretation of the 'power' of Jesus or the kingdom is more or less faithful to the historical Jesus and compatible with Paul's view. That would require an in-depth study of Luke's christology, a task outside the scope of my effort here.

148. Obviously Paul's belief in the general resurrection of the dead was not original in itself. It is part of the prepaschal message of Jesus himself, and it was a belief

shared by the Pharisees as a group in contrast to the Sadducees.

149. See 2 Cor 5:4.

150. As I have already noted, it is worth noting how John's gospel, long after Paul, tends to vacillate between the two views. On the one hand Jesus, like the Father, has the power to give life (Jn 5:21); hence he can promise his followers that he will raise them up on the last day (Jn 6:39-40; 11:25). On the other hand the author alludes to a general resurrection for the purpose of judgment leading to life or condemnation (Jn 5:28-29).

Chapter VI

151. In choosing to investigate Paul's christology through a study of Romans 1-8, I am obviously making a theological option. Not everyone would say that these eight chapters go together, or see an obvious reason why they should be separated from the later chapters (9-11 in particular). Note this comment, for example: "It is no doubt an arguable question how far these later chapters [Romans 6-8] can rightly be included under the same category as the earlier. Dr. Liddon, for instance, summarizes their contents as 'Justification considered subjectively and in its effects upon life and conduct. Moral consequences of Justification. (A) The Life of Justification and sin (6:1-14). (B) The Life of Justification and the Mosaic Law (6:15-7:25). (C) The Life of Justification and the work of the Holy Spirit (8)'. The question as to the legitimacy of this description hangs together with the question as to the meaning of the term Justification. If Justification = *Justitia infusa* as well as *imputata,* then we need not dispute the bringing of chaps. 6-8 under that category. But we have given the reasons which compel us to dissent from this view. The older Protestant theologians distinguished between Justification and Sanctification; and we think that they were right both in drawing this distinction and in referring chaps. 6-8 to the second head rather than the first" (ICC 1:38). I maintain that the content of the first five chapters would remain incomplete, superficial, and devoid of specifically 'anthropological' meaning without the next three chapters. That is my strong argument for rejecting any differentiation of content, and for including justice (or sanctification) in the term 'justification' as used by Paul (see Chapter IX). Moreover, we can readily see that in Romans 6-8 Paul reiterates most of the fundamental data of the earlier chapters. This suggests that he was not aware of having changed his content or moved on to a second part. He is still confronting the same problematic and challenge he was confronting in the first few chapters.

152. Bultmann feels that this was the prevailing idea in the Jewish world. We see it in the baptism for the remission of sins used by John the Baptist, in the baptism of Jewish proselytes, and even in the mentality of the church community in Jerusalem (Acts 2:38). With some reason, which we cannot go into here since it deals with other matters, Bultmann sees a tendency in Paul to deritualize the Christian community. Thus Paul turns Baptism, for example, into a memorial of, and incorporation into, the life, death, and resurrection of Jesus of Nazareth. Bultmann thinks Paul got the image of water as the source of life from the Hellenistic mystery religions. That is how he came to see complete immersion and then emersion as an identification of the Christian initiate with the death and resurrection of Jesus (Bultmann, I, 140f.). Both the present form of baptismal administration and cultural differences make it hard for us to see symbolism that was readily comprehensible in Paul's own day.

153. "Some would limit the reference of *en tō thnētō humōn sōmati* to the physical body, but it is better to understand Paul to mean by *sōma* the whole man in his

fallenness" (ICC 2:317). To this we might add what Ortega y Gasset calls the 'circum-stance' of the human being: everything that surrounds the human being and forms an integral part of its life. As I noted earlier, Paul probably used 'body' instead of 'flesh' in some passages because he felt that those of Greek culture would understand the former term better, even though it might give rise to misunderstandings. This proves, I would suggest, that it is not true that "the facts of language are inexorable" (see end of note 125).

154. The term 'sanctification' can have two meanings in Paul. One, deriving from biblical usage, refers to what is 'holy' or 'sanctified' as something set apart from the profane and consecrated to God. The other, deriving more from Hellenistic usage, refers more to moral perfection. Paul's argument holds for either usage here.

155. It might be better to designate the two respective causalities as *efficient* rather than final. It is indicative and highly significant that the Greek term *telos,* so crucial for comprehending the final result of human action vis-à-vis that of God, is not explicated by our ICC commentators. I think you have to force Paul's vocabulary and thinking a great deal to turn 'justification' into a mere extrinsic declaration of justice that leaves the human being as such right where it was before. On the other hand we should not assume that the 'justified' human being becomes just automatically and totally. This point should be obvious from what we are seeing in Paul's text here. What Paul makes clear here, it seems to me, is that a line of just conduct begins and grows in the justified human being, and that it has both immediate and mediate ends or results.

156. ". . . *ho nomos* is here used in a limited sense—'the law (as condemning us)', 'the law ('s condemnation)'. That this is what is mainly intended is suggested by the way in which Paul continues his argument in 8:1 with *ouden ara nun katakrima tois en Christō Iēsou* (7:7-25 is to be understood as a necessary clarification of 7:1-6). But perhaps there is the further thought of the law, in so far as, by men's misuse of it, it has become a bondage. That—*pace* many commentators—the meaning is not that we have been discharged from the law *simpliciter* is clear enough from v. 25b (cf. vv. 12 and 14a; also 3:31; 8:4; 13:8-10)" (ICC 2:338).

This exegesis is subtle and cryptic. The ICC commentator seems to be suggesting that the Law must maintain its sway for the human being to continue being a sinner. But Paul repeatedly states that we are no longer 'under the Law'. Moreover, Romans 7:1-13 makes clear that we are liberated *simpliciter*—about as *simpliciter* as it is possible to be liberated—from the Law. The only thing to be kept in mind is that the *simpliciter* refers to the liberated, not to the disappearance or uselessness of the Law (see 3:31). We are liberated *simpliciter* from the Law in that we switch places with it; instead of being under it, we now stand over it as children of God. Here *simpliciter* means 'plainly and simply', not 'easily', as the latter half of Romans makes quite clear.

157. The *Nueva Biblia Española* translates Gal 5:4 sensibly as: "You have fallen into dis-Grace." Another correct and literal translation might be: "You have been degraded from Grace."

158. For exegetical reasons that are hard to explain, Bultman begins with a relatively clear term like 'body' instead of going directly to the stranger term 'flesh'. He does ultimately suggest their closeness, but in the last analysis he fails to see that Paul is often resorting to a Greek term to make clear to his audience what is meant by Hebrew *basar.* Thus Paul's usage fluctuates between a literal translation of the latter Hebrew term, which might be fairly incomprehensible to the uninitiate, and an equivalent term ('body') with its advantages and disadvantages. See note 153 above.

159. That brings up a point important for our study here. In the Old Testament, the

term 'flesh' and its content has both negative and positive connotations. The negative connotation has to do with what we today might call a tendency towards 'secularization': i.e., the creature in its actions tries to find efficacy in the created. Thus Isaiah accuses Israel of looking to Egypt for aid rather than looking to Yahweh: "Egypt is human, not divine, and its horses *flesh,* not spirit" (Is 31:3). On the other hand ancient Israel values the 'religious' attitude whereby individuals and groups, realizing they are created, fear and worship the transcendence of the Creator. Note the eschatological hope of Trito-Isaiah: "From new moon to new moon and from sabbath to sabbath, all *flesh* will come to prostrate itself before me, says Yahweh" (Is 66:23). The originality of Paul here lies in the fact that he gave a negative evaluation to *both* the secularizing and the religious tendencies of the 'Flesh'.

160. Contrary to what some modern translations suggest, Paul does not say that the Spirit makes us *serve.* The Greek text indicates that the meaning is: so that we *can* serve (see ICC 1:175). This accentuates the anthropological content of the passage: something has changed and we are now capable of something of which we were not capable before.

161. The most clear, precise, and succinct formulation of this function of faith is to be found in Reinhold Niebuhr's work (I, 272): "This 'I' and 'Thou' relationship is impossible without the presupposition of faith for two reasons: (1) Without freedom from anxiety man is so enmeshed in the vicious circle of egocentricity, so concerned about himself, that he cannot release himself for the adventure of love" (I, 272).

162. Human *moral* action, according to the exegesis of Paul's own time. It is modern exegesis that has brought out the nature of the decalogs as civic constitutions (see Von Rad, *Old Testament Theology,* I, 190f.). Thus 'Thou shalt not covet' did not refer to an internal sin but to overt attempts to rob the property of another (see Mic 2:2).

163. This is correctly understood by the *Nueva Biblia Española* which translates it as 'no desearás'. The Greek verb used by Paul does not so much refer to a precept of the decalog; rather, it connotes an uncontrolled *instinct, a passion.*

164. There is no reason to think that the mere fact of prohibiting something makes it automatically attractive (see ICC 2:350). The ICC commentator suggests that the precept limits human freedom and hence causes inconvenience. I think that is just another version of the first explanation that I rejected above. Another possible explanation is that there is an implicit reference to the serpent of Paradise, who incites the human being to disobedience by false lines of reasoning and by darkening the human heart. The implicit reference lies in the fact that Sin is singular, hence personalized in a sense (ICC 2:350).

165. "It is more straightforward to understand Paul's meaning to be that, while men do actually sin in the absence of the law, they do not fully recognize sin for what it is, apart from the law (cf. 3:20), and that, while they do indeed experience covetousness even though they do not know the tenth commandment, it is only in the light of that commandment that they recognize their coveting for what it is—that coveting which God forbids, a deliberate disobeying of God's revealed will" (ICC 2:348–349).

This might be more 'straightforward', but it clashes with everything Paul says about Christian freedom. I suggest we do better with a different view. By coming to know covetousness through the letter of the Law, human beings fall prey to the mechanisms that prevent them from 'recognizing' their own work. The focusing of their attention on covetousness prevents them from pushing ahead with the projects of their inner humanity, so that those projects eventually fall under the control of the impersonal mechanisms of the 'outer' flesh (see 7:14–25).

166. This may help us to explain a question that we have left unanswered so far. Paul

boasts to the Philippians that he is 'irreproachable' with respect to the justice of the Law. In other words, he has fulfilled it, presumably in accordance with the intention of his 'I' or 'inner humanity'. That seems to contradict his assertions in Romans: that no one will be justified by the works of the Law; that no one is just; that we all are under Sin, etc. Here in Romans 7 we may have an answer to the seeming contradiction. Though it may be difficult, human beings can keep the *letter* of the Law in an irreproachable way. But at what price? At the price of not fulfilling its sense or spirit, of becoming even more enslaved to Sin, to the point where they may fail to realize that its meaning and culmination is to be found in Jesus Christ. Lost in self-deception and seeking security in the letter of the Law, people ignore the presence of the God who revealed that Law and its import. Paul was under Sin in the same way, and for the same reason, that the Pharisees who persecuted Jesus and his group were under Sin before him. Thus K. Stendahl points out that the only 'sin' weighing on Paul's conscience is that of having persecuted the Church of God (1 Cor 15:9; Gal 1:13-14). In the period of writing Romans and other contemporary letters, Paul never offers excuses for that sin. In a later letter (1 Tm 1:13) he claims 'ignorance' as the reason for his 'blasphemy' (the term itself is noteworthy). But there are doubts that this later letter was written by Paul, and the proffered excuse may well indicate the hand of a disciple of his.

167. Romans 7, particularly verses 14–25, is obviously introspective and explores the anthropological depths of the human being. Hence it constitues the strongest argument against the thesis proposed by Krister Stendahl, as he himself recognizes to some extent (see note 78).

Chapter VII

168. "It is difficult to think of this as exactly St. Paul's own experience: as a Christian he seems above it, as a Pharisee below it—self-satisfaction was too ingrained in the Pharisaic temper . . . But St. Paul was not an ordinary Pharisee . . . and his experience as a Christian would throw back a lurid light on those old days 'of which he was now ashamed' " (ICC 1:183). Paul, in other words, is offering a first-person description of his earlier experiences as a Pharisee, in the light of the Christian faith. In this chapter I give reasons why I do not share this opinion of the ICC commentator. Apparently it is not too convincing in the eyes of that commentator either, as we shall see in the next note.

169. It is Paul's summary in 7:25 that the ICC commentator finds hardest to apply to Paul as a Christian. It seems to describe "the state of things prior to the intervention of Christ" (ICC 1:184). Aside from that verse, which I suggest should be interpreted in the light of the victory that glimmers in Romans 6, the rest of the passage refers to human existence as such. Thus the ICC commentator aptly remarks: "But here, whether the moment described is before or after the embracing of Christianity, in any case abstraction is made of all that is Christian. Law and soul are brought face to face with each other, and there is nothing between them. Not until we come to ver. 25 is there a single expression used which belongs to Christianity. And the use of it marks that the conflict is ended" (ICC 1:186). Perhaps it would be better to say that the *description* of the conflict is ended. As the experience of any Christian will confirm, we still seem to face the situation described in 7:15: "I do not recognize what I accomplish [*katergadzomai*]." Note the same root as the Greek word for 'work' *(ergon)*.

170. Paul refers to this as the 'law of the mind', i.e., the mainspring of our 'inner humanity'. It is hard to find a correct translation for the Greek term *nous* in our modern

languages, since we tend to confuse or equate 'mind' with 'reason' or 'thought produc-tion'. In the original Greek 'mind' would mean the innermost reality of the human being as a thinking and willing being. Thus it is related to the Hebrew biblical notion of 'heart'. But there is an important shade of difference between the two terms. By virtue of its semantic content or the fact that it is the connecting link between the human 'I' and the Spirit of God at work there, the 'mind' seems to heed only the voice of a human being's innermost 'I'. That is how Paul depicts it at any rate, and this suggested connection with the Spirit (see 8:16) seems to be confirmed from the opposite end by the possibility of having a 'reprobate mind' (1:28). The 'heart', on the other hand, seems to be situated a little more towards the outside (though admittedly in Romans 1 Paul is describing human behavior insofar as it is not guided by the Spirit). While the 'heart' may also be the source of thoughts and decisions, it is also the place where the 'cravings' of the 'flesh' show up in full force; and we learn in 7:25 that the 'flesh' is opposed to the law of the mind. Taking all that into account, the best translation for the term might be 'spirit' in small letters, suggesting but not necessarily presupposing the guiding action of the Spirit that proceeds from God.

171. That would in no way permit us to say that this necessity derives from 'pure human nature' rather than from the gift of Grace. To call this crucial human dimension a 'gift' might surprise some people because we are so used to regarding a 'gift' as something 'scarce' that is granted only now and then, as something very different from what we always have for a certainty. Here we would be dealing with a gift given to 'all' the brothers and sisters (8:29), hence a *gratuitous* anthropological dimension. It is our customary equation of 'grace' with 'scarcity' that prompts us to see a *restrictive* decision in the 'predestination' mentioned in 8:30, though that goes completely against the most obvious and clearcut drift of Paul's thought.

172. In the interpretation we are studying, the equivalent would go something like this. The agreement of our inner humanity with the Law would mean that our 'I' would spontaneously and automatically be in basic agreement with the precepts of the decalog rather than just because the letter of the Law said so. In and of itself, it would find killing, robbing, lying, and so forth, repugnant. And this is what Paul is suggesting when he says: "I am in agreement with the Law that it is good" (7:16).

173. Right off it differs basically with Paul insofar as it devalues freedom and creativity. Jeremiah makes it clear that the value of the new covenant lies in the effective fulfillment of the Law (or of its letter, to be more exact), sparing the human being the difficult and dangerous intermediate step of *deliberating* and then *deciding* what it is that God wants.

174. It is apropos here to call attention to the ambivalence of many of these terms, both in technical and ordinary usage. An example of the former would be the term *superego*. An example of the latter would be the French word *moeurs,* which can mean both the moral behavior that should be practiced and the behavior that actually is practiced by most people: i.e., both the patterns of behavior associated with freedom and those associated with statistics.

175. This does not mean failing to recognize ideologically the differences that society imposes to more easily conceal and justify inhuman relations between human beings. It means relativizing the concrete form they take so as to create new ones of a more truly human sort.

176. At the start of this chapter (p. 115) I said that clarification of the major antitheses would probably help us to clarify lesser ones as well. I think that is the case and has been done. Readers should at least be able to judge what I think of various translations of

these terms. The *Nueva Biblia Española,* for example, often does an excellent job. But you can guess what I think of it when it translates 'flesh' as 'lower instincts' (7:18), 'members' as 'body' (7:23), 'body' (= flesh) as 'this being of mine' (7:24), and 'mind' as 'reason' (7:23.25).

177. At first glance Paul might seem to be far from original here. Indeed Bultmann succumbs to the temptation of citing Ovid here: *Video meliora proboque, deteriora sequor*—I see and approve the better but follow the worse. But the similarity is completely fallacious. Ovid is simply noting the gap between free will in the abstract and actual practice dominated by the passions. As I have tried to bring out, Paul at the very least is trying to say something very different. As he sees it, every human being is faced with the question of knowing what point there is to having a freedom designed to be creative in an already created world of instruments that operate on their own, disregard human freedom, and overwhelm it with the statistically dominant power of the easy way.

178. Bultmann and the *Nueva Biblia Española* do not hesitate to resort to the facile solution of assuming that the order of the verses has been mixed up. So the *Nueva Biblia* arranges them this way (25b, 24, 25a): "En una palabra, yo de por mí, por un lado, con mi razón, estoy sujeto a la Ley de Dios; por otro, con mis bajos instintos, a la ley del pecado. ¡Desgraciado de mí! ¿Quién me librará de este ser mío, instrumento de muerte? Pero ¡cuántas gracias le doy a Dios por Jesús, Mesías, Señor nuestro!"

To begin with, there is no trace of doubt about the order of these verses in our most ancient manuscripts or later ones. And this, despite the fact that minor adverbial alterations indicate that the copyists and the Fathers of the Church citing them were aware of the difficulty. Secondly, the basic principle that *the more difficult reading* is to be regarded as the genuine one should be respected here. Thirdly, there is an even more profound and subtle reason for rejecting any alteration in the order of these verses, as my discussion in this chapter and the start of the next chapter should make clear. Paul has to indicate how the situation he has described earlier has changed, if he is to begin his chapter on victory (Romans 8) with a connective 'so'. A mere exclamation, 'Thanks be to God', will not suffice. He must be specific in some way, indicating why the exclamation is appropriate. We are forced to conclude that he does so when he asserts: "With the mind I myself serve the Law of God." If you put that part of the verse elsewhere, as does the *Nueva Biblia,* you do nothing less than miss the reason for the victory.

179. Readers will surely recall my reasons for insisting that we must rule out any and every solution of a magical sort. Paul's framing of the issues is clearly anthropological, so we must assume that his solution to them is anthropological too.

Chapter VIII

180. Note that Paul uses the co-called 'divine passive' here, since God is the agent of the action involved. Thus Paul does not say that the Christian human being fulfills the Law. He says that God, or God's Spirit, fulfills the Law in the human being. With God's help something becomes possible for the human being that was not possible for the weakness of the flesh.

181. The parable of the wheat and the chaff might allude to this. But it deals more with the necessity of tolerating evil until the eschatological time than with the way in which God's judgment is to be made.

182. There is a latent dualism in other statements or images dealing with judgment, but they do not have the contextual importance or elaboration we find in 1 Cor 3:10–15. See, for example, 1 Cor 6:9–10.

183. Indeed Paul ends the passage with a verse that is very difficult for exegesis insofar as it seems to take away all definitiveness from this judgment insofar as the person of the human being is concerned (or of the Christian, if you will, since the context deals specifically with that; see 1 Cor 3:4–9.11). Paul states that even the person whose work has been burned up will be saved, but as one passing through fire (1 Cor 3:15). This concentration of God's judgment on 'the work' of the human being shows up in another verse we have seen earlier (see Chapter IV, pp. 65f.), and it is important because it confirms our suspicion that some images of Paul are exaggerated if we take them too literally. Romans 4 might seem to suggest that Abraham did not work, since the Promise he received was not a *wage*. In 1 Corinthians 3:8, by contrast, Paul tells us that each will receive a *wage* according to his or her *effort* or *labor.* The word 'wage' is the same in both passages. The other term comes through in languages such as English which distinguish work/labor (French, *travail/labeur*), the latter term in each case suggesting heavy, burdensome toil that is not recompensed proportionately. If we take the image literally here, we would seem to have the very opposite exaggeration. But the whole context suggests clearly that once again Paul is talking about work as a 'vocation', not work done for the sake of pay. Paul's point is that the result will not be lost if the labor is good; it will have the certainty or security of a *wage*. This point deserves highlighting because otherwise Paul would seem to be saying contradictory things. And some readers might think my talk about exaggeration in his image is based on a preconceived theological position rather than on a strictly exegetical standpoint.

184. It should be pointed out that one negative remnant of the Reformation controversies is that some Lutheran theologians regard any and all human cooperation with God (synergism) as a theological deviation. Such is the case with Jürgen Moltmann in his "Open Letter" to José Míguez Bonino about Latin American theology. Actually Moltmann is alluding specifically to my final remarks in my article, "Capitalism Versus Socialism," which was originally published in *Concilium.* There can be no denying that Martin Luther rediscovered central features of Paul's theology. But his juridical, magical view of justification by faith led him to a position that is thoroughly anti-Pauline, in my opinion. His view of *soli Deo gloria* implies that God's glory is protected all the more, the less human causality collaborates with God's plans.

185. And why not? The pointedly conflictive nature of Jesus' mission, his harshness with opponents, and the nationalistic narrowness of his message and work would seem to suggest that his work 'visibly' succumbed to the objective mechanisms of Sin, however much *subjective* innocence may have been his.

186. One important point deserves to be brought up here. The 'likeness of a Flesh of Sin' does not disappear with the so-called triumph of Christianity and the Church. This is clearly suggested by Paul himself insofar as he keeps shifting between a positive and negative response to the question whether the Christian is free from Sin. See my commentary on Romans 6.

187. My statements here might seem to be very close to other formulations of classic eschatology: e.g., Oscar Cullmann's 'already but not yet'. There is a profound difference, however. Because of underlying theological or ideological presuppositions, his 'already but not yet' does not show up as an *anthropological* dimension of action in history. It tells us that Christ has already triumphed but we cannot yet see the consequences of his victory. Those consequences are hidden in the mystery of God, as it were, and have no connection with, or impact on, human involvement in history. Indeed they seem to dispense wholly with it. If human beings nevertheless *ought* to get involved, it is

a *moral* duty deriving indirectly from justification (see note 198). It is not that the victory *has need of* our human involvement and commitment.

188. Paul tells us that 'peace' is properly the work of the Spirit. This 'spiritual mentality' seems to have a very important anthropological sense. It is related to 'life' (8:6), to unblocking the human being who is paralyzed by anxiety. Thus peace signifies the security needed to act for the sake of the intrinsic value of what is being done rather than to chalk up points on the scoreboard of salvation: "Peace (eirēnē), as we have seen, is not only (i) the state of reconciliation with God, but (ii) the sense of that reconciliation which diffuses a feeling of harmony and tranquillity over the whole man" (ICC 1:196). I think that peace, as liberation from anxiety, deserves more serious attention. Note the remarks of Reinhold Niebuhr cited earlier, for example (see note 161).

189. We thus come back to the hope of an Abraham in its fullest realization. 'Hoping against hope' means hoping for resurrection in its fullest anthropological sense: the shift from Sin as breeder of uselessness and corruption to Faith in the work of Grace that gives life, usefulness, and incorruption to love. "That resurrection has two sides or aspects: it is not only physical, a future rising again to physical life, but it is also moral and spiritual, a present rising from the death of sin to the life of righteousness" (ICC 1:117). This very apt commentary is vitiated a bit by the unreal and unsubstantial addition of the word 'present'. In the 'present' there is no *visible* change whatsoever (see 8:24-25).

190. I say 'all', not only because the parallelism between Adam and Christ suggests that clearly, but also because Paul reaffirms that explicitly in his summary of the parallelism in 1 Cor 15:22-23.

191. That is how the principal manuscripts present it, interpolating 'adoption as child'. The interpolation reinforces my argument since 'adoption as child' and 'redemption of our *body*' cannot be synonymous unless 'body' has the meaning of 'flesh' and takes in the whole human being and what surrounds it.

192. We saw, for example, the Yahwist writer's description of the origin of matrimony. The spouses are to separate from their respective families and become 'one flesh' (Gn 2:23-24). That is an allusion to the complete affective unity of the pair, wherein everything is shared in common and the other party's feeling and reality is felt as one's own (see Eph 5:28-31).

193. See Chapter IV, pp. 74-75; Chapter V, pp. 96-98.

194. See Chapter IV, p. 74.

195. Ibid., pp. 74-75.

196. Ibid.

197. Bultmann (I, 301-302) notes this from his own peculiar viewpoint without deducing all its phenomenological consequences: "He—unlike the Hermetic tractates with their initial cosmological teachings—does not first present the salvation-occurrence, the credibility of which would first have to be acknowledged. Instead he begins by exposing the plight of mankind, so that then the proclamation of God's salvation-deed becomes a decision-question. . . . The union of believers into one *soma* with Christ now has its basis not in their sharing of the same supernatural substance, but in the fact that in the word of proclamation Christ's death-and-resurrection becomes a possibility of existence in regard to which a decision must be made . . ."

198. "Nothing more is required of us than that we should cry to the one true God 'Abba, Father' with full sincerity and with full seriousness. That this necessarily includes seeking with all our heart to be and think and say and do what is well-pleasing to Him and to avoid all that displeases Him, should go without saying. In the accom-

plishment of this work of obedience the *dikaiōma tou nomou* is fulfilled (cf. v. 4) and God's holy law established" (ICC 2:401–402). I would only point out that the 'necessarily includes' is a moral, hortatory conclusion. The ICC commentator does not seem to see there a distinct *anthropological* situation.

199. Note that the terminology of father-child relationship, and even the use of the word 'Abba', goes back to the vocabulary of Jesus himself. Paul did not invent this attitude of filial maturity vis-à-vis God, but he did go far beyond the Synoptic writers in drawing out its consequences.

200. Maturity is manifested in *faith* (Gal 3:23–25), in the attitude of Abraham. It is no accident that Abraham became the inheritor of the world (4:13). See my following Chapter IX.

201. Even though the authorship of the letter to the Ephesians is disputed, Paul's influence on it is not denied. Granting that it may represent a later stage of his christology, we note that the 'recapitulation' of the whole universe in Christ (Eph 1:9–10) is to take place in the 'fullness of time' (see Chapter VII, p. 120). In Galatians 4:3–4, however, we learn that the 'fullness of time', identical with the time of full human maturity and freedom, is already here in the present, though not yet manifested in glory.

202. The idea of a creation that is incomplete and for the moment condemned to uselessness, not good *in itself,* seems to be original with Paul, who is often alleged to be close to the Stoics. In the 'Christian' Middle Ages the prevalent idea was that creation or nature represents the good, that the possibility of evil lies only in the freedom of the human being. In *The Flies,* Jean-Paul Sartre offers us a Thomist image of God in Jupiter. After Orestes kills Clytemnestra and Aegistus, Jupiter speaks to him as follows: ". . . The world is good. I created it after my own will, and I am good. But you, you have done evil, and things accuse you with their petrified voices. Good is everywhere . . . in you, outside you . . . it is what permits the success of your evil undertaking . . . And the evil of which you are so proud, what is it but a reflection of being, a wrong turn, a deceitful image whose very existence is sustained by the good? . . . *Return,* my son . . ."

203. Exegetes debate the identity of 'the one who subjected' creation to uselessness: God, Satan, Adam, or humanity. It does not matter for our purposes here. The point is that in any case God has left creation dependent on human decision, and that only the glorious manifestation of the freedom of God's children will restore to creation its usefulness.

204. Bultmann rightly stresses that Paul sees justification or the 'declaration of justice' as already present (I, 274f.). But Bultmann renders this present much too easy when he turns justification into a (mythical) *forensic* happening (I, 276). What becomes of Bultmann's happening when we reinsert it in the anthropological dimension where Paul is at home?

205. And turning the human elements necessarily associated with the Christian faith into a system of religious efficacy, a religious ideology.

206. I reject and disregard the third answer, which found its way into theology as the famous but gloomy theory of *predestination:* i.e., in his foreknowledge God voluntarily destined some human beings to exist in order to be declared just and saved, and others to exist in order to be declared culpable and condemned. Whatever speculative support may be found for such a theory in abstract notions—i.e., God's eternal, non-temporal knowledge of what takes place in time—there is *not the slightest* justification for it as an exegesis of Paul. Both his explicit and his implicit christology *are opposed to any such conception.* Note, for example, my remarks on Romans 5:6–9, pp. 78f.

207. This is one of the rare passages where Paul seems to lean towards a magical kind

of declaration of justice—one which Abraham, for example, could not possibly have attained. It does not seem to harmonize with the overall thought of Paul or the depth of his anthropology. I agree with many exegetes, including Bultmann (I, 81 and 125), that the literary genre suggests that Paul is citing a creedal formula already being used by the Church. Indeed this formula would dovetail well with the religious and apocalyptic conception of Jesus' resurrection that we find in the early Jerusalem Church. See Acts 2:28 and my discussion in Appendix II of Volume II of this work.

208. Even within the Christian community, however, it seems quite clear that Paul did not succeed in moving beyond the social barriers that marginalize women (see 1 Cor 14:34; 11:3f.). Here we have another example of the ideological limitations of any and every faith.

209. That is why Paul advises the Corinthians against circumcision, even though it is not bad or evil (see 1 Cor 7:18-19). That is why he forbids it in the case of the Galatians (Gal 5:2-4), since it seems to signify that one is still looking for justice from 'the works of the Law'.

210. In *Mission et grâce* (p. 214f.), Karl Rahner looks at this question and suggests that Paul would answer 'no', but that his answer would not hold up today. I myself am not so sure that Paul's answer would be no. Here is what Rahner writes: "It is not possible for Christians living in the present age of church history to share the pessimistic ideas of St. Paul about the salvation of Non-Christians . . . Paul thought that human beings who did not attain Baptism were lost. It is true that Paul did not spell out any dogma on this point, but in practice it was an evident truth for him."

211. Two likely sociological factors might lend support to this view, though they remain circumstantial: (1) the rapid expansion of the Christian community in the pagan world at the time; (2) the first incursions of a christology 'from above', with its ideas of expiation, redemption, and reconciliation associated both chronologically and causally with the death of Jesus of Nazareth 'for our sins'.

212. Myth tends to explain what actually occurs *later*. The *before* of a myth is not a temporal before but a contrastive explanation of the original, like the setting of a jewel.

213. That is the function of the 'word' or 'message', which is added to what is actually operative in reality. Thus, for example, God is reconciling the world or the impious to himself (2 Cor 5:19; Rom 5:6). To this process is added the 'word' or 'message' of reconciliation (2 Cor 5:19) and the ministry of it. It is nothing else but what we in Latin America call *conscientization:* i.e., making people consciously aware of a process that is going on without their knowing it.

214. The consequences, duties, responsibilities, and service roles that fall to us as part of this plan, and that constitute a Christian community as such, were the topics of my earlier work, *The Community Called Church.*

Chapter IX

215. Remember: Sin *(he hamartia)* as opposed to 'sins' in the plural or other equivalent terms such as 'offenses' and 'transgressions'.

216. This takes in equivalent terms such as 'believer' or 'one who believes'.

217. Even in the rest of Romans it shows up only a few times with the same meaning and the same relationship to justification or salvation. See 9:30-31 and 10:4-10.

218. The term 'nature' here should include our 'second nature', the sociocultural realm created by human beings. Paul actually is interested in the differences of attitude and behavior that have thus been introduced between Jews and Greeks, slaves and free

persons, males and females. See Gal 3:28; Rom 10:12; 1 Cor 12:13; Col 3:11; Eph 4:24.

219. I have already given my reasons for preferring this second hypothesis in Chapter I (see pp. 18–21). I might add another important observation here. Human 'desires' or 'cravings' obviously exist before the option for idolatry, but they are contained, as it were, by recognition of an Absolute that holds them in check. When this check is removed by the self-deceiving idolatry of human beings, then human beings are 'handed over' to the forces dwelling in them by their own bad faith. No punitive intervention by God is required. It is in that sense that God *has* to 'hand over' human beings to the mechanisms that darken their heart.

220. And to that extent the Law was fashioned to be fulfilled by 'working good'. Commenting on Romans 2:7, the ICC says: "The expression *ergon agathon* has been variously interpreted. Some understand Paul to mean such goodness of life as would be a real fulfilling of God's law and would actually merit salvation, but to be speaking here from a pre-evangelical point of view (not taking account of the revelation of the *dikaiosunē theou* referred to in 1:17; 3:21f.) and also hypothetically (such goodness of life not in fact being found among men), the purpose of what is here said being merely to contribute to the demolishing of the Jews' claims; others take him to be referring to faith as being the good work required by God; and others—and this is perhaps the most likely interpretation—think the reference is to goodness of life, not however as meriting God's favour but as the expression of faith. It is to be noted that Paul speaks of those who seek . . . glory, honour and incorruption, not of those who deserve them" (ICC 2:147). The very last interpretation is in fact the one that does justice to Paul's subtle anthropological analysis and the place of *Faith* in it.

221. Even the subordination of justification to Faith, if improperly understood, could turn Faith into a new sacred 'instrument' and lead to a corresponding obsession with fulfilling the *precept*. Only now the precept would be reduced to 'believing' or 'having Faith'. Here is what one ICC commentator writes: "We may then understand Paul's meaning to be that the correct answer to the question 'By what kind of law (has such glorying been excluded)?' is 'By God's law (i.e. the law of the OT)—that is, by God's law, not misunderstood as a law which directs men to seek justification as a reward for their works, but properly understood as summoning men to'. There is confirmation of the rightness of this interpretation in 9:31f. . . ." (ICC 2:220). All well and good, but a few questions come to mind. Why give that precept to human beings? If justification or salvation were magical, then there would be no need even for Faith. And if they aren't magical, if Faith is required because it implies a radical change of conduct, a new 'anthropological' attitude, what exactly is that changed reality? What sort of human existence does Faith make possible?

222. From the very moment that the word 'faith' first appears in Romans, some commentators think they can define precisely what it means even though nothing in the context suggests such a thing. "Nygren has rightly warned against thinking of faith as being 'prior to the gospel and independent of it. It arises only through one's meeting with the gospel'. It is not a qualification which some men already possess in themselves so that the gospel, when it comes to them, finds them eligible to receive its benefits. Faith, in the sense in which the term is used here, can exist only as response to the gospel (or its OT foreshadowing). And it is also wrongly conceived, if it is thought of as being, as a man's response to the gospel, a contribution from his side which, by fulfilling a condition imposed by God, enables the gospel to be unto salvation for him. In that case, faith would itself be in the last resort a human meritorious work, a man's establishment of his own claim on God by virtue of something in himself. But it is of the very essence of

faith, as Paul understands it, that it is opposed to all human deserving, all human establishing of claims on God (cf., e.g., 3:20–22, 28; 4:2–5; 9:32; Gal 2:16; 3:2,5). For Paul man's salvation is altogether—not almost altogether—God's work; and the faith spoken of here is the openness to the gospel which God Himself creates, the human response of surrender to the judgment and unmerited mercy of God which God Himself brings about—God who not only directs the message to the hearer but also Himself lays open the hearer's heart to the message. And yet this faith, as God's work in a man, is in a real sense more truly and fully the man's own personal decision than anything which he himself does of himself; for it is the expression of the freedom which God has restored to him—the freedom to obey God. But it is not till chapter eight that this secret of faith is revealed" (ICC 2:89–90).

As is characteristic of a verse-by-verse commentary, the above note comes with the first meeting of the word 'faith' in Paul's text, not where the characteristics of faith are treated by Paul explicitly by the commentator's own admission. Indeed when we get to Romans 8, we find that what Paul can say about faith has lost much of its importance for the commentator, given that some doubt is raised that Romans 6–8 continue the problem of *justification,* of how faith is to be understood, that was being explained in Romans 1–5. "The fact that sanctification is not mentioned as an intermediate link between justification and glorification certainly does not mean that it was not important to Paul: the earlier part of this chapter—not to mention chapter 6 and 12:1–15:13— is clear evidence to the contrary. . . . He may perhaps have felt that *edoksasen* covered sanctification as well as glorification" (ICC 2:433). But wouldn't it be much more logical for readers to think that the sense of 'sanctification' was already present in the chapters that dealt with justification, unless they had special theological reasons of their own for not doing so?

223. Although Krister Stendahl (*Paul Among Jews and Gentiles,* pp. 16–17) attacks the anthropological key I use here, he rightly notes the importance of this historical argument: for three centuries after Paul, no one thought of opposing *faith* to *works* and giving faith the decisive role in the face of God's judgment.

224. With respect to 2:5–11, for example, theological presuppositions as to what Paul *cannot* possibly mean oblige our commentators to proffer no less than ten interpretations of this passage. The first is particularly noteworthy because it assumes quite simply that Paul is inconsistent and contradicts himself.

Verses 6–11 have been variously interpreted. There seem to be at least ten possibilities which ought to be considered:
(i) That Paul is inconsistent, and, whereas elsewhere he maintains that God will justify *ek pisteōs* or *dia tēs pisteōs* (3:30) and that no one will be justified on the ground of his works, he is here expressing the thought that the final judgment will be according to men's *deserts* and there will be some (both Jews and Gentiles) who will have *earned* God's approval by their goodness of life.
(ii) That Paul is here speaking hypothetically, leaving the gospel out of account and arguing from the presuppositions of the Jew, whom he is apostrophizing (this is how—on the Jew's own presuppositions—the judgment will be), in order to show that his present conduct (see vv. 3 and 4) will, even on his own presuppositions, bring disaster.
(iii) That Paul means by *erga* in v. 6 faith or lack of faith and in vv. 7 and 10 is referring to Christians, meaning by the *ergon agathon* of v. 7 and *to agathon* of v. 10 the good work of faith.

(iv) That Paul is referring in vv. 7 and 10 to Christians, but means by the *ergon agathon* and *to agathon* not their faith itself but their conduct as the expression of their faith, and similarly by *erga* in v. 6 each man's conduct as the expression either of faith or of unbelief.

Interpretations (v) and (vi) understand the reference of vv. 7 and 10 to include OT believers as well as Christians, otherwise agreeing with (iii) and (iv) respectively.

(vii) and (viii) understand the reference of vv. 7 and 10 to include, in addition to Christians, not only OT believers but also some heathen Gentiles who in some mysterious way believe with a faith known only to God, but otherwise agree respectively with (iii) and (iv).

And lastly (ix) and (x), which also agree with (iii) and (iv) respectively with regard to *erga,* the *ergon agathon* and *to agathon,* take vv. 7 and 10 to refer to OT believers and these mysterious believers among the heathen, but not to Christians at all.

Of these (i) may surely be rejected at once. While it would be extremely rash to claim that there are no inconsistencies in the Pauline epistles, the inconsistency which this explanation attributes to Paul is altogether too colossal and too glaring to be at all likely. The explanations (iii), (v), (vii) and (ix) should also be set aside as unlikely on the ground that, though Jn 6:29 affords an example of the use of *ergon* with reference to faith, there seems to be no evidence of such a use elsewhere in the Pauline epistles. It would indeed be so foreign to Paul's usage . . . that it would be very surprising if he employed *ergon* here in this sense. In favour of (ii) it may be said . . . but the fact that there is no indication whatsoever . . . that what is being said is hypothetical tells strongly against it. With regard to (x), it is difficult to see. . . . It seems likely, then, that the choice should be between (iv), (vi) and (viii). On the whole, we are inclined to think that (iv) is the most probable, and that in vv. 7 and 10 Paul was probably actually thinking only of Christians . . . [ICC 2:151–152].

225. The first alternative was to view Faith as an arbitrarily fixed condition so as to wipe away human sinfulness with a magic sponge, as it were. But would this be faith in God, in Jesus Christ, or what? The second alternative, which I chose, was to view Faith as a crucial attitude in terms of its results in human action and God's later judgment. That judgment would be gratuitous, but not arbitrary or magical; in it God would declare human beings just or impious.

226. The whole passage on Christian 'knowing' is of even greater anthropological value: ". . . *knowing* that affliction [the trouble that is worthwhile or not, depending on the transcendent datum we accept] produces endurance [quality of action that points to permanence], endurance maturity [mark of the Christian anthropological stage], maturity hope; and the hope is not delusory because *the love* proceeding from God [anthropological faith in my terminology, that which seeks and supports the transcendent datum which justifies it in turn] has been poured into our hearts . . ." (5:3–5).

227. This is brought out clearly in Paul's summary treatment of the antithetical parallelism between Adam and Christ in 1 Corinthians: "As by a human being came death, so by a human being comes the resurrection of the dead. For as in Adam all die, so in Christ will all be made alive" (1 Cor 15:21–22). We might add, then, that Sin and Death must be defeated in all human beings if Christ is not to be a failure vis-à-vis Adam. And that could not be the case if the human being—a single human being—were

to go through existence without being able to recognize at least some of its works as its own. See section III of this chapter.

228. We find another example of the relative degree of the *force* of this transcendent datum in a Non-Christian character in literature: Kirillov. He refuses, *methodically* as it were, to believe in the resurrection of Jesus. Yet he finds himself more or less compelled by what I would call his *anthropological faith* to reach the same conclusion. This passage from Dostoyevsky's novel might well be compared with Proust's passage about 'hostages' in Volume II, Appendix I, section II. Kirillov is talking to Pyotr Stepanovitch Verkhovensky: "Listen to a great idea: there was a day on earth, and in the midst of the earth there stood three crosses. One on the Cross had such faith that he said to another, 'To-day thou shalt be with me in Paradise'. The day ended; both died and passed away and found neither Paradise nor resurrection. His words did not come true. Listen: that Man was the loftiest of all on earth, He was that which gave meaning to life. The whole planet, with everything on it, is mere madness without that Man. There has never been any like Him before, or since, never, up to a miracle. For that is the miracle, that there never was or never will be another like Him. And if that is so, if the laws of nature did not spare even Him, have not spared even their miracle and made even Him live in a lie and die for a lie, then all the planet is a lie and rests on a lie and on mockery. So then, the very laws of the planet are a lie and the vaudeville of devils. What is there to live for? Answer, if you are a man" (F. Dostoyevsky, *The Possessed*, pp. 633–34).

229. As far as I can tell, Vatican II's *Gaudium et spes* is the first document of the Roman Catholic magisterium that picks up Paul's thinking about the eschatological resurrection in its full historical extension: "Then, with death overcome, the children of God will be raised up in Christ. What was sown in weakness and corruption will be clothed with incorruptibility. While charity and its fruits endure, all that creation which God made with humanity in mind will be freed from the bondage of uselessness. . . . For after we have obeyed the Lord, and in his Spirit nurtured on earth the values of human dignity, brotherhood/sisterhood, freedom, and indeed all the good fruits of our nature and enterprise, we will find them again, but freed from taint, illumined, and transfigured . . . when Christ hands over the kingdom to the Father" (GS:39). Note that in writing 'charity' the Council was disregarding the present-day connotation of the word to preserve the Greek distinction between love as self-giving *(agapē)* and love as sensual attraction *(eros)*. It was referring to 'love' as *agapē*.

230. Paul's anthropological key does not stop him from using *religious* language, which was more normal in his culture than it is for us today. We would tend to separate religious language from straight-forward anthropological language. In particular, when Paul moves from his existential analysis of Sin and Faith to the transcendent datum based on the paschal experiences that constituted Jesus 'Son of God in power' (Rom 1:4), the language he uses might suggest to some people that only those who are already on the *religious* plane and accept the existence of God by faith or reasoning could follow the further developments of Paul's thought and accept his conclusions. This commonplace misunderstanding or mistaken assumption is one that I dealt with in Volume I. Mentioning 'God' by name is not what will unlock the door for people today so that they can understand the import of Paul's christology. The 'transcendence' of certain data in his christology is far more important than explicit mention or acceptance of God. That still leaves a problem which *was* crucial in Paul's eyes: knowing what content is to be given to the word 'God'. The attribution of 'divinity' to Jesus is an issue I shall consider in Volume IV, Chapter I.

231. Readers might object that I am simply retrojecting the miracle to the start of

creation or of humanity's appearance in it, however evolutionary we may conceive things *after* that. Even granting that, however, I think that such a shift merits two brief considerations here. First, we should not minimize the importance of shifting from a merely extrinsic, magical explanation to an intrinsic one such as evolution, with all the analogies the mind notices between that anthropological transformation and other similar processes of nature. Second, the idea, however vague, of someone linked by love to this hostage we know as the human being immersed in history is most important. Whether we give the name 'God' to that someone or not, it is a transcendent datum that is at least tacitly present in every commitment to values that face death with hope and maintain hope above, beyond, and in spite of death.

232. We are indebted to Luther, and particularly to his conception of the human being as *simul justus et peccator,* for having perceived the radical opposition of Paul's thinking to any simplistic reduction of the problem of Sin. In that he surpassed Augustine. Contrary to what Krister Stendahl maintains, I don't think Luther was indebted to Augustine for the *introspective* character of his interpretation. What he did borrow from Augustine was the legalistic or *juridical* bent characteristic of Roman, not Hebrew, thought. That gave him a facile solution for an antinomy that deserved a better deal from him, considering Paul's own thought on the matter.

233. That continues to be the theological temptation for any interpretation that assumes as its premise what was one of the more offbase conclusions of classical Reformation theology. I have already cited Bultmann's 'premise' as an example. Before any exegetical effort has been made, he defines the kingdom or reign of God as "a miraculous event which will be brought about *by God alone without the help of men" (Theology of the New Testament,* I, 4).

234. I readily admit that my own effort to move from an investigation of the historical Jesus in Volume II to one single christology of the New Testament in this volume is enormously limited. However rich Paul's christology may be, a method is not learned with one example and one effort of this sort. But everything is limited, including our lives as individuals. I can only urge others to join in this common effort. It will take team work to fill the christological gap we see today.

235. There are many different interpretations of the *key* used by the author or authors of the fourth gospel (see Raymond E. Brown, *The Gospel According to John [I-XII],* pp. lii-lxxvi). The one that remains most satisfying to me overall is the now classic work of C. M. Dodd, *The Interpretation of the Fourth Gospel.*

236. *To a certain extent* the non-dialectical materialism of the eighteenth and nineteenth centuries is an exception, as is its first cousin, the positivism of the nineteenth and twentieth centuries. But they are exceptions only to a certain extent because they sought to immerse *homo* totally in the general framework of nature. Since they lacked more subtle and dialectical categories, this immersion was such a blatant *reductionism* that more serious philosophical thought continued to stress the strangeness, solitude, and anxiety of the human condition within the apparent order of nature.

237. Consider this text: "Everything works together for the good of those who love God" (Rom 8:28). Some might say that nothing has really changed in our *cognition.* It is simply that hope now puts all its energy into trusting that things will turn out differently or look different on another plane that is now totally invisible or totally non-existent insofar as historical reality is concerned. But the whole thought of Paul goes against such an assumption, as his view of human liberation from the Law should indicate. Paul is trying to make clear to us that here we have a change in our way of *interpreting* events, i.e., our way of *knowing* them. He is talking about a *premise* which, through the attitudes of 'peace and joy', causes a human being to see things differently, to draw

different conclusions from events, to 'punctuate' the sequence of events differently and thus profoundly affect the 'ecology of mind'. See the remarks on Bateson's view in Volume I, Chapter IV, pp. 91-95.

Appendix

238. Readers are referred back to my discussion of terminology—faith, ideologies, transcendent data—in Volume I.

239. As we shall see in more detail in Chapter I of Volume IV, this in no way strips Jesus' message of its character as *'divine* revelation', with corresponding guarantees of truth and life. But it does oblige us, *for those very reasons,* to insert his message into the process of *learning how to learn* that is embodied in the whole Old and New Testaments and that does not end there. See Volume I, Chapter III, section II, pp. 70f.; and my work, *The Liberation of Theology,* Chapter Four, section IV, 4, pp. 118f.

240. I don't think this advice of Paul's is mainly or wholly due to eschatological imminence (see, in the same context, 1 Cor 7:36.39). The brevity of a human life might suffice to prompt Paul, in this chapter, to calculate the energy costs entailed in various social situations insofar as human transformation as envisioned in his christology is concerned. That would account for his comparison of different 'preoccupations'. See section III of this appendix.

241. This conception must also be embodied, confirmed, and 'signified' in the behavior of the Christian community. Otherwise the latter would lose its proper character (see 1 Cor 11:17-22; Philemon).

242. Not to mention existentialist topics, which are congenitally linked to Paul. The links run from Paul to Augustine, from Augustine to Luther, from Luther to Kierkegaard, and from Kierkegaard to the existentialists of our time. That would include even atheistic existentialists such as J. P. Sartre.

243. See Gustavo Gutiérrez, *A Theology of Liberation,* Chapter Three and *passim.* This denunciation of an overly individualistic and private context and other superficial similarities have led some to mistakenly classify Latin American liberation theology as a branch of European political theology, and to assert the chronological dependence of the former on the latter. The problem has been compounded by the mistake of situating the origin of Latin American liberation theology in the appearance of Gutiérrez's book. The fact is that his book appeared almost a decade after the major themes of liberation theology had surfaced. His book systematized those themes and gave them a label that stuck. In his work he also cited European theologians engaged in political theology, who were unknown in the decade when the first discussions and writings of the new Latin American theology were taking place.

244. Reacting against the alleged apoliticalness of Jesus, some tried to get beyond the impasse by inflating sparse data and proving a possible connivance between Jesus and the Zealots. On this subject see two works by Oscar Cullmann, especially the second: *The State in the New Testament; Jesus and the Revolutionaries.*

245. Two examples are his advice to slaves and his exhortation to obey public authorities. His assumption, very uncritical if he actually held it, might have been that the latter were really carrying out the theoretical function they were supposed to carry out. To some extent his discrimination against women in practice might also be considered 'political'. But remember that in theory he declares that any basis for discriminating against women has been destroyed in Christ.

246. "Every day human interdependence grows more tightly knit and worldwide. As

a result, the common good . . . today assumes an increasingly universal cast, implying rights and duties with respect to the whole human race" (GS:26). "Let them fight energetically against any kind of slavery, be it social or political . . ." (GS:29). "The more unified the world becomes, the more do the duties of the human being extend beyond the limits of specific groups and gradually embrace the whole universe" (GS:30).

247. So when this impact is not involved, as is the case with laws regarding divorce, abortion, birth control, etc., we find the Church and churchmen adopting clear and concrete positions on political matters. In so doing, they often confuse or equate, at times *ex professo*, the realm of moral licitness and the realm of social coercion. These positions lead to the drawing of party lines when people differ on the issues. Even Vatican II retreated from one of the most logical conclusions to be drawn from the function of *Faith* as an essential feature of the Church. It did so in this statement: "Christ gave his Church no proper mission in the political, economic, or social order. The purpose he assigned it is religious . . ." (GS:42). If we take the work 'proper' with each of the realms mentioned in isolation, then we may be able to salvage an unfortunately worded statement; but the fact is that it has been used *ad nauseam* to justify stances of the most apolitical, conservative, and reactionary sort. Let us go back a bit earlier in the conciliar document and see what Vatican II was bold enough to say about *Faith* as the proper element of the Church: "Faith . . . thus directs the mind toward *solutions that are fully human"* (GS:11). But where are those problems demanding fully human solutions if not in "the political, economic, or social order"? On this fear of drawing concrete political conclusions from faith see my book, *The Hidden Motives of Pastoral Action.*

248. I think that Ignacio Ellacuría *(Freedom Made Flesh)* and Jon Sobrino *(Christology at the Crossroads)* are the Latin American theologians who did most to focus theology and exegesis on the historical Jesus and the political key as the tool of interpretation. I think it is unfortunate, however, that Ellacuría seems to follow the lead of European exegetes in seeking the historical significance of Jesus in his possible connection with the Zealots.

249. "Among both the exegetes and the theologians of liberation, there is some uncertainty about the interpretation of the Bible in the milieu of liberation theology." After rejecting the image of the Exodus as a present-day solution, author and exegete J. Konings goes on to say: "And proving that Jesus of Nazareth was directly a political liberator is a task rejected by almost all true exegetes. . . . Fortunately, the 'big names' of liberation theology are more circumspect . . ." (Konings, "Hermeneutica Biblica," p. 5).

250. In its defense it should be pointed out that liberation theology was often led to such unbalance by the incredibly superficial and ideological dichotomies of the opposite camp: e.g., structural changes are worthless without conversion of heart; defense of human rights without any class struggle; revolution in freedom by majority consent rather than by violence, which always engenders greater violence, etc.

251. Praxis, and 'practice' as another term for it, specifically means practice grounded in a theory. In turn, theory is nurtured and revised by new elements discovered in experiential practice.

252. Tending toward that is the method of reflection used by many Christian groups as the only one compatible with the primacy of praxis over theology: 're-examination of life'. The disconnectedness of the problems supposedly presented by praxis, together with the subjective selection and manipulation of biblical passages used to spell out the

viewpoint of faith, leads to a parody of the function that Gustavo Gutiérrez aptly described as a 'critical reflection on praxis' (*A Theology of Liberation*, Chapter I). The fact is that *praxis* is not the superficial, ingenuous flow of events and problems. Nor does 'critical' mean choosing some biblical passage, isolated from its immediate context and the whole biblical process, in order to confirm the option proposed.

253. The failure of this excess is a widespread experience in Latin America. And by failure I am referring to an irrelevant crisis of faith produced by the trivial answers derived from faith when used in the wrong way. It is silly and fruitless to look to Jesus for examples, norms, and solutions that bypass real praxis and the need for autonomy in constructing ideologies today, and that refuse to leave room for the dose of pragmatic gratuitousness implied in any profound educational process.

254. This situation is much more widespread than many theologians are willing to admit. Indeed some have proposed the need for a theology of *captivity*. As an alternative to a theology of liberation, such a proposed theology must certainly be rejected. No one wants to canonize captivity merely because liberation seems to be moving farther away. But the proposal does make sense insofar as some Latin American theologians talk about liberation in triumphalist terms, as if it were already within our grasp, when the overall situation of Latin America indicates the need for a bridge between reality and theologizing. Consider the ever increasing misery of the poor, their obvious lack of orientation, and the growing evidence and signs of further oppression and repression. I must confess that I detect such triumphalism in Gustavo Gutiérrez's more recent work. Despite his many critical-minded specifications, the very title of the work strikes me as offbase: *The Power of the Poor in History*. What 'power' is he talking about? Where has this 'power' been hiding for the past four centuries, since the days of European colonialism? Where has it been hiding for the past century and a half, since the days of political independence? Why doesn't he analyze the how, why, and wherefore of the *powerlessness* of the poor in history instead?

255. In an equally artificial way I am not taking into account other important vehicles of information and unconscious valuation: e.g., the child or adolescent perceives that his parents *submit* meekly to the existing social structures, thereby repeatedly rejecting in practice the criteria they are teaching their children to respect.

256. It is fairly common practice in many places, not just in Latin America, to criticize (e.g.) people who look to the official Communist Party to find tranquilizing certitude of a religious sort, and who are therefore willing to accept at face value its contradictory directives. But in Volume I, Chapter V, I made the point that any conception of religious faith claiming not to need ideologies is in pretty much the same category.

257. There is much empty rhetoric in superficially dazzling formulas that are all the rage in Latin America today. People are invited, for example, to put themselves 'under the discipleship of the Poor'. Flying in the face of the tragic history of Latin America, some extol the imperviousness of the authentic 'People' to the ideologies of the ruling classes. Gustavo Gutiérrez himself brandishes a dazzling argument, in fairly nuanced terms, that others will use in a more 'realistic' and demagogic sense: "What is to be done away with is the intellectualizing of the intellectual who has no ties with the life and struggle of the poor—the theology of the theologian who reflects upon the faith precisely from the point of view of those from whom the Father has hidden his revelation: the 'learned and clever' (Matt. 11:25). Paul announces the annihilation of thought, but it is not the thought of the 'little ones', the poor. For it is only to the poor that the grace of receiving and understanding the kingdom has been granted. To the lowly—to those who cannot or are not allowed to speak—the word of God is given, so

that they can go and proclaim the kingdom. The illogical language of the cross is death for the wisdom of the wise—for those who do not understand the word. Reflection on the faith that does not accept that illogicality, that folly, reflection that does not accept death, that does not accept the revelation granted to the poor, mistakes its way" (*The Power of the Poor in History,* p. 103).

I might also add that even methods of 'conscientization' or 'consciousness-raising', stemming of course from minorities and shaping minorities by virtue of their very content, have had to beg pardon for their lack of appreciation of the common people and talk about 'mutual conscientization' (e.g., the method of Paulo Freire). Yet this fails to respect what Bateson, following Russell, would call the 'difference of logical levels' involved in any such reciprocity. If readers find it paradoxical that theologies of liberation generally do *not* engage in a political reading of the gospels, the reason is simple enough: the gospels run counter to populist tendencies, as Paul realized and said in his own key.

258. Without this dialectic, we would bypass the necessary quantitative base for any qualitative transformation. This is an important element that has been examined far too little up to now in attempts to elaborate christology. One then *does* fall into the 'elitism' that some have tried to pin on any 'minority' function, so as to reject the latter.

259. I am not trying to ignore the terribly long time it took to abolish slavery in the West, nor the curious way it was effected. In most Latin American countries, for example, the formal abolition of slavery came only in the nineteenth century. At the same time we must try to avoid anachronisms. More than once in these volumes I have alluded to some of the reasons behind the long paralysis of 'Christian' creativity in political and moral matters. For centuries Christianity had to provide the European masses with a civic morality, one which in fact upheld the institutions of the State and government. As a result, it was a seemingly Non-Christian current that pushed for the abolition of slavery, as the French Revolution might suggest. The Christian community did not recognize its own principles in such movements. But the situation of the slave was not always improved when he or she ceased being property and became a wage contractor. One need only read Volume I of *Capital* to realize that. Here again we find seemingly Non-Christian and even Anti-Christian forces undertaking the effort to find effective ideologies for implanting certain basic Christian values regarding the human being.

260. The widespread reluctance to present Jesus in a political key stems largely from a fear of *comparisons* that will not turn out well. I am referring to a problem discussed in Volume I: the habit of comparing a faith and an ideology. While a faith is presented through concrete ideologies, it nevertheless transcends them. An ideology may be presented as such, independent of any faith, even an anthropological one. Comparing a faith and an ideology really violates Russell's principle of different logical levels. Some rightly fear that people will opt for the ideology, which is concerned with problems of efficacy, and abandon a faith insofar as it looks like an ineffective ideology.

261. Notice the big difference between *determining the way in which the specific Christian contribution is to be brought out in each individual case* and *deciding in advance what the specifically Christian contribution is in any and every circumstance.* See my book, *The Liberation of Theology,* Chapter Three, section IV.

262. Reviewing the course of a theological conference held in São Paulo (Brazil) in February 1980, the theme of which was basic ecclesial communities, one article in the press noted that P. Libanio "said that in popular communities the process of conscientization involved three steps. The first step was the discovery that they could interpret the

word of God by themselves. 'That is the conquest of the word', said Libanio." Of course the press has a tendency to oversimplify things. We find a more nuanced formulation of this notion by Gustavo Gutiérrez: "The gospel, read from the viewpoint of the poor, from the viewpoint of the militancy of their struggles for liberation, convokes a popular church—that is, a church born of the people, the 'poor of the earth', the predilect of the kingdom, 'God's favorites'. It is a church rooted in a people that snatches the gospel from the hands of the great ones of this world. It prevents it from being utilized henceforward as an element in the justification of a situation contrary to the will of the Liberator-God" (*The Power of the Poor in History,* p. 208).

From the hermeneutic side, it is rather curious that Gutiérrez does not ask himself why Jesus did not succeed in his own day in getting his own people, his own poor people, to snatch God's revelation, the Law and the Prophets, from the hands of the great ones of Israel.

Reference Bibliography

1. Works Cited by Abbreviations

DS.   Denzinger, Bannwart, and Schoenmetzer. *Enchiridion Symbolorum.* Segundo cites the Spanish edition: *El magisterio de la Iglesia,* Barcelona: Herder, 1955.

GS.   *Gaudium et spes.* Vatican II, Pastoral Constitution on the Church in the Modern World, December 7, 1965.

ICC 1.   International Critical Commentary. W. Sanday and A. C. Headlam, *A Critical and Exegetical Commentary on the Epistle to the Romans,* Edinburgh: T & T Clark, 1895.

ICC 2.   International Critical Commentary. C. E. B. Cranfield, *A Critical and Exegetical Commentary on the Epistle to the Romans,* Edinburgh: T & T Clark, 1975.

JB.   *The Jerusalem Bible.* Garden City, NY: Doubleday, 1966.

2. Anthologies and Works Cited by Title

Dios llega al hombre. Nuevo Testamento de Nuestro Señor Jesucristo: Versión popular. Sociedades Bíblicas en América Latina, 1966.

Nueva Biblia Española. Edición Latinoamericana. Spanish translation edited by L. A. Schoekel and J. Mateos, Madrid: Ed. Cristiandad, 1976.

3. Works Cited by Author

Bauer, W. *Griechisch-Deutsches Woerterbuch . . .* Eng. trans., *A Greek-English Lexicon of the New Testament and Other Early Christian Literature,* Chicago: University of Chicago Press, 1969.

Brown, R. E. (ed. and trans.). *The Gospel According to John (I–XII).* Doubleday Anchor Bible 29. Garden City, NY: Doubleday, 1966.

Bultmann, R. *Theology of the New Testament.* Eng. trans., New York: Scribner's, 1951 and 1955. Two volumes.

Cullmann, O. *Jesus and the Revolutionaries.* Eng. trans., New York: Harper & Row, 1970.

Cullmann, O. *The State in the New Testament,* Eng. trans., New York: Scribner's, 1956.

De Fuenterrabía, F. *Nuevo Testamento: Traducción de los textos originales.* Estella: Ed. Verbo Divino, 1969.

Dodd, C. H. *The Interpretation of the Fourth Gospel.* New York: Cambridge University Press, 1953.

Dostoyevsky, F. *The Possessed.* Eng. trans., New York: Dell/Laurel, 1961.

Durrwell, F. X. *The Resurrection.* New York: Sheed & Ward, 1960.

Eagleson & Torres (eds.). *The Challenge of Basic Christian Communities.* Maryknoll, NY: Orbis Books, 1981.

Ellacuría, I. *Freedom Made Flesh: The Mission of Christ and His Church.* Eng. trans., Maryknoll, NY: Orbis Books, 1976.

Gibellini, R. (ed.). *Frontiers of Theology in Latin America.* Eng. trans., Maryknoll, NY: Orbis Books, 1978.

Gutiérrez, G. *The Power of the Poor in History.* Eng. trans., Maryknoll, NY: Orbis Books, 1983.

Gutiérrez, G. *A Theology of Liberation.* Eng. trans., Maryknoll, NY: Orbis Books, 1973.

Konings, J. "Hermeneutica Biblica e Teologia de Libertação," *Revista Eclesiástica Brasileira,* March 1980, fasc. 157.

Léon-Dufour, X. *Les Évangiles et l'histoire de Jésus,* Paris, 1963. English version, *The Gospels and the Jesus of History,* Garden City, NY: Doubleday Image Book.

Léonard, E. G. *A History of Protestantism.* Vol. 1. Eng. trans., Indianapolis, IN: Bobbs-Merrill, 1968.

Marx, K. *Capital.* Vol. 1. Eng. trans., New York: Vintage Books, 1977.

Moltmann, J. "An Open Letter to José Míguez Bonino," *Christianity and Crisis,* March 29, 1976, pp. 57–63.

Niebuhr, R. *The Nature and Destiny of Man.* 2 vols. New York: Scribner's, 1964.

Ogden, S. *The Reality of God.* New York: Harper & Row, 1977.

Pannenberg, W. *Jesus—God and Man.* Second edition. Eng. trans., Philadelphia: Westminster Press, 1977.

Rahner, K. *Mission et grâce.* French trans., Tours: Mame, 1962.

Sartre, J. P. *Les Mouches* (The Flies).

Segundo, J. L. "Capitalism Versus Socialism: Crux Theologica," Chapter 11 in Gibellini (see above).

Segundo, J. L. *The Community Called Church.* Vol. 1 of A Theology For Artisans of a New Humanity. Eng. trans., Maryknoll, NY: Orbis Books, 1973.

Segundo, J. L. *Faith and Ideologies.* Vol. I of Jesus of Nazareth Yesterday and Today. Eng. trans., Maryknoll, NY: Orbis Books, 1984.

Segundo, J. L. *The Hidden Motives of Pastoral Action.* Eng. trans., Maryknoll, NY: Orbis Books, 1977.

Segundo, J. L. *The Historical Jesus of the Synoptics.* Vol. II of Jesus of Nazareth Yesterday and Today. Eng. trans., Maryknoll, NY: Orbis Books, 1985.

Segundo, J. L. *The Liberation of Theology.* Eng. trans., Maryknoll, NY: Orbis Books, 1976.

Stendahl, K. *Paul Among Jews and Gentiles.* Philadelphia: Fortress Press, 1976.

Von Rad, G. *Estudios sobre el Antiguo Testamento.* Spanish trans., Salamanca: Ed. Sígueme, 1975. German original: *Gesammelte Studien zum Alten Testament,* Munich, 1958.

Von Rad, G. *Old Testament Theology.* 2 vols. Eng. trans., New York: Harper & Row, 1962.

Zerwick, M. *Analysis Philologica Novi Testamenti Graeci.* Rome: Ed. Pont. Inst. Bibl., 1957.

The English Text of Romans 1:16–8:39

Romans 1:16–32

1   (16) I am not ashamed of the gospel. For it is the saving power of God for everyone who believes, for the Jew first and (also) for the Greek. (17) Because in it the justice *that proceeds* from God is being revealed from faith to faith, as it is written: "The one who is just by faith will live."

(18) For the wrath of God is being revealed from heaven against every *type of* impiety and injustice of human beings who are holding truth shackled in injustices. (19) For what is knowable of God is manifest in their midst, because God has made it manifest to them. (20) The fact is that since the creation of the world the invisible (_____pl.) of his are seen intellectually by means of (his) works, both his eternal power and divinity, so that they have no excuse, (21) because even though they have known God, they did not glorify him as God or give him thanks, but have become entangled in their own reasonings and their uncomprehending hearts have been darkened.

(22) Claiming to be wise, they have shown themselves to be fools, (23) and exchanged the glory of the incorruptible God for the likeness of the image of (the) corruptible human being, birds, quadrupeds, and reptiles. (24) For this, God handed them over to the cravings of their hearts, *delivered over* to the impurity of dishonoring their bodies among themselves.

(25) They actually exchanged the truth of God for the lie, and adored and worshipped the creature instead of the Creator, who is blessed forever, amen. (26) For this, God handed them over to passions that bring dishonor: for, on the one hand, their females have exchanged natural relations for anti-natural ones (27) and, on the other hand, the males, having abandoned natural relations with the female, have burned with cravings for one another, males with males committing the unseemly and receiving in their own selves the due *negative* consequence of their aberration.

(28) And since they did not deign to recognize God, God handed them over to a reprobate mind, to do the unsuitable, (29) replete with every injustice, wickedness, outrage, full of envy, murder, quarreling, deceit, malice, gossipers, (30) slanderers, haters of God, insolent, haughty, boastful, inventive in wickedness, disobedient to their parents, (31) senseless, disloyal, unloving, pitiless. (32) They know the just *decree* of God, that those who practice such things are deserving of death; but not only do they do them, they also approve those who do them.

Romans 2:1–28

2   (1) For *all* that you have no excuse, human being, whoever you may be, you who judge *others*, for in judging the other *person* you condemn yourself because you pass judgment *in spite of* doing the very same things *the other* does. (2) And we know that

God's judgment, in accordance with the truth, is levelled against those who do such things. (3) You, human being, who pass judgment on those who do such things and do the same yourself, do you think you will escape God's judgment? (4) Or do you think little of the wealth of his kindness, patience, and forbearance, not choosing to recognize that his kindness *seeks* to lead you to conversion? (5) Because of the hardness and impenitence of (your) heart, you are storing up wrath for yourself on the day of wrath and the manifestation of the just judgment of God, (6) who will give to each *human being* according to its works. (7) To those who seek glory, honor, and incorruption, (God will give) eternal life. (8) But for those who (are) egotists, indocile to the truth but docile to injustice, (there will be) wrath and indignation. (9) For every human being who works evil, the Jew first and also the Greek, (there will be) tribulation and anguish; (10) glory, honor, and peace, on the other hand, for everyone who works good, for the Jew first and also for the Greek. (11) Because there is no partiality on God's part.

(12) Those who have sinned without law will perish without law, and those who have sinned in *the system of* the law will be judged by *the criterion of* the law. (13) For it is not those who hear the law who (are) just before God, but *only* those who practice it will be declared just. (14) For when *some* Gentiles, without having law, naturally do *what is commanded by* the law, they are law for themselves *even* without having a law. (15) They prove thereby that they have the work of the law written in their hearts, witness being provided by their own conscience and their inner thoughts, which will accuse and even defend them (16) on the day when God will judge the secrets of human beings through Christ Jesus, as per my good news.

(17) But if you call yourself Jew, and rely on the law, and glory in God, (18) and know his will, and discern *the essential*—having been instructed by the law, (19) and claim to be guide for the blind, light for those who dwell in darkness, (20) *moral* educator of the foolish, teacher of uninformed beginners, because in the law you have the very pattern of knowledge and truth— (21) well, teaching others, you do not teach yourself; preaching one should not steal, you steal; (22) saying one should not commit adultery, you commit adultery; *claiming* to abhor idols, you commit sacrilege. (23) Glorying in the law, you dishonor God by transgressing the law; (24) and so, on account of you, God's name is blasphemed among the Gentiles, as it is written.

(25) Circumcision is certainly useful if you fulfill the law; but if you are a violator of the law, your circumcision becomes uncircumcision. (26) Now if uncircumcision keeps the just precepts of the law, will not that uncircumcision be reckoned as circumcision? (27) Physical uncircumcision that fulfills the law will judge you who, possessing the letter *of the law* and circumcision, are a transgressor of the law. (28) Because being a Jew is not in the outer, nor is circumcision the outer in the flesh; being a Jew (is) in the inner, and circumcision of the heart (is) in the spirit, not in the letter, and its praise (comes) not from human beings but from God.

Romans 3:1–31

3 (1) What is the Jew's advantage, then? Or what is the usefulness of circumcision? (2) A great deal, from every point of view. First of all, God's oracles were entrusted to their faithfulness. (3) So if some of them were unfaithful, does their unfaithfulness render ineffective the faithfulness of God? (4) Never! God must be true, though every human being be false, as it is written: "That you may be declared just in your words and win out, on being judged."

(5) But if our injustice sets the justice of God in relief, what *are we to say* then? (That)

God is unjust when he inflicts his wrath on us?—I am speaking in human terms— (6) Never! Because, otherwise, how is God to judge the world? (7) But if the truthfulness of God *is made manifest* even more to his glory by my lie, why am I still judged as a sinner? (8) Might it not then be the case, as some people slanderously allege that we say: "Let us do evil that good may come (of it)"? The condemnation of such people is just.

(9) What then? Do we *Jews* have a head start? Not entirely. Because we have already made the accusation that we all, Jews and Greeks, are under sin, (10) as it is written: "There is no one (who is) just, (11) no one (who has) sense, no one who seeks God. (12) All have gone astray, (all) together have become useless, there is no one who does good, not even one. (13) An open grave is their throat, with their tongues they are in the habit of deceiving, snake poison (is) under their lips. (14) Their mouth is full of curses and bitterness. (15) Their feet (are) swift to shed blood, (16) destruction and misery *pile up* along their ways, (17) and they have not known the way of peace, (18) there is no fear of God before their eyes."

(19) But we know that whatever the law says, (it says it) speaking to those who are in *the system of* the law, in order that every mouth be stopped and the whole world present itself guilty before God. (20) Because no flesh, through the works of the law, will be declared just before him. Since with the law *comes* knowledge of sin.

(21) But now, independently of the law, the justice of God has been manifested, in accordance with the testimony of the law and the prophets, (22) that is, the justice of God through faith in Jesus Christ for all who believe. There is no distinction, you see. (23) Because all have sinned and lack the glory of God, (24) being declared just by the gift of his grace through the redemption *accomplished* by Christ Jesus (25) whom God destined to be, in his own blood, expiation through faith, so as to prove the justice of God in overlooking earlier sins (26) during the patience of God: *i.e.*, to prove his justice at the right moment, so that he might be just and declare just one who believes in Jesus.

(27) Where, then, the glorying? It has been ruled out. By what law? By the law of works? No, but by the law of faith. (28) We maintain, you see, that the human being is declared just by faith independently of the works of the law. (29) Is God (God) only of the Jews, and not of the Gentiles as well? Of course of the Gentiles as well! (30) So if God is one (and only), (it is God) who will declare just circumcision in accordance with faith, and uncircumcision by means of faith. (31) Do we then invalidate the law with faith? Never! Rather, we make it stand.

Romans 4:1–25

4   (1) Then what shall we say happened in the case of Abraham, our ancestor according to the flesh? (2) Because if Abraham was declared just by works, he has ground for glorying. But *it is* not *so* before God. (3) After all, what does the Scripture say? "And Abraham had faith in God, and it was credited to him as justice." (4) Now to one who works, the wage is not counted as a gift but as something due. (5) But to one who does not work, who has faith in the one who declares just the impious, his faith is credited to him as justice. (6) David, too, talks about the happiness of the human being to whom God credits justice without works: (7) "Happy are they whose iniquities have been pardoned and whose sins have been covered up. (8) Happy the human being against whom God will not debit sin."

(9) Now *does* this declaration of happiness *apply* (only) to circumcision, or to uncircumcision as well? After all, we say that faith was credited to Abraham as justice. (10) But how was it credited? After he was circumcised or before? Not with circumci-

sion, but in (a state of) uncircumcision. (11) He received the sign of circumcision as the seal of the justice of faith *that he had* (in the state of) uncircumcision; so that he could be the father of all who have faith in (a state of) uncircumcision and thus have it credited to themselves as justice, (12) as well as the father of circumcision, *i.e.*, of those who not only are circumcised but also follow the trail that was our father Abraham's even in (the state of) uncircumcision.

(13) It wasn't through the law, you see, that the promise (was made) to Abraham and his seed that the world would be his inheritance; it was through the justice of faith. (14) If the inheritance (is due) to the law, then faith is made an empty thing and the promise is nullified. (15) For the law produces wrath. But where there is no law, there is no transgression either. (16) So it is due to faith, that the promise might be a gratuitous gift guaranteed to all his offspring, not only those of the law but also those of the faith of Abraham, who is the father of us all— (17) as it is written, "I have made you the father of many nations"—in the eyes of God, in whom he had faith as a God who gives life to the dead and who calls into being what does not have being. (18) Hoping against hope, he had faith, and so he became the father of many nations as he had been told: "So shall your offspring be." (19) He did not falter in his faith when he considered his own body, almost a corpse—he was almost a hundred years old—and the deadness of Sarah's womb. (20) Insofar as God's promise (was concerned), he did not lapse into unbelief. He grew strong in faith, (21) giving glory to God and fully convinced that (God) has the power to do what he has promised. (22) And so this was credited to him as justice.

(23) But the "it was credited to him" was not written for his sake alone, (24) but for our sake also. To us it will be credited, who have faith in the one who raised from the dead Jesus our Lord, (25) who had been handed over for our misdeeds and resurrected that we might be declared just.

Romans 5:1–20

5   (1) And so, having been declared just by reason of faith, we are at peace with God through our lord Jesus Christ, (2) through whom we also have gained access with faith to this grace in which we persevere, and we glory in the hope of God's glory. (3) Not only that, we glory even in our afflictions, knowing that affliction produces endurance, (4) endurance maturity, maturity hope; and the hope is not delusory (5) because the love proceeding from God has been poured into our hearts by the holy spirit that has been given to us.

(6) When we were still without power, Christ died at the right moment for the impious.— (7) It is hardly conceivable someone would die for a just person, though one might chance it for a good person.— (8) But God proved his love for us, since Christ died for us while we were still sinners. (9) With all the more *reason*, then, we shall be saved by him from the wrath, since we have been declared just by his blood. (10) If we were reconciled with God while still God's enemies by the death of his son, with all the more *reason* we, *already* reconciled, will be saved by his life. (11) Not only that, we glory in God through our lord Jesus Christ, thanks to whom we have now received reconciliation.

(12) So you see, just as sin entered the world through one human being (only), and through sin death, and thus death reached all human beings because all sinned— (13) For sin was *already* in the world before the law and, even though sin was not computed since there was no law, (14) death nevertheless reigned from Adam to Moses, even over those who did not sin the way Adam had, who was a type of the one to come— . . .

(15) But there is no equation between the offense and the gift. Because if by the offense of one (only) the many died, the grace of God and the gratuitous gift of one human (only), Jesus Christ, did much more abound in the many. (16) And there is no equation between the result of the one's aberration and the gift. Because the judgment following from the one (only) *ended in* condemnation, whereas the (work of) grace, following the many offenses, *ended in* a declaration of justice. (17) If by the offense of one (only) death reigned on account of one, much more will those who receive the abundance of grace and the gift of justice reign in life by one (only), Jesus Christ. (18) So you see, as the offense of one (only) *turned out to be cause of* condemnation for all human beings, so the justice of one (only) *turned out to be cause of* justice bringing life for all human beings. (19) As by the disobedience of one (only) the many were made sinful, so by the obedience of one (only) the many will be made just.

(20) *As for* the law, (it) intervened to increase the offense. But where sin abounded, grace abounded even more; with the result that, as sin reigned in death, so grace will reign by means of justice for eternal life, through Jesus Christ our lord.

Romans 6:1–7:13

6 (1) So what *are we* to say? That we should continue in sin so that grace may increase? (2) Never! How could we, who have died to sin, still live in it? (3) Do you not realize that all of us who have been baptized in Christ Jesus have been baptized in his death? (4) We have been buried with him by baptism in death so that, as Christ was resurrected from the dead by the glory of the father, we too might operate in the newness of life. (5) For if we have been assimilated to the form of his death, so we will be to the form of the resurrection, (6) knowing this: that our old humanity was crucified with him so that the body of sin might be destroyed and we might not be slaves to sin any longer. (7) Because one who is dead is declared just of sin.

(8) If we have died with Christ, we believe we shall also live with him, (9) knowing that Christ, once resurrected from the dead, will never die again and (that) death no longer has dominion over him. (10) Dying, he died to sin once and for all; living, he lives for God. (11) So you too should count yourselves dead to sin, but alive for God in Christ Jesus.

(12) Don't let sin reign in your mortal body, so that you obey its cravings (13) or offer your members to sin as weapons of injustice; offer yourselves to God as alive from the dead, and your members to God as weapons of justice. (14) For sin will no longer have dominion in you, since you are no longer under the law but under grace.

(15) What then? Are we going to sin because we are not under the law but under grace? Never! (16) Don't you realize that to whomever you offer your obedience as slaves, you become that one's slaves: either of sin, toward death; or of obedience, toward justice? (17) But, thank God, you who were slaves to sin have wholeheartedly obeyed the standard of teaching to which you have been transferred (18) and, liberated from sin, you have made yourselves slaves of justice—I speak in human terms because of the weakness of the flesh *in* you—. (19) Just as you offered your members (as) slaves to impurity and iniquity, to *live in* iniquity; so now offer your members (as) slaves to justice, to *live in* sanctification. (20) When you were slaves of sin, you were free of justice. (21) What fruit did you reap then? (Things) of which you are now ashamed, since their end is death. (22) But now, having been liberated from sin and made slaves of God, the fruit you have is sanctification, and the end is eternal life. (23) For the wage of sin (is) death, whereas the gift of God (is) eternal life in our lord Jesus Christ.

7   (1) Don't you know, brothers,—I am speaking to *people* who know about *laws*—that law has dominion over a human being only so long as that being lives? (2) A married woman, for example, is bound to her husband (while he is) alive; but if the husband dies, she is free of the husband law. (3) While her husband is alive, she will be treated as an adulteress if she becomes another man's; but if her husband dies, she becomes free of the husband law, so that she does not commit adultery if she becomes another man's. (4) In like manner, my brothers, you have died to the law, by the body of Christ, to become another's—the one who was resurrected from the dead—and to bear fruit for God. (5) When we were in the flesh, the passions of sins *roused* by the law were at work in our members, so that we bore fruit for death. (6) Now, on the other hand, we have been liberated from the law, having died to what bound us, so that *we can* serve in the newness of the spirit, not in the oldness of the letter.

(7) What shall we say, then? That the law is sin? Never! Admittedly, I did not know sin except through the law. I would not *have come* to know *what* covetousness *was*, if the law had not said: "Thou shalt not covet." (8) But sin, seizing its opportunity, by means of the precept aroused in me every *kind of* covetousness. Without law, you see, sin (is) dead. (9) Once upon a time I was alive without law. Then the precept came and sin began to live. (10) I, on the other hand, died. And the result for me was that the very precept given for life served for death. (11) Sin, seizing its opportunity, by means of the precept deceived me and thereby killed me.

(12) So, now, the law itself is holy and the precept holy, just, and good. (13) If that is the case, did the good turn into death for me? Never! But sin, to be manifestly clear as sin, produced death in me by means of something good; so that sin, by means of the precept, might turn into something exaggeratedly sinful.

Romans 7:14–25

7   (14) We know that the law is spiritual, but I am fleshly, made a slave *of the power* of sin. (15) I do not recognize what I accomplish because I do not perform what I want to do, I perform what I hate. (16) Now if I perform what I don't want to do, I am in agreement with the law that it is good. (17) But if that is the case, then it is not I who accomplish *that*, but sin that dwells in me. (18) For I know that the good does not dwell in me, i.e., in my flesh, since wanting it is within my capacity but accomplishing good is not. (19) I do not perform the good I want to do; I perform the evil I don't want to do. (20) But if I perform *precisely* what I don't want, then it is no longer I who accomplish it but sin that dwells in me.

(21) So I discover the law: wanting to do good, I find it is evil that is within my capacity. (22) I am delighted with the law of God in my inner humanity, (23) but I observe another law in my members warring against the law of my mind and making me prisoner of the law of sin that is in my members. (24) Wretched human that I am! Who will deliver me from this body of death? (25) Thanks be to God, through Jesus Christ our Lord! So with the mind I myself serve the law of God, but with the flesh I serve the law of sin.

Romans 8:1–39

8   (1) So there is no longer any condemnation for those who are in Christ Jesus, (2) since the law of the spirit of life has liberated you in Christ Jesus from the law of sin and death. (3) For God sent his own son in the likeness of a flesh of sin and, with respect to sin, condemned sin in the flesh—something the law was incapable of doing, because weak on account of the flesh— (4) so that the just precept of the law might be fulfilled in us, who walk not according to the flesh but according to the spirit.

(5) Those who live according to the flesh focus on the things of the flesh; those who (live) according to the spirit (focus on) the things of the spirit. (6) The mentality of the flesh is death; the mentality of the spirit, on the other hand, (is) life and peace. (7) Hence the mentality of the flesh is enmity with God because it is not subject to the law of God, nor indeed is it capable of that, (8) and those who are in the flesh cannot please God. (9) But you are not in the flesh; (you are) in the spirit, since the spirit of God dwells in you.—If one does not have the spirit of Christ, one is not Christ's— (10) Now if Christ is in you, the body (is) dead because of sin, to be sure, but the spirit lives because of justice. (11) And if the spirit of the one who resurrected Jesus from the dead dwells in you, the one who resurrected Christ Jesus from the dead is going to bring to life your mortal bodies as well by his spirit dwelling in you.

(12) So, my brothers, we are not debtors to the flesh that we *have to* live according to the flesh. (13) If you live according to the flesh, you will die; but if with the spirit you put to death the praxis of the body, you will live.

(14) You see, all who are guided by the spirit of God are children of God. (15) You did not receive a spirit of slavery, to *fall back* into fear again. You received a spirit of adoption *as child*, by which we cry out: Abba, Papa! (16) The spirit itself joins in to testify with our spirit that we are children of God; (17) and if children, heirs as well, heirs of God and joint heirs with Christ, assuming that we suffer with him so that we may also be glorified with him. (18) Because I think the sufferings of the present moment are not worth considering vis-à-vis the coming glory to be revealed in us.

(19) For the anxious expectation of creation yearns for the manifestation of God's children, (20) since creation was subjected to uselessness not by *its own* will, but on account of the one who subjected it, with the hope (21) that creation itself would be liberated from the slavery of corruption to *pass to* the freedom of the glory of God's children. (22) We know that all creation together is groaning and in travail up to now. (23) But not only it. We ourselves also, possessing the first-fruits of the spirit, groan within ourselves as we long for adoption, i. e., the redemption of our body. (24) *It was* in hope we were saved. But a hope seen is not hope. Why hope for what one already sees? (25) But if we hope for what we do not see, we do so with patient yearning.

(26) In the same way the spirit, too, helps our weakness, We do not even know what we should pray for, but the spirit itself intercedes *for us* with unspeakable groanings. (27) The one who scrutinizes hearts knows the intention of the spirit, and that it is interceding for the saints in accordance with God.

(28) We know that everything works together for the good of those who love God, those who were called in accordance with his resolve. (29) For those whom he knew beforehand, he also destined them beforehand to reflect the image of his son so that the latter might be the firstborn of many brothers and sisters. (30) Those he destined beforehand, he also called; and those he called, he also declared just; and those he declared just, he also glorified.

(31) What shall we say after all that? If God (is) for us, who (will be) against us? (32) The one who did not spare even his own beloved son, but handed him over for all of us— how will he not gift us with everything besides him? (33) Who will be the accuser of God's chosen ones? When God declares just, (34) who will accuse (them)? It is Jesus Christ, who died, or rather who was resurrected, who is at the right hand of God and who is also interceding for us. (35) Who will separate us from the love Christ *has for us*?

Affliction or anxiety or persecution or hunger or nakedness or danger or the sword? (36) As it is written: "For your sake we are being put to death all day long, we are counted as sheep (for) slaughter." (37) But in all these things we come out superwinners, through him who loved us. (38) I am convinced that neither death nor life nor angels nor principalities nor present nor future nor powers (39) nor height nor depth nor any other creature will be able to separate us from the love of God (that is) in Christ Jesus, our lord.

Index of Scriptural References
(Excluding Romans 1–8)

237

General Index

Other Orbis Books . . .

THE LIBERATION OF THEOLOGY
by Juan Luis Segundo
Juan Luis Segundo analyzes the methodology of liberation theology, which is integrally linked to the structural realities of Latin American societies, and challenges the supposed impartiality of academic theology in Europe and North America.
   "Makes for exciting reading and should not be missing from any theological library."
Library Journal

no. 286-8   **248pp. pbk.**   **$10.95**

FACES OF JESUS
Latin American Christologies
edited by José Míguez-Bonino
The most extensive part of this book is devoted to describing and analyzing the christologies that have been present in Latin America throughout history. A fascinating picture emerges of how Jesus functions within establishment, traditional peasant, and revolutionary sectors of the population. Boff, Casalis, Segundo, Croatto, Assmann, and others contribute to this ecumenical effort.
   "If one thinks, or is tempted to think, that Christian theology is boring, stale, repeating the eternal, unchanging truths, then this book will shatter the myth."   *America*
no. 129-2   **192pp. pbk.**   **$10.95**

HERALDS OF A NEW REFORMATION
The Poor of South and North America
by Richard Shaull
Foreword by Paul Lehmann
Richard Shaull interprets Latin American liberation theology for first world Christians and shows how it relates to our situation. The one-time Princeton Professor of Ecumenics includes a moving account of how his own life plan and faith have been altered by his encounter with the poor of the Americas over four decades.
   "For those of us in the 'First World,' living as we do 'in a society deeply troubled because it can dream of no future beyond the continuation of what it is now—and is in danger of losing,' this book is a timely and renewing account of the vision of the people of the 'Third World,' and of the new future which their vision can offer to us as well."
Paul Lehmann, from the Foreword
no. 345-7   **160pp. pbk.**   **$8.95**

CHRISTOLOGY AT THE CROSSROADS
A Latin American Approach
by Jon Sobrino
A landmark contribution to contemporary christological thought and action that is rooted in the historical Jesus and in the Latin American situation of oppression, injustice, and exploitation.

"The most thorough study of Christ's nature based on Latin America's liberation theology." *Time Magazine*
no. 076-8 **458pp. pbk.** **$12.95**

THE IDOLS OF DEATH AND THE GOD OF LIFE
A Theology
by Pablo Richard, et. al.
Ten Latin Americans look at the biblical, economic, and ideological implications of a liberating, life-giving God in contrast to "the false gods of the system," which through militarism, oppression, and economic exploitation deny life and usher in death. Richard, Croatto, Pixley, Sobrino, Araya, Casanas, Limon, Betto, Hinkelammert, and Assmann contribute to this ecumenical endeavor.

"Even where their way is not our way, we need to listen to what they have learned. These essays make an excellent listening post." *Walter Wink,*
Auburn Theological Seminary
no. 048-2 **240pp. pbk.** **$12.95**

JESUS CHRIST LIBERATOR
A Critical Christology for Our Time
by Leonardo Boff
"An excellent introduction to the basics of contemporary liberation Christology and thought, written from a position of deep faith . . . particularly helpful in its biblically faithful assessment of the politics of Jesus." *The Christian Century*
no. 236-1 **335pp. pbk.** **$9.95**